FIGHTERS OF THE UNITED STATES AIR FORCE

FIGHTERS OF THE UNITED STATES AIR FORCE

From World War I Pursuits to the F-117

Robert F. Dorr & David Donald

Military Press
New York

Originally published in Great Britain in 1990
by The Hamlyn Publishing Group Limited,
a division of the Octopus Publishing Group,
Michelin House, 81 Fulham Road, London SW3 6RB

This 1990 edition published by Military Press
Distributed by Crown Publishers, Inc.,
225 Park Avenue South, New York, New York 10003

Produced by Mandarin Offset
Printed and bound in Hong Kong

ISBN: 0-517-66994-3

h g f e d c b a

Produced by Aerospace Publishing Ltd,
179 Dalling Road, London W6 0ES, UK

All correspondence concerning the content of this
volume should be addressed to Aerospace Publishing
Ltd. Trade enquiries should be addressed to Crown
Publishers, Inc.

Picture acknowledgements

The publishers would like to thank the
following for their kind help in supplying
photographs for this book:

United States Air Force
United States Department of Defense
United States Navy
Imperial War Museum
General Dynamics Corporation
Lockheed Aeronautical Systems Company
McDonnell Douglas
Northrop Corporation Aircraft Group
Rockwell International
Bruce Robertson

CONTENTS

Baptism of Fire

For the nation that started the story of the aeroplane, the United States was woefully slow to appreciate the military value of the flying machine. It took involvement in World War I to show the way ahead.

For the nation which first achieved the goal of powered flight, it is amazing just how backward the United States came to be during the years which followed Orville Wright's history-making flight on 17 December 1903. Much of this can be traced back to the last years of the 19th century, when the US Army gave official blessing (and money) to Samuel P. Langley, in order to develop and fly a powered aircraft.

The US Army was no stranger to aerial warfare, having used balloons during the Civil War. In 1898 Langley was commissioned to build his 'Aerodrome', and following successful model tests, it was ready for flight in October 1903. Unfortunately this attempt failed, as did another in December, leaving the Wright Brothers to carry off the prize of first powered flight. As the first aircraft paid for by public funds, the 'Aerodrome' was soundly criticised by the public and politicians alike, and this coloured the thoughts of military leaders with regard to aviation long after the Wrights had flown their machine.

The first aircraft

It was not until February 1908 that the Army issued a request for a Wright biplane, and this Model A was eventually handed over to the military on 2 August 1909, going to the newly-formed Aeronautical Division. For two years this was the sole aircraft in the inventory, and it was not until 1912 that authorisation was received for more machines. By 1913 the 1st Aero Squadron had formed, and this was used in the Mexican border war. In 1914, the Division was renamed the Aviation Section of the Signal Corps, and numbered some 320 men!

While war raged in Europe, and pilots such as Boelcke, Immelmann and Lanoe Hawker forged the rules of air combat that would stand for all time, the US military appeared blissfully unaware of these developments, pursuing only a small-scale expansion of the Aviation Section with no attempt at providing combat aircraft. The first overseas units were formed in the Philippines and Panama. On 6 April 1917, the United States entered World War I, and found its Aviation Section virtually useless against the modern fighting machines fielded by Germany and its allies.

The pathetic state of US military aviation (at the time only the 14th largest air force in the world) was offset slightly by a group of US volunteers who had fought with the Allies as the *La Fayette* squadron, and these hardened veterans provided a nucleus of

The best-known US pilot of the war stands by the best-known aircraft type of the best-known squadron. Captain Eddie Rickenbacker of the 94th Aero Squadron ('Hat-in-the-Ring') was the leading US pilot, with 22 aircraft and four balloon kills, most in the SPAD XIII.

Grand plans were made as the United States entered the war to mass-produce British and French types. In the event only the de Havilland D.H.4 was built in quantity. One of the types for production was the Bristol F.2B Fighter, shown here in US markings.

combat-ready pilots around which to form a pursuit squadron. In February 1918, they were absorbed into the Aviation Section as the 103rd Aero Squadron.

Other pilots were hastily trained for war, but without the expertise of their instructors, the product was often lacking. No indigenous pursuit fighters were available, so the standard allied fighters were used, these being of French origin (SPAD, Nieuport) or British (Camel, S.E.5). Fresh units were first sent to Toul, where the opposition was weak and the unit could achieve some combat proficiency without suffering large attrition. The first US-trained fighter unit arrived at Toul on 9 April 1918, the 94th Aero Squadron ('Hat-in-the-Ring') under Captain Eddie Rickenbacker, a year and three days after the US entered the war.

During the World War I involvement, the American fighters were largely tied to air support of the Army, yet they managed to run up impressive combat records. Large-scale production of Allied aircraft designs was ordered, but only the de Havilland D.H.4 bomber was built in any reasonable numbers.

Rising stars

In the summer of 1918, the Germans were still capable of launching stinging attacks, and the first American units were sent to take part in the battle of Château-Thierry. Here the first taste of real war was experienced by the fighter pilots, and while most units lost large numbers, stars began rising in the US camp. Rickenbacker and Luke rose to prominence, the latter a young and irrepressible genius, who scored 18 kills before falling to a combined air and ground assault on 29 September.

By the time the war ended, the Aviation Section had been renamed the Air Service, and was to be operating briefly as an autonomous service. Its fighters had accounted for 781 enemy aircraft and 73 balloons, a splendid tribute to the commitment of the young men who had been trained and thrown into combat in a matter of months. These men were the very reason that the US Air Force rose quickly to a position of prominence, and they are widely honoured today.

The phenomenal growth in strength has not been seen before or since. In 1916 the Aviation Section numbered 311 personnel: at the Armistice in November 1918 there were 195,023. But suddenly without a war to fight, the budgetary axe started to swing, gathering force as the months passed until the Air Service was almost back to where it started.

142 Fokker D.VIIs were captured intact during World War I, and impressed into service after the end of the conflict. Some were given US-built engines, and these spawned the PW-6 development.

SPAD VII and SPAD XII

History and notes

SPAD – initials famous in aviation history – at first identified the French company Société Pour les Appareils Deperdussin which was established in 1910 at Bétheny, near Rheims by Armand Deperdussin. Keenly interested in aviation (as well as its potential to increase his not insignificant fortune) this middle-aged silk merchant first came into contact with aviation engineer Louis Béchéreau when, in 1909, he persuaded Béchéreau to provide an aeroplane as an eye-catching Christmas display for his elegant Bon Marché store in the centre of Paris. Soon Deperdussin financed the establishment at Bétheny, where Béchéreau and a then unknown André Herbemont became responsible for running this company. Their efforts soon made European aviation aware that SPAD spelt innovation and achievement – efforts that were dashed in 1913 when Deperdussin was arrested for embezzlement, resulting in the SPAD company being declared bankrupt in 1915. Louis Blériot then took it over, changing the name to Société Pour l'Aviation et ses Dérivés, thus retaining the well-known initials.

By then Europe was at war, and after some early experimentation the new SPAD company was soon busy supplying aircraft to France and its allies. Its first real success came with the single-seat SPAD VII, a conventional biplane of wood and fabric construction (except for aluminium panels covering the forward fuselage). Its configuration included tailskid-type landing gear, and power was provided by a Hispano-Suiza Vee engine. The initial production version (built to a total of more than 500) had a 150-hp (112-kW) Hispano-Suiza 8Aa engine. The second version (about 6,000 built by SPAD and sub-contractors) had the

more powerful Hispano-Suiza 8Ac. Not surprisingly the AEF was keen to acquire SPAD aircraft, but, with a lower priority than the home air force, it was only able to procure 189, the first of them received in December 1917. They were used to equip, fairly briefly, six or seven squadrons until, three months later, deliveries to the AEF began of the more cap-able SPAD XIII, at which time many SPAD VIIs were returned to the USA for use in a training role.

At the request of Capitaine Georges Guynemer (the French ace), one SPAD VII was modified as a cannon-armed fighter, with a 37-mm cannon mounted between the two cylinder banks of the engine. At the same time, the wing span was

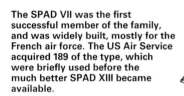

The SPAD VII was the first successful member of the family, and was widely built, mostly for the French air force. The US Air Service acquired 189 of the type, which were briefly used before the much better SPAD XIII became available.

After their brief service with front-line squadrons, the majority of the SPAD VIIs were channelled into fighter pilot training. Due to the similarity to the SPAD XIII for which most aircrew were headed, they were particularly admirable in this role.

SPAD VII and XII

increased by 1 ft 3¾ in (0.40 m), and a more powerful version of the Hispano-Suiza engine was installed. This variant of the SPAD VII was to become designated the SPAD XII and 300 aircraft were produced. Only a single example was procured by the AEF, which shipped it to the USA for study and evaluation of the cannon armament.

Specification
SPAD VII
Type: single-seat fighter
Powerplant: one 180-hp (134-kW) Hispano-Suiza 8Ac Vee piston engine
Performance: maximum speed 118 mph (190 km/h) at 6,560 ft (2,000 m); service ceiling 18,045 ft (5,500 m); endurance 2 hours 15 minutes
Weight: maximum take-off 1,664 lb (755 kg)
Dimensions: span 25 ft 7.9 in (7.82 m); length 20 ft 8 in (6.30 m); height 7 ft 8.5 in (2.35 m)
Armament: one fixed forward-firing synchronised 0.303-in (7.7-mm) Vickers machine-gun

SPAD 7 cutaway drawing key

1 Steel wire trailing edge
2 Rudder construction
3 Rudder post
4 Sternpost
5 Rudder hinge control
6 Starboard elevator
7 Elevator construction
8 Elevator hinge control
9 Tailplane construction
10 Fin construction
11 Tailskid
12 Steel shoe
13 Elastic cord shock absorber
14 Port elevator
15 Port tailplane
16 Fin attachment
17 Fuselage fabric covering
18 Dorsal construction
19 Dorsal stringers
20 Top longeron
21 Tailplane control cables
22 Vertical spacers
23 Bottom longeron
24 Fuselage stringers
25 Diagonal wire bracing
26 Headrest fairing
27 Plywood decking
28 Headrest
29 Padded cockpit coaming
30 Fuel filler cap
31 Used cartridge belt storage drum
32 Exhaust pipe tail fairing
33 Control cable pulleys
34 Pilot's seat
35 Safety hardness
36 Underfloor fuel tank
37 Starboard upper wing panel construction
38 Upper wing spars
39 Compression rib
40 Internal wire bracing
41 Aileron horn control
42 Starboard aileron

43 Leading edge carry-round
44 Leading edge stiffeners
45 Interplane strut
46 Aileron control rod
47 Aileron rod crank
48 Lower wing spars
49 Compression rib
50 Internal wire bracing
51 Leading edge rib construction
52 Flying wire bracing
53 Flying wire support strut
54 Spar root fixing

55 Fuselage wing root rib
56 Cockpit floor panel
57 Rudder pedal bar
58 Fuselage keel member
59 Control column
60 Instrument panel
61 Gun cocking lever
62 Engine throttle
63 Centre section strut
64 Windscreen
65 Padded trailing edge section
66 Service fuel tank
67 Steel wire trailing edge
68 Port aileron
69 Aileron horn
70 Port upper wing panel construction
71 Spar section joint
72 Interplane strut
73 Flying wires
74 Flying wire bracing strut
75 Lower wing panel fabric covering
76 Radiator header tank
77 Ammunition drum
78 Ammunition belt feed chute
79 Engine compartment bulkhead
80 0.303-in (7.7-mm) Vickers machine gun
81 Engine blister fairing
82 Radiator filler cap
83 Engine access panel
84 205 hp Hispano-Suiza 8Ab Vee-engine
85 Exhaust pipe
86 Engine bearer construction
87 Ventilation air intake panel
88 Nose cowlings
89 Radiator cowling ring
90 Water radiator
91 Radiator shutters
92 Propeller fixing bolts
93 Propeller hub
94 Two-bladed wooden propeller
95 Port mainwheel
96 Laminated wooden main undercarriage legs
97 Undercarriage leg top fixing
98 Undercarriage bracing wires
99 Fixed axle beam
100 Swing axle fixing
101 Elastic cord shock absorber
102 Wheel hub fixing
103 Fabric wheel disc fairing
104 Tyre inflation valve
105 Starboard mainwheel

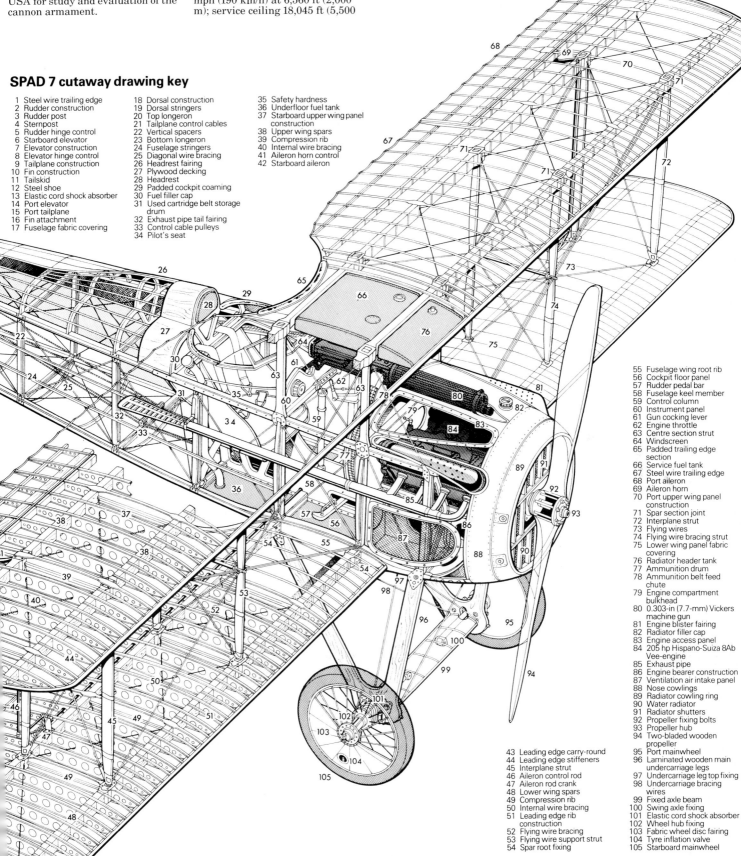

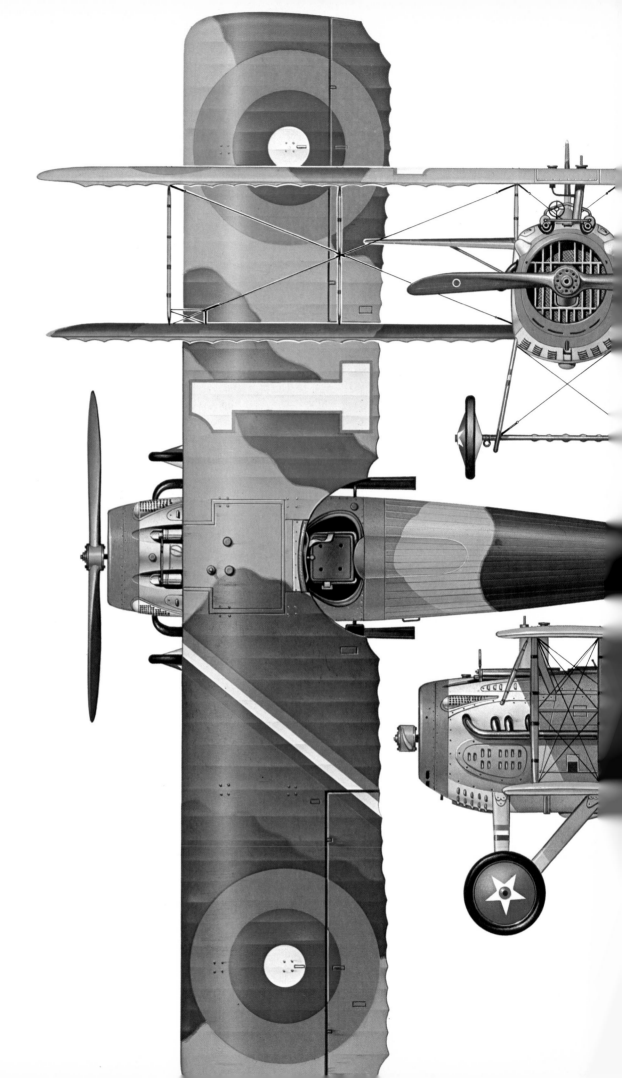

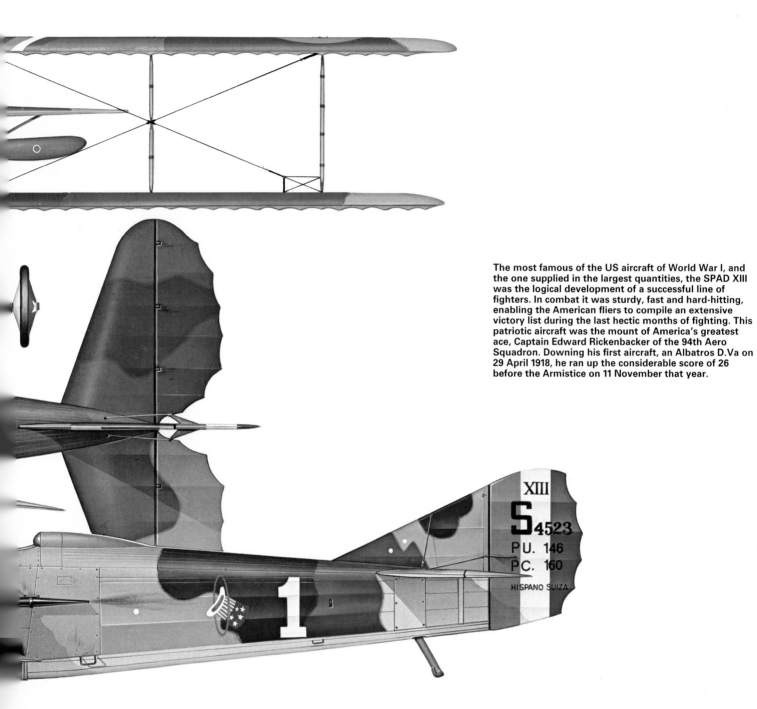

The most famous of the US aircraft of World War I, and
the one supplied in the largest quantities, the SPAD XIII
was the logical development of a successful line of
fighters. In combat it was sturdy, fast and hard-hitting,
enabling the American fliers to compile an extensive
victory list during the last hectic months of fighting. This
patriotic aircraft was the mount of America's greatest
ace, Captain Edward Rickenbacker of the 94th Aero
Squadron. Downing his first aircraft, an Albatros D.Va on
29 April 1918, he ran up the considerable score of 26
before the Armistice on 11 November that year.

SPAD XIII

History and notes

With more than 6,500 examples built, the SPAD VII could be regarded as a definite success and, not surprisingly, it was decided to develop the same basic design to produce a new single-seat fighter. In adopting such an approach at a period of time when a day saved could be of vital importance to the course of the air war, the company was able to 'lean upon' the best features of the SPAD VII, and gain enhanced performance from a combination of improvements and more power. Thus in basic configuration there was little difference between the SPAD VII and the new version, which was given the designation SPAD XIII. Except for some structural reinforcement, the improvements were largely of an aerodynamic nature, with the wing span increased by 11 in (28 cm), the introduction of improved ailerons, an increase in the area of tail surfaces, plus other aerodynamic refinements that resulted largely from cleaning up the existing structure. A more powerful version of the Hispano-Suiza 8 engine was adopted and, in this form, the prototype was flown for the first time on 4 April 1917.

Test and evaluation of the prototype showed an improvement of some 18 per cent in maximum speed and a 19 per cent increase in ceiling, with the additional power making it possible to carry a second machine-gun yet retaining the excellent handling and manoeuvrability that had been the secret of the SPAD VII's success. Orders flowed in from France's allies, with initial deliveries starting at the beginning of June 1917. By the time that production ended a total of 8,472 had been built and orders outstanding for more than

In all some 893 SPAD XIIIs were supplied to the American Expeditionary Force, and they were the most successful fighter type. Following Rickenbacker, the next most successful ace was Frank Luke, a flamboyant Lieutenant from Arizona, who was renowned for balloon-busting exploits.

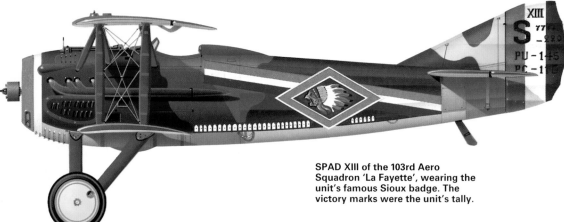

SPAD XIII of the 103rd Aero Squadron 'La Fayette', wearing the unit's famous Sioux badge. The victory marks were the unit's tally.

A scene typical of the late air war in France as USAS SPAD XIIIs rest between missions. Resembling its forebears closely, the SPAD XIII introduced a more powerful engine and significant aerodynamic improvements.

10,000 aircraft were cancelled at the Armistice.

AEF procurement of the SPAD XIII totalled 893, which was by far the largest number of any single type which the US Army acquired from any of its allies during World War I. The type eventually equipped 16 squadrons and the first was delivered in March 1918 to the 1st Pursuit Group, which comprised the 27th, 94th, 95th and the 147th Aero Squadrons based in the Toul Sector. SPAD XIIIs helped top American aces Eddie Rickenbacker, Frank Luke and Raoul Lufbery to reach their respective totals of 26, 21 and 17 combat victories, but the type saw little more than five months' front-line service before the Armistice brought an end to the fighting, and surviving SPAD XIIIs were shipped to the USA. There they were used for a short period as first-line fighters before they were relegated to a training role. Unreliability of the Hispano-Suiza engine hastened their withdrawal from service, but in 1922 a small number were re-engined with a 180-hp (134-kW) direct-drive Wright E (licence-built Hispano-Suiza) to become redesignated the SPAD 13E.

Specification
SPAD XIII

Type: single-seat fighter
Powerplant: one 220-hp (164-kW) Hispano-Suiza 8Be Vee piston engine
Performance: maximum speed 139 mph (224 km/h) at 6,560 ft (2,000 m); climb to 13,125 ft (4,000 m) in 12 minutes 30 seconds; service ceiling 21,815 ft (6,650 m); range 185 miles (298 km)
Weight: maximum take-off 1,863 lb (845 kg)
Dimensions: span 26 ft 6.9 in (8.1 m); length 20 ft 8 in (6.3 m); height 7 ft 8.5 in (2.35 m)
Armament: two fixed forward-firing synchronised 0.303-in (7.7-mm) Vickers machine-guns

The SPAD XIII continued in US service long after the war, mostly as fighter trainers. Several were re-engined with Wrights to prolong their useful lives, being redesignated SPAD 13E in the process. Here three wear post-war markings.

The classically pugnacious lines of the SPAD XIII were the epitome of the glamorous fighter in 1918. Visibility was not as good as in other fighters, the low set upper wing impairing forward view but improving upward view. In all 8,472 of this superb fighter were produced for the Allies, of which the United States took 893.

Nieuport 17, 21 and 23

History and notes

Founded at Issy-les-Moulineaux, Paris, in 1910, the Société Anonyme des Etablissements Nieuport was active during the early stages of European aviation. By the time of the outbreak of war with Germany in August 1914, it was sufficiently well established to design and manufacture a series of fighter aircraft that saw extensive use by the French and its Allies.

Designed by Gustave Delage, the Nieuport 17 was what would now be regarded as a typical single-seat fighter biplane of the early stages of World War I. A braced single-bay biplane, its fuselage structure was basically of wood but introduced a forward section of welded steel tubing which was covered by aluminium cowlings to the pilot's cockpit. Aft of that the wooden structure was fabric covered, as were the wings and tail surfaces, with the narrow-chord lower 'sesquiplane' wing having half the area of the upper wing. The landing gear was of tailskid type, the main unit comprising wire-braced Vee struts supporting a through axle. The initial Nieuport 17 was powered by a 110-hp (82-kW) Le Rhône 9J rotary engine or, in the case of the Nieuport 17-bis, by the

Escadrille N 124 of the French air force was staffed by American volunteers, and was transferred to the USAS in February 1918 to become the first pursuit squadron in action. Officially the 103rd Aero Squadron, they were far better known as the 'La Fayette' squadron.

130-hp (97-kW) Clerget 9B. Extensively operated by the Allies, AEF procurement was limited to 75 Nieuport 17s which were used for training, and a single Nieuport 17-bis which was shipped to the USA for test and study.

The Nieuport 21, which was a variant of the 17, introduced an 80-hp (60-kW) Le Rhône 9C engine and enlarged ailerons, but otherwise differed only in small details. Two versions were acquired by the AEF, the initial Nieuport 21 (to a total of 181), plus 17 of a variant with the Le Rhône 9J engine, all 198 being used in the training role. Final direct version of this family was the Nieuport 23, a slightly more robust (and consequently heavier) version of the Nieuport 17. AEF procurement of this totalled only 50 (again for training) comprising variants with the Le Rhône 9C (total 47) and 9J (3).

Specification
Nieuport 17

Type: single-seat fighter
Powerplant: one 110-hp (82-kW) Le Rhône rotary piston engine
Performance: maximum speed 106 mph (170 km/h) at 6,500 ft (1,980 m); climb to 13,125 ft (4,000 m) in 19 minutes 30 seconds; service ceiling 17,550 ft (5,350 m); range 155 miles (250 km)
Weights: empty 825 lb (374 kg);

maximum take-off 1,235 lb (560 kg)
Dimensions: span 26 ft 10.75 in (8.2 m); length 19 ft 7 in (5.97 m); height 8 ft 0 in (2.44 m); wing area 158.77 sq ft (14.75 m²)
Armament: one fixed forward-firing 0.303-in (7.7-mm) Lewis gun mounted above the upper wing centre-section to fire clear of the propeller disc; subsequently, after the introduction of synchronising gear, one 0.303-in (7.7-mm) Vickers machine-gun

Nieuport 24 and 27

History and notes

The close relationship between the Nieuport 17/21/23 and the Nieuport 24/27 is illustrated by the fact that the Nieuport 23 served as the prototype for the generally similar Nieuport 24. This last differed primarily by introducing a rounded fuselage structure and efforts had been made to reduce drag by more careful attention to streamlining. The other noticeable external changes saw the adoption of rounded wingtips and the introduction of a small fixed vertical fin forward of the rudder, the first time that such a feature had been used on a production version of this related family of aircraft, although this tail unit configuration had been tested on an experimental aircraft which the company identified as the Nieuport 18.

Still desperately short of single-seat advanced trainers, the AEF procured 121 Nieuport 24s from the French government and the initial deliveries were made during November 1917, more or less simultaneously with the first deliveries of a batch of 140 Nieuport 24-bis. This variant of the Nieuport 24 reverted to the more angular wingtips of the

Nieuport 17 and, reportedly, also adopted again the tail unit of that aircraft (the type without a fixed tail fin). There appears to be no documentary evidence able to confirm this last report, and one historian was provoked to comment: "... The distinction between the latter 24-bis and the Nieuport 24 is consequently difficult to establish and doubtful at best."

Last in this line of Nieuport sesquiplane V-strut fighters was the Nieuport 27, for which the AEF was the best customer by procuring a total of 287. The reason for this was clear, even though far more capable fighter aircraft were beginning to enter service and were being adopted by the air arms of the European allies. The AEF needed them for advanced training rather than

The Nieuport 27 was largely outclassed by other fighters at the time of its production, but the USAS needed large numbers of aircraft to support the large training effort under way. It was procured mainly for this reason, and it became the main operator.

combat, and for such a role the Nieuport 27 was still a valuable asset. Basically the same as the Nieuport 24, the 27 introduced a revised tailskid type landing gear, and all three variants noted here shared the same Le Rhône 9Jb powerplant.

Specification
Nieuport 27

Type: single-seat fighter
Powerplant: one 120-hp (89-kW) Le Rhône 9Jb rotary piston engine
Performance: maximum speed 110

mph (177 km/h) at sea level; service ceiling 17,715 ft (5,400 m); range 155 miles (250 km)
Weights: empty 838 lb (380 kg); maximum take-off 1,289 lb (585 kg)
Dimensions: span 26 ft 10.75 in (8.20 m); length 19 ft 2.3 in (5.85 m); height 7 ft 11.3 in (2.42 m); wing area 158.77 sq ft (14.75 m²)
Armament: one fixed forward-firing synchronised 0.303-in (7.7-mm) Vickers machine-gun and/or one 0.303-in (7.7-mm) Lewis gun mounted above the upper wing centre-section

Nieuport 28

History and notes

The Nieuport 28, of which the first of the four prototypes was flown initially on 14 June 1917, marked the introduction of a new configuration which differed in several important respects from the family of Nieuport single-seat fighters that had preceded it. Most conspicuous of the changes was the adoption of conventional biplane wings, the lower wings more nearly equal in size to that of the upper wing and to which

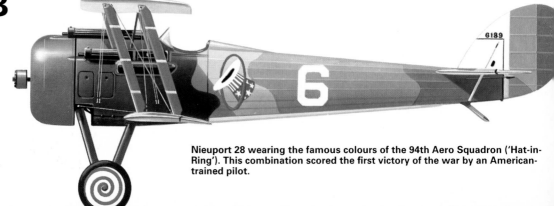

Nieuport 28 wearing the famous colours of the 94th Aero Squadron ('Hat-in-Ring'). This combination scored the first victory of the war by an American-trained pilot.

Nieuport 28

it was linked by parallel interplane struts. By comparison with the Nieuport 24/27, it had a more slender circular-section fuselage and a new, well-proportioned tail unit. The landing gear had also undergone revision, the main gear struts forming a true vertical Vee, and in consequence giving the aircraft a very different appearance in side elevation. The powerplant was the Gnome 9N rotary, with some 33 per cent more power than the Le Rhône of its immediate predecessor and offering much improved performance. However, by the time the Nieuport 28 was in service, SPAD fighters were proving far more agile. This accounted for several attempts to boost performance of the Nieuport 28 by a series of flight tests with more powerful engines.

With priority in delivery of SPADs going to the home air force, the AEF's need for fighter aircraft had become so urgent that 297 Nieuport 28s were procured from the French government, the first being delivered in early March 1918. The type was to serve with the 27th, 94th, 95th and 103rd Aero Squadrons, but it was with the 94th 'Hat-in-Ring' Squadron that it is renowned in US Air Force history. This moment came on 14 April 1918 (which was the 94th's first day of operations) when Lieutenant Douglas Campbell and Lieutenant Alan F. Winslow were left on standby at the Squadron's base at

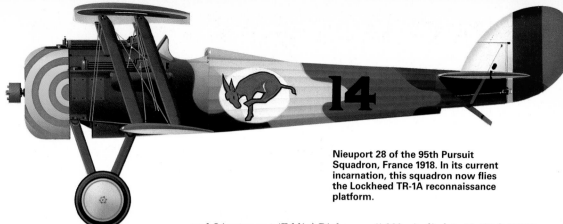

Nieuport 28 of the 95th Pursuit Squadron, France 1918. In its current incarnation, this squadron now flies the Lockheed TR-1A reconnaissance platform.

Toul after three of the 94th's aircraft had been despatched on a patrol over enemy lines. Within a short time of their take-off a telephone message from an outpost at Lironville warned Toul that two enemy single-seaters were headed their way. Lieutenants Campbell and Winslow were in the air within a few minutes and almost at once were in contact, with guns 'a-blazing'. It was a short encounter, and within minutes both of the German aircraft had been damaged so extensively that they made crash landings (one in flames) near the airfield at Toul.

Thus Douglas Campbell achieved the second of his three 'firsts' in AEF records. On 19 March (only days after receiving their Nieuport 28s) he had accompanied the squadron commander, Major Raoul Lufbery,

and Lieutenant 'Eddie' Rickenbacker (US 'ace-of-aces' during World War I) on the first American air patrol over enemy lines. Campbell's was the first combat victory by an American-trained pilot. With his fifth 'score' on 31 May 1918 he became the first 'ace' to have served exclusively with the American forces.

For the 14 April 1918 incident alone the Nieuport 28 has an honoured place in USAF annals, and because of the type's achievements many were shipped back to the USA after the war's end.

Specification
Nieuport 28

Type: single-seat fighter
Powerplant: one 160-hp (119-kW) Gnome 9N rotary piston engine
Performance: maximum speed 133 mph (214 km/h) at 6,500 ft

(1,980 m); climb to 16,405 ft (5,000 m) in 16 minutes 30 seconds; service ceiling 17,060 ft (5,200 m); range 249 miles (400 km)
Weights: empty 1,172 lb (532 kg); maximum take-off 1,631 lb (740 kg)
Dimensions: span 26 ft 3 in (8 m); length 20 ft 4.1 in (6.2 m); height 8 ft 1.6 in (2.48 m); wing area 215.29 sq ft (20 m²)
Armament: two fixed forward-firing synchronised Vickers 0.303-in (7.7-mm) machine-guns

Although bearing a similarity in fuselage line to the 27, the Nieuport 28 featured a revised wing layout with equal-span upper and lower wings, and twin struts between them in place of the Vee-strut. They saw widespread action with the AEF during the last year of the war.

Sopwith F.1 Camel

History and notes

Regarded as the most famous Allied aircraft of World War I, the Sopwith Camel (known at first as the Sopwith Biplane F.1) had the unique distinction of recording more combat victories (over 2,800 claimed by pilots of the Royal Flying Corps, Royal Naval Air Service and the Royal Air Force) than any other single type of aircraft involved in the war. Basically a development of the Sopwith Pup, which it superseded in

Although the experienced fighters of the Royal Flying Corps and Royal Naval Air Service (both later joined as the Royal Air Force) found the Camel a superb air-to-air machine, it was disliked by US pilots, who found its handling characteristics vicious.

service and with which it was generally similar, it differed primarily by having an empty weight some 18 per cent greater but had as

Sopwith Camel

standard an engine developing just over 60 per cent more power. The Camel also had its ammunition, fuel, pilot and powerplant concentrated within a compact area of a fuselage that was slightly shorter than that of the Pup. This resulted in superb manoeuvrability, an attribute which, enhanced by the torque of its large rotary engine, made snap turns to starboard so fast that many experienced pilots found it quicker (and more confusing to the enemy) to make a 270° turn to starboard than a 90° turn to port.

The Camel first entered service with the RFC and RNAS in mid-1917, which was about the same time that the first detachment of the AEF reached France. It did not take the AEF long to appreciate the capability of the Camel in British hands, but almost a year elapsed before any of the 143 procured entered service with them. The first units to equip with the Camel were the 17th Aero Squadron (20 June 1918) and the 148th Aero Squadron (1 July 1918). Of greater historical interest was the transfer of the 185th Aero Squadron to the 1st Pursuit Group at Rembercourt, France, as an embryo night fighter squadron (known then as a 'Night Chasse Squadron'). Commanded by 1st Lieutenant Seth Low, the task of 185th Aero was to 'establish a barrage over our line of searchlights against enemy night bombing machines'. The squadron's first operation was flown on the night of 18/19 October, but with bad weather limiting operations to just eight nights before the 11 November Armistice, only a total of 21 sorties was made. Enemy bomber aircraft were contacted only on the night of 24/25 October, when one pilot made five (apparently unsuccessful)

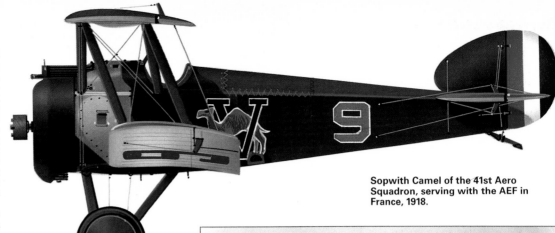

Sopwith Camel of the 41st Aero Squadron, serving with the AEF in France, 1918.

The Sopwith Camel led the British contingent of aircraft supplied to the AEF, with 143 examples. Used sparingly, it was not as effective in American hands as the SPAD XIII. A pair of Vickers machine-guns provided the punch, mounted above the rotary engine.

attacks on them.

With the war over, the Camel did not survive long in either British or US service, apart from a number used for experimental purposes. A machine that had been born during the 'war to end all wars' was not thought to have any useful remaining purpose after the end of that conflict.

Specification
F.1

Type: single-seat fighter
Powerplant: one 130-hp (97-kW)

Clerget rotary piston engine
Performance: maximum speed 115 mph (185 km/h) at 6,500 ft (1,980 m); climb to 10,000 ft (3,050 m) in 8 minutes 30 seconds; service ceiling 19,000 ft (5,790 m); endurance 2 hours 30 minutes
Weights: empty 929 lb (421 kg); maximum take-off 1,453 lb (659 kg)

Dimensions: span 28 ft 0 in (8.53 m); length 18 ft 9 in (5.72 m); height 8 ft 6 in (2.59 m); wing area 231 sq ft (21.46 m^2)
Armament: two fixed forward-firing synchronised 0.303-in (7.7-mm) machine-guns, plus up to four 25 lb (11.3 kg) bombs carried externally

Sopwith 5F.1 Dolphin

History and notes

A shortcoming of the typical single-seat biplane fighter was the limited upward and forward field of view imposed by its upper wing. Sopwith's 5F.1 Dolphin was designed to remove this limitation by introducing a deep-section fuselage with the upper wing mounted close to it. This allowed the pilot to be seated so that his head protruded through the wing centre-section, providing a superb all-round and upward view, though at the cost of a reduction in his field of view beneath the aircraft, this factor being considered less vital for a single-seat fighter. The Dolphin thus appeared somewhat unorthodox from the start, but since the

adoption of this configuration 'fixed' the position of the upper wing, the lower wing had to be moved forward to maintain the correct relationship between lift and the centre of gravity. This resulted in a backward-stagger biplane, regarded with grave suspicion by all pilots who usually subscribed to the aircraft engineers' tenet that, 'if it looks right, it is right'. It didn't look right, and this delayed its acceptance and the discovery that it was a pleasant aircraft to handle. In other respects the Dolphin was of conventional construction and built in the Mk I (powered by a geared version of the 200-hp/149-kW Hispano-Suiza Vee engine), Mk II (built in small num-

bers in France with a 300-hp/224-kW direct-drive Hispano-Suiza engine) and Mk III (direct-drive 200-hp/149-kW engine) versions.

Following the first flight of the prototype Dolphin Mk I in May 1917, a total of 1,532 was built, of which 621 entered service before the end of World War I and were used operationally with the RFC/RAF, the remainder were placed in storage. Procurement by the AEF was limited to just five examples, one of them being used for test and evaluation in France during October 1918. With the war's end, the other four were shipped to the USA for further test and study of their unusual configuration.

Specification
Dolphin Mk I

Type: single-seat fighter
Powerplant: one 200-hp (149-kW) Hispano-Suiza Vee piston engine
Performance: maximum speed 122 mph (196 km/h) at 10,000 ft (3,050 m); climb to 6,500 ft (1,980 m) in 6 minutes 5 seconds; service ceiling 20,000 ft (6,095 m); endurance 1 hour 45 minutes
Weights: maximum take-off 2,008 lb (911 kg)
Dimensions: span 32 ft 6 in (9.91 m); length 22 ft 3 in (6.78 m); height 8 ft 6 in (2.59 m); wing area 263.25 sq ft (24.46 m^2)
Armament: two fixed forward-firing synchronised 0.303-in (7.7-mm) machine-guns, plus one or two 0.303-in (7.7-mm) Lewis guns on the forward spar of the upper wing centre-section, firing forwards and upwards over the propeller disc

Royal Aircraft Factory S.E.5a

History and notes

A product of the Royal Aircraft Factory at Farnborough, Hampshire, England, the S.E.5 single-seat fighter was designed by H.P. Folland. The first production aircraft were delivered to the Royal Flying Corp's No.56 Squadron on 13 March 1917 and less than a month later, on 7 April, the squadron had moved to France. Of what was then typical biplane configuration with tailskid-

type landing gear, the S.E.5 was powered by a new 150-hp (112-kW) Hispano-Suiza V-8 piston engine. The improved S.E.5a which followed soon after, had detail airframe revisions and a more powerful version of the Hispano-Suiza engine driving a four-blade propeller. From June 1917 they began to replace the S.E.5s with No.56 Squadron. Unfortunately it took some time for both the engine and the Constantinesco

interrupter gear to settle down to a reasonable standard of reliability, a state not achieved until the early months of 1918. Even before that time, however, the S.E.5a had begun to gain an enviable reputation for its capability as a dog-fighter in the hands of such well-known aces as Major Edward ('Mick') Mannock and Captain J.T.B. McCudden.

With the arrival in France on 5 June 1917 of the US Army's First

Aeronautic Detachment, the process began of procuring from the Allies suitable combat aircraft to equip what was to become a growing American force. The capability of the S.E.5a ensured that this aircraft was numbered among procurement plans although only 38 were acquired from the British government for service in France (with units that included Nos 17, 25 and 148 Aero Squadrons). However, the

Royal Aircraft S.E.5a

S.E.5a was chosen by the Bolling Commission for mass production in the United States, and the Curtiss Aeroplane and Motor Company was contracted to produce 1,000. Only one of these was built (serial no 43153) before the Armistice brought cancellation of the remainder. Subsequently, Curtiss modified and assembled 57 S.E.5a airframes received from the UK. These, plus the surviving S.E.5a aircraft that the AEF squadrons brought back to the USA after the Armistice, provided the nation's first-line pursuit force until indigenous fighters became available at the beginning of the 1920s. In 1923 50 of these aircraft were rebuilt by the Eberhart Aeroplane & Motor Company to become redesignated SE-5E. In the process they acquired a plywood-covered fuselage structure and more power in the form of a Wright E engine, which was a licence-built version of the 180-hp (134-kW) Hispano-Suiza.

Specification
S.E.5a

Type: single-seat fighter
Powerplant: one 200-hp (149-kW) Hispano-Suiza V-8 piston engine
Performance: maximum speed 138 mph (222 km/h) at sea level; service ceiling 19,500 ft (5,945 m); endurance 3 hours
Weights: empty 1,400 lb (635 kg); maximum take-off 1,955 lb (887 kg)
Dimensions: span 26 ft 7.5 in (8.12 m); length 20 ft 11 in (6.38 m); height 9 ft 6 in (2.9 m); wing area 244 sq ft (22.67 m^2)
Armament: one fixed forward-firing Vickers 0.303-in (7.7-mm) synchronised machine-gun on the port upper forward fuselage, and one 0.303-in (7.7-mm) Lewis gun on a Foster mounting above the upper wing centre-section

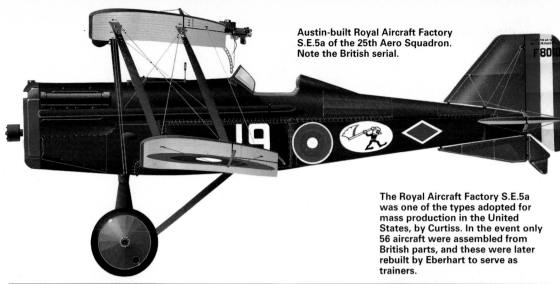

Austin-built Royal Aircraft Factory S.E.5a of the 25th Aero Squadron. Note the British serial.

The Royal Aircraft Factory S.E.5a was one of the types adopted for mass production in the United States, by Curtiss. In the event only 56 aircraft were assembled from British parts, and these were later rebuilt by Eberhart to serve as trainers.

Fokker D.VII

History and notes

Germany's most successful fighter of World War I, the D.VII was designed by Reinhold Platz to compete in a single-seat fighter competition. His V11 prototype drew heavily on the Fokker Dr.I, being of similar fuselage profile and construction. The undercarriage remained unchanged while the tail surfaces were tailored to the new design. Central to the design was the use of a more powerful, and consequently heavier, engine to provide a suitable increase in performance. Therefore the wings would have to be larger than the D.VI biplane it succeeded. Early aircraft were completed with the Mercedes D.III engine, although the more powerful BMW III was substituted.

Winning the fighter competition in January 1918, the D.VII was ordered into immediate production, and some 700 were delivered by the Armistice on 11 November. In service it proved immensely popular and a high performer. On the Allied side only the Sopwith Snipe and SPAD XIII could get near it. During the signing of the Peace Treaty, it was stipulated that all D.VIIs (and Zeppelins) must be surrendered to the Allies, such was the potential of the type. Despite this Fokker managed to restart production in Hol-

The high-climbing Fokker D.VII impressed US plane-makers, and it was carefully studied to aid post-war pursuit design. Fokker produced the PW-6, an improved version.

land, providing many post-war air forces with fighters.

Of those confiscated, 142 were shipped to the United States, where they were impressed into service as pursuits after evaluation. These helped provide a fighter force during the immediate post-war years when the air force was being rapidly run down. Several were re-engined with American powerplants, these including the Liberty 6, Packard 1A-1116 and Packard 1A-1237. One aircraft was a two-seater powered by a 290-hp Liberty 8. Six of the aircraft were transferred to the US Marine Corps for trials, and plans for a further six to the Navy were cancelled.

The best mass-produced German fighter of the war was the Fokker D.VII, and large numbers were shipped back to the United States after the war to serve as fighters or trainers.

Specification
Fokker D.VII

Type: single-seat pursuit aircraft
Powerplant: one 185-hp (138-kW) BMW III 6-cylinder inline piston engine, watercooled
Performance: maximum speed 124 mph (200 km/h) at 3,280 ft (1000 m); climb to 16,404 ft (5000 m) in 16 minutes; service ceiling 22,966 ft (7,000 m); endurance 1 hour 30 minutes
Weights: empty 1,620 lb (735 kg); maximum take-off 1,940 lb (880 kg)
Dimensions: wing span 26 ft (8.12 m); height 9 ft (2.75 m); wing area 221 sq ft (20.50 m^2)
Armament: two fixed forward-firing 0.31-in (7.92-mm) LMG 08/15 machine-guns

Thomas-Morse S-4

History and notes

Among early US aircraft builders were the brothers Oliver and William Thomas, who completed their first aeroplane during the winter months of 1910-1. This led to the formation of the Thomas Brothers Aeroplane Company in 1912. A number of designs were originated to meet the early require-

The attractive Thomas-Morse S-4 bore a close resemblance to the Sopwith Pup, and featured the same Gnome rotary engine. It was originally built to answer the call for a new fighter.

ments of the US Army. The growing capability of Thomas Brothers brought a merger with the Morse Chain Company, to establish the Thomas-Morse Aircraft Corporation at Ithaca, New York, in January 1917.

In Europe a major conflict had been raging since the summer of 1914, one which historians were later to label as World War I, but it was not until 6 April 1917 that the United States declared war on Germany. Ill-prepared to participate, the most urgent requirements of the Aviation Section of the US Army Signals Corps were aircraft, and

trained pilots to fly them. Thomas Brothers had designed a single-seat scout, but after evaluation by the Aviation Section it was regarded as unsuitable for combat and was instead ordered from the Thomas-Morse company as an advanced trainer. Designated S-4B, initial procurement ran to 100 examples of these stagger-wing single-bay biplanes. They had a basic structure of wood with fabric covering, landing gear of tailskid type, and power provided by a 100-hp (74.6-kW) Gnome rotary engine (then being licence-built in the USA). The S-4C which followed had improved

ailerons and aileron control system, but only the first 50 of the 1,050 contracted retained the somewhat temperamental Gnome engine. The remainder had a Le Rhône rotary, but only 497 S-4Cs had been delivered at the time of the Armistice and the 553 then outstanding were cancelled. Ten examples of the S-4B and four of the S-4C were also acquired by the US Navy for use as advanced trainers.

Regarded as superior to the renowned Curtiss 'Jenny', S-4Cs soon found buyers when offered in the post-war surplus market. They saw much use until the late 1920s when more stringent safety regulations brought their era to an end.

Specification
S-4C

Type: single-seat advanced trainer
Powerplant: one 80-hp (59.7-kW) Le Rhône rotary piston engine
Performance: maximum speed 95 mph (153 km/h) at sea level; initial climb 10 minutes to 7,500 ft (2,285 m); service ceiling 15,000 ft (4,570 m); endurance 2 hours 30 minutes
Weight: maximum take-off 1,373 lb (623 kg)
Dimensions: span 26 ft 6 in (8.08 m); length 19 ft 10 in (6.05 m); height 8 ft 1 in (2.46 m); wing area 145 sq ft (13.47 m^2)
Armament: normally one camera gun, occasionally one Marlin 0.3-in (7.62-mm) machine-gun

Thomas-Morse MB-3

Thomas-Morse MB-3A of the 43rd School Squadron, Kelly Field, Texas in 1925.

History and notes

In the early months of 1918 the US Army decided it was desirable that the nation's industry got down to the task of designing and building aircraft for its use, rather than continuing to rely upon the purchase or licence manufacture of aircraft designed and produced by its Allies and plans were made to bring this about. At the war's end, when the Army Air Service returned to the USA, one of the most urgent requirements was a replacement for the French-built SPAD XIII, 893 of which the AEF had procured and the survivors returned to the USA after the Armistice for first-line use.

Among the US manufacturers approached was the Thomas-Morse Aircraft Corporation whose design proposal was for a single-seat biplane which the company designated MB-3. Retaining some similarity to the SPAD XIII that it was intended to replace, the MB-3 also had a basic structure of wood with fabric covering, tailskid type landing gear and power provided by a 340-hp (254-kW) Hispano-Suiza Vee engine. The USAAS acquired initially four prototypes for test and evaluation with the first of them (40092) making the type's maiden flight on 21 February 1919. Its performance was sufficiently impressive to win a contract for 50 production MB-3s, but when an additional 200 were ordered it was The Boeing Airplane Company at Seattle, Washington, which gained the contract under a competitive bidding system that had then been introduced. The aircraft produced by Boeing had the designation MB-3A and they incorporated a number of

The Thomas-Morse MB-3 can be regarded as the first serious US attempt to produce an indigenous fighter. This is an MB-3A with smaller wing and other improvements. Most ended their days as advanced trainers.

refinements. An external identification feature was substitution of the MB-3's upper wing-mounted radiator by two smaller radiators, one on each side of the fuselage adjacent to the cockpit. The last 50 of the Boeing contract introduced an enlarged tailfin, and all 200 had been delivered by the end of 1922.

The 94th Pursuit Squadron, then based at Selfridge Field, Michigan, was one of the first squadrons to operate the MB-3A, and a number of these aircraft also equipped units at overseas bases. However, with the

MB-3/3As being little changed from a design of the 1916 era, they were soon replaced by more capable aircraft, and after redesignation as MB-3M they were employed at Kelly Field, Texas, until 1928 in various advanced training roles. There was growing interest in national air races and it is interesting that the Army selected the MB-3 for participation in these events. Three were given clipped wings and an uprated Wright H-3 engine developing 400-hp (298-kW) to become redesignated MB-6. A fourth conversion

with the same powerplant and with the introduction of an unusual Alula monoplane wing (which had been developed in the UK) produced the one-off MB-7 which had a top speed of 180 mph (290 km/h).

Specification
MB-3A

Type: single-seat fighter
Powerplant: one 300-hp (224-kW) Wright H-3 Vee piston engine
Performance: maximum speed 141 mph (227 km/h) at sea level;

cruising speed 125 mph (201 km/h); initial climb rate 1,235 ft (376 m) per minute; service ceiling 19,500 ft (5,945 m); endurance 2 hours 15 minutes
Weights: empty 1,716 lb (778 kg); maximum take-off 2,529 lb (1,152 kg)
Dimensions: span 26 ft 0 in (7.92 m); length 20 ft 0 in (6.1 m); height 7 ft 8 in (2.34 m); wing area 228.5 sq ft (21.23 m²)
Armament: two fixed forward-firing synchronised 0.3-in (7.62-mm) machine-guns

Orenco D

History and notes
During the closing stages of World War I the little-known Ordnance Engineering Corporation of Baldwin, New York, designed a single-seat fighter biplane. This proved of interest to the new US Army Air Service which had been formed on 24 May 1918. Designated by the company as the Orenco D, it was a robust-looking twin-bay biplane of all-wooden construction with the fuselage skinned with plywood, its tailskid-type landing gear including heavy Vee struts for the through-axle main landing gear. Selected powerplant was the Wright Model H, this being a licence-built version of the Hispano-Suiza 300-hp (224-kW) V-8 liquid-cooled engine, which in the case of the Orenco D was given a nose radiator installation.

Only four prototypes (40107-40110) were procured from Ordnance Engineering (which failed to make any other sales and soon went out of business), and delivery of these began in January 1919. The type was given a thorough evaluation before, later in 1919, the USAAS requested US aircraft manufacturers to tender

for the production of a batch of 50, the contract eventually being awarded to the Curtiss Aeroplane and Motor Company of Buffalo, New York. Only minor modifications were introduced by Curtiss, the most noticeable being a slight increase in span of the upper wing and the introduction of horn-balanced ailerons. Delivery of these aircraft (63281-63330) began in 1920 and was completed during the following year. Before delivery of the Curtiss-built Orenco Ds the USAAS had introduced a new system of type nomenclature, pursuit aircraft with

liquid-cooled engines being known as Type I and given PW designation prefixes. These designations were not applied to aircraft already delivered although the Orenco D was listed as a Type I aircraft. Lack of documentation would suggest that it was far from successful in service and that it was soon taken out of use.

Specification
Orenco D

Type: single-seat fighter
Powerplant: one 200 PS (220-kW) Wright H V-8 engine

Performance: maximum speed 139 mph (224 km/h); cruising speed 134 mph (215 km/h); climb to 1,227 ft (374 m) in one minute; service ceiling 12,468 ft (3800 m); range 342 miles (550 km)
Weights: empty 1,907 lb (865 kg); maximum take-off 2,820 lb (1279 kg)
Dimensions: span 33 ft (10.06 m); length 21 ft 6 in (6.54 m); wing area 273 sq ft (25.36 m²)
Armament: two fixed synchronised 0.3-in (7.62-mm) Browning machine-guns

Orenco built four prototypes of their D Pursuit for the Army, and these led to a production order for 50 aircraft built by Curtiss. Light bombs could be carried between the undercarriage struts.

Loening PA-1

History and notes
Identified as the PA-1, the one and only PA (Pursuit Air-cooled engine) designation to be allocated by the

US Army Air Service, two aircraft were ordered from the Loening Aeronautical Engineering Company in 1921. This single-seat

biplane had thick section wings and was powered by a Curtiss-Wright R-1454 engine of 350-hp (261-kW). Testing of the first aircraft during 1922 would appear to have proved unsuccessful as records indicate that the second example was cancelled.

Specification
PA-1

Performance: maximum speed 124 mph (200 km/h); maximum take-off weight 2,463 lb (1,117 kg)
Dimensions: span 28 ft 0 in (8.53 m); length 19 ft 9 in (6.02 m)

Aeromarine PG-1

History and notes
Designed by the Engineering Division of the US Army Air Service, the PG-1 single-seat biplane built by the Aeromarine Plane and Motor Company Inc. was the only aircraft included in this PG (Pursuit, Ground attack) category. Powered by a Wright K-2 Vee engine of 330-hp (246-kW), for the ground attack role these aircraft were armed by a 37-mm cannon mounted in the Vee of the two cylinder banks of the engine. No production aircraft followed test and evaluation of the three PG-1 prototypes, which were delivered during 1922.

Specification
PG-1

Performance: maximum speed 124 mph (200 km/h); maximum take-off weight 3,918 lb (1,777 kg)
Dimensions: span 40 ft 0 in (12.19 m); length 24 ft 6 in (7.47 m)

The single aircraft in the 'PG'/ Pursuit, Ground Attack' category was the Aeromarine PG-1, an Engineering Division design. For its attack role it was to have carried a 37-mm cannon in the propeller shaft and shackles for bombs. Only three were completed.

Political Struggle

With the war in Europe over, massive demobilisation took place. Despite spirited fighting from men like Billy Mitchell, the fortunes of the US Army Air Service and its fighters took a nose-dive.

11 November 1918: the war in Europe is over, and the United States Air Service has played a massive part in the final proceedings. A phenomenal effort in both industry and the training of aircrew has resulted in a huge force of victorious fliers, but now there is nothing for them to do, and they must face the political music back home.

Temporarily divorced from the Army, leaders of the Air Service were quick to try to retain some of the autonomy and power with which they had been entrusted in 1917/18. Certainly the war in Europe had proved that air power was the military force of the future, and to ignore it now was to commit military suicide. Leading light of these protagonists was Brigadier-General Billy Mitchell, who fought tooth and nail to establish a separate air force, and to sway the traditionalist Army and Navy top brass into believing that bombers were mightier weapons than tanks or battleships. From 1918 onwards, a political battle erupted over the question of the air arm.

Post-war cutback

From the moment of the Armistice, demobilisation took precedence over defence, and personnel strengths were decimated almost overnight. Orders from US manufacturers standing at thousands of aircraft were cut at a stroke, leaving the air arm's suppliers almost bankrupt. The large number that had been built for the war effort were either burned in France (rather than pay the shipping fee back to the States) or sold off at ridiculous rates, brand-new crated fighters going for a few dollars to lucky private individuals. Ironically the large numbers of out-of-work pilots and the availability of aircraft sparked off the 'barnstorming' revolution, which did more than anything to raise the level of aviation consciousness in the United States.

Congress was cutting defence budgets left, right and centre. A 1918 plan for an Air Service with 24,000 personnel and an appro-

Brigadier-General Billy Mitchell had been the commander of the AEF in France, and after the war fought fanatically for the recognition of air power and the establishment of a separate Air Force. Now regarded as an enlightened hero, his career ended in a court martial. Here he is seen proudly displaying a Curtiss PW-8.

Dominating the immediate post-war period were the designs of Curtiss and Boeing. Two classic lines of fighters were developed which ran in parallel throughout the 1920s. Here are the two starting blocks, the Boeing PW-9 (left) and Curtiss PW-8 (right).

priate number of aircraft was slashed to less than one-third, and by 1920 the total strength was only 12,000. There was no money for new aircraft, so squadrons still flew aircraft left over from the war. To hit back against this misguided policy, Mitchell and his Air Service arranged record-breaking flights to prove the speed and potential of the warplane, but throughout his fight he was outgunned by Army and Navy officials in terms of rank, and he would never overcome this handicap. In June 1920 the Army regained control of the aircraft, the new body becoming the US Army Air Service. Things became bleaker and bleaker for Mitchell.

Designation system

Earlier, in September 1919, the Air Service had introduced its first formal means of identifying aircraft types. Until the introduction of this classification system, US military aircraft had been known by their manufacturers' names, but the 1919 system introduced classes according to the aircraft's role. In the case of the fighters, these became PA (pursuit, aircooled), PG (pursuit, ground attack), PN (pursuit, night), PS (pursuit, special alert) and PW (pursuit, watercooled). This system lasted until 1924, although aircraft so designated retained their designations after that time.

At the start of the 1920s, Mitchell was ever more fanatical over his argument for air power, arguing that there was no point buying expensive battleships when his fighters could strafe them and his bombers sink them. Luckily for him, some Navy admirals shared his view, and the Navy instigated a small exercise against a surplus battleship. The results were good, but the Navy top brass suppressed them to avoid publicity. In January 1921 Mitchell went before the Appropriations Committee to argue his case that " . . . we can either destroy or sink any ship in existence today. . . . all we want is a chance to demonstrate these things . . ."

Another area of inspiration for fighter designers was the high-performance observation aircraft. The Loening M.8 two-place spotter was developed into this, the PW-2 single-seat fighter, one of a number of pursuit designs that remained only in prototype form.

The Secretary of the Navy, Josephus Daniels, stated in reply that he would gladly stand bare-headed on the deck of any battleship while under attack from the air. This statement came to backfire on Daniels, for some German warships were turned over to the Navy for air attack trials, in which Mitchell and his bombers took part. In a series of attacks, the Air Service claimed a destroyer, a light cruiser and finally the battleship *Ostfriesland*. After an onslaught with two thousand-pound bombs, the mighty ship went down. Mitchell had been proved right.

Throughout this period, the bomber was

seen as the main instrument of airpower, with the pursuits acting as escorts to ensure that the '. . . bomber will always get through'. Nevertheless, development of fighters was slowly gearing up during the early 1920s, culminating in the Curtiss PW-8 and Boeing PW-9. Each initiated a line of fighters that would dominate the fighter scene for the next few years.

Designs proliferated in the 1920s, with designs for the prestige air races spawning fighters, as well as fighters being developed for racing. The Engineering Division-Verville VCP-1 was developed as both a fighter (PW-1) and racer (R-1).

Curtiss PN-1

History and notes

Designed by the Engineering Division of the US Army Air Service, the PN-1 was intended for a night interception role, hence its designation PN (Pursuit, Night). In finalising its design, the Engineering Division had clearly been influenced by the configuration of the highly successful Fokker D.VII of World War I but, unusually, this single-seat biplane was expected to maintain its structural integrity without the use of interplane struts. Curtiss gained the contract to build these two aircraft, but only the first prototype was completed with the second being cancelled. As prepared for testing, the sole PN-1 had a basic fuselage structure of welded steel tube with fabric covering, this being the first time that Curtiss had been involved in this mode of construction. Power was to have been provided by a 230-hp (172-kW) Liberty 6 engine, but in fact the PN-1 never flew, its service use limited to static testing.

Specification
PN-1

Performance: maximum speed estimated 108 mph (174 km/h); maximum take-off weight, estimated 2,310 lb (1,048 kg)
Dimensions: span 30 ft 10 in (9.40 m); length 23 ft 6 in (7.16 m)

Dayton-Wright PS-1

History and notes

Obviously intending to explore the potential of single-seat interceptor aircraft, the US Army Air Service finalised a contract in 1921 with the Dayton-Wright Airplane Company of Dayton, Ohio, for the design and construction of three prototypes to meet this requirement. Interestingly, at that time Orville Wright was the company's consulting engineer. The intended role for the PS-1 aircraft is highlighted by the designation (Pursuit, Special alert). These short-range parasol-wing monoplanes, powered by the 200-hp (149-kW) Lawrance J-1 nine-cylinder air-cooled radial engine, were delivered during 1922-3 as XPS-1 prototypes, and were either inadequate in performance or ahead of their time. Little was heard of them and they remained the only examples of the PS category.

Specification
PS-1

Performance: maximum speed 145 mph (233 km/h); maximum take-off weight 1,715 lb (778 kg)
Dimensions: span 30 ft 0 in (9.14 m); length 19 ft 2 in (5.84 m)

The 'PS' designation stood for 'Pursuit, Special Alert' and was applied only to the Dayton-Wright PS-1. This category was intended for short-range interceptors of important targets (a discipline known today as point defence). Only three PS-1s were built.

Engineering Division PW-1

History and notes

What was to become the first member of the PW (Pursuit, Water-cooled engine) family of US Army Air Service aircraft, the PW-1 was the work of Alfred 'Fred' V. Verville, a designer who came to the Engineering Division late in World War I. From his Verville Chasse Plane was evolved the VCP-1 fighter (only one of the two prototypes was flown). The VCP-1 formed the basis for the two VCP-2 prototypes (64349 and 64350) of which the first was used for static tests. A typical single-seat biplane of the period with a 350-hp (261-kW) Packard 1A-1237 12-cylinder Vee engine, 64350 was first flown in early 1920 and shortly after was redesignated PW-1. Hoping to improve

Between 1919 and 1924, all watercooled pursuits were designated 'PW', and the first member of the category was the PW-1. This photograph shows the single PW-1 modified to PW-1A standard with straight-chord wings designed by Fokker.

performance, the aircraft was tested with straight-chord wings incorporating a thicker aerofoil section and was redesignated the PW-1A at this time, but reverted to PW-1 when the original wings were refitted. A PW-1B variant with tapered wings of revised aerofoil section was planned but was cancelled.

Specification
PW-1

Performance: maximum speed 146 mph (235 km/h); maximum take-off weight 2,005 lb (1,363 kg)
Dimensions: span 32 ft 0 in (9.75 m); length 22 ft 6 in (6.86 m)

Here the PW-1 exhibits the tapering wings with which it was initially built. In addition to the sole flying aircraft, another static test airframe was built. The type had been developed from the VCP-1, and was originally known as the VCP-2.

Loening PW-2

History and notes

During 1918 the Loening Aeronautical Engineering Company had designed the M.8, a two-seat shoulder-wing monoplane intended for use in an observation role. It gained a US Army Air Service contract, but with the war's end only two were built. From this basic design the company developed a new single-seater to meet a post-war requirement of the USAAS for a fighter in the PW (Pursuit, Watercooled) category. Three PW-2 prototypes were built, the first (64139) being used for static testing. Evaluation of 64140 and 64141 led to a contract for 10 PW-2A production aircraft, with modifications to the rear fuselage and tail unit, and with power provided by the 320-hp (239-kW) Wright H engine. After one of the first four production aircraft lost its wings in flight, the remaining six were cancelled. One of the PW-2As was subsequently reworked with wings of reduced span and given a 350-hp (261-kW) Packard 1A-1237 engine, and was tested for a period under the designation PW-2B.

Specification
PW-2A

Performance: maximum speed 136 mph (219 km/h); maximum take-off weight 2,799 lb (1,270 kg)
Dimensions: span 39 ft 9 in (12.12 m); length 26 ft 1 in (7.95 m)

Above: The Loening PW-2 was not a successful design, production amounting to just six flying and one static aircraft. The monoplane layout could not match the manoeuvrability of the biplane, with little advance in performance.

Below: In an attempt to improve the poor performance of the PW-2, this PW-2A was modified to PW-2B standard with cropped wings and a more powerful (350 hp) Packard 1A-1237 engine. Note the beautifully crafted four-blade propeller.

Orenco PW-3

History and notes

The third type to be procured by the US Army Air Service in its PW category was a single-seat biplane fighter designated PW-3 from Orenco (Ordnance Engineering Corporation). Known by the company as the Model D2, this design was evolved from the earlier Orenco D, and was to have been powered by the 320-hp (239-kW) Wright H engine. Only one of these aircraft was delivered to McCook Field during 1921 but it was never flown, and in the same year all three were condemned and scrapped.

Specification
PW-3

Performance: maximum weight, estimated 2,670 lb (1,211 kg)
Dimensions: span 27 ft 9 in (8.46 m); length 23 ft 10 in (7.26 m)

Developed from the D Pursuit, the Orenco PW-3 was an unsuccessful fighter design which was destined never to fly. Three aircraft were ordered from Orenco, but in the event only one was delivered to the Air Service. All three airframes were scrapped shortly after.

Gallaudet PW-4

History and notes

The Gallaudet Engineering Company had built some interesting prototypes for the US Navy during 1917-8. The newly-named Gallaudet Aircraft Corporation received a contract from the US Army Air Service in 1921 covering the design and supply of three PW-4 single-seat biplane fighters of all-metal construction. Intended powerplant was the 350-hp (261-kW) Packard 1A-1237, but after the first example (64385) had been delivered to McCook Field in 1922 and failed to survive its static tests, the two remaining examples were cancelled.

Specification
PW-4

Performance: maximum speed, estimated 145 mph (233 km/h); maximum take-off weight, estimated 3,076 lb (1,395 kg)
Dimensions: span 29 ft 10 in (9.09 m); length 22 ft 8 in (6.91 m)

The interesting Gallaudet PW-4 was of all-metal construction, with a bulky fuselage and large Packard engine. The structure was its undoing, for this could not take the strain of static load tests. The prototype was scrapped without flying, and the other two were scrapped before completion.

Fokker PW-5, PW-6 and PW-7

History and notes

The famous Fokker company, which was established in the Netherlands on 21 July 1919, was soon to win a contract from the US Army Air Service. This occurred in 1920 after the USAAS had completed evaluation of one or more of the 142 Fokker D.VII biplane fighters that had been captured in Europe and returned to the USA. It resulted in procurement from the Dutch company of two aircraft based on the Fokker F.VI and these (identified by Fokker as V.40) were single-seaters of highwing monoplane configuration with Wright-Hispano engines and two Browning machine-guns. Under test at McCook Field the first of these (64231) crashed during 1922, but clearly the evaluation was sufficiently promising for the USAAS to order 10 more from Fokker, these being given the designation PW-5. Generally similar to the two V.40s and each powered by a 335-hp (250-kW) Wright H2 engine, they were delivered towards the end of 1922 and used for a time by the 1st Pursuit Group in an advanced training role.

Other procurements from Fokker at that time included the company's D.IX prototype (a development of

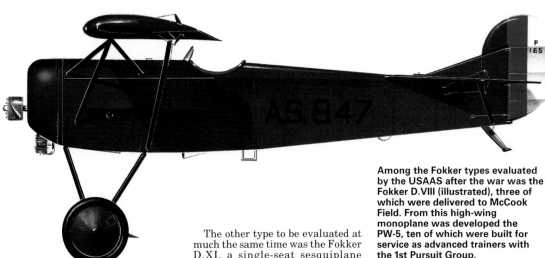

the D.VII biplane) which had a basic fuselage structure of metal, slightly greater wing area and a 320-hp (239-kW) version of the Wright H2 engine. Designated the PW-6, this was evaluated at McCook Field as a potential replacement for the in-service captured D.VIIs.

The other type to be evaluated at much the same time was the Fokker D.XI, a single-seat sesquiplane fighter of which three examples were procured under the designation PW-7. Powered by the 440-hp (328-kW) Curtiss D-12 engine and armed with two 0.30-in (7.62-mm) machine-guns, their evaluation by the USAAS did not result in the procurement of any production examples.

Among the Fokker types evaluated by the USAAS after the war was the Fokker D.VIII (illustrated), three of which were delivered to McCook Field. From this high-wing monoplane was developed the PW-5, ten of which were built for service as advanced trainers with the 1st Pursuit Group.

Specification
PW-5
Performance: maximum speed 137 mph (220 km/h); maximum take-off weight 3,015 lb (1,368 kg)
Dimensions: span 39 ft 5 in (12.01 m); length 27 ft 2 in (8.28 m)

Curtiss PW-8

History and notes

The Curtiss Hawks, well-known single-seat fighters of the US Army during the 'inter-war' years, were used by both the US Army Air Service which had been established in World War I, and the US Army Air Corps which superseded it on 2 July 1926. The Hawk family originated as a private venture in 1922 when Curtiss designed and built the prototype of a new single-seat fighter

which it was hoped would prove of interest to the US Army. This was a difficult period for aviation manufacturers, when large numbers of surplus aircraft from World War I were still in storage and air arms had no funds to procure more-modern aircraft.

Designated by the company as the Model 33, the new single-seat two-bay biplane had all-wooden wings and introduced a fuselage structure

of wire-braced welded steel tube, as well as tail surfaces based upon aluminium frame structures with fabric covering. Landing gear was of tailskid-type, powerplant comprised the new Curtiss D-12 Vee engine, and unique for a military aircraft were the wing surface radiators for the engine coolant, a feature handed over from Curtiss racing aircraft.

In due course the US Army tested a Model 33 and, impressed with its

The Curtiss Model 33 emerged in USAAS service as the PW-8, and can be regarded as one of the first successful US-designed and built pursuits. To demonstrate its versatility, this aircraft was fitted with skis for snow operations.

performance by comparison with the ex-World War I aircraft in service, bought it in April 1923, and ordered two more. All three were duly de-

Curtiss PW-8 of the 17th Pursuit Squadron, 1st Pursuit Group. It wears the number '60' for participation in the 1924 Mitchell Trophy race.

One PW-8 was retained by Curtiss for modifications to the radiators system and for new wings. It is seen here as the XPW-8B, with short-span lower wings and tunnel radiator mounted beneath the engine. As such it was to serve as the prototype for the important P-1 series.

signated PW-8 (Pursuit, Water-cooled, the 8th of the type procured), but becoming redesignated XPW-8 in 1924 when the X (experimental) designation prefix letter was adopted. On 25 September 1923 the army ordered 25 production PW-8s, and these incorporated a number of features introduced in the second prototype, including revised main landing gear, strut-connected ailerons and unbalanced elevators. Delivered from June 1924, one PW-8 (24-204) is distinguished in USAAS history when on 23 June 1924, piloted by Lieutenant Russell Maughan, it achieved the first dawn-to-dusk crossing of the United States.

The third XPW-8 prototype was retained by Curtiss for installation of single-bay wings incorporating a radiator in the upper wing centre-

This standard PW-8 was used for the first dawn-to-dusk crossing of the United States, as noted by the emblem on the fuselage side. Performing this feat on 23 June 1924, the aircraft was flown by Lieutenant Russell Maughan. Note the heavy strut connecting upper and lower ailerons.

section. It was delivered on 4 September 1924 and redesignated XPW-8A. Tests showed the cooling radiator to be inadequate, and it was soon changed to a tunnel-type radiator mounted beneath the engine. This aircraft was later given tapered wings, then becoming redesignated XPW-8B. These wings and the tunnel radiator became recognition features of the subsequent Hawk series.

Specification
Curtiss PW-8

Type: single-seat fighter
Powerplant: one 435-hp (324-kW) Curtiss D-12 Vee piston engine
Performance: maximum speed 171 mph (275 km/h) at sea level; maximum cruising speed 136 mph (219 km/h); initial climb rate 1,830 ft (558 m) per minute; service ceiling 20,350 ft (6,200 m); range 544 miles (875 km)

Weights: empty 2,185 lb (991 kg); maximum take-off 3,155 lb (1,431 kg)
Dimensions: span 32 ft 0 in (9.75 m); length 23 ft 1 in (7.04 m); height 9 ft 1 in (2.77 m); wing area 279.3 sq ft (25.95 m²)
Armament: two, usually one 0.3-in (7.62-mm) and one 0.5-in (12.7-mm), fixed forward-firing synchronised machine-guns mounted within the engine cowling

Boeing PW-9

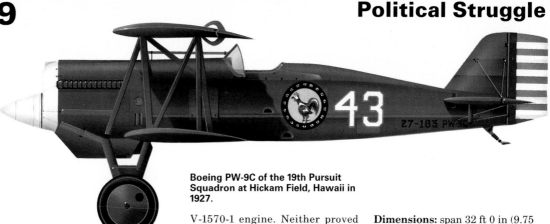

Boeing PW-9C of the 19th Pursuit Squadron at Hickam Field, Hawaii in 1927.

History and notes

At the same period that Curtiss was designing and building its private venture Model 33 in the hope of winning a military contract from the US Army Air Service, The Boeing Airplane Company was pursuing a similar course for precisely the same reason. Boeing, however, was in a better position to adopt such a policy, as the company had already gained considerable experience from its production of the Thomas-Morse MB-3A (which see), and in addition had recently developed an arc welding process which held considerable promise for the manufacture of robust steel tube structures. Thus Boeing was reasonably certain that it could produce a better fighter than anything then in service with the USAAS, when it decided to proceed with the private venture to design and construct a single-seat fighter prototype under the company designation Model 15.

The prototype which emerged (flown for the first time on 29 April 1923) was a single-seat biplane with tapered wings of unequal span that were of fabric-covered wooden construction. The fuselage and tail unit both had basic metal structures with fabric covering. The landing gear was of tailskid-type with through-axle main units. Power was provided by a Curtiss D-12 with a tunnel radiator below the engine. USAAS testing of this prototype during the summer of 1923 resulted in a contract covering the purchase of this aircraft and two additional prototypes, later designated XPW-9. The third of these, of slightly heavier construction and with divided-axle main landing gear, was of the configuration adopted for the initial

Boeing produced a superb aircraft with the PW-9, this exhibiting performance and manoeuvrability with no major disadvantages. This is the first of three prototypes, displaying to advantage the sesquiplane layout.

production batch of 12 (later increased to 30) PW-9s which was ordered on 19 September 1924.

The first PW-9s entered service from October 1925, and were followed subsequently by the PW-9A (25 built) with a Curtiss D-12C engine and minor changes. One was completed instead with a 180-hp (134-kW) Wright E-4 (Hispano-Suiza) engine for use as an advanced trainer, becoming designated AT-3, and one temporarily flown with a Curtiss D-12D engine was redesignated PW-9B during its test and evaluation period. The designation PW-9C (40 built) applied to what was virtually a production version of the PW-9B, but which also introduced structural strengthening and larger wheels.

Final production version for the USAAS was the similar PW-9D, then some 8 per cent heavier than the original PW-9, and which had a new coolant radiator, a balanced rudder, revised cowlings and introduced wheel brakes to landing wheels of the same size as the PW-9A. Variants included the XP-4, which was a PW-9D converted to a 500-hp (373-kW) Packard 1A-1500 turbocharged engine, and a second PW-9D converted to XP-7 configuration with a 600-hp (447-kW) Curtiss

V-1570-1 engine. Neither proved successful and the XP-7 was reworked as a PW-9D.

Specification
Boeing PW-9D

Type: single-seat fighter
Powerplant: one 435-hp (324-kW) Curtiss D-12D Vee piston engine
Performance: maximum speed 155 mph (249 km/h) at sea level; cruising speed 124 mph (200 km/h); climb to 5,000 ft (1,525 m) in 4 minutes; service ceiling 18,230 ft (5,555 m); range 390 miles (628 km)
Weights: empty 2,328 lb (1,056 kg); maximum take-off 3,234 lb (1,467 kg)

Dimensions: span 32 ft 0 in (9.75 m); length 23 ft 5 in (7.14 m); height 8 ft 2 in (2.49 m); wing area 241 sq ft (22.39 m^2)
Armament: two fixed forward-firing synchronised 0.3-in (7.62-mm) machine-guns; some with one 0.3-in (7.62-mm) and one 0.5-in (12.7-mm) machine guns

Boeing's PW-9 became the leading home-produced fighter during the mid-1920s. Although only small numbers were produced, the budgetary cuts prevalent at the time meant that it was a relative success. This machine is typical of early production PW-9s, which entered service in 1925.

Hawks High

Stemming from the PW-8, the Curtiss Hawk blossomed into one of the most important aircraft of the 1920s. Boeing designs followed soon after to challenge the classic biplane.

As the 1920s progressed, Billy Mitchell and his Air Service fought ever harder for budgetary recognition in order to build a realistic air force. Their superb efforts against the surplus German ships had proved once and for all that the warplane was a force to be reckoned with, and that it should be regarded as at least an equal of land and naval equipment. Of course, the senior ranking officers of those services thought otherwise, and the air arm continued to be squashed.

Following the tests against the German ships, more tests were conducted with similar results, and with similar reactions from the top brass. Mitchell grew more impatient and more abrasive, and was effectively exiled from the public eye by a posting to San Antonio. However, even from this backwater he sounded a broadside when a giant dirigible, the USS *Shenandoah*, crashed killing 14 crewmen in 1925. In a press release, Mitchell blamed the accident, and

others, on the "... incompetence, criminal negligence and almost treasonable administration of the national defence by the War and Navy Departments".

This was too much for the officials to bear, and on 7 September 1925 the orders for Mitchell's court martial were announced. Found guilty, he was suspended from the Army. He died on 19 February 1936, never to see the ultimate proof of his far-sighted concepts in the bombing onslaughts on Europe

Another well-known photograph, showing a Curtiss P-1B Hawk cavorting over Washington D.C. More than ten years after the war, the US air arm was still a small force. At least with aircraft like the P-1 they had good machines.

and Japan during World War II.

With their most articulate and most fanatical spokesman gone, the Air Service did not put up so much fight against the

One of the best-known and evocative photographs of the period shows Curtiss P-6Es of the 17th Pursuit Squadron, 1st Pursuit Group from Selfridge Field, Michigan. The 'snowy owl' insignia was well-known, and was augmented by white talons on the mainwheel spats.

One of the many Hawk variants was the XP-3A, fitted with a Pratt & Whitney R-1340-9 Wasp radial. This is the second of two XP-3As, with a fully-cowled engine. It achieved second place in the 1929 Thompson race.

Army and Navy. The Air Service remained at much the same size throughout the decade, comprising one Pursuit Group, one Bomber Group and one Observation Group. With no threat of war there was no need for any expansion, although this policy can easily be seen as foolhardy in hindsight.

During this period, the service changed its name. In 1926 the title United States Army Air Corps was adopted. Two years previously, it introduced a system of nomenclature to simplify the previous classifications. To confuse the issue, however, aircraft designated previously (such as the PW-8), retained their old designations. Pursuits were, from May 1924, designated P (or PB for a handful of 'Biplace' aircraft), while bombers received 'B', transports 'C', advanced trainers 'AT' and so forth.

Dominating the first run of the Pursuit series were designs from Curtiss and Boeing, which used the PW-8 and PW-9 respectively as their starting points to create two lines of aircraft that provided the fighter units with their machines well into the 1930s.

Curtiss was the first to show, claiming the P-1 to P-6 designations for successive variants of the Hawk biplane. The two main production versions were the P-1 and P-6, the latter being the definitive Hawk, and in its P-6E version one of the best-looking biplane fighters ever built. New designations were dished out to seemingly minor variants of the Hawk like confetti, and further numbers used up were the P-11, 17, 20, 21, 22 and 23.

Boeing fighters

More purposeful and less graceful were the Boeing fighters, which evolved from the PW-9. Boeing was a major supplier of fighters to the Navy, and the development tended to follow the naval path rather than the air force, but variants were produced of the FB, F2B and F4B for the Air Corps. In particular the last of these was a classic, the P-12, and it was built in large numbers (for the day) in the early 1930s.

Following these two classics in the designations list were a number of experimental fighters from other manufacturers, none of which showed any great potential. The Hawk and Boeing families had taken the biplane fighter about as far as it could go, and the way ahead for fighter development lay with the monoplane. During the 1930s, this was to become a reality.

Curtiss P-1 Hawk

History and notes

The Curtiss P-1 Hawk enjoys the distinction of being first in the hallowed line of pursuit/fighter aircraft designated under a system adopted by the US Army Air Corps (USAAC) in 1924 and continued to the present day, with changes in 1948 and 1962. An improvement of pioneer Glenn Curtiss' earlier XPW-8B, first ordered in a batch of 10 on 7 March 1925, the sturdy biplane fighter with limited bomb-carrying capacity was ready for tests at McCook Field, Ohio, by 17 August. The first machines served with the 27th and 94th Pursuit Squadrons, 1st Pursuit Group (commanded by Major Thomas G. Lanphier), at Selfridge Field, Michigan.

Development of the basic airframe, considered tough and reliable by pilots, led to the P-1A with a slightly lengthened fuselage, 25 of which were ordered in September 1925. Two of these machines were later diverted to other roles, one becoming the sole XAT-4 advanced trainer. Soon after, 23 P-1Bs were ordered in August 1926 and again stationed at Selfridge with the 27th Pursuit Squadron under Major Ralph Royce. The P-1B had the V-1150-3 engine, improved radiator, larger tyres, and slightly increased normal loaded weight.

Success of the design led to contracts for 33 P-1Cs with the same

The 27th Pursuit Squadron at Selfridge was the recipient of the 23 Curtiss P-1Bs ordered in 1926. The early Hawks were produced in rapid succession with relatively minor modifications between models, so deliveries of the P-1B began only two months after the order.

Curtiss P-1B of the 27th Pursuit Squadron, 1st Pursuit Group at Selfridge Field, Michigan.

engine, slightly increased weight, and wheel brakes. The XP-1C designation was assigned to one airframe equipped with a one-off Heinrich radiator and Prestone cooling system.

P-1D and P-1E fighters, actually converted from machines built originally as AT-5 trainers, totalled 40 and equipped the 43rd Pursuit Squadron, known as the Hornets, at Kelly Field, Texas. Similar conversions of the AT-5A trainer, powered by the Wright R-790 engine, became the P-1F. An additional P-1F airframe resulted from conversion of an airframe which had had other incarnations as a P-3A, XP-3A and XP-21.

These early single-bay biplane Hawks, close kin to the Curtiss racers of the late 1920s and early 1930s, were considered advanced for their period and had a special reputation for ruggedness. Related machines in the series would encompass several early pursuit designations and cul-

minate in the classic P-6E Hawk. But the liquid-cooled engine did not enjoy full favour at this time and the change to a radial powerplant with the P-3 Hawk was to be the next major development. With the reversion of 52 trainers and four later P-2 airframes to P-1 standard, a total of 149 P-1 Hawks was manufactured.

Covered with icicles, this P-1C rests on its skis on Lake St. Clair. The aircraft is from the 1st Pursuit Group Arctic Patrol Flight, on a trip from its Selfridge base to Spokane in 1930.

Specification

P-1B

Type: single-seat pursuit aircraft
Powerplant: one 435-hp (324.4-kW) Curtiss V-1150-1 liquid-cooled 12-cylinder Vee piston engine driving a fixed-pitch two-blade propeller
Performance: maximum speed 159.6 mph (256.8 km/h) at 10,000 ft (3048 m); cruising speed 128 mph (206 km/h); stalling speed 58 mph (93 km/h); initial climb rate 1,400 ft (427 m) per minute; service ceiling 21,000 ft (6401 m)
Weights: empty 2,041 lb (925.8 kg); normal loaded 2,932 lb (1330 kg)
Dimensions: span 31 ft 6 in (9.60 m); length 22 ft 11 in (6.98 m); height 8 ft 11 in (2.72 m); wing area 252 sq ft (23.41 m^2)
Armament: one 0.3-in (7.62-mm) and one 0.5-in (12.7-mm) fixed, synchronized, forward-firing machine-guns firing through propeller disc

Curtiss P-2 Hawk

History and notes

'Fastest pursuit ship in the world!' proclaimed Curtiss literature shortly after signing of the 7 March 1925 contract authorising an XP-2 plus four P-2 Hawk airframes, the same order which had begun the life of the earlier P-1 Hawk. An exaggeration, even though the speed of 185 mph (297.7 km/h) was more than respectable, the claim was built around an exhaust-driven turbocharger mounted on the right side of the fuselage nose with exhaust from

the Curtiss V-1400 engine ducted through the turbine to compress the air rammed into the carburettor. Turbo-charging did enhance both the speed and altitude capability of the ubiquitous biplane Hawk, but the engine itself was fraught with teething problems. A decision was made to limit installation of the turbocharger to the sole XP-2, serial number 25-420.

The remaining four P-2 airframes, serials 25-421 to 25-424, briefly saw operational service. Displeasure

with the powerplant made their life brief. One was involved in a rather spectacular crack-up, although it was fully repaired. All were re-engined with the proven Curtiss V-1150 to be redesignated P-1 and, as a further switch in the many name changes of early Curtiss fighters, one example, serial 25-423, was further redesignated XP-6 when the Curtiss V-1550 Conqueror engine became available.

Though turbo-charging did not succeed with this fabric-covered,

single-bay biplane fighter, through no flaw in the notion itself but rather due to an unsatisfactory powerplant match-up, turbocharging would prove one way to enhance combat performance of later fighters. From the very first flight of the XP-2 in December 1925, through tests at McCook Field, Ohio, in which the pursuit ship operated under firm control at altitudes as high as 32,790 ft (9994 m), it was apparent that if the XP-2 design itself was not the answer, Glenn Curtiss's design teams were at least addressing the right questions. Major Leroy Jackson, who flew the XP-2 briefly and had later experience with the super-charged P-6D, says, "The potential was definitely there. The P-2 would have been able to fight any adversary we knew about at that time. In mock dogfights, I was almost always able to gain the upper hand."

Like all Curtiss Hawk pursuit ships of the period, the P-2 wore standard Army olive-drab camouflage. The open cockpit was roomy

and comfortable. High nose and fixed gear required some patience when taxying, but the craft was sturdy enough to withstand a 'hard' landing by an unskilled pilot. Such were common attributes of the Hawk series. But the P-2 appellation would be relegated to history with but five airframes completed.

Specification
XP-2

Type: single-seat pursuit aircraft
Powerplant: one 600-hp

(447.4-kW) Curtiss V-1400 liquid-cooled 12-cylinder Vee piston engine with turbo-charger driving a ground-adjustable two-blade Hamilton propeller
Performance: maximum speed 185 mph (297.7 km/h) at 20,000 ft (6096 m); cruising speed 130 mph (212 km/h) at 20,000 ft (6096 m); stalling speed 58 mph (93 km/h); initial climb rate 2,400 ft (732 m) per minute; service ceiling 24,500 ft (7468 m); maximum ceiling 32,790 ft (9994 m); range 570 miles

(917 km)
Weights: empty 2,081 lb (943.9 kg); normal loaded 2,869 lb (1301.4 kg)
Dimensions: span 31 ft 7 in (9.63 m); length 22 ft 10 in (6.96 m); height 8 ft 7 in (2.62 m); wing area 252 sq ft (23.41 m²)
Armament: one 0.3-in (7.62-mm) and one 0.5-in (12.7-mm) fixed, synchronized, forward-firing machine-guns firing through propeller disc

Curtiss P-3 Hawk

History and notes
A round cowl with a distinctive Townend ring housing, radial engine, and further juggling of aircraft designations in the prolific Curtiss Hawk series characterised the broad-nosed, ungainly P-3 fighter design. No fewer than three engine types were tried on the Curtiss P-3 Hawk and three other designations (XP-21, XP-22, AT-5A) eventually adorned a bulky and unpopular variation on a theme, perhaps best remembered because it introduces the Pratt & Whitney name to US Army fighters of the period.

The XP-3, serial 26-300, which had begun life as the final P-1A, was conceived for the 390-hp (290.8-kW) Curtiss R-1454 air-cooled radial engine which, like several of the powerplants of the late 1920s, failed to reach fruition for practical use. Instead, the 410-hp (305.7-kW) Pratt & Whitney R-1340-9 Wasp radial was installed and this aircraft was tested extensively both uncowled and with a variety of deep-chord NACA cowls. The second airframe, XP-3A serial 28-189, was built with a streamlined cowling and propeller hub to reduce drag and add much-needed cosmetic relief to a far from eyecatching configuration. This machine finished second in the 1929 Thompson Trophy Race, achieving a speed of 186.84 mph (300.7 km/h) with a US Army pilot at the controls.

Four further P-3A aircraft had their R-1340-3 exposed radial engines shielded by Townend ring cowlings, which enhanced airflow but severely impeded visibility. Pilots of Major Ralph Royce's 94th Pursuit Squadron, briefly equipped with the P-3A, noted that on the ground, taxying was an ordeal; in flight the pilot needed to 'jink' constantly to see ahead. The basic

Although the Hawk pursuits were mainly powered by liquid-cooled engines, many attempts were made to successfully fit radials although none reached production status. The Wasp engine of the P-3 destroyed the pugnacious lines of this classic fighter.

fabric-covered, single-bay biplane design was retained but P-3A experience seems, to some extent at least, to have quelled voices advocating air-cooled power for the ever-adaptable Hawk. Performance was somewhat inferior to that of the liquid-cooled Hawk contemporaries, and the dismal visibility frayed pilots' tempers. Even when further experimentation and modification led to the XP-21 and XP-22 develop-

ments of the Hawk design, as well as the forgettable AT-5A trainer, the intrinsic drawbacks of the P-3 were never overcome. The Pratt & Whitney name would go on to glory and by 1931, radial-engine design would be proven in the Boeing P-12 fighter, but more experience and more work would, first, lie ahead. The Curtiss P-3 Hawk thus was to become another footnote to history, a total of only six airframes being completed.

Specification
P-3A

Type: single-seat pursuit aircraft
Powerplant: one 450-hp (355.6-kW) Pratt & Whitney R-1340-3 Wasp air-cooled 9-cylinder radial piston engine

driving a fixed-pitch two-blade propeller
Performance: maximum speed 153 mph (246.2 km/h) at 20,000 ft (6096 m); cruising speed 122 mph (196.3 km/h) at 20,000 ft (6096 m); stalling speed 58 mph (93 km/h); initial climb rate 1,800 ft (549 m) per minute; service ceiling 23,000 ft (7070 m); range 490 miles (789 km)
Weights: empty 1,956 lb (887.2 kg); normal loaded 2,788 lb (1264.6 kg)
Dimensions: span 31 ft 7 in (9.63 m); length 22 ft 5 in (6.83 m); height 8 ft 9 in (2.67 m); wing area 252 sq ft (23.41 m²)
Armament: two synchronized, forward-firing machine-guns were planned but apparently not installed

Boeing P-4

History and notes
The Boeing XP-4 was the first machine in the US Army's pursuit series to emanate from the manufacturing giant founded in 1916 by William E. Boeing (1881-1956) and, as late as 1929, still privately-owned. A remarkable decade of success for Boeing in the single-engine fighter field began around 1922 with the PW-9 series, designated under an earlier system where 'W' meant the use of a water-cooled engine. The US Army's fascination with turbocharging in the mid-1920s led to the one-off XP-4, itself not a success but another offshoot of a long period of

trial and error.

The XP-4 seems to have been too many things to too many people: turbocharging for better performance, wing guns to break away from the obstacle of a spinning propeller, and a strut arrangement for its biplane wings patterned curiously after World War I's German Fokker D VII. Boeing's engineering colleague Michael Gilead seems to have been strongly influenced by the Fokker fighter, more than a decade old in 1926 when the US Army acquired the XP-4 by modifying a PW-9 airframe, serial 25-324.

So that the XP-4, like the Curtiss P-2 Hawk before it, could be used to

evaluate a turbo-charger, a blown 510-hp (380.3-kW) Packard 1A-1530 liquid-cooled engine was equipped with the turbocharger in the right front fuselage. Flight testing carried out at McCook Field, Ohio, (a grass strip of some historical import then, later to become the flight test centre at Wright-Patterson Air Force Base) indicated that the boosted powerplant was a mismatch for this particular tube-construction, fabric-covered, single-bay biplane design and only 4.5 hours of flying were actually logged. Unique features of the nose-heavy and decidedly unpretty XP-4, including its wing guns and double sets of wing ailerons for

improved manoeuvrability, were never fully tested. Performance generally was regarded as a sour disappointment, comparing favourably neither with the Curtiss Hawk series nor the Boeing design from which the XP-4 had been developed.

Boeing's reputation as a constructor of bombers and airliners, at this time, lay far in the future and the XP-4 was a noteworthy exception to a tradition of success which had aroused the best competitive instincts of Curtiss and other fighter manufacturers.

The final disposition of the XP-4 is not recorded but, as may have seemed inevitable from the outset,

Boeing P-4

Certainly not the most attractive aircraft ever built, the Boeing XP-4 was based on the PW-9 but featured wing guns and a turbocharger, the engine driving a large four-blade propeller. It was a low performer, and development proceeded no further.

the XP-4 ended its career with only one machine having been built.

Specification
XP-4

Type: single-seat pursuit aircraft
Powerplant: one 510-hp (380.3-kW) Packard 1A-1530 liquid-cooled piston engine with supercharger driving a four-blade wooden propeller
Performance: maximum speed 168 mph (270.4 km/h); cruising speed 120 mph (193.1 km/h); initial climb rate 1,400 ft (427 m) per minute; service ceiling 22,000 ft (6706 m); maximum ceiling

22,850 ft (6965 m); range 375 miles (604 km)
Weights: empty 2,783 lb (1262.4 kg); maximum take-off 3,650 lb (1655.6 kg)

Dimensions: span 32 ft 1 in (9.78 m); length 23 ft 11 in (7.29 m); height 8 ft 10 in (2.69 m); wing area 245 sq ft (22.76 m²)
Armament: one 0.3-in (7.62-mm)

and one 0.5-in (12.7-mm) fixed nose machine-guns firing through propeller disc, plus two 0.3-in (7.62-mm) forward-firing, fixed wing machine-guns

Curtiss P-5 Hawk

History and notes

The Curtiss P-5 Hawk, yet another twist on a familiar theme of Curtiss dominance in the fighter field in the late 1920s, illustrated the US Army's fixation on turbo-charged fighters. The P-5 also added to the seemingly endless practice of assigning separate designations for each slightly different machine in the Hawk series.

The sole XP-5 and four P-5 airframes, serials 27-327 to 27-331, were intended to combine the speed and altitude advantages of supercharging with the new Curtiss D-12F engine then seen as the powerplant which would stretch the service potential of the Hawk series. It came to pass that the Curtiss V-1570 Conqueror engine being developed separately was likely to

become available sooner, and work on the D-12F was discontinued.

The P-5 single-bay biplane fighters were completed, in the end, with power supplied by the now-familiar Curtiss V-1150-3 engine with supercharging. First ordered on 27 May 1927, the machines were delivered in 1928 to the 94th Pursuit Group, then operating a diverse stable of Curtiss designs. Almost immediately, two were lost in crashes. Still, the P-5 showed impressive combat performance and gained pilots' respect.

Now that pursuit ships were venturing to greater heights, the P-5 was equipped with two oxygen bottles. Engine heat was channelled into the cockpit from the supercharger and a tarpaulin cape, secured to the cockpit rim by metal

snaps, was used to enclose the pilot inside what was otherwise an open cockpit. In tests, this early method of providing heat for the pilot's comfort was shown not to seriously hinder his ability to manoeuvre the aircraft for flying and fighting.

Although slower than earlier types at sea level, the somewhat awkward-looking and nose-heavy P-5 exceeded all contemporary aircraft types in airspeed in level flight above 20,000 ft (6096 m). In the standard olive-drab of the period with red and white horizontal stripes on its rudder surface, the XP-5 was rated as 'extremely promising' in 1928 evaluations at McCook Field, Ohio, (soon to be renamed Wright Field), while its sister ships were slicing through Michigan skies with the 94th Group.

With a fuel capacity of 100 US gal (378.5 litres) in two internal tanks, the P-5 had a combat radius of 115 miles (185 km), a respectable if not dramatic capability.

The two surviving P-5 machines demonstrated the inherent durability of the basic Hawk design by soldiering on with the 94th Pursuit Group until April 1932, when they were finally retired. They had shown enormous potential as high-altitude fighters, and had garnered public support for the US Army at several air shows. But they would be remembered, above all, because, under the system of designating pursuit ships, the P-5 came immediately before the definitive and unforgettable version of the Curtiss Hawk.

Specification
XP-5

Type: single-seat pursuit aircraft
Powerplant: one supercharged 435-hp (324.4-kW) Curtiss V-1150-3 liquid-cooled 12-cylinder Vee piston engine driving a two-blade propeller
Performance: maximum speed 144 mph (231.7 km/h) at sea level, and 166 mph (267.1 km/h) at 25,000 ft (7620 m); service ceiling 26,700 ft (8138 m); maximum ceiling 33,100 ft (10090 m); range 245 miles (394 km)
Weights: empty 2,699 lb (1224.3 kg); maximum take-off 3,349 lb (1519.1 kg)
Dimensions: span 31 ft 6 in (9.60 m); length 23 ft 8 in (7.21 m); height 9 ft 3 in (2.82 m); wing area 252 sq ft (23.41 m²)
Armament: machine-gun armament was contemplated but apparently not installed

Fitted with turbocharger, rudimentary cockpit heating and oxygen bottles, the P-5 was a high-altitude development of the basic Hawk series. Although ungainly, the four P-5s served with the 94th Pursuit Group at Selfridge. Two of them battled on into the 1930s.

Curtiss P-6 Hawk

The 'Prestone' cooling system identified the Curtiss P-6D variant of the Hawk. It served with the 8th Pursuit Group at Langley Field.

The turbocharged P-6D variant was not a success, only 10 airframes being converted to this standard. As might be expected from the look of the aircraft, the powerplant installation was very heavy, although maximum speed was high (317 km/h).

History and notes

The Curtiss P-6 Hawk was the success that other Hawk designs tried to be. It was the first important indigenous American fighter. It was the most numerous of the Curtiss pursuits and the most important biplane until the Boeing P-12 came along. In the early 1930s, it was also the outer limit of stretching potential for the basic Hawk design.

The XP-6 (25-423) and XP-6A (26-295) were actually a converted P-2 and P-1A respectively, re-engined with the 600-hp (447.4-kW) Curtiss V-1570 Conqueror, the long-awaited definitive engine, for the 1927 National Air Races held in Spokane, Washington. The latter airframe boosted the image of US Army aviation by winning the unlimited race at a speed of 201 mph (323.5 km/h), the XP-6 coming in second at 189 mph (304.2 km/h). Although the XP-6A was lost in a crash the following year, the effectiveness of the Conqueror powerplant was proven and on 3 October 1928 the US Army ordered 18 YP-6s, delivered to the 1st Pursuit Group under Lieutenant Colonel Frank M. Andrews at Selfridge Field, Michigan, the following year.

As a time-saving measure, nine of these machines were delivered with water-cooled V-1570-17 engines. Eight were subsequently re-engined with the V-1570-23 and redesignated P-6A, some employing three-blade variable-pitch propellers. Two further P-6s were produced by converting three P-11 airframes (following) to the intended V-1570-23 glycol-cooled powerplant. One machine (29-263) was assigned to radiator trials as the XP-6A no. 2, while a later Hawk (29-259) became the XP-6B. Better known as the Hoyt Hawk Special, intended for a long-distance New York-Alaska flight by Captain Ross G. Hoyt, the XP-6B was unsuccessful in the marathon effort and was later relegated to test duties. For a time, this airframe also held the P-6C designation.

The P-6D Hawk series all had turbochargers. The XP-6D (29-260), a converted P-6A, was fitted with a supercharged V-1570C and attained a speed of 197 mph (317 km/h) at 15,000 ft (4572 m). Nine further P-6Ds, converted from earlier Hawks and delivered to the 8th Pursuit Group at Langley Field, Virginia, under Major Byron Q. Jones in April 1932, differed from the XP-6D in having three-blade propellers.

The all-time favourite Curtiss Hawk fighter, and the most elegant, was the P-6E variant. The prototype YP-6E (29-374) went through various incarnations as an XP-11, a YP-20 and, eventually, with a revised landing gear, as the sole XP-6F. It set the stage for the P-6E, best remembered for its resplendence in yellow wings and tail, white-trimmed khaki fuselage and red/white striped rudder. Perhaps the best-recalled Hawk of all is this P-6E, often illustrated with a short-lived Arctic snow owl painted in white on its rear fuselage and corresponding beak and talons painted up front.

The developed P-6E had tapered wings and fuselage that faired gracefully into the liquid-cooled Conqueror engine with its three-blade variable-pitch propeller. The initial order was for 46 P-6E variants (32-233/278) and most were delivered to Andrews' 1st Pursuit Group at Selfridge in 1932. Single-leg landing gear and a flush, belly-mounted radiator gave the P-6E a streamlined appearance and distinguished it from other Hawks. Also, the P-6E had a tail wheel rather than the tail skid which, until then, was standard on biplane fighters.

Classic fighter

The P-6E was to be an all-time classic, and some remained in service as late as 1938, but the series did not stop there. The experimental XP-6F, fastest of all Hawks, had turbocharged V-1570-55 Conqueror and a new feature which spoke of things to come, namely an enclosed cockpit. Slightly heavier than other Hawks, in 1933 the XP-6F attained the then phenomenal speed of 232 mph (373.4 km/h) at 18,000 ft (5486 m). Engine cooling problems brought an end to XP-6F operations in August 1933.

The sole XP-6G (32-254) was a P-6E with supercharging deleted. It eventually reverted to service in P-6E standard. The XP-6H (32-233) carried six 0.3-in (7.62-mm) machine-guns in lieu of the usual two, but tests with this 'flying arsenal' proved unproductive.

Eight P-6 airframes were exported to the Netherlands East Indies and about a dozen went to Cuba with Pratt & Whitney R-1340 radial engines. A single Hawk was purchased in about 1931 by Mitsubishi in Japan, where the technical inspector was Jiro Horikoshi, later the design genius behind the Mitsubishi A6M5 Zero fighter.

Curtiss P-6E Hawk of the 33rd Pursuit Squadron, 8th Pursuit Group, Langley Field, Virginia.

As will be seen in this narrative, there were endless variations on the Curtiss Hawk theme, such as the already-mentioned final P-11 aircraft (which was completed as the YP-20 and became the XP-6E and XP-6F) and the sole XP-22 (ordered into production as the Y1P-22 but delivered as the P-6E). Some of the one-off variations had so many designations, powerplants and changes in nomenclature that no complete history may ever be written about all. The important point is that by the time the principle P-6E production variant (originally YP-20, XP-22) was being delivered in numbers to the US Army Air Corps, the Boeing P-12 was also being supplied. The Curtiss P-6 and Boeing P-12 would form the major biplane fighting force of the American air arm in the years between world wars.

In all, the variants of the P-6 encumbered fewer than 90 individual airframes, including the many which bore other designations at one time or another, yet the P-6 left a mark which far exceeds its numbers. One P-6E Hawk is beautifully restored today at the US Air Force Museum in Dayton, Ohio.

Specification

P-6E

Type: single-seat pursuit aircraft

Powerplant: one 600-hp (447.4-kW) Curtiss V-1570-23 liquid-cooled 12-cylinder Vee piston engine driving a three-blade propeller

Performance: maximum speed 197 mph (317 km/h) at sea level; initial climb rate 2,400 ft (732 m) per minute; service ceiling 24,700 ft (7529 m); range 570 miles (917 km)

Weights: empty 2,699 lb (1224.3 kg); maximum take-off 3,392 lb (1538.6 kg)

Dimensions: span 31 ft 6 in (9.60 m); length 23 ft 2 in (7.06 m); height 8 ft 10 in (2.69 m); wing area 252 sq ft (23.41 m²)

Armament: two 0.3-in (7.62-mm) fixed machine-guns with 600 rounds per gun on sides of nose firing through propeller disc

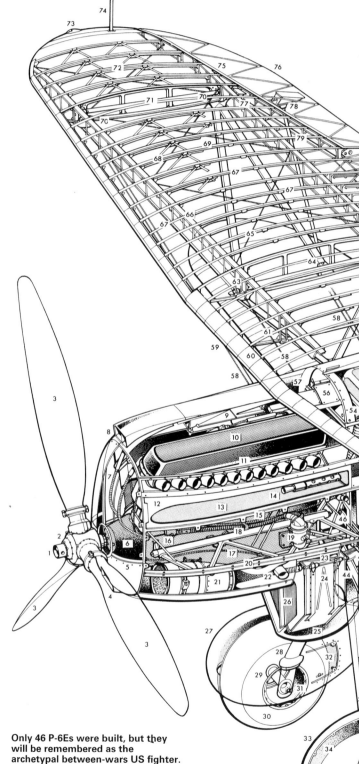

Only 46 P-6Es were built, but they will be remembered as the archetypal between-wars US fighter. This is the best-known scheme, the 'snowy owl' of the 17th Pursuit Squadron from Selfridge Field.

Hawks High

A handful of P-6Es staggered on with the Pursuit Squadrons after re-equipment with other types. This 33rd PS aircraft was still serving in 1938, probably as a communications 'hack'.

Curtiss P-6E Hawk cutaway drawing key

1. Starter dog
2. Propeller hub
3. Three-blade Hamilton Standard metal propeller
4. Oil cooler chin intake
5. Nose cowling front panel line
6. Gear housing
7. Front curved panel
8. Carburettor air intake
9. Intake trunk
10. Curtiss V-1570-C Conqueror engine
11. Exhaust stubs (2 per cylinder)
12. Stainless steel trough surround
13. Gun trough
14. Machine-gun muzzle
15. Cowling access panel line
16. Diagonal brace
17. Struts
18. Main engine support bearer
19. Filter
20. Lower panel lines
21. Oil cooler assembly
22. Telescopic access/servicing step
23. Radiator attachment mounts
24. Prestone radiator
25. Radiator fairing
26. Intake
27. Starboard mainwheel spat
28. Starboard undercarriage strut
29. Axle
30. Starboard low-pressure mainwheel tyre
31. Anchor point
32. Inboard access panel (brake servicing)
33. Port mainwheel spat
34. Flathead screw panel line
35. Port axle assembly
36. Port low-pressure mainwheel tyre
37. Hub assembly forging
38. Angled undercarriage strut
39. Removable spat half-section
40. Undercarriage leg fairing
41. Strut/fairing attachment
42. Strut support forged frame member
43. Strut pivot
44. Hinged cover plate
45. Front wires fuselage attachment
46. Engine accessories
47. Fuselage forward frame
48. Port ammunition magazine (600 rounds per gun)
49. Deflector panel
50. Cartridge chute
51. Gun support strut
52. Ammunition feed fairing
53. Oleo shock strut/rebound spring
54. Upper pivot point
55. Cabane forward attachment
56. Oil access point
57. Bulkhead panel
58. Starboard wires
59. Aluminium leading-edge panels
60. Upper wing centre-section
61. Cabane struts
62. Cabane wires
63. Cabane upper wing attachment points
64. Reinforced strut
65. Starboard lower wing plan
66. Front spar
67. Interplane 'N'-struts
68. Upper wing ribs
69. Internal bracing wires
70. Interplane strut upper attachment points
71. Reinforced rib
72. Outer rib assemblies
73. Starboard navigation light
74. Aerial mast
75. Aileron/rear spar join
76. Welded steel aileron (fabric-covered)
77. Aileron hinge link
78. Metal plate
79. Aileron interplane actuating link
80. Aileron profile
81. Rear spar
82. Trailing-edge rib assembly
83. Centre-section cut-out
84. Handhold
85. Telescopic gunsight
86. Gunsight supports
87. Hinged fuel access panel
88. Filler neck
89. Fuselage main fuel tank (50 US gals/189 litres)
90. Engine controls
91. Port 0.30-in (7.62-mm) Browning machine-gun
92. Lower longeron
93. Fuel tank bearer
94. Lower wing front spar attachment
95. Wingroot walkway
96. Diagonal strut frame
97. Lower wing rear spar attachment
98. Aileron control linkage
99. Hanging rudder pedal assembly
100. Control column
101. Fuselage frame
102. Cabane rear attachment
103. Instrument centre panel
104. Main instrument panel
105. Windscreen
106. Control grip
107. Side switch panel
108. Engine control quadrant
109. Throttle lever
110. Upper wing trailing-edge
111. Padded forward coaming
112. Cockpit cut-out
113. Headrest/turnover frame
114. Bad-weather cover (snap-on rubber tarpaulin)
115. Oxygen access panel (starboard)
116. Pilot's seat
117. Seat support frame
118. Inspection 'Vee' panel
119. Cockpit floor
120. Fuselage diagonal side frames
121. Oxygen cylinder (starboard)
122. Metal door flap
123. Parachute flare stowage (port)
124. Baggage compartment hinged side door
125. Hasp and lock
126. Baggage compartment hinged upper panel
127. Snap fasteners
128. Fuselage top frames
129. All-metal dorsal decking
130. Diagonal brace wires
131. Elevator control cables
132. Rudder control cables
133. Fuselage structure
134. Pulleys
135. Cross-member
136. Dorsal cross-section transition (round/point)
137. Tailplane front beam attachment
138. Bearer frame
139. Tailfin front beam attachment
140. Tailfin leading-edge
141. Starboard tailplane
142. Aerials
143. Tailfin structure
144. Tailplane brace wires
145. Rudder balance
146. Aerial post
147. Tail navigation light recess
148. Rudder upper hinge
149. Rudder frame
150. Spacers
151. Rudder post
152. Elevator control horns
153. Tailfin rear beam attachment
154. Elevator control cable
155. Rudder control horns
156. Port elevator frame
157. Brace wire attachment
158. Port (adjustable) tailplane
159. Tailplane front beam
160. Tail dolly lug
161. Swivel/steerable tailwheel
162. Axle fork
163. Metal grommet collar
164. Fuselage strut
165. Tailwheel shock-strut leg
166. Leather grommets (elevator control cables)
167. Tailwheel leg upper attachment
168. Access 'Vee' panel
169. Diagonal brace wires
170. Lower longeron
171. Ventral skinning
172. Port aileron
173. Aerial mast
174. Lower wingroot cut-out
175. Ventral tank aft fairing
176. Rear spar
177. Interplane 'N'-struts
178. Upper wing leading-edge
179. Drop tank filler cap
180. Drop tank (41.6 Imp gal/189 litres)
181. Vent
182. Lower wing aluminium leading-edge panels
183. Nose ribs
184. Wire turnbuckle clamp
185. 'N'-strut lower attachments
186. Port navigation light
187. Reinforced rib
188. Aileron actuating linkage
189. Lower wing trailing-edge
190. Rear spar
191. Outer rib assemblies
192. Front spar
193. Wingtip structure
194. Handling point

© Pilot Press Limited

Curtiss P-6

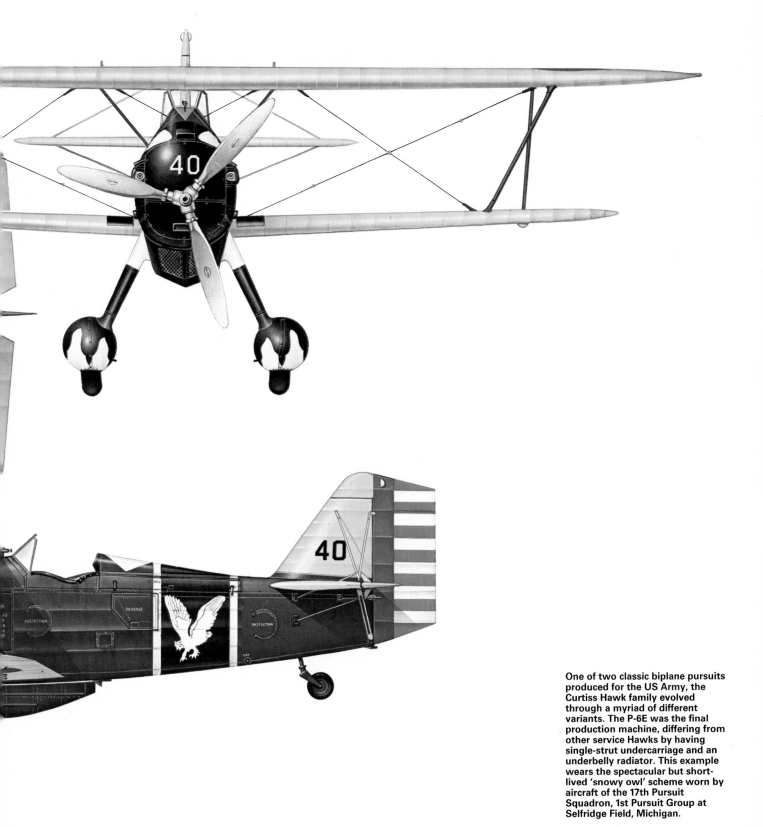

One of two classic biplane pursuits produced for the US Army, the Curtiss Hawk family evolved through a myriad of different variants. The P-6E was the final production machine, differing from other service Hawks by having single-strut undercarriage and an underbelly radiator. This example wears the spectacular but short-lived 'snowy owl' scheme worn by aircraft of the 17th Pursuit Squadron, 1st Pursuit Group at Selfridge Field, Michigan.

Boeing P-7

History and notes

As competition intensified for pursuit orders from a budget-starved US Army in the late 1920s, Boeing decided to take advantage of the availability of the Curtiss V-1570 Conqueror engine. It was not an easy notion to accept, the engine being a product of the era's other principal maker of pursuit ships. The V-1570-1 water-cooled powerplant of 1928, delivered 600 hp (447.4 kW), had proven generally more reliable and easier to service than other engines of the period, and would surely improve the fighting potential of any proven airframe, or so it seemed.

Boeing mated the promising Curtiss engine to its final PW-9D (28-41). But the PW-9 series, like the similar machines which served the US Marine Corps and US Navy as the FB-1 to FB-5, had run its course; the PW-9D design had been stretched to the limits of its capability. The new fighter, the XP-7, or Boeing Model 93, distinguished from the production PW-9D by a shorter, deeper nose, was an idea whose time had come too late. Although the new engine gave the lighter XP-7 a speed advantage of 14 mph (22.5 km/h) over the PW-9,

By fitting a Curtiss Conqueror engine in a PW-9D, Boeing produced the P-7, which showed a small increase in performance. However, more important advances in structure were being undertaken by the company (and Curtiss), rendering the aircraft obsolete before it had flown.

its overall performance was unenviable at best and dismal in some respects. The aircraft clearly lacked the promise of the Curtiss P-6 and Boeing P-12 series, both of which were being developed contemporaneously.

The XP-7, an attractive biplane fighter but with the familiar nose-heavy look and a few too many struts and wires marring its clean lines, made its first flight in November 1928. A preliminary look at performance aroused enough interest for plans to be made to produce four P-7s for service tests. But these plans were set aside when it became evident that other pursuit ships would out-fly and out-fight the P-7.

Eventually, the sole XP-7 airframe finished its flight test programme. The Conqueror engine was removed and replaced by a Curtiss

D-12, the aircraft reverting to its former status as a PW-9D.

Specification
XP-7

Type: single-seat pursuit aircraft
Powerplant: one 600-hp (447.4-kW) Curtiss V-1570-1 Conqueror liquid-cooled 12-cylinder Vee piston engine driving a two-blade propeller
Performance: maximum speed 167.5 mph (269.6 km/h) at sea level;

initial climb rate 1,940 ft (591 m) per minute; service ceiling 22,500 ft (6858 m); range 155 miles (249 km)
Weights: empty 2,323 lb (1053.7 kg); maximum take-off 3,260 lb (1478.7 kg)
Dimensions: span 32 ft 0 in (9.75 m); length 24 ft 0 in (7.32 m); height 9 ft 0 in (2.74 m); wing area 241 sq ft (22.39 m²)
Armament: two fixed 0.3-in (7.62-mm) machine-guns were contemplated but not installed

---

Boeing P-8

History and notes

In the spirit of innovation typical of biplane fighter development of the period, William Boeing's design team created the XP-8 on its own initiative. Few of the 'one off' biplane fighters were more radical in appearance. The XP-8 was almost bullet-nosed with its thin engine cowl and with the cooling radiator located across a broad section of the lower wing. The sole XP-8 airframe (28-359), powered by an inverted Packard 2A-1530 engine, looked

sleek enough to prevail in a dogfight against any adversary. But appearance was deceiving.

The XP-8 was covered by an Army contract dated April 1925 and was delivered in July 1927. It was essentially a private venture, financed by Boeing funds allocated in 1926, and was given the company designation Model 66. Pilots who wrung out the Boeing XP-8 in simulated combat at McCook Field (later Wright Field) beginning in January 1928 were impressed with the pursuit ship's

spacious cockpit and easy handling characteristics. Their enthusiasm rubbed off on the US Navy, which ordered an almost identical machine under the designation F2B-1. The naval version, different in engine configuration, flew with VB-2B squadron on the carrier USS *Saratoga* (CV-3) and made an impressive showing in the 1928 National Air Races, held in Los Angeles.

But the Packard engine of the XP-8 simply did not live up to expectations. Deficient in performance, it also required excessive maintenance time. While manufacturers continued to compete fiercely with each other for limited contracts for pursuit aircraft in the middle and late 1920s, Boeing decided to concentrate on other designs. The XP-8 proved to be the last Packard-powered Army fighter. It was also the final Boeing design which had tapered wings for the Army. The sole airframe contributed to knowledge of fighter design until it was scrapped in June 1929.

Specification
XP-8

Type: single-seat pursuit aircraft
Powerplant: one 600-hp (447.4-kW) Packard 2A-1530 liquid-cooled inverted piston engine driving a two-blade Hamilton Standard propeller
Performance: maximum speed 176 mph (283.2 km/h) at 6,000 ft (1829 m); cruising speed 148 mph (238.2 km/h); initial climb rate 1,750 ft (533 m) per minute; service ceiling 20,950 ft (6386 m); range 325 miles (523 km)
Weights: empty 2,390 lb (1084.1 kg); maximum take-off 3,421 lb (1551.8 kg)
Dimensions: span 30 ft 1 in (9.17 m); length 23 ft 5 in (7.14 m); height 9 ft 0 in (2.74 m); wing area 260 sq ft (24.15 m²)
Armament: one 0.3-in (7.62-mm) and one 0.5-in (12.7-mm) fixed nose-mounted machine-guns firing through the propeller disc

The single XP-8 showed a novel approach to fighter design, with a low drag Packard engine installation with a large radiator underneath. General characteristics were favourable, but the engine proved unreliable and the performance mediocre.

Boeing P-9

History and notes

Almost certain to be remembered for little else, Boeing's XP-9 pursuit ship of 1930 enjoys the distinction of being the first monoplane in the series covered by the USAAC system for designating fighters. Eventually, a monoplane would be the last great fighter turned out by this builder, but at the time the monoplane was only beginning to come along. In 1923, a Verville-Sperry monoplane had been clocked at a respectable 210 mph (338 km/h) and soon thereafter every major manufacturer was at least thinking seriously about monoplanes. In 1928, the prolific Boeing design team began work on its entry, the company's Model 26, designated XP-9. Other manufacturers were still

thinking; none as yet had so radical an aircraft under construction.

As is so often the case, appearance was deceiving. Despite a plethora of struts and wires so commonplace in its day, the XP-9 looked rather potent, but turned out to be a disappointment. Delivery of the sole machine (28-386) was postponed until June 1929, then until April 1930, and finally to September 1930. Once delivered, the XP-9 with its revolutionary semi-monocoque fuselage and monoplane wing turned out to be less a pacemaker than a hazard. The bulky wing joined at the top of the fuselage and made the pilot virtually blind! The aircraft had poor control characteristics. Its cramped cockpit had a control stick too low and short for comfort and

square rudder pedals not contoured for the pilot's shoes or boots. Though it finally flew successfully (more or less) on 18 November 1930, the XP-9 never made more than token journeys into the air.

Its Curtiss V-1570-15 Conqueror engine was the only proven feature in the fighter's design and enabled it to reach 213 mph (342.8 km/h). Still, the XP-9 was perhaps the least popular of all experimental prototypes of the period.

Specification
XP-9

Type: single-seat pursuit aircraft
Powerplant: one 583-hp (434.7-kW) Curtiss V-1570-15 Conqueror liquid-cooled 12-cylinder

Vee piston engine driving a two-blade propeller
Performance: maximum speed 213 mph (342.8 km/h) at 12,000 ft (3658 m); initial climb rate 2,430 ft (741 m) per minute; service ceiling 25,300 ft (7711 m); range 180 miles (287 km)
Weights: empty 2,669 lb (1210.7 kg); maximum take-off 3,623 lb (1643.4 kg)
Dimensions: span 36 ft 6 in (11.13 m); length 25 ft 1¾ in (7.66 m); height 7 ft 9 in (2.36 m); wing area 210 sq ft (19.51 m²)
Armament: two 0.3-in (7.62-mm) or 0.5-in (12.7-mm) fixed machine-guns mounted behind engine and firing through troughs at the side

Curtiss P-10

History and notes

In the late 1920s, the manufacturing firm created by Glenn L. Curtiss was turning out an astonishing variety of fighter, transport and other aircraft. One of the most pleasing to the eye was the XP-10, a biplane fighter with plywood wings joined in gull fashion to the fuselage. In most respects cleaner and more aerodynamically functional than the early monoplanes of the period, and powered by the eminently successful V-1710 Conqueror engine, the sleekly shaped XP-10 gave its pilot comfort and excellent visibility.

The sole XP-10 (28-387) was the result of an 18 June 1928 contract from the USAAC which emphasized manoeuvrability as well as vision for the pilot. Delivered in August 1928 and first flown in September by pilot Melvin Pobre, the XP-10 achieved the fairly modest top speed of only 170 mph (273.6 km/h), but in most other respects was a solid performer, particularly impressive in the close-in dogfight situation. Pobre reported that it 'tore the pants' off Curtiss Hawk biplanes in mock air battles.

Though its engine was reliable, the XP-10's cooling method created problems. A cooling system comprising brass sheet wrapped around the upper wings, ribbed to form channels through which liquid coolant was pumped, eliminated radiator drag almost entirely but proved dif-

With its gull-shaped upper wing and sleekly-cowled Conqueror engine, the XP-10 was a handsome machine. Curtiss had managed to remove the radiator, substituting surface cooling blankets instead. These were to prove the design's undoing, being temperamental in operation.

ficult to maintain and prone to breakdown. Worse, it meant that the XP-10, if hit in the cooling area by gunfire, could be felled by a single bullet or a short burst. Recurring difficulty with the piping of coolant water plagued the XP-10 test pro-

gramme, and experiments with other kinds of coolant failed to remedy the situation. This prevented an otherwise highly promising pursuit ship from reaching production status.

Specification
XP-10

Type: single-seat pursuit aircraft
Powerplant: one 600-hp (447.4-kW) Curtiss V-1570-15 liquid cooled 12-cylinder Vee piston engine driving a two-blade propeller
Performance: maximum speed

170 mph (273.6 km/h) at 5,000 ft (1524 m); cruising speed 130 mph (209.2 km/h); initial climb rate 1,940 ft (591 m) per minute; ceiling 19,610 ft (5977 m); range 195 miles (312 km)
Weights: empty about 2,900 lb (1315 kg); maximum take-off about 3,400 lb (1542 kg)
Dimensions: span 33 ft 0 in (10.06 m); length 24 ft 6 in (7.47 m); height 10 ft 10 in (3.30 m); wing area about 238 sq ft (21.1 m²)
Armament: 0.3-in (7.62-mm) and 0.5-in (12.7-mm) machine-guns were planned

Curtiss P-11

History and notes

The dubious historical claim of the Curtiss XP-11 Hawk variant is that it is the first among 131 aircraft types in the pursuit/fighter series which were not built, although three airframes intended as XP-11s were completed and flown with other designations. No more than a brief episode in the long and diverse experimentation carried out in the Curtiss Hawk period, the XP-11 was ordered on 3 October 1928 as part of procurement decisions made in the P-6 Hawk programme. A somewhat 'fattened' Hawk, unpleasing to the eye, the XP-11 was to have been powered by the new, unproven Curtiss H-1640-1 Chieftain engine. It remains unclear why the Curtiss

fighter team prepared engineering studies and actually began construction of airframes with a powerplant which seemingly would have offered no improvement in performance, especially when proven engines sold by the firm already powered most Hawk variants. In the event, the XP-11 was a false start.

The Chieftain engine, flown with some trepidation on a converted Curtiss XO-18 Falcon testbed, was prone to overheating. The 12-cylinder inline air-cooled radial was configured with a second bank of cylinders directly in line with the first and cooling simply did not work. A test pilot flying the XO-18 recommended against further development. Ground testing of the

bulky, cantankerous powerplant was also unsuccessful. By 1929, a decision was reached to terminate Chieftain development and to divert the three planned XP-11 airframes to more effective use.

Two planned XP-11s (29-367/368) were completed as P-6D fighters, powered by supercharged Curtiss V-1570-23 Conqueror engines. The third XP-11 (29-374) came from the manufacturer's line as the sole YP-20 pursuit ship.

Specification
XP-11

Type: single-seat pursuit aircraft
Powerplant: (planned) one 600-hp (447.4-kW) Curtiss H-1640-1

Chieftain air-cooled 12-cylinder radial piston engine driving a two-blade propeller
Performance: (estimated) maximum speed 190 mph (305.7 km/h) at sea level; initial climb rate 1,500 ft (457 m) per minute; service ceiling 20,000 ft (6096 m); range 425 miles (684 km)
Weights: (estimated) empty about 2,200 lb (998 kg); maximum take-off about 2,400 lb (1089 kg)
Dimensions: (approximately) span 32 ft 0 in (9.75 m); length 23 ft 0 in (7.01 m); height 8 ft 6 in (2.59 m); wing area 250 sq ft (23.23 m²)
Armament: 0.3-in (7.62-mm) and 0.5-in (12.7-mm) machine-guns planned for installation

Boeing P-12

History and notes

The Boeing P-12 was the US Army Air Corps' last great biplane fighter. The single-bay biplane design proved a classic in Navy/Marine Corps service, where 160 examples through the F4B-4 were still operational on the eve of World War II, yet the Army's variants were twice as numerous, 366 airframes being delivered to fulfil contracts awarded between 1929 and 1933. This pursuit ship had caught the attention of the Navy first; the initial order for 10 P-12 airframes came only after Army pilots at Bolling Field, adjacent to NAS Anacostia in Washington, DC, had a chance to evaluate the very promising F4B-1. Powered by the reliable 500-hp (372.85-kW) Pratt & Whitney R-1430-7 Wasp radial piston engine, the first P-12 (29-353) flew on 11 April 1929 and nine P-12s (Boeing Model 102) had been delivered when the tenth airframe was completed as the XP-12A (Model 101) with minor modifications and a more powerful engine.

Maiden flight

The XP-12A was equipped with a long-chord NACA cowling enclosing its 525-hp (391.41-kW) Pratt & Whitney R-1340-9 engine. First flown 10 May 1929, the XP-12A was formally turned over to the US Army the following day but was destroyed on 18 May 1929 in a mid-air collision with another P-12. Development then progressed to the P-12B variant, 90 of which were funded in June 1929. The P-12B (Boeing Model 102B) was slightly heavier but otherwise offered few innovations over the basic Boeing biplane design.

The P-12C (Boeing Model 222), ordered in June 1930, introduced a Townend ring encircling the engine cowl, a feature which was retroactively fitted to some P-12Bs. This variant also introduced a spreader-bar main landing gear, loose in flight but taut and sturdy on the ground. In all, 96 P-12C machines were built before produc-

The first production version for the Air Corps of this classic biplane was the P-12B, this differing little from the F4B Navy fighter. Although not as elegant as the P-6, the P-12 radiated pugnacious purpose, and was to be built in much larger numbers.

tion shifted to the P-12D (Boeing Model 227) powered by a 550-hp (410.14-kW) R-1340-17 engine. In 1932, one P-12D (31-273) was retroactively fitted with a 550-hp (410.14-kW) Pratt & Whitney XGRS-1340-E Wasp commercial powerplant and modified tail surfaces, and was redesignated XP-12H.

Based on a Boeing private venture which became the USAAC's one-off XP-925A, the P-12E ordered in March 1931 (Boeing Model 234) was the most widely employed of all P-12 variants and was in service with operational fighter squadrons until replaced by the Boeing P-26A 'Peashooter' monoplane in 1935. The P-12E had a monocoque fuselage, pilot's headrest faired by a turtleback, and the more powerful engine of the P-12D. Some 25 further airframes also ordered in March 1931 (Boeing Model 251) were delivered as the

This evocative photograph captures the P-12Es of the 27th Pursuit Squadron from Selfridge Field, Michigan. This variant introduced the 'turtleback' headrest, as well as a more powerful engine. One hundred and ten of this variant were built.

P-12F. The last of these was fitted with an experimental closed cockpit and sliding canopy.

One re-engined P-12E flew with the designation P-12J. Seven P-12Es were redesignated YP-12K when Q-2 fuel injectors were fitted to their R-1340-7 engines. This increased maximum speed to 192 mph (309 km/h) at 4,000 ft (1219 m) and maximum take-off weight to 2,815 lb (1276.9 kg). One P-12K was further modified to become the single XP-12L when an F-7 turbocharger was added, and the remaining six became known as P-12Ks before eventually reverting to P-12E standard. A total of 23 P-12s was turned over to the US Navy in 1940 for use as F4B-1A target drones.

King Kong

The P-12 seems, looking back, a symbol of an age between wars when military men were rough-hewn and underpaid, fighter squadrons were identified by bright and colourful markings (diagonal red fuselage stripes and a pouncing tiger adorned a P-12E of the 24th Pursuit Squadron in the Panama Canal Zone) and imaginations were vivid enough to enable biplane fighters to shoot a Hollywood gorilla, King Kong, from atop the Empire State Building. At least one P-12 seems to have served as the personal mount of Major General Benjamin D. Foulois, Chief of the Air Corps from December 1931, and another P-12 has been noted in unique checkerboard markings with the US Army's Command and Staff College, Fort Leavenworth, Kansas. Some P-12s appeared in elaborate disruptive camouflage schemes such as those in desert sand/green/grey used in war games at March Field, California, November 1935. P-12Es of the 'Skylarks' aerobatic team, Maxwell Field, Alabama, carried the US Army's message to the public in 1937.

P-12 airframes were still in existence, albeit long out of operational service, well into the 1940s. There appear to be no significant instances of the Boeing biplane fighter being used in combat. A few P-12s are thought to have reached Latin American air forces and may have done some fighting there. In 1983, a P-12E (31-559) restored in the markings of the 6th Pursuit Squadron, Hawaii, was added to the US Air Force Museum collection in Dayton, Ohio.

The last production version was the P-12F, similar to the P-12E except for an uprated engine and the adoption of a tailwheel. This last feature was later retrofitted to many P-12Es. The short Townend ring round the cylinder heads was a feature of all P-12s apart from the A and B series.

Specification

P-12E

Type: single-seat pursuit aircraft
Powerplant: one 550-hp (410.14-kW) Pratt & Whitney R-1340-17 Wasp air-cooled 7-cylinder radial piston engine driving a two-blade propeller
Performance: maximum speed 189 mph (304.2 km/h) at 7,000 ft (2134 m); initial climb rate about 2,000 ft (610 m) per minute; service ceiling 23,600 ft (7193 m); range about 540 miles (869 km)
Weights: empty 1,999 lb (906.7 kg); maximum take-off 2,690 lb (1220.2 kg)
Dimensions: span 30 ft 0 in (9.14 m); length 20 ft 3 in (6.17 m); height 9 ft 0 in (2.74 m); wing area 227.5 sq ft (21.13 m^2)
Armament: two 0.3-in (7.62-mm) fixed forward-firing machine-guns

Thomas-Morse P-13 Viper

History and notes

The unsuccessful XP-13 Viper brings the name of a new manufacturer to the pursuit/fighter designation series, although the Thomas-Morse Aircraft Corporation was, in fact, far from new as a builder of combat aeroplanes. Thomas-Morse was by 1929 an established and respected maker, having turned out the MB-3 and MB-6 observation craft of 1919 and 1923 respectively. As the lean years between world wars were made leaner by the Depression, Thomas-Morse's fortunes, in fact, were on the decline.

The firm's sole XP-13 Viper single-bay biplane fighter (29-453) was begun as a private venture and delivered to the USAAC in 1929. The airframe design offered good performance potential but the XP-13 was doomed from the start because of its reliance on the 600-hp (447.4-kW) Curtiss H-1640-1 Chieftain, the same powerplant which posed insoluble problems for the Curtiss P-11 and P-14. Cooling difficulties with the complex Chieftain were never resolved.

Having earlier made the S-4 and MB-3 fighters, Thomas-Morse attempted to break the Curtiss/Boeing stranglehold with the XP-13 Viper. The use of the Curtiss Chieftain engine doomed this attempt from the start, although the aircraft was re-engined before it crashed.

After tests apparently conducted at McCook Field (Wright Field) near Dayton, Ohio, the XP-13 Viper was re-engined with a 450-hp (331.6-kW) Pratt & Whitney R-1340C engine and given the new designation XP-13A. This enabled the sole airframe to continue flight tests until it was lost to an in-flight fire in 1931. Though a Curtiss-built Viper called the XP-14 was planned, it was never built and in time the Thomas-Morse firm was absorbed by Consolidated.

Specification

XP-13

Type: single-seat pursuit aircraft
Powerplant: one 600-hp (447.4-kW) Curtiss H-1640-1 Chieftain air-cooled 12-cylinder piston engine driving a two-blade Hamilton Standard propeller
Performance: maximum speed 173 mph (278.4 km/h) at 5,000 ft (1524 m); cruising speed 130 mph (209.2 km/h); initial climb rate about 1,700 ft (518 m) per minute; service ceiling 21,100 ft (6431 m); range 193 miles (312 km)
Weights: empty 2,262 lb (1026.0 kg); maximum take-off 3,256 lb (1476.9 kg)
Dimensions: span 28 ft 0 in (8.53 m); length 23 ft 6 in (7.16 m); height 8 ft 5 in (2.57 m); wing area 189 sq ft (17.56 m^2)
Armament: 0.3-in (7.62-mm) machine-guns planned for installation

Enter the Monoplane

The Boeing and Curtiss pursuit families reached their zenith with the P-6 and P-12, but development continued along the same lines. All these new fighters could not hide the fact that monoplanes were the fighters of the future.

With Curtiss Hawks and Boeing P-12s equipping the pursuit squadrons of the early 1930s, the United States Army Air Corps had a well-equipped and well-trained air defence force, although the numbers involved were so small as to make the notion of defending the United States against aerial attack somewhat laughable. Centred around bases in Virginia, California and Michigan, the air defence force could not be expected to protect large tracts of the nation.

This position began to change during the 1930s with a gentle increase in force levels, and with the introduction of the monoplane fighter the force also began to push to the forefront of equipment technology. Central to this push was the remarkable Boeing P-26. Of course, in 1931 when the Boeing Airplane Company showed its proposals to the USAAC, there was much caution and scepticism concerning the new monoplane

fighter.

The biplane fighter had progressed just about as far as it could by this time, the later Curtiss Hawk and Boeing P-12 variants being considered the last word in biplane design given the available powerplants. The P-26 promised to be far better, and even the most diehard Army official could not ignore the monoplane any longer. When it emerged in March 1932, the P-26 was a remarkable machine. Although possessing an externally-braced wing with its attendant forest of bracing wires, it looked sleek and streamlined compared with the biplanes in service. Its faired undercarriage and rotund fuselage gave it a pugnacious look, while the 'Peashooter' gunsight and Townend ring cowling gave it its distinctive character.

What astounded most who saw these early aircraft was the wing, beautifully crafted in an elliptical fashion but, above all, very

short. In fact the span of the P-26 was around 0.6-m shorter than that of the biplane P-12 it was intended to replace. All these points put together made it around 40 km/h faster on similar engines, and the short wing gave a good roll rate. Even the unit cost of the aircraft was slightly less than a P-12! On the down side was the landing speed, which rose alarmingly. Nevertheless, the Army pilots took to their new mounts in 1934 with verve, finding them sensitive, manoeuvrable, fast and unbeatable. The monoplane was here to stay.

The 'Peashooter' remained the Army's main pursuit ship during the mid-1930s

The 1930s are best-remembered for the Boeing P-26, the first all-metal fighter and first monoplane fighter. That it went on to take a mauling from the Japanese air force in 1941 rather clouds its momentous achievements a few years earlier.

An interesting concept originally introduced by the Berliner-Joyce P-16 was that of the two-seat fighter, with heavy forward-firing armament and a rear-facing gunner. The next aircraft in this category was the Consolidated P-30 (right), which also served into the 1940s.

before Seversky P-35s and Curtiss P-36s were introduced from 1938 onwards. The P-26 went on to fight in the early stages of the war, where it was severely mauled by the sleek and modern fighters of the Japanese. This ignominious end marred the reputation of what had been an historic aircraft: America's first all-metal fighter.

Two-man fighter

Only pursued on a small scale, other moves were afoot to break with fighter tradition. Pursuits had always been single-place ships, and in the 1920s it was almost heresy to suggest otherwise. At the end of the decade, however, the Berliner-Joyce company not only suggested the concept of a two-seat fighter, but also managed to sell them to the Army. Based along accepted fighter lines, the P-16 was a sturdy and high-performing biplane with forward-firing armament, but also adding a second cockpit for a rear-gunner. So good was the performance that it could match the single-seat fighters then in service, and was ordered in small numbers for the Army.

Somewhat despised by the crews who rather craved the glamour of single-seat flying, the P-16 proved the concept of two-seat fighters, and this led to a batch of designs for others. These were led by the Lockheed P-24, which adopted the monoplane layout, and were followed by a series of Consolidated aircraft which culminated in the P-30. Seen as the successor to the P-16, a small production run was ordered, and these gave sterling service into the 1940s. To further fuel the derision felt for two-seat fighters, the P-16 and P-30 were assigned their own 'Pursuit, Biplace' category in 1935, becoming the PB-1 and PB-2 respectively.

As the 1930s progressed, the spectre of war was looming over the world, although it was paid only grudging respect in the United States. The pace of aeronautical achievement was quickening in Europe and Japan, and while the P-26 was state-of-the-art in 1934, by 1938 it was decidedly outdated. As well as its 'firsts', it must be remembered that the 'Peashooter' was also the last open-cockpit and fixed-undercarriage fighter in the USAAC. What the United States needed now were new fighters that it could take to war.

Above: Throughout the 1930s the Curtiss and Boeing biplanes were still a regular sight around the pursuit fields. This Boeing P-12 was seen at March Field in 1935. It is wearing special camouflage for participation in aerial exercises.

Below: Pilots were proud of their P-26 'Peashooters', finding it good to fly and more than a match for any biplane opposition put up against them. This photograph shows aircraft of the 17th Pursuit Group at March Field, California in 1935.

Curtiss P-14

History and notes

P-14 is the second in the pursuit/fighter designation series applied to an aircraft which, though planned and funded, was never built. In the definitive history *US Army Aircraft 1908-1946* by James C. Fahey, the P-14 designation is covered by a brief note reading '29-cc', meaning that the aircraft was cancelled in 1929.

The XP-14 had been ordered as a Curtiss-built version of the Thomas-Morse XP-13 and, so far as can be determined, would have been identical to the latter. Like the XP-11 and XP-13 before it, the XP-14 was a victim of the failings of the Curtiss Chieftain engine, a powerplant which never worked properly because of cooling problems. Although Curtiss would continue as a major manufacturer and innovator in the fighter aircraft field for two more decades, its P-14 was one of the briefest footnotes in its history, a machine whose time had passed.

Specification

XP-14

Type: single-seat pursuit aircraft
Powerplant: (planned) one 600-hp (447.4-kW) Curtiss H-1640-1 Chieftain air-cooled 12-cylinder piston engine driving a two-blade Hamilton Standard propeller
Performance: (estimated) maximum speed 173 mph (278.4 km/h) at 5,000 ft (1524 m); cruising speed 130 mph (209.2 km/h); initial climb rate about 1,700 ft (518 m) per minute; service ceiling 21,100 ft (6431 m); range 195 miles (312 km)
Weights: (estimated) empty 2,262 lb (1026 kg); maximum take-off 3,256 lb (1476.9 kg)
Dimensions: span 28 ft 0 in (8.53 m); length 23 ft 6 in (7.16 m); height 8 ft 5 in (2.57 m); wing area 189 sq ft (17.56 m²)
Armament: 0.3-in (7.62-mm) machine-guns planned for installation

Boeing P-15

History and notes

The Boeing XP-15 became the second monoplane in the pursuit series, following the same manufacturer's XP-9. It was also the first to feature an attractive but troublesome parasol wing, raised on struts above the fuselage.

First flown in January 1930 and a private venture, like so many aircraft of the period, the XP-15 bore civil registry number NX270V and was never assigned a USAAC serial. Owing its ancestry less to the monoplane XP-9 than to the biplane P-12 then still in production, the XP-15 was really little more than a P-12 fuselage with the parasol wing and was initially tested with a vertical stabilizer from a P-12C before its own tail design was installed. Like many fighters of the period, the XP-15 was put through its paces at McCook Field (Wright Field) in Dayton, Ohio, and was popular with pilots. Data obtained from test flights, including mock dogfights, were used to improve the characteristics of late P-12 machines still being assembled.

Initially flown without an enclosed cowling for its 525-hp (391.5-kW) Pratt & Whitney R-1340 Wasp, the XP-15 was retrofitted with a Townend ring cowling which added weight but reduced drag, improving performance marginally. Somewhat underpowered but highly manoeuvrable, the XP-15 was a serious candidate for a production order, but tight-fisted budgeting intervened.

On 7 February 1931 the sole example of the XP-15 was lost when a propeller blade failed during a speed run and the engine was torn from its mounts.

Specification

XP-15

Type: single-seat pursuit aircraft
Powerplant: one 525-hp (391.5-kW) Pratt & Whitney R-1340-D Wasp air-cooled 7-cylinder radial piston engine driving a fixed-pitch two-blade propeller
Performance: maximum speed 185 mph (297.7 km/h) at 8,000 ft (2438 m); initial climb rate 1,845 ft (562 m) per minute; service ceiling 26,550 ft (8092 m); range 195 miles (312 km)
Weights: empty 2,050 lb (929.9 kg); maximum take-off 2,790 lb (1265.5 kg)
Dimensions: span 30 ft 6 in (9.30 m); length 21 ft 0 in (6.40 m); height 9 ft 0 in (2.74 m); wing area 157 sq ft (14.59 m²)
Armament: two 0.3-in (7.62-mm) machine-guns planned but not installed

The fuselage of the Boeing P-15 was basically that of the P-12 biplane, with a new parasol wing fitted. Although this gave some trouble, the aircraft performed well and was enjoyed by most who flew it. The sole prototype was destroyed in 1931.

Berliner-Joyce P-16

History and notes

The Berliner-Joyce P-16 brings to the pursuit series the name of yet another aircraft manufacturing firm. More importantly, it introduces a concept verging on heresy, the two-seat fighter. Not until the McDonnell F-4 Phantom II of nearly a half-century later would it be widely accepted that air-combat aircraft (and not just single-role interceptors) should carry two crewmen. In April 1929 when the US Army held a two-seat fighter competition and obtained design submissions from Boeing, Curtiss and Berliner-Joyce, American brass hats responsible for air combat doctrine envisioned skies filled with twisting, turning aircraft doing battle at very close range with little flight discipline, each pursuit ship essentially fighting alone. The XP-16 prototype (29-326), delivered in October 1929 after being built with remarkable speed, was intended to protect itself in such an intense battle environment, having not merely nose 0.5-in (12.7-mm) guns but, also, a rearward-firing, flexible 0.3-in (7.62-mm) machine-gun operated by the extra crewman. The P-16 was a gull-winged biplane fighter, one of the most attractive of the period, and its XP-16 progenitor exceeded all expectations in tests at Wright Field. Again, as was so often the case, the winning fighter design was powered by a 600-hp (447.4-kW) Curtiss V-1570 Conqueror engine.

The USAAC ordered a pre-production batch of 25 aircraft designated Y1P-16, these differing from the prototype in having a three-bladed propeller but no supercharger. This slight change in configuration, coupled with introduction of one 75-US gal (283.9-litre) external fuel tank, increased the range of the Y1P-16 from around 200 miles (322km) to no less than 630 miles (1014km), an impressive figure for any fighter at the outset of the 1930s. Once service trials had been completed, the Y1P-16 airframes were redesignated P-16. Later, to distinguish them from single-seat pursuit aircraft, they were removed from the pursuit sequence of designations entirely and redesignated PB-1, meaning pursuit, bi-place. In fact, the Berliner-Joyce P-16 was in every respect as fast, as manoeuvrable, and as deadly in the air combat arena as contemporary machines which carried only one crewman. In simulated dogfights, P-16 pilots were often able to 'shoot down' men at the controls of the seemingly more nimble Boeing P-12. But although the P-16's performance was satisfactory in every respect, the type was not developed

further. The Berliner-Joyce name eventually faded from the scene, the manufacturer being absorbed by a predecessor firm of today's Rockwell International.

In the late 1940s, World War II having intervened, no surviving P-16 airframe could be located when the US Air Force Museum sought to find an example of one of the first successful two-seat fighters.

Specification
XP-16

Type: two-seat pursuit aircraft
Powerplant: one 600-hp (447.4-kW) Curtiss V-1570-25

Conqueror liquid-cooled 12-cylinder Vee piston engine driving a two-blade propeller
Performance: maximum speed 186 mph (299.3 km/h) at 5,000ft (1524 m); cruising speed 151 mph (243.0 km/h); initial climb rate about 1,700 ft (518 m) per minute; service ceiling 26,200 ft (7986 m); range on internal fuel about 195 miles (312 km)
Weights: empty 2,803 lb (1271.4 kg); maximum take-off about 4,000 lb (1814.4 kg)
Dimensions: span 34 ft 0 in (10.36 m); length 28 ft 2 in (8.59 m); height about 9 ft 0 in (2.74 m); wing area 279 sq ft (25.92 m²)

Armament: two fixed cowl-mounted 0.5-in (12.7-mm) machine-guns and one flexible rear-mounted 0.3-in (7.62-mm) machine-gun, plus provision for 225 lb (102 kg) of bombs on external wing racks

The P-16 was one of the best-looking aircraft of the period, its gull upper and inverted-gull lower wing giving it a distinctive look. It was also a surprisingly good performer, being able to match many of the single-place fighters of the period.

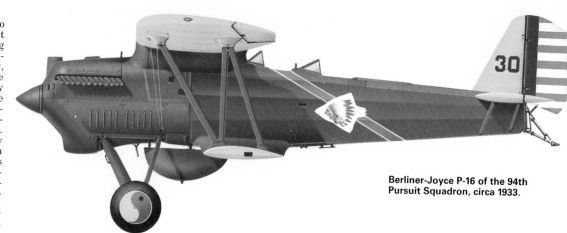

Berliner-Joyce P-16 of the 94th Pursuit Squadron, circa 1933.

Curtiss P-17

History and notes

The pursuit designation XP-17 was applied, retroactively and by administrative fiat, to the first Curtiss P-1 Hawk (24-410) late in its operational life at a point when this airframe was concluding a long career as a testbed for various powerplants. This began in 1926 with the 435-hp (324.4-kW) Curtiss V-1150D-12, continued later in 1926 with the 410-hp (305.73-kW) Allison-Liberty air-cooled engine, and culminated (in

1930 when the XP-17 designation was formally assigned) with the 550-hp (410.14-kW) Wright V-1460-3.

A further example of the experimenting, the shifts in nomenclature, and the constant changes in the Curtiss Hawk programme, the XP-17 seems to have been only one more in a parade of Curtiss Hawks used for a variety of tests at Wright Field and elsewhere. While still known as a

P-1 and driven by the Curtiss engine, this pursuit ship attained 176.18 mph (283.53 km/h) in the rigidly disciplined 1926 Rotary Club Trophy Race in Kansas City, Kansas, a respectable speed at that time under closed-course pylon racing conditions, although pilot Lieutenant William McKierman was later disqualified on a technicality.

In June 1930, when it acquired the inverted Wright powerplant and the

XP-17 appellation, this pursuit ship also assumed an awkward, tacky appearance. Its engine, wider than the fuselage, was enclosed by a crude, flush metal sheet which served as a cowl. Lloyd S. Jones, an author on US fighters, calls the XP-17 cowling 'toy-like' in appearance. Apparently a sleeker and more aerodynamic cowl could have been fitted. It was not precisely because the airframe was a 'dogship', or test

Curtiss P-17

Despite being given a designation in the Pursuit series, the XP-17 was little more than a re-engined Curtiss P-1 Hawk, and it was never intended for production for the Air Corps. Its main characteristic was the crude triangular cowling.

machine, and there never existed any possibility that the XP-17 would be ordered into production. In March 1932, the XP-17 was officially withdrawn from service. The sole aircraft was subsequently scrapped.

By the early 1930s, the Curtiss Hawk's once-remarkable performance was no longer up to the standard of newer fighters and all of the many variants of the Curtiss fighter were living on borrowed time.

Specification
XP-17
Type: single-seat pursuit aircraft

Powerplant: one 550-hp (410.14-kW) Wright V-1460-3 liquid-cooled inverted-Vee piston engine driving a two-blade Hamilton Standard propeller
Performance: maximum speed 165 mph (265.5 km/h) at 1,000 ft (305 m); cruising speed 128 mph (206.0 km/h); stalling speed 58 mph

(93 km/h); initial climb rate about 1,800 ft (549 m) per minute; service ceiling 21,400 ft (6523 m); range 570 miles (917 km)
Weights: empty 2,204 lb (999.7 kg); maximum take-off 2,994 lb (1358.1 kg)
Dimensions: span 31 ft 6 in (9.60 m); length 22 ft 10 in (6.96 m); height 8 ft 7 in (2.62 m); wing area about 250 sq ft (23.23 m²)
Armament: 0.3-in (7.62-mm) or 0.5-in (12.7-mm) machine-guns planned but apparently not installed.

Curtiss P-18

History and notes
The P-18 designation is the third applied to an aircraft never actually built (following the Curtiss XP-11 and P-14) and is, in turn, followed by the P-19 which also existed on paper only. In 1930, the US Army Air Corps had created a requirement for a pursuit ship to be powered by the proposed Wright V-1560-1 12-cylinder engine, and had tentatively planned on obtaining two aircraft types to test the powerplant. The Curtiss P-18 would have been a single-bay biplane fighter similar in size to the Hawk series but otherwise new in design. When, by late 1930, it was evident that the powerplant was not going to be developed successfully, the Curtiss P-18 was cancelled before reaching an advanced design stage.

Specification
XP-18
Type: single-seat pursuit aircraft
Powerplant: (planned) one 600-hp (447.4-kW) Wright V-1560-1 air-cooled 12-cylinder piston engine
Performance: never specified
Weights: never specified
Dimensions: never specified
Armament: never specified

Curtiss P-19

History and notes
The P-19, a Curtiss monoplane fighter, never even reached the 'drawing board' stage. Like the P-18 before it, the aircraft had been conceived by the Army to be powered by the proposed Wright V-1560 engine.

Apart from the decision that it would have been of single-seat monoplane configuration, the Curtiss P-19 was cancelled before any details of its specification could be decided.

Specification
XP-19
Type: single-seat pursuit aircraft
Powerplant: (planned) one 600-hp (447.4-kW) Wright V-1560-1 air-cooled 12-cylinder piston engine
Performance: never specified

Weights: never specified
Dimensions: never specified
Armament: never specified

Curtiss P-20

History and notes
The sole Curtiss YP-20 service-test pursuit ship (29-374) had been conceived as the third Chieftain-powered P-11. While still under construction, it acquired the YP-20 appellation when the original powerplant failed to materialize. Yet another of the seemingly incessant one-off variations on the Curtiss Hawk theme, it was completed with outsized wheel spats for both main gear and tailwheel and a Townend cowl ring encircling its 650-hp (484.7-kW) Wright R-1820-9 Cyclone radial, and was painted in the standard khaki scheme of the time with 'US Army', designation and serial presented on the rear fuselage side. Ordered in 1929 and flown in 1930, the fighter showed potential and, before its chequered

Another fighter test-bed, the airframe which at one time was designated XP-20 saw many different configurations. In XP-20 form it had a Wright radial engine and large spats over not only the mainwheel but also the tailwheel. It was converted to XP-6E standard.

life was over, contributed substantially to the ongoing P-6 Hawk programme.

The much-used 600-hp (447.4-kW) Curtiss V-1570 Conqueror engine was planned for the YP-20 after it flew with the Wright powerplant and yet a further designation, XP-22, was planned for this airframe. Although a different Hawk airframe eventually was built as the sole complete XP-22, the YP-20 did acquire the Conqueror engine by late 1930, was again redesignated to

become the XP-6E and, as noted earlier, pioneered the way for the superb P-6E Hawk series of fighters. Still another change took place later, an enclosed cockpit structure being added and this airframe becoming the sole XP-6F.

By the time it was withdrawn from duty and scrapped in 1932, the YP-20 had been intended for three different powerplants and had held five designations (P-11, YP-20, XP-22, XP-6E, XP-6F). Few test machines experienced as much

diversity or contributed so much knowledge to fighter aviation.

Specification
YP-20

Type: single-seat pursuit aircraft
Powerplant: one 650-hp (484.7-kW) Wright R-1820-9 Cyclone air-cooled 9-cylinder radial piston engine driving a two-blade propeller
Performance: maximum speed 186 mph (299.3 km/h) at 5,000 ft

(1524 m); initial climb rate 2,410 ft (735 m) per minute; service ceiling about 24,000 ft (7315 m); range 540 miles (869 km)
Weights: empty 2,477 lb (1123.6 kg); maximum take-off 3,233 lb (1466.5 kg)
Dimensions: span 31 ft 6 in (9.60 m); length 23 ft 9 in (7.24 m); height 8 ft 10 in (2.69 m); wing area 252 sq ft (23.41 m²)
Armament: two 0.3-in (7.62-mm) fixed forward-firing nose machine-guns

Curtiss P-21

History and notes
The designation XP-21 was assigned to a pair of 300-hp (224-kW) Pratt & Whitney Wasp-powered (and, in reality, underpowered) Curtiss Hawk airframes converted from their initial incarnation as XP-3A pursuit ships. Again, perhaps with a view to deceiving holders of Congressional purse strings as the Depression deepened, the 1929-31 period of trial and experimentation with the Curtiss Hawk series caused a proliferation of fighter designa-

tions. No fewer than 12 'P for pursuit' designations were held by various Hawks.

The two XP-21 airframes (28-188/189) joined the diverse stable of fighters being judged at Wright Field, Ohio, but appear to have offered no significant improvement over the P-3A, let alone over the other Curtiss design then in production. It was this design, the P-6E Hawk, which would be remembered long after 1931 when the two XP-21s were retired from service.

Specification
XP-21

Type: single-seat pursuit aircraft
Powerplant: one 300-hp (223.7-kW) Pratt & Whitney R-985-1 Wasp Junior air-cooled radial piston engine driving a two-blade propeller
Performance: maximum speed 137 mph (220.5 km/h) at 10,000 ft (3048 m); cruising speed 122 mph (196.3 km/h); initial climb rate 1,400 ft (427 m) per minute; service ceiling

about 23,000 ft (7010 m); range 426 miles (686 km)
Weights: empty 1,956 lb (887.2 kg); maximum take-off 2,590 lb (1174.8 kg)
Dimensions: span 31 ft 7 in (9.63 m); length 22 ft 3 in (6.78 m); height 8 ft 9 in (2.67 m); wing area 252 sq ft (23.41 m²)
Armament: one 0.3-in (7.62-mm) fixed forward-firing machine-gun believed planned but not installed

Curtiss P-22

History and notes
The XP-22 designation, intended originally for the sole YP-20 (29-374), was assigned to the third production P-6A (29-262) when it became apparent that the latter airframe could be completed first with the 600-hp (447.4-kW) Curtiss V-1570 Conqueror liquid-cooled engine. Again, a designation was encumbered by yet another variant of the Curtiss Hawk biplane fighter, this one being converted by Curtiss in St Louis, Missouri, in 1931. The resulting configuration was virtually identical to what became the

production P-6E Hawk.

In June 1931, a US Army Air Corps team evaluating Hawk variants chose the YP-22 for production and ordered 45 Y1P-22 airframes. Most sources indicate that the Y1P-22s were redesignated P-6E before completion, although historian James C. Fahey suggests that some may have actually taken to the air bearing the Y1P-22 designation. In the event, the XP-22, like so many other machines, was but a footnote in history on the route to the P-6E Hawk.

Specification
XP-22

Type: single-seat pursuit aircraft
Powerplant: one 600-hp (447.4-kW) Curtiss V-1570-23 Conqueror liquid-cooled 12-cylinder Vee piston engine driving a three-blade Hamilton Standard propeller
Performance: maximum speed 200 mph (321.86 km/h) at 4,000 ft (1219 m); initial climb rate 2,480 ft (756 m) per minute; service ceiling 24,700 ft (7529 m); range 570 miles (917 km)
Weights: empty about 2,300 lb (1043.3 kg); maximum take-off

3,436 lb (1558.6 kg)
Dimensions: span 31 ft 6 in (9.60 m); length 23 ft 2 in (7.06 m); height 8 ft 10 in (2.69 m); wing area 252 sq ft (23.41 m²)
Armament: two 0.3-in (7.62-mm) fixed forward-firing nose machine-guns

The neatly-cowled engine and three-blade propeller were virtually identical to those of the production P-6E Hawk, and there is some contention whether the first P-6Es were actually designated Y1P-22 during their first flights.

Curtiss P-23

History and notes

The Curtiss XP-23 was the last biplane in the pursuit series. In most respects an entirely new design and a very graceful one, it was altered on the production line from the final airframe (32-278) among the 45 which were ordered as Y1P-22 but redesignated P-6E. The ubiquitous 600-hp (447.4-kW) Curtiss V-1570 Conqueror was again called-up for service, initially with a turbo-charger and three-blade propeller. Delivered 16 April 1932 and evaluated by operational fighter pilots at Wright Field, the XP-23 seems to have performed very well, subject only to the limitations of the double-wing configuration. Some reports that the XP-23 was excessively heavy, with maximum take-off weight as high as 4,300 lb (1950.5 kg) appear to be based on an erroneous interpretation of Curtiss documents from the period. The XP-23 flew like it looked, a sleek, potent fighter denied a production contract only because, in 1932, it was competing not with other biplanes but with the monoplane Boeing P-26 'Peashooter'.

The aircraft reached the service-test stage with turbo-charger removed, two-blade propeller retrofitted, and its designation changed to YP-23. Eventually, despite speed and manoeuvrability fully competitive with that of the Boeing monoplane, it became clear that the US Army would choose the latter as its standard fighter of the early 1930s. Ultimately, the YP-23 was deleted

from Army inventory and turned back to Curtiss, where its wings were retained for use on the prototype US Navy XF11C-1 shipboard fighter. It may be symbolic that the wings lasted longer than the fuselage: never again would paired wings adorn a pursuit/fighter aircraft.

Specification
XP-23

Type: single-seat pursuit aircraft
Powerplant: one 600-hp (447.4-kW) Curtiss V-1570-23 Conqueror liquid-cooled 12-cylinder Vee piston engine driving a two-blade propeller
Performance: maximum speed 203 mph (326.7 km/h) at 4,000 ft (1219 m); initial climb rate about 1,500 ft (457 m) per minute; service ceiling about 26,000 ft (7925 m); range 435 miles (700 km)
Weights: empty 2,900 lb (1315.4 kg); maximum take-off 3,400 lb (1542.2 kg)
Dimensions: span 31 ft 6 in (9.60 m); length 23 ft 10 in (7.26 m); height 9 ft 6 in (2.90 m); wing area about 250 sq ft (23.23 m²)

The end of an era in more ways than one, the Curtiss YP-23 was not only the final expression of the famous Hawk series, but was also the last biplane in the pursuit series. Despite being a superb fighter, the monoplanes were too well advanced for it to gain a production order.

Armament: one 0.3-in (7.62-mm) and one 0.5-in (12.7-mm) fixed forward-firing machine-guns, plus provision for 500 lb (227 kg) of bombs

Lockheed P-24

History and notes

The sole YP-24 (32-320), delivered to the Army on 29 September 1931, was the first fighter designed by the Lockheed firm at Burbank, California, founded by Allan Lockheed (originally Loughead) and renowned for its Vega and Orion monoplane airliners. Initially designated XP-900, the YP-24 was a low-wing monoplane two-seater with retractable landing gear seen as a heavier and faster replacement for the Berliner-Joyce P-16, which had equipped the 94th Pursuit Squadron at Selfridge Field, Michigan. The ever-familiar Curtiss Conqueror was again employed as powerplant. Although of composite wood and metal construction, the Lockheed P-24 in a production version would almost certainly have been an all-metal machine. Though it carried 'extra' weight in the person of a rear gunner and his weapon, the YP-24 with its top speed of 214 mph (344.4 km/h) was the fastest fighter in the United States in 1931. The YP-24 was also uncommonly big for a fighter, with a wing span of 42 ft 9 in (13.03 m) and a maximum take-off weight of 4,360 lb (1977.7 kg).

The Burbank design team under engineer Robert Wood had created an exceptionally promising heavy aircraft with potential as a pursuit ship and even more promise for the attack role. It was to be company finances, not the merits of the design, which doomed the YP-24 to 'one-off' status. In March 1929, the Lockheed firm had been acquired by Detroit Aircraft Corporation, seek-

Representing the first venture into fighter design by the Lockheed company, the YP-24 was an attempt to provide a heavy biplace fighter to replace the Berliner-Joyce P-16. By all accounts it was a good aeroplane, being fast and heavily-armed, but financial matters ensured it stayed a one-off.

ing to build what would today be called a conglomerate. In October 1932, at the lowest point in the Depression, the Detroit firm filed for bankruptcy. That same year, the Lockheed firm would separate from both its founder and its parent company, and would be rescued and reorganized by a new chief executive, Robert Gross. But by then it was too late for the YP-24. The Army ordered five Y1P-24s and five further airframes to be built as YA-9 attack

bombers, but none was ever completed.

During a test flight on 19 October 1931, the YP-24 experienced a mechanical problem with its landing gear partially lowered. The landing gear could not be made to lower fully and lock into place. The pilot was able to retract the gear and was contemplating a belly landing, but onwatchers were concerned that the low-slung engine radiator would dig in, flipping the heavy aircraft on its back. The pilot was ordered to parachute to safety and the YP-24 was lost.

Specification
YP-24

Type: two-seat pursuit aircraft
Powerplant: one 600-hp (447.4-kW) Curtiss V-1570-23 Conqueror liquid-cooled 12-cylinder Vee piston engine driving a three-blade Hamilton Standard propeller
Performance: maximum speed 214 mph (344.4 km/h) at 5,000 ft (1524 m); cruising speed 180 mph (289.7 km/h) at 5,000 ft (1524 m); stalling speed 58 mph (93 km/h); initial climb rate about 2,600 ft (792 m) per minute; service ceiling 26,400 ft (8047 m); range 556 miles (895 km)
Weights: empty 3,010 lb (1365.3 kg); maximum take-off 4,360 lb (1977.7 kg)
Dimensions: span 42 ft 9 in (13.03 m); length 28 ft 9 in (8.76 m); height 8 ft 2 in (2.49 m); wing area 292 sq ft (27.13 m²)
Armament: one 0.3-in (7.62-mm) and one 0.5-in (12.7-mm) fixed forward-firing machine-guns, and one 0.3-in (7.62-mm) flexible rear machine-gun

Consolidated P-25

History and notes

The P-25 was built by Consolidated, a manufacturer founded in Buffalo, New York, in 1923 as successor to the Dayton-Wright Airplane Company. The P-25 was externally almost a replica of the Lockheed P-24 but slightly larger and heavier. One of Robert Wood's design engineers moved from Lockheed to Consolidated and retained the goal of creating a fast, two-seat tandem fighter to replace the Berliner-Joyce P-16. The US Army Air Corps in 1932 was sufficiently interested to order two Consolidated Y1P-25 airframes (32-321/322), although the second was soon given the attack function and redesignated Y1A-11. A cantilever low-wing monoplane of all-metal construction (unlike its partly wood Lockheed forbear), the Y1P-25 had retractable landing gear, the familiar Curtiss Conqueror engine, and a rearward-facing machine-gunner. The engine was supercharged, making possible a top speed of 247 mph (397.5 km/h) at 15,000 ft (4572 m).

First flown in 1932, the Y1P-25 (32-321) crashed on 13 January 1933 and was written off. The Y1A-11 was also lost that same month. But in its short test life the Y1P-25 had shown sufficient promise for the USAAC to seek further development. Indeed, by May 1932 the service had decided to explore the basic design further. The Y1P-27 and Y1P-28 variants, to be powered by Pratt & Whitney Wasp engines of different marks, were seriously contemplated but

never built. Four Conqueror-powered service-test machines were completed as P-30s and later machines were redesignated PB-2 (for pursuit, biplace). The basic design, after being allocated several designations, became the principal USAAC two-seat fighter between world wars.

Specification
Y1P-25

Type: two-seat pursuit aircraft
Powerplant: one turbo-charged 600-hp (447.4-kW) Curtiss V-1570-27 Conqueror liquid-cooled 12-cylinder Vee piston engine driving a three-blade Hamilton Standard propeller
Performance: maximum speed 247 mph (397.5 km/h) at 15,000 ft (4572 m); cruising speed about 180 mph (289.7 km/h) at 15,000 ft (4572 m); initial climb rate about 2,600 ft (792 m) per minute; service ceiling about 27,000 ft (8230 m); range about 580 miles (933 km)
Weights: empty 3,887 lb (1763.1 kg); maximum take-off 5,110 lb (2318 kg)

Showing great similarity to the Lockheed P-24, the P-25 was designed to perform a similar job, although its armament was not quite as heavy. The two Y1P-25 test aircraft showed sufficient promise for the type to be further developed.

Dimensions: span 43 ft 10 in (13.36 m); length 29 ft 4 in (8.94 m); height 8 ft 7 in (2.62 m); wing area about 300 sq ft (27.87 m²)
Armament: two 0.3-in (7.62-mm) fixed forward-firing machine-guns, and one 0.3-in (7.62-mm) flexible rear machine-gun

Boeing P-26

History and notes

Just after Pearl Harbor, when Philippine air force pilots in the Boeing P-26 were outclassed and outfought by the formidable Mitsubishi Zero, it was fashionable to berate the 'Peashooter' as a dated and doughty pursuit ship. The P-26 had fixed landing gear with heavy, high-drag wheel pants. It was festooned with bracing wires. Its armament of two 0.3-in (7.62-mm) or one 0.3-in (7.62-mm) and one 0.5-in (12.7-mm) machine-guns seemed hopelessly inadequate. P-26s battled Japanese invaders in the Philippines and in China (which acquired 11 export machines) but were badly mauled. In those dark days of World War II, it would have been easy to forget that the P-26 of 1931 had been a bold new venture in fighter design: the first all-metal fighter and the first monoplane fighter to enter

squadron service. The P-26 was also the final production fighter built by Boeing, which had dominated the field for nearly two decades.

Ordered by the US Army on 5 December 1931 initially with the designation XP-936, the 'Peashooter' made its first flight on 20 March 1932. The prototype machine (32-412), one of three covered by the contract, differed from the familiar production model (Boeing Model 266) in having a lower headrest for its open canopy, and wheelpants which extended behind the main landing gear struts. No beauty, with a huge Townend ring enclosing its 525-hp (391.5-kW) Pratt & Whitney R-1340-21 radial air-cooled engine, an im-

The 'Kicking Mule' insignia identify these P-26s as being from the 95th Pursuit Squadron, today a Lockheed TR-1 operator. The P-26 was notable for its raised and strengthened headrest, incorporated to protect the pilot if the aircraft nosed over.

Boeing P-26

A new era for United States fighter aviation was ushered in on 20 March 1932, when the first P-26 took to the air. It was also to be the end of an era, for the P-26 was Boeing's last USAF fighter. This aircraft served with the 95th Pursuit Squadron, 17th Pursuit Group at March.

proved version of the powerplant used by the P-12 biplane fighter, the P-26 nevertheless impressed the onwatcher with its sleekness by comparison with biplane fighters of the time, including the P-12 itself which was still in production. Shortly after the third machine (32-414) reached Selfridge Field, Michigan, on 25 April 1932 to be evaluated by operational pilots, the Army formally purchased the first three airframes from Boeing and designated them XP-26, later YIP-26 to indicate the service-test function and, later yet, simply P-26. With improved headrest and other minor changes, the P-26A was ordered into production on 28 January 1934 with an initial buy of 111 airframes (33-28/138). There followed two P-26Bs with fuel injection (33-179 and 33-185) and 23 P-26Cs (33-181/203), the latter with 600-hp (447.4-kW) R-1340-27 engines.

Some 'greats' of the era flew the P-26. Lieutenant Colonel Ralph Royce (later a major general) at Selfridge Field, Michigan, was fond of it. Major General Frank O. Hunter of the 17th Pursuit Group at March Field, California, sung its praises. Major Armin F. Herold of the 20th Pursuit Group at Barksdale Field, Louisiana, led formations in a P-26A gaudy with blue, yellow and red bands around the engine cowl. In fact, 'Peashooters' appeared widely with elaborate paint schemes. Those of the Bolling Field Detachment, Washington, DC, had alternating blue and gold squares on their Townend rings and around the capitol insignia on the rear fuselage, with yellow tail and red/white striped rudder surfaces. Perhaps most impressive were the mostly blue machines, with red, yellow and gold trim, operated by the 95th Attack Squadron at Selfridge. Major Peter Schwenk, a pilot with that unit, recalled that his Boeing 'looked like a flying neon sign'. In all, 'Peashooters' served with the 3rd, 16th, 17th, 18th, 19th, 20th, 27th, 32nd, 34th, 38th, 55th, 73rd, 77th, 79th, 94th and 95th squadrons.

'Hot' ship

In the 1930s, the Boeing monoplane was a 'hot' ship. With a maximum level speed of 227 mph (365.3 km/h) at 10,000 ft (3048 m) and an initial climb rate of 2,300 ft (701 m) per minute, it was highly manoeuvrable. It outclassed the biplane P-12 in every performance regime. On landing, where it required careful control and did not forgive the lax flier, the P-26 was too hot. Its 82.5 mph (132.8 km/h) landing speed made it difficult to handle until flaps were developed by the Army, reducing landing speed to 70 mph (112.7 km/h). The flaps were retrofitted on P-26As and installed on P-26B and P-26C machines on the production line.

Flying the P-26 was a thrill. "That open cockpit and high manoeuvrability kept you in touch with the elements," says Schwenk. The high, sturdy headrest found on the fourth airframe onward resulted from an accident when an early P-26 flipped violently on its back and killed the pilot with almost no structural damage to the aircraft. "It was sturdy," says Schwenk. "Though we never flew it in combat, we had the feeling it could take punishment." Though its landing gear was stalky and its approach characteristics, as noted, were demanding, the P-26 was easy on the touch once aloft and pilots were pleased that it evoked a feeling of power and toughness. It was a mainstay between world wars until replaced by the Seversky P-35 and Curtiss P-36 in the late 1930s.

In addition to the Philippines, US Army P-26s ended up in the air forces of Panama and Guatemala. The latter country was valiantly flying 'Peashooters' as late as 1957. The final variant, the Boeing Model 281, did not enter US service or receive a P-26 designation, although identical to the US machine: 11 went to China and one to Spain. A P-26 occupies a place of pride at the US Air Force Museum in Dayton, Ohio.

Specification

P-26C

Type: single-seat pursuit aircraft
Powerplant: one 600-hp (447.4-kW) Pratt & Whitney R-1340-27 Wasp air-cooled 9-cylinder radial piston engine driving a two-blade propeller
Performance: maximum speed 234 mph (376.6 km/h) at 7,500 ft (2286 m); initial climb rate 2,600 ft (792 m) per minute; service ceiling 27,400 ft (8352 m); range 560 miles (901 km)
Weights: empty 2,196 lb (996.1 kg); maximum take-off 3,015 lb (1367.6 kg)
Dimensions: span 27 ft 11.5 in (8.52 m); length 23 ft 10 in (7.26 m); height 10 ft 5 in (3.17 m); wing area 149.5 sq ft (13.89 m²)
Armament: one 0.3-in (7.62-mm) and one 0.5-in (12.7-mm) fixed forward-firing machine-guns, plus provision for two 100-lb (45.36-kg) or five 30-lb (13.61 kg) bombs

Boeing P-26A cutaway drawing key

1 Starter dog
2 Propeller hub sleeve
3 Sleeve attachment
4 Two-blade propeller
5 Engine face plate
6 Cooling inlets
7 Engine cowling ring

8 Pratt & Whitney R-1340-27 Wasp engine
9 Cylinder heads
10 Gun barrel blast tube extension
11 Exhaust pipes
12 Engine bearer ring
13 Louvred exhaust stacks
14 Carburettor cold air intake
15 Engine bearer upper support struts
16 Starter primer access
17 Cowling panel fasteners
18 Hot air intake
19 Cockpit heater
20 Exhaust stub
21 Gun blast tube
22 Oil cooler
23 Lower panel access
24 Wingroot stub
25 Port gun barrel
26 Bulk head/lower longeron attachment
27 Fuselage forward frame
28 Air intake/starter controls
29 Support strut attachment
30 Cooling louvres
31 Oil tank, capacity 8 US gal (30 litres)

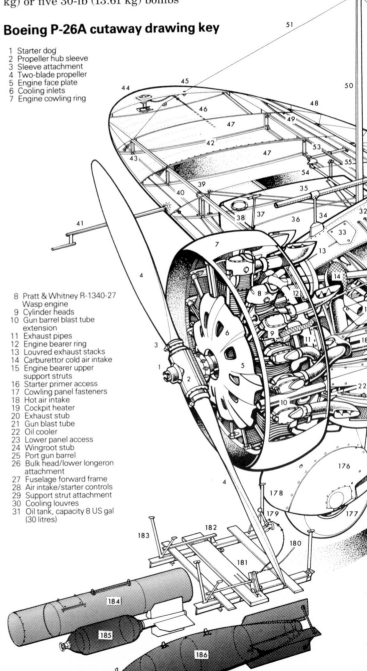

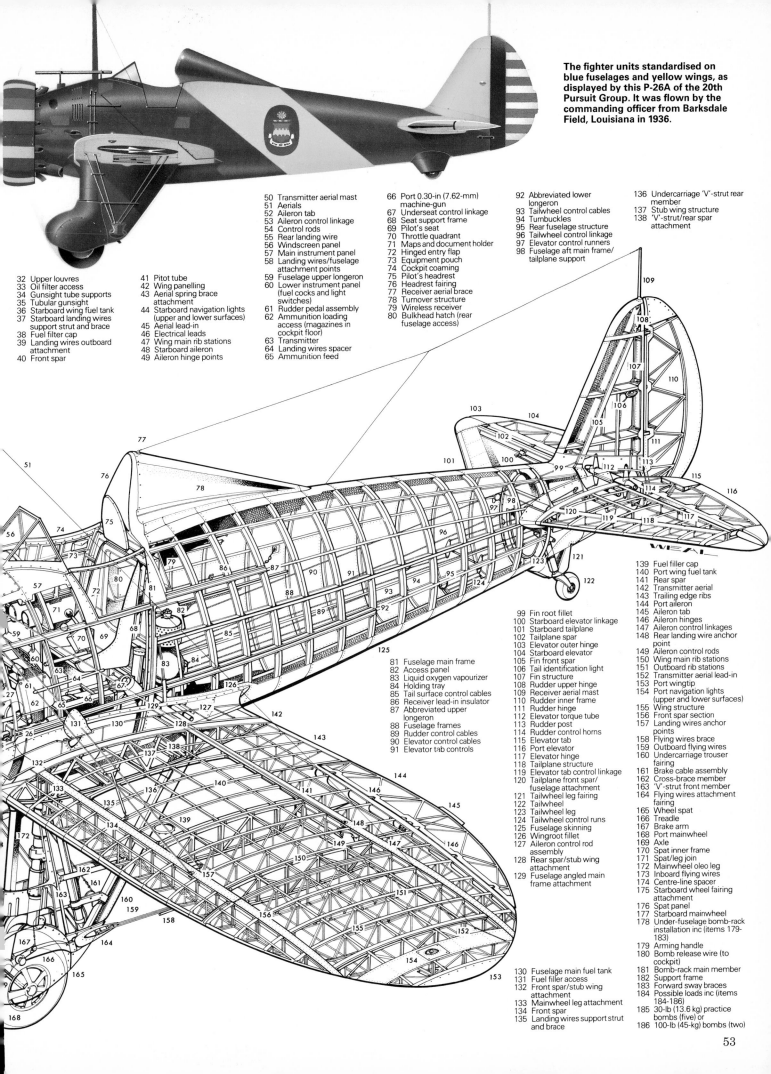

The fighter units standardised on blue fuselages and yellow wings, as displayed by this P-26A of the 20th Pursuit Group. It was flown by the commanding officer from Barksdale Field, Louisiana in 1936.

32 Upper louvres
33 Oil filter access
34 Gunsight tube supports
35 Tubular gunsight
36 Starboard wing fuel tank
37 Starboard landing wires support strut and brace
38 Fuel filter cap
39 Landing wires outboard attachment
40 Front spar
41 Pitot tube
42 Wing panelling
43 Aerial spring brace attachment
44 Starboard navigation lights (upper and lower surfaces)
45 Aerial lead-in
46 Electrical leads
47 Wing main rib stations
48 Starboard aileron
49 Aileron hinge points

50 Transmitter aerial mast
51 Aerials
52 Aileron tab
53 Aileron control linkage
54 Control rods
55 Rear landing wire
56 Windscreen panel
57 Main instrument panel
58 Landing wires/fuselage attachment points
59 Fuselage upper longeron
60 Lower instrument panel (fuel cocks and light switches)
61 Rudder pedal assembly
62 Ammunition loading access (magazines in cockpit floor)
63 Transmitter
64 Landing wires spacer
65 Ammunition feed

66 Port 0.30-in (7.62-mm) machine-gun
67 Underseat control linkage
68 Seat support frame
69 Pilot's seat
70 Throttle quadrant
71 Maps and document holder
72 Hinged entry flap
73 Equipment pouch
74 Cockpit coaming
75 Pilot's headrest
76 Headrest fairing
77 Receiver aerial brace
78 Turnover structure
79 Wireless receiver
80 Bulkhead hatch (rear fuselage access)

81 Fuselage main frame
82 Access panel
83 Liquid oxygen vapourizer
84 Holding tray
85 Tail surface control cables
86 Receiver lead-in insulator
87 Abbreviated upper longeron
88 Fuselage frames
89 Rudder control cables
90 Elevator control cables
91 Elevator tab controls

92 Abbreviated lower longeron
93 Tailwheel control cables
94 Turnbuckles
95 Rear fuselage structure
96 Tailwheel control linkage
97 Elevator control runners
98 Fuselage aft main frame/tailplane support

99 Fin root fillet
100 Starboard elevator linkage
101 Starboard tailplane
102 Tailplane spar
103 Elevator outer hinge
104 Starboard elevator
105 Fin front spar
106 Tail identification light
107 Fin structure
108 Rudder upper hinge
109 Receiver aerial mast
110 Rudder inner frame
111 Rudder hinge
112 Elevator torque tube
113 Rudder post
114 Rudder control horns
115 Elevator tab
116 Port elevator
117 Elevator hinge
118 Tailplane structure
119 Elevator tab control linkage
120 Tailplane front spar/fuselage attachment
121 Tailwheel leg fairing
122 Tailwheel
123 Tailwheel leg
124 Tailwheel control runs
125 Tailwheel skinning
126 Wingroot fillet
127 Aileron control rod assembly
128 Rear spar/stub wing attachment
129 Fuselage angled main frame attachment

130 Fuselage main fuel tank
131 Fuel filler access
132 Front spar/stub wing attachment
133 Mainwheel leg attachment
134 Front spar
135 Landing wires support strut and brace

136 Undercarriage 'V'-strut rear member
137 Stub wing structure
138 'V'-strut/rear spar attachment

139 Fuel filler cap
140 Port wing fuel tank
141 Rear spar
142 Transmitter aerial
143 Trailing edge ribs
144 Port aileron
145 Aileron tab
146 Aileron hinges
147 Aileron control linkages
148 Rear landing wire anchor point
149 Aileron control rods
150 Wing main rib stations
151 Outboard rib stations
152 Transmitter aerial lead-in
153 Port wingtip
154 Port navigation lights (upper and lower surfaces)
155 Wing structure
156 Front spar section
157 Landing wires anchor points
158 Flying wires brace
159 Outboard flying wires
160 Undercarriage trouser fairing
161 Brake cable assembly
162 Cross-brace member
163 'V'-strut front member
164 Flying wires attachment fairing
165 Wheel spat
166 Treadle
167 Brake arm
168 Port mainwheel
169 Axle
170 Spat inner frame
171 Spat/leg join
172 Mainwheel oleo leg
173 Inboard flying wires
174 Centre-line spacer
175 Starboard wheel fairing attachment
176 Spat panel
177 Starboard mainwheel
178 Under-fuselage bomb-rack installation inc (items 179-183)
179 Arming handle
180 Bomb release wire (to cockpit)
181 Bomb-rack main member
182 Support frame
183 Forward sway braces
184 Possible loads inc (items 184-186)
185 30-lb (13.6 kg) practice bombs (five) or
186 100-lb (45-kg) bombs (two)

53

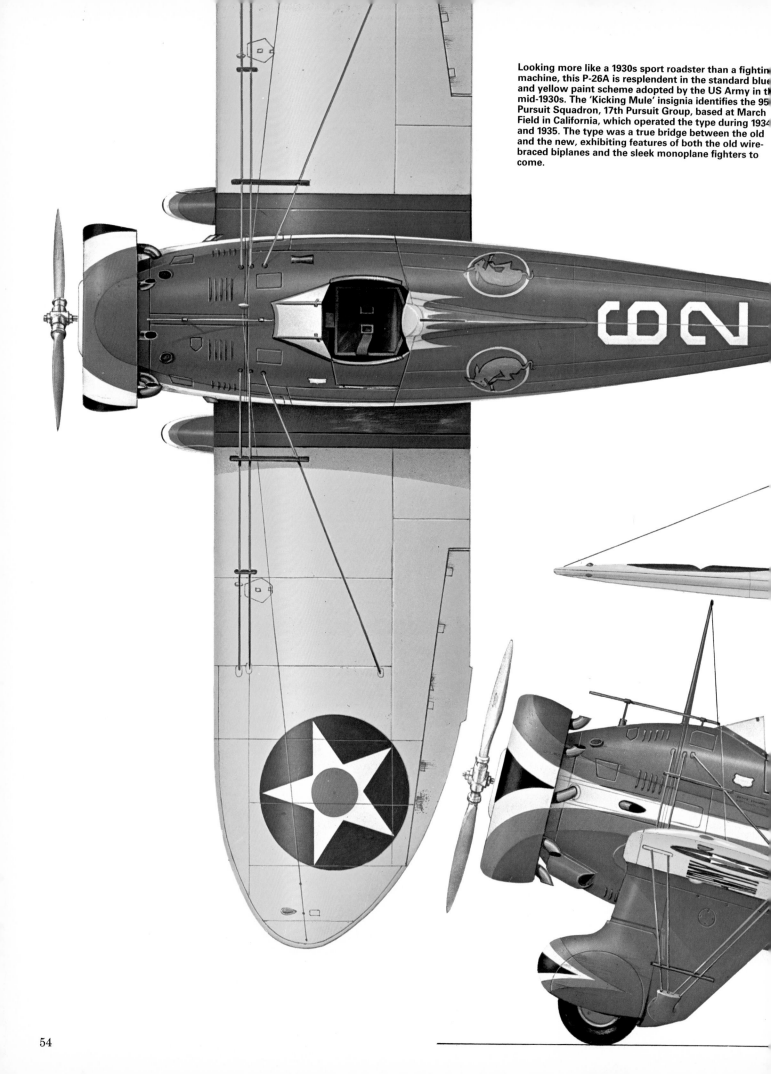

Looking more like a 1930s sport roadster than a fighting machine, this P-26A is resplendent in the standard blue and yellow paint scheme adopted by the US Army in the mid-1930s. The 'Kicking Mule' insignia identifies the 95th Pursuit Squadron, 17th Pursuit Group, based at March Field in California, which operated the type during 1934 and 1935. The type was a true bridge between the old and the new, exhibiting features of both the old wire-braced biplanes and the sleek monoplane fighters to come.

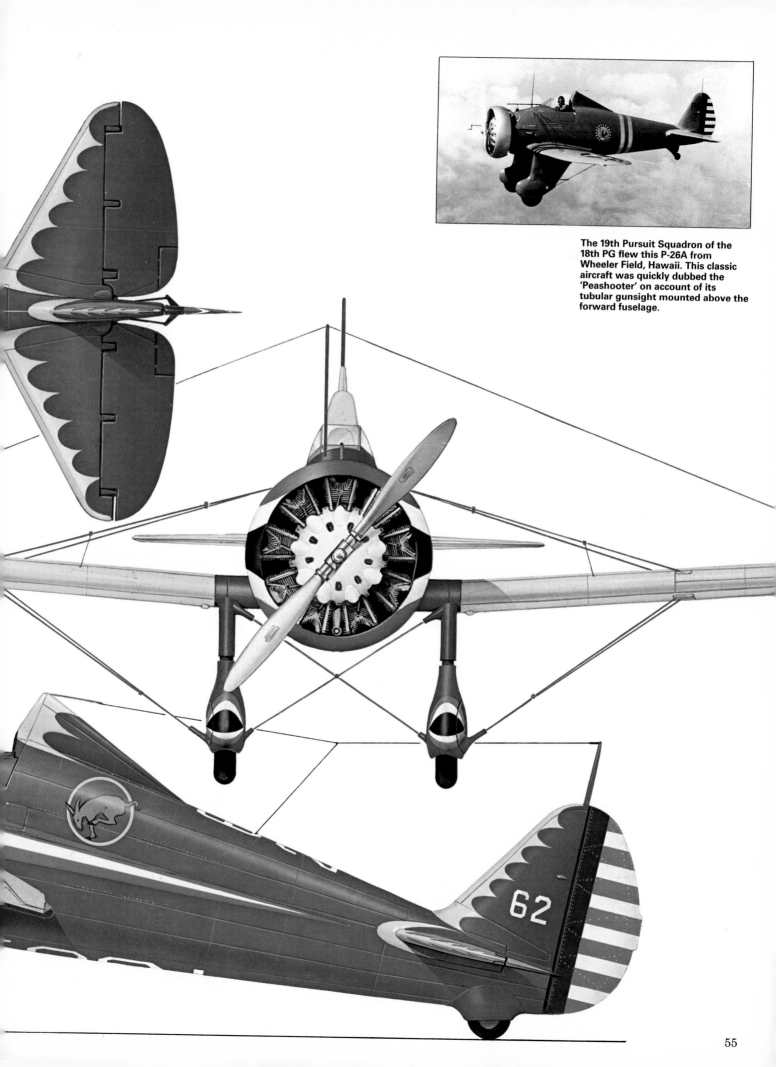

The 19th Pursuit Squadron of the 18th PG flew this P-26A from Wheeler Field, Hawaii. This classic aircraft was quickly dubbed the 'Peashooter' on account of its tubular gunsight mounted above the forward fuselage.

Consolidated P-27

History and notes

The P-27 designation, more specifically Y1P-27, went to the USAAC's proposed version of the Consolidated P-25 to have been powered by a 550-hp (410.1-kW) Pratt & Whitney R-1340-21 Wasp air-cooled radial engine, a concept which seems to have been inspired by the single-seat Boeing P-26. This would have given the two-seat tandem fighter a fattened look, destroying the sleek lines of liquid-cooled, Conqueror-powered variants, and it seems unlikely that the design top speed of 250 mph (402.3 km/h) at 15,000 ft (4572 m) would actually have been attained.

Although ordered in 1932, the Y1P-27 was not built and was thus only a paper concept in the long chain of two-seat fighter development which included YP-24, Y1P-25, Y1A-11, P-27, P-28, P-30 and PB-2.

Specification

Y1P-27

Type: two-seat pursuit aircraft
Powerplant: (planned) one 550-hp (410.1-kW) Pratt & Whitney R-1340-21 Wasp air-cooled 9-cylinder radial piston engine driving a three-blade propeller
Performance: (estimated) maximum speed 250 mph (402.3 km/h) at 15,000 ft (4572 m); cruising speed about 180 mph (289.7 km/h) at 15,000 ft (4572 m); initial climb rate about 2,600 ft (792 m) per minute; service ceiling about 27,000 ft (8230 m); range about 580 miles (933 km)
Weights: (estimated) empty 3,887 lb (1763.1 kg); maximum take-off 5,110 lb (2317.9 kg)
Dimensions: (planned) span 43 ft 10 in (13.36 m); length 29 ft 4 in (8.94 m); height 8 ft 7 in (2.62 m); wing area about 300 sq ft (27.87 m²)
Armament: (planned) two 0.3-in (7.62-mm) fixed forward-firing machine-guns, and one 0.3-in (7.62-mm) flexible rear machine-gun

Consolidated P-28

History and notes

The P-28 was to have been another Consolidated, Wasp-powered variation on the two-seat tandem fighter theme begun with the Lockheed YP-24, continued with the Consolidated Y1P-25, and including the unbuilt Consolidated Y1P-27. The Y1P-28 would have been powered by a 600-hp (447.4-kW) Pratt & Whitney R-1340-19 Wasp air-cooled radial engine. This second unbuilt proposal of its kind, and second which would have lacked the sleek lines of Conqueror-powered variants, the Y1P-28 was cancelled before construction began and was bypassed by the P-30.

Specification

Y1P-28

Type: two-seat pursuit aircraft
Powerplant: (planned) one 600-hp (447.4-kW) Pratt & Whitney R-1340-19 Wasp air-cooled 9-cylinder radial piston engine driving a three-blade Hamilton Standard propeller
Performance: (estimated) maximum speed 250 mph (402.3 km/h) at 15,000 ft (4572 m); cruising speed about 180 mph (289.7 km/h) at 15,000 ft (4572 m); initial climb rate about 2,600 ft (792 m) per minute; service ceiling about 27,000 ft (8230 m); range about 580 miles (933 km)
Weights: (estimated) empty 3,997 lb (1813.1 kg); maximum take-off 5,110 lb (2317.9 kg)
Dimensions: (planned) span 43 ft 10 in (13.36 m); length 29 ft 4 in (8.94 m); height 8 ft 7 in (2.62 m); wing area about 300 sq ft (27.87 m²)
Armament: (planned) two 0.3-in (7.62-mm) fixed forward-firing machine-guns, and one 0.3-in (7.62-mm) flexible rear machine-gun

Boeing P-29

History and notes

The P-29 or company Model 264 was a Boeing effort to improve upon the already impressive performance of the P-26 'Peashooter'. It dispensed with the latter's drag-inducing fixed gear, struts and bracing wires. A low-set cantilever wing monoplane pursuit ship with retractable landing gear, the P-29 looked more formidable than the production P-26, and one of the three machines built attained a speed of 234 mph (376.6 km/h) at 7,500 ft (2286 m) with its 550-hp (410.1-kW) Pratt & Whitney R-1340-35 engine. Initially flown on 20 January 1934, the first of the three airframes was originally designated XP-940 and was built with an enclosed, flush canopy, a concept apparently ahead of its time.

The canopy design proved unpalatable. Boeing pilot Billy Acker asserted that it 'rattled like a bird cage'. After brief flight tests in which Army pilots also judged the canopy impracticable, this first airframe was returned to the manufacturer, rebuilt with the more traditional open cockpit, and redesignated YP-29A

The second airframe, designated YP-29, added landing flaps to the basic design while the third, the YP-29B, added greater dihedral to the wings.

In its various incarnations, the P-29 was an advanced fighter and received considerable attention. But flight tests confirmed that the P-29, which was heavier than the P-26, offered at best only a very marginal improvement in performance. On balance, it was deemed not to warrant further development. Though the three airframes were exhaustively tested well into the mid-1930s and contributed to institutional knowledge about fighter design, they were eventually deleted from inventory and scrapped.

Specification

YP-29

Type: single-seat pursuit aircraft
Powerplant: one 550-hp (410.1-kW) Pratt & Whitney R-1340-35 Wasp air-cooled 9-cylinder radial piston engine driving a two-blade propeller
Performance: maximum speed 234 mph (376.6 km/h) at 7,500 ft (2286 m); cruising speed 200 mph (321.9 km/h); initial climb rate 2,360 ft (719 m) per minute; service ceiling 24,400 ft (7437 m); range 520 miles (832 km)
Weights: empty 2,573 lb (1167.1 kg); maximum take-off 3,572 lb (1620.3 kg)
Dimensions: span 29 ft 4½ in (8.95 m); length 25 ft 0 in (7.62 m); height 7 ft 8 in (2.34 m); wing area 177 sq ft (16.44 m²)
Armament: two 0.3-in (7.62-mm) fixed forward-firing machine-guns, plus provision for 327 lb (148.3 kg) of bombs

An attempt to wring more performance from the P-26 resulted in the P-29, which featured a cantilevered wing, dispensing with the considerable array of bracing wires of the 'Peashooter'. However, its weight countered any appreciable increase in performance. This is the YP-29A.

Consolidated P-30

History and notes

The P-30 appellation was another signpost on the route toward operational service for the two-seat fighter concept which had begun with the Lockheed YP-24 and continued with the Consolidated Y1P-25. By 1933, the YP-24's builder was out of the fighter business, the Y1P-25 and Y1A-11 had crashed, and the Y1P-27 and Y1P-28 were soon to be cancelled. Still, the Army had confidence in the cantilever low-wing monoplane design with all-metal construction (except for control surfaces), controllable-pitch propellers, retractable landing gear, enclosed heated cockpit (for pilot) and exhaust-driven supercharger. Turning to the 675-hp (503.3-kW) supercharged Curtiss V-1710-57 Conqueror inline engine, the USAAC ordered four Consolidated airframes (33-204/207) under the designation P-30.

By 1934, flight tests of the P-30 were under way, the aeroplane carrying an officer/pilot and enlisted man/gunner. Pilots bred on the romance and appeal of the single-seat pursuit ship were not readily won-over by a two-seat machine. Gunners found their semi-open perch aboard the P-30 distinctly uncomfortable and, at high altitude, very cold. Reports that rear gunners sometimes 'blacked out' during high-g manoeuvres appear erroneous, but the heavy clothing, required to keep the gunner from freezing, seriously impaired his effectiveness. For this and other

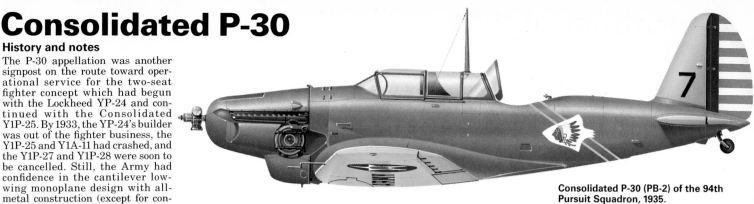

Consolidated P-30 (PB-2) of the 94th Pursuit Squadron, 1935.

reasons, the P-30 was never effective at high altitude, the very regime where USAAC doctrine called for it to fly and fight. Development of the parallel A-11 attack aircraft was suspended after delivery of four airframes and some airmen argued that the P-30, too, had reached the limit of its usefulness. But on 6 December 1934, the Army placed a firm contract for a production batch of 50 P-30As (35-1/50) and made plans for the 1st Pursuit Group at Selfridge Field, Michigan, to operate the type. The operational machines received the 700-hp (522-kW) Curtiss V-1570-61 powerplant. They became a familiar sight in war games at USAAC aerodromes during the 1930s.

A single P-30A was built as a single-seater and competed without success in the 1936 fighter competition which produced the Curtiss P-36 Mohawk. Shortly after the

P-30A entered service, the 'pursuit bi-place' category was closed, surviving P-30 airframes becoming PB-2s and the single-seat P-30A becoming the PB-2A. This heavy and heavily-armed fighter was to take in one further designation in an unbuilt variant, XP-33, before passing into history. A few PB-2As (former P-30As) are thought to have remained in service as late as the eve of Pearl Harbor.

Specification
P-30A

Type: two-seat pursuit aircraft
Powerplant: one 700-hp (522-kW) Curtiss V-1570-61 Conqueror liquid-cooled 12-cylinder Vee supercharged piston engine driving a three-blade Curtiss constant-speed propeller
Performance: maximum speed 275 mph (442.6 km/h) at 25,000 ft

(7620 m); cruising speed 215 mph (346 km/h); initial climb rate 2,800 ft (853 m) per minute; service ceiling 28,000 ft (8534 m); range 510 miles (821 km)
Weights: empty 4,306 lb (1953.2 kg); maximum take-off 5,643 lb (2559.7 kg)
Dimensions: span 43 ft 11 in (13.39 m); length 30 ft 0 in (9.14 m); height 8 ft 3 in (2.51 m); wing area 297 sq ft (27.59 m²)
Armament: two 0.3-in (7.62-mm) fixed forward-firing machine-guns, and one 0.3-in (7.62-mm) flexible rear machine-gun

The first service monoplane biplace fighter was the P-30, quickly redesignated PB-2 to reflect the accommodation. It was a useful heavy fighter, particularly at low level, and it remained in service beyond 1940.

Build-up to War

The build-up to war was slow in the United States, so in 1941 the Air Force was ill-equipped for the task it faced in the Pacific. Nevertheless, some excellent aircraft had been taking shape on the drawing boards.

During the 1930s world fighter development was moving at a rapid pace, particularly in Japan and Germany, where the expansionist aims were provoking the requirement for world-beating aircraft. Other European nations were spurred to produce better and better fighters to counter any potential threat. The Hurricane, Spitfire, A6M Zero and, above all, the Messerschmitt Bf 109 were all products of the 1930s fighter race.

In the United States, the nation was still basking in the technical achievement of the Boeing P-26, which although a potential world-beater when it appeared, within two years was rendered obsolete by other types around the world. Such was the pace of this development that it was not only marginally obsolete, but totally outclassed. The need for a new USAAC fighter was paramount.

Unfortunately for the pursuit community, the 'top brass' of the Air Corps were far more interested in bombers, and in particular the Boeing B-17. Such was the performance of this splendid machine that it could outrun

Initially defeated in a fighter contest by the Seversky P-35, the Curtiss P-36 'Mohawk' was in many ways a better machine, and soon gained sizeable orders at home and overseas. In USAAC service it was the main fighter immediately before the war.

the P-26 easily. Instead of this fact suggesting rather strongly that the USAAC needed a new fighter urgently, it spurred the build-up of bomber forces. While the B-17 went on to do as much for the Allied war effort as any other aircraft, it certainly held back US fighter development considerably, a fact that was to be felt chronically at the beginning of the next decade.

General apathy ruled fighter development in the mid-1930s in the United States, to the point that when a superb private venture aircraft was submitted for evaluation in May 1935, it was shelved for eleven months before a suitable competitor could be found for fly-off trials. The unlucky aircraft was the Curtiss Model 75, a thoroughly modern pursuit with radial engine, retractable undercarriage and enclosed cockpit.

Seversky winner

When the competition got under way eventually in April 1936, the Model 75 was pitted against a similar yet more ungainly aircraft, the Seversky AP-1. This had all the features of the Model 75, but they were executed in a considerably less graceful fashion, giving the aircraft a stocky appearance that did not engender much enthusiasm. The performance of the two aircraft was similar, and the Seversky machine was chosen in preference to that from Curtiss. Designated P-35, the winning design was procured to the tune of 77 aircraft, the first entering service in July 1937. Comparing these aircraft with the sleek Bf 109s across the Atlantic gives some idea of the state of the US fighter at the time.

The P-35 became one of the two mainstay fighters of the pre-war Air Corps, but it never stood much chance when it was eventually called into action in 1941, receiving a severe mauling at the hands of the Japanese in the Philippines. Subsequently it undertook no more operational missions, but it had established a design lineage that would culminate in the much underrated P-47 Thunderbolt.

Offsetting the obsolescence of the P-35 to some degree was the eventual procurement of the Model 75. After losing the fighter competition, Curtiss had been awarded, by way of compensation, a contract for three further aircraft, designated Y1P-36. These were so successful that soon after the initial competition they were ordered into production. This was no small order, for 210 examples of the P-36A were to be built, the largest US peacetime contract for pursuits. When it entered service in April 1938, the P-36 exhibited beautifully harmonised controls and better performance than the P-35. Had fighters been given more prominence in the 1930s USAAC, this excellent machine could have been in service two years earlier, and the US would have had a fighter that matched contemporary designs.

As it was, while it became the main fighter of the Air Corps, it too was severely outclassed by the end of the decade. It fared better in wartime than its partner, but mainly through the tenacity and skill of its pilots rather than its performance. Serving with many air arms, it compiled a long kill list, but only at the expense of many of its number. In USAAC service it was found desperately wanting against the well-equipped and battle-hardened Japanese, and was swiftly relegated to training duties in 1941.

At least towards the end of the 1930s, American designers were taking lessons from those in Europe, and were producing designs that reflected the state-of-the-art elsewhere in the world. However, it would be some time before these became available to the fighter squadrons, and in many cases it would be just in time. While the designs varied from the excellent (Lockheed P-38) through the mediocre (Curtiss P-40) to the poor (Bell P-39), at least the next crop of US fighters could meet the new enemies on roughly equal terms.

Left: Seversky P-35s of the 27th Pursuit Squadron, 1st Pursuit Group line up outside their hangar at Selfridge Field, Michigan. When it was introduced into service, the P-35 was the USAAC's first single-seat, all-metal retractable undercarriage pursuit.

Right: The first of the three great US wartime fighters was Lockheed's 'forked-tail devil' – the P-38 Lightning. This long-legged fighter was a match for most Axis types, and also proved adept in the fighter-bomber role.

Curtiss P-31

History and notes

The XP-31 or Curtiss Shrike of 1932-3 was an all-metal, low wing, strut-braced fighter design which drew heavily upon the characteristics of the manufacturer's A-8 Shrike (enclosed cockpit, trailing edge flaps and leading-edge slots), but failed to attain the A-8's production status. The sole prototype XP-31 (33-178), at first designated XP-934, marked a step forward for Glenn L. Curtiss's fighter team but arrived on the scene just when the comparable Boeing P-26 'Peashooter' had already proven itself superior in most aspects of performance.

First flown in July 1932 with a 700-hp (522-kW) Wright R-1820-4 Cyclone engine, the XP-31 was immediately found to be underpowered. Though the purpose seems unclear, the sole airframe was re-engined with a 600-hp (447.4-kW) Curtiss V-1570 Conqueror powerplant which, in 1933 flight tests, offered no improvement of any kind. Slower than the P-26, short-legged with its scant 370-mile (595-km) range, the XP-31 helped Curtiss to upgrade its design and structural thinking at a time when the monoplane was clearly the aircraft of the future. But it was also, in many respects, an anachronism. Its non-retractable landing gear and drag-inducing wing struts were the last to appear on a USAAC fighter. Furthermore the XP-31, although very small by comparison with other pursuit ships of its day, was unduly heavy. Swift in name only and apparently very demanding on maintenance resources, the XP-31 was rigorously tested and underwent various minor modifications in the

early 1930s, but it belonged to the past more than the future. It was not chosen for production and did not, directly, lead to any later designs. The existing XP-31 is understood to have been scrapped in 1935.

Specification
XP-31

Type: single-seat pursuit aircraft

Powerplant: one 600-hp (447.4-kW) Curtiss V-1570-53 Conqueror liquid-cooled 12-cylinder Vee piston engine driving a two-blade propeller

Performance: maximum speed 208 mph (334.7 km/h) at 10,000 ft (3048 m); initial climb rate about 2,000 ft (610 m) per minute; service ceiling 24,400 ft (7437 m); range 370 miles (595 km)

Weights: empty 3,334 lb (1512.3 kg); maximum take-off 4,143 lb (1879.3 kg)

Dimensions: span 36 ft 0 in (10.97 m); length 26 ft 3 in (8.00 m); height 7 ft 9 in (2.36 m); wing area 203 sq ft (18.86 m²)

Armament: four 0.3-in (7.62-mm) fixed forward-firing machine-guns, two mounted in cowl and two in blisters beside cockpit

Originally designated XP-934, the Curtiss XP-31 prototype was the company's first attempt at a monoplane fighter, but it failed due to poor performance and heavy weight. It had the misfortune of appearing at the same time as the Boeing P-26.

Boeing P-32

History and notes

The P-32 designation was assigned to an unbuilt development of the Boeing pursuit aircraft of the early 1930s, the configuration which had begun with the P-26 'Peashooter' and continued with the service-test YP-29. The P-32 would have been a YP-29 airframe re-engined with the then-unproven 700-hp (522-kW) Pratt & Whitney R-1535 radial

engine. For various reasons, including the plethora of other experimental and service-test pursuit aircraft being tested during budget-lean years, an early decision was made not to proceed with the P-32 programme. The specification which follows must be regarded as provisional. Actual construction of the aircraft never began and by 1934 the project had been cancelled.

Specification
XP-32

Type: single-seat pursuit aircraft

Powerplant: (planned) one 700-hp (522-kW) Pratt & Whitney R-1535-1 air-cooled radial engine driving a two-blade propeller

Performance: (estimated) maximum speed 250 mph (402.3 km/h) at 7,500 ft (2286 m); initial climb rate 2,500 ft (762 m)

per minute; service ceiling 25,000 ft (7620 m); range 520 miles (832 km)

Weights: (estimated) empty 2,500 lb (1134.0 kg); maximum take-off 3,500 lb (1587.6 kg)

Dimensions: (planned) span 29 ft 4½ in (8.95 m); length 25 ft 0 in (7.62 m); height 7 ft 8 in (2.34 m); wing area 177 sq ft (16.44 m²)

Armament: never decided

Consolidated P-33

History and notes

The P-33 appellation was the eighth in the US Army Air Corps pursuit series (following P-11, P-14, P-18, P-19, P-27, P-28, P-32) for which no actual airframe was constructed or converted from an existing aircraft. The Consolidated P-33 was to have been a radial-powered, and therefore far less rakish, development of the two-seat fighter line which began with the Lockheed YP-24 and also encumbered the P-25, P-27, P-28, and P-30 designations (as well

as A-11 and PB-2). With the two-seat fighter concept enjoying only very limited support and funding during the cost-sensitive years between world wars, the 800-hp (596.6-kW) Pratt & Whitney R-1830-1 Twin Wasp proposed for the P-33 was not thought to offer a breakthrough in performance, and the project was terminated at an early stage.

Specification
XP-33

Type: two-seat pursuit aircraft

Powerplant: (planned) one 800-hp (596.6-kW) Pratt & Whitney R-1830-1 Twin Wasp air-cooled 14-cylinder radial piston engine driving a three-blade Curtiss Electric constant-speed propeller

Performance: (estimated) maximum speed 250 mph (402.3 km/h) at 15,000 ft (4572 m); initial climb rate 2,600 ft (792 m)

per minute; service ceiling 27,000 ft (8230 m); range 580 miles (933 km).

Weights: (estimated) empty 3,887 lb (1763.1 kg); maximum take-off 5,110 lb (2317.9 kg)

Dimensions: (planned) span 43 ft 10 in (13.36 m); length 29 ft 4 in (8.94 m); height 8 ft 7 in (2.62 m); wing area about 300 sq ft (27.87 m²)

Armament: (planned) two 0.3-in (7.62-mm) fixed forward-firing machine-guns, and one 0.3-in (7.62-mm) flexible rear machine-gun

Wedell-Williams P-34

History and notes

The P-34, had it been built when first conceived, at 308 mph (495.7 km/h) would have been the fastest pursuit aircraft of its day. Its conception dates to 1932 and the XP-34 designation was assigned in 1936 when the US Army acquired design rights to a racer promoted by the Wedell-Williams Company. The years between ate up the speed advantage of pressing a racer into pursuit service and, while the influence of the National Air Races on

Army thinking remained great, not enough consideration was given to the limited military application of the Wedell-Williams XP-34.

Initially conceived with a 700-hp (522-kW) Pratt & Whitney R-1535-1 Twin Wasp Junior radial, the XP-34 was later planned for a 900-hp (671.1-kW) XR-1830-C Twin Wasp from the same engine supplier. The resulting airframe would have been uncommonly heavy, yet capable of only limited range and weapons-carrying potential. Racers did in-

fluence other fighter designs from Seversky and Curtiss, but the Wedell-Williams XP-34 proved a non-starter and was cancelled before construction began.

Specification
XP-34

Type: single-seat pursuit aircraft
Powerplant: (planned) one 900-hp (671.1-kW) Pratt & Whitney XR-1830-C Twin Wasp air-cooled 14-cylinder radial piston engine

driving a two-blade propeller
Performance: (estimated) maximum speed 308 mph (495.7 km/h) at 10,000 ft (3048 m); other performance characteristics not determined
Weights: (estimated) empty 3,400 lb (1542.2 kg); maximum take-off 4,250 lb (1927.8 kg)
Dimensions: span 37 ft 8½ in (11.49 m); length 23 ft 6 in (7.16 m); height 10 ft 9 in (3.28 m); wing area about 200 sq ft (18.58 m²)
Armament: none planned

Seversky P-35

History and notes

The P-35 marks the debut of Seversky (later Republic) of Farmingdale, Long Island, as a major builder of fighters and introduces the work of the firm's chief designer, Alexander Kartveli. The Seversky P-35 was the first single-seat all-metal pursuit plane with retractable landing gear and enclosed cockpit to go into service with the US Army Air Corps. It was a major step forward, albeit one which was short-lived as war approached. The type began as the company SEV-1XP, one of several machines flown as pursuit prototypes and racers in the 1930s by Major Alexander P. de Seversky, Jacqueline Cochran and others. The P-35 won out over the Curtiss Hawk Model 75 (later P-36) for a 16 June 1936 US Army contract for 77 airframes (36-354/430), powered by the 950-hp (708.4-kW) Pratt & Whitney R-1830-9 Twin Wasp 14-cylinder radial engine. The final airframe in this batch was diverted to become the sole Seversky XP-41. The first P-35 was delivered to Wright Field, Ohio, for tests, and the remaining 75 went initially to the 1st Pursuit Group at Selfridge Field, Michigan. There, the type was received with considerable enthusiasm which lingered even after six machines had been lost in accidents during 1938. Only by later, wartime standards would it become evident that the P-35 was unstable, underarmed, and lacking both armour protection for the pilot and self-sealing fuel tanks.

The company EP-106 export variant attracted Sweden's attention and 120 machines were ordered with the Flygvapen designation J9. These were powered by the 1,050-hp (783-kW) Pratt & Whitney R-1830-45 Twin Wasp radial. When President Roosevelt announced his 10 October 1940 embargo on fighter shipments to Scandinavia,

only half (FV serials 2101/2160) had been delivered. The remainder were seized by the US Army as the P-35A.

P-35A pursuit ships served with various USAAC units, but by late 1941 about 50 were with First Lieutenant Joseph H. Moore's 20th Pursuit Squadron, 24th Pursuit Group, at Clark Field in the Philippines. Second Lieutenant Max Louk wrote to his parents in mid-1941 that the squadron was undergoing 'a very strenuous programme' of flying 'up to eight hours a day' in the P-35A. Incredibly, some P-35As arrived at Clark still painted in Swedish markings and still wore them during the 8 December 1941 Japanese assault, which was synchronised with the attack on Pearl Harbor.

Combat

The P-35 was flown by a few memorable pilots, including First Lieutenant 'Buzz' Wagner, commander of the 17th Pursuit Squadron, Nichols Field, Philippines, the first American ace of the war. But by December 1941 the type had become dated and inadequate. Pilots of the P-35 started with the disadvantage of an unforgiving mount. 1939 Technical Order No. 01-65 BA-1 had imposed mind-boggling limitations on the P-35, proscribing inverted flight, inverted spins, and outside loops, and similar caveats applied to the slightly more powerful P-35A. Group Captain Christopher Clarkson, the UK's Royal Air Force test pilot on the US east coast in 1940, logged six hours on P-35 variants and ("I'm sorry to report") utterly rejected the machine for the RAF. "It had some of the nastiest high speed and high loading stall characteristics I've ever encountered. It would have been quite impossible to 'dogfight' it as, as soon as you got it into a tight turn and pulled any 'G' at all, it flicked over into a

At the time of its introduction, the P-35 offered the USAAC a modern monoplane fighter, and as such it had a short period of popularity and success. Nevertheless, as other monoplanes became available, the overall shortcomings of the design became readily apparent.

P-35 of the 94th Pursuit Squadron, 1st Pursuit Group, Selfridge Field, Michigan. The rear fuselage bands denoted the commanding officer's aircraft.

Seversky P-35

spin which took a turn to recover." Americans in P-35As in the Philippines simply could not stay with or effectively fight the Mitsubishi and Nakajima fighters that swarmed down on them. Some died ignominiously: First Lieutenant Samuel W. Marrett, commander of the 34th Pursuit Squadron at Del Carmen Field, Philippines, was killed 10 December 1941 when an ammunition barge he was strafing exploded beneath him over Lingayen Gulf, Northern Luzon.

Swedish pilots guarding their nation's neutrality faced a different problem. Hans Westerberg, now a furniture dealer in Stockholm, flew the J9 (P-35A) and, in 1944, intercepted a crippled American B-24 Liberator struggling away from a target in Germany. "I could just keep speed with the bomber. I closed in to use hand signals to tell him that his crew could land and be interned in Sweden. All of his guns turned towards me and he was an instant away from opening fire before he understood. The problem was that from some angles my [P-35A] looked exactly like a Focke-Wulf Fw 190."

Specification

P-35A

Type: single-seat pursuit aircraft
Powerplant: one 1,050-hp (783-kW) Pratt & Whitney R-1830-45 air-cooled 14-cylinder radial piston engine driving a three-blade Hamilton Standard propeller
Performance: maximum speed 310 mph (498.9 km/h) at 14,300 ft (4359 m); service ceiling 31,400 ft (9571 m); maximum range 950 miles (1529 km)
Weights: empy 4,575 lb (2075.2 kg); maximum take-off 6,723 lb (3049.6 kg)
Dimensions: span 36 ft 0 in (10.97 m); length 26 ft 10 in (8.18 m); height 9 ft 9 in (2.97 m); wing area 220 sq ft (20.44 m²)
Armament: two 0.5-in (12.7-mm) and two 0.3-in (7.62-mm) fixed forward-firing machine-guns, plus provision for up to 350 lb (158.8 kg) of bombs carried externally

Above: 27th Pursuit Squadron P-35s formate for the camera, demonstrating the squat appearance and semi-retractable undercarriage of the type. The first major work by Alex Kartveli, the P-35 showed many of the features to be found later in the superb P-47 Thunderbolt.

P-35A (embargoed Swedish aircraft) of the 17th Pursuit Squadron, 24th Group, Luzon, Philippines in 1941.

Right: This 27th Pursuit Squadron P-35 wore temporary, soluble paint for war games in 1939.

Curtiss P-36

Curtiss P-36A of the 79th Pursuit Squadron, 20th Pursuit Group based at Moffett Field, California in late 1939.

History and notes

The P-36 or Curtiss Model 75 Hawk, commonly called the Mohawk, began life as a private venture, soldiered bravely in foreign colours, and enjoyed modest if unspectacular success as the last major USAAC fighter before the outbreak of hostilities in World War II. A monoplane low-wing pursuit ship with retractable landing gear and an enclosed cockpit, the Model 75 prototype was powered by a 900-hp (671.1-kW) Wright XR-1670-5 engine and was initially scrutinised by the US Army in May 1935 but not ordered, although Curtiss obtained permission to provide details to several foreign governments. Re-engined with an 850-hp (633.8-kW) Wright R-1820 Twin Wasp radial and called Model 75B, the craft was re-examined by the Army in April 1936, when it lost a major production order to the similar Seversky P-35. As consolation, Curtiss received a contract for three service-test Y1P-36s (37-68/70), delivered in February 1937.

Based on Y1P-36 evaluation at Wright Field, Ohio, there followed in July 1937 a production order for 210 P-36A airframes, the Army's largest fighter contract since World War I. Delivery began in April 1938 at about the same time that 112 examples of a less complex export version, the Hawk Model 75M, were purchased by the Chinese Nationalist air force; 12 similar Hawk Model 75N and 29 Hawk Model 75O aircraft went to Siam and Argentina respectively, a further 20 being assembled locally in the latter country. Two export Hawk Model 75Qs went to China, one being presented to General Claire Chennault by Madame Chiang Kai-shek. In the USA, the relatively new P-36As were rapidly considered obsolescent as war clouds gathered.

The sole P-36B (38-20), a converted P-36A model, was powered by a 1,000-hp (745.7-kW) Pratt & Whitney R-1830-25 radial. The XP-36D was tested with two cowl-mounted 0.5-in (12.7-mm) and four wing-mounted 0.3-in (7.62-mm) guns. The XP-36E was also a solitary armament test ship with one nose 0.5-in (12.7-mm) and no fewer than eight wing 0.3-in (7.62-mm) guns. The XP-36F, also a one-off conversion, had two underwing 23-mm Madsen cannon plus one 0.3-in (7.62-mm) and one 0.5-in (12.7-mm) nose guns. Production efforts shifted to 31 examples of the P-36C with engine improvements.

Following the failure of the Model 75 prototype in the USAAC fighter evaluation, three Y1P-36 evaluation airframes were ordered from Curtiss. Further tests led to a major production order for the P-36A fighter. This is one of the Y1P-36s.

P-36C of the 27th Pursuit Squadron, Selfridge Field, in special scheme.

Curtiss P-36

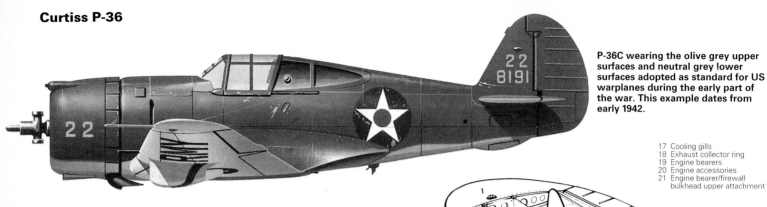

P-36C wearing the olive grey upper surfaces and neutral grey lower surfaces adopted as standard for US warplanes during the early part of the war. This example dates from early 1942.

Examples of the Hawk Model 75A went to France and a few fell into Vichy French hands, resulting in aircraft of this type confronting each other in combat. The bulk of the French order was diverted to the UK's Royal Air Force, which assigned the familiar Mohawk nickname and operated the type with lack-lustre results. A total of 24 Hawk Model 75A-6 machines reached Norway before a 1940 embargo by President Roosevelt on US fighter deliveries to Scandinavia. The 30 P-36G aircraft had been intended as export Hawk Model 75As for Norway but were operated by the USAAC.

Worldwide use

The US Army dispersed its modest fleet of 243 P-36s widely. The 18th and 20th Pursuit Groups operated the P-36A, the latter employing no fewer than three squadrons at Barksdale Field, Louisiana. As late as 1942, while war raged in the Aleutians, the 28th Composite Group operated P-36As in Alaska. The XP-36B was tested exhaustively at Wright Field, Ohio. The 1st Pursuit Group, Selfridge Field, Michigan, despatched a dozen P-36Cs to the National Air Races in Cleveland, Ohio, in September 1939, each machine painted in an elaborate, one-of-a-kind camouflage scheme which, ironically, was never used in actual exercises or war games. Although the basic design was by then long in the tooth and no match for the fighters of Messerschmitt and Mitsubishi, the XP-36D, XP-36E and XP-36F were included in a major exposition of 'modern' fighters at Bolling Field, Washington, DC, in January 1940. P-36 or Hawk 75 variants also served, sooner or later, with the air arms of the Netherlands, Finland, India, Portugal and South Africa, and a pristine example is on display at the Air Force Museum in Dayton, Ohio. As Admiral Isoru Yamamoto's fleet approached the Hawaiian Islands, a handful of P-36s was also located amid the heat and red clay of Wheeler Field, Hawaii.

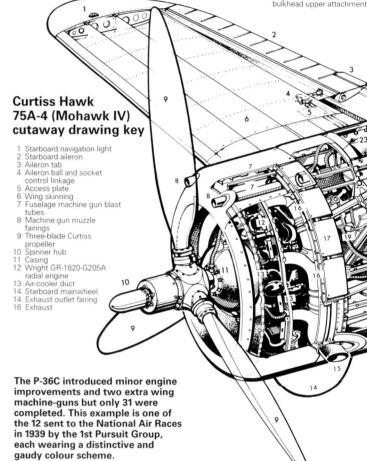

Curtiss Hawk 75A-4 (Mohawk IV) cutaway drawing key

1 Starboard navigation light
2 Starboard aileron
3 Aileron tab
4 Aileron ball and socket control linkage
5 Access plate
6 Wing skinning
7 Fuselage machine gun blast tubes
8 Machine gun muzzle fairings
9 Three-blade Curtiss propeller
10 Spinner hub
11 Casing
12 Wright GR-1820-G205A radial engine
13 Air-cooler duct
14 Starboard mainwheel
14 Exhaust outlet fairing
16 Exhaust

17 Cooling gills
18 Exhaust collector ring
19 Engine bearers
20 Engine accessories
21 Engine bearer/firewall bulkhead upper attachment

The P-36C introduced minor engine improvements and two extra wing machine-guns but only 31 were completed. This example is one of the 12 sent to the National Air Races in 1939 by the 1st Pursuit Group, each wearing a distinctive and gaudy colour scheme.

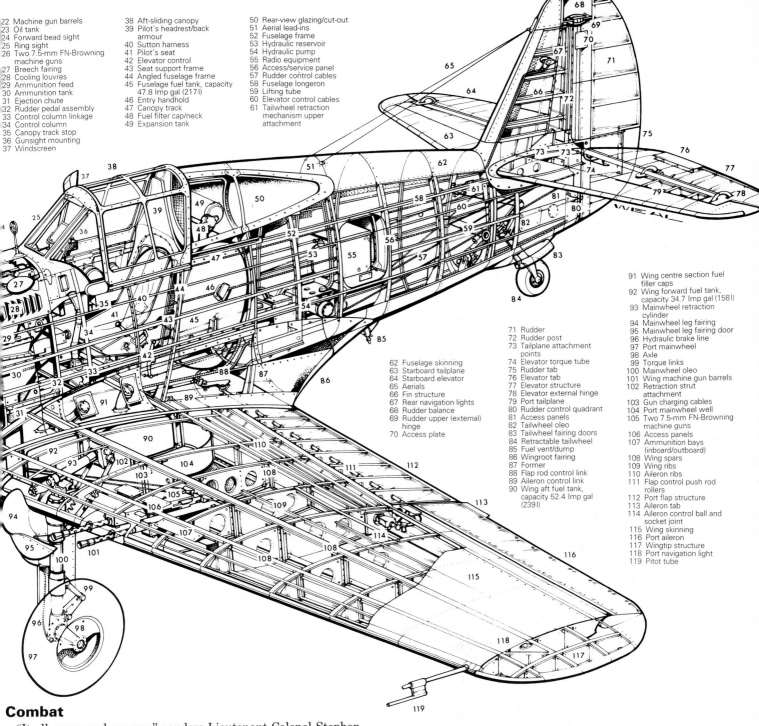

22 Machine gun barrels
23 Oil tank
24 Forward bead sight
25 Ring sight
26 Two 7.5-mm FN-Browning machine guns
27 Breech fairing
28 Cooling louvres
29 Ammunition feed
30 Ammunition tank
31 Ejection chute
32 Rudder pedal assembly
33 Control column linkage
34 Control column
35 Canopy track stop
36 Gunsight mounting
37 Windscreen

38 Aft-sliding canopy
39 Pilot's headrest/back armour
40 Sutton harness
41 Pilot's seat
42 Elevator control
43 Seat support frame
44 Angled fuselage frame
45 Fuselage fuel tank, capacity 47.8 Imp gal (217 l)
46 Entry handhold
47 Canopy track
48 Fuel filter cap/neck
49 Expansion tank

50 Rear-view glazing/cut-out
51 Aerial lead-ins
52 Fuselage frame
53 Hydraulic reservoir
54 Hydraulic pump
55 Radio equipment
56 Access/service panel
57 Rudder control cables
58 Fuselage longeron
59 Lifting tube
60 Elevator control cables
61 Tailwheel retraction mechanism upper attachment

62 Fuselage skinning
63 Starboard tailplane
64 Starboard elevator
65 Aerials
66 Fin structure
67 Rear navigation lights
68 Rudder balance
69 Rudder upper (external) hinge
70 Access plate

71 Rudder
72 Rudder post
73 Tailplane attachment points
74 Elevator torque tube
75 Rudder tab
76 Elevator tab
77 Elevator structure
78 Elevator external hinge
79 Port tailplane
80 Rudder control quadrant
81 Access panels
82 Tailwheel oleo
83 Tailwheel fairing doors
84 Retractable tailwheel
85 Fuel vent/dump
86 Wingroot fairing
87 Former
88 Flap rod control link
89 Aileron control link
90 Wing aft fuel tank, capacity 52.4 Imp gal (239 l)

91 Wing centre section fuel filler caps
92 Wing forward fuel tank, capacity 34.7 Imp gal (158 l)
93 Mainwheel retraction cylinder
94 Mainwheel leg fairing
95 Mainwheel leg fairing door
96 Hydraulic brake line
97 Port mainwheel
98 Axle
99 Torque links
100 Mainwheel oleo
101 Wing machine gun barrels
102 Retraction strut attachment
103 Gun charging cables
104 Port mainwheel well
105 Two 7.5-mm FN-Browning machine guns
106 Access panels
107 Ammunition bays (inboard/outboard)
108 Wing spars
109 Wing ribs
110 Aileron ribs
111 Flap control push rod rollers
112 Port flap structure
113 Aileron tab
114 Aileron control ball and socket joint
115 Wing skinning
116 Port aileron
117 Wingtip structure
118 Port navigation light
119 Pitot tube

Combat

"It all seems so long ago," ponders Lieutenant Colonel Stephen Barneyback, running his eyes over Wheeler Field where the first blows were struck. "This place was a tropical paradise. We were not ready. We had no idea what was coming." Barneyback recalls that P-36 pilots were half-awake, stunned, and totally outclassed, neither as manoeuvrable nor as well-armed as the incoming waves of Mitsubishi Zeros. "If Sanders hadn't given the order to disperse some of the P-36s the night before, all of them would have been caught on the ground."

Amid the 7 December 1941 Japanese carrier strike on nearby Pearl Harbor, First Lieutenant Lewis M. Sanders, commander of the 46th Pursuit Squadron, got aloft from Wheeler Field with four P-36As and led his men in shooting down three attacking aircraft. Second Lieutenant Philip M. Rasmussen was credited with one of the kills, as was Second Lieutenant George H. Sterling, Jr, who was killed in the action, one of the first American fatalities of the conflict. The era of pursuit fighter development between world wars was over, and the Curtiss P-36 had ended its American combat service the moment a new era arrived.

Specification
P-36G

Type: single-seat pursuit aircraft

Powerplant: one 1,200-hp (894.8-kW) Wright R-1820-G205A Cyclone air-cooled 9-cylinder radial piston engine driving a three-blade propeller

Performance: maximum speed 322 mph (518.2 km/h) at 15,200 ft (4633 m); cruising speed 261 mph (420 km/h); climb to 15,000 ft (4572 m) in 6 minutes; service ceiling 32,350 ft (9860 m); range 650 miles (1046 km)

Weights: empty 4,675 lb (2120.6 kg); maximum take-off 5,880 lb (2667.2 kg)

Dimensions: span 37 ft 0 in (11.28 m); length 28 ft 6 in (8.69 m); height 9 ft 3 in (2.82 m); wing area 236 sq ft (21.92 m²)

Armament: four wing-mounted 0.3-in (7.62-mm) and two fuselage-mounted 0.5-in (12.7-mm) fixed forward-firing machine-guns

Build-up to War

By a strange quirk of fate, the Curtiss Model 75 was to fight on both sides during World War II, serving with France, Great Britain, the Netherlands and the United States on the Allied side, and those exported to Norway being seized and used by the Luftwaffe on the Axis side. This P-36A is seen in more peaceful colours while assigned to the 35th Pursuit Squadron at Langley Field, Virginia, in 1939. A few P-36s, together with some P-40s, managed to scramble during the Japanese raid on Pearl Harbor, claiming 10 of the attackers.

Curtiss P-37

History and notes

The 'long-nosed' P-37 was a Curtiss attempt in the late 1930s to couple the P-36 Mohawk design with the 1,330-hp (991.8-kW) Allison V-1710-21 inline engine. The result was a pursuit ship with some promise but with a few serious drawbacks, including poor visibility from its far-aft enclosed cockpit. The sole XP-37, ordered in 1937 with a supercharged V-1710-11 powerplant, was nothing more than a P-36 airframe with the engine change. It was quickly apparent that the pilot not only could not see well in flight but also on the ground he could scarcely see at all! It was hoped that some improvement would be offered by the 13 service-test YP-37 airframes (38-472/484) which were 22 in (0.56 m) longer and had the V-1710-21 engine.

The YP-37 aircraft went through rigorous tests at Wright Field, Ohio, including gunnery tests, but the visibility problem was not resolved and the YP-37s were not as stable as Army pilots wanted. Serious consideration was given to further development, but at the time Curtiss was also about to come forth with the P-40 which offered an inline powerplant without the drawbacks. Though they contributed to knowledge gained by fighter designers and tacticians, the YP-37s never reached operational service as other types appeared with greater

Re-engining the P-36 with a V-1710-11 engine improved the performance, but was very unpopular with test pilots due to the appalling visibility from the aft-placed cockpit. Fourteen P-37s were built in all, but they merely paved the way for the more practical P-40.

promise. As world conflict loomed, multi-role missions were now being foreseen for aircraft once intended solely to chase other aircraft, and machines capable of a range of combat functions would increasingly become known not as pursuit ships but as fighters.

Specification
YP-37
Type: single-seat pursuit aircraft
Powerplant: one 1,150-hp (857.6-kW) Allison V-1710-21 liquid-cooled 12-cylinder Vee piston engine driving a three-blade propeller
Performance: maximum speed 340 mph (547.2 km/h) at 25,000 ft (7620 m); initial climb rate about 2,500 ft (762 m) per minute; service ceiling 34,000 ft (10363 m); range 870 miles (1400 km)
Weights: empty 5,723 lb (2596.0 kg); maximum take-off 7,178 lb (3,255.9 kg)
Dimensions: span 37 ft 4 in (11.38 m); length 32 ft 10 in (10 m); height 9 ft 6 in (2.90 m); wing area 236 sq ft (21.92 m²)
Armament: one 0.3-in (7.62-mm) and one 0.5-in (12.7-mm) fixed forward-firing machine-guns

Lockheed P-38 Lightning

History and notes

On 27 January 1939 at March Field in Riverside, California, the prototype XP-38 (37-457) was taken aloft on its maiden flight by Lieutenant Benjamin S. Kelsey. With Thunderbolt and Mustang, the name Lightning has become synonymous with American fighter aviation. A total of 9,895 Lockheed Lightnings was manufactured for US forces by VJ-Day, and the twin-boom 'forked-tail devil' fought in every theatre of war, a potent and adaptable air-combat machine not easily defeated in battle, not even by Axis fighters developed considerably later.

Lockheed's Burbank, California, design team headed by H. L. Hibbard, including Clarence L. (Kelly) Johnson and prodded by chief executive Robert Gross, shaped the XP-38 to meet a 1938 US Army specification for a high-altitude pursuit ship capable of 360 mph (579.3 km/h) at 20,000 ft (6096 m). Its twin-boom configuration freed the fighter's nose for unsynchronised guns and produced a broad, sturdy warplane with respectable range able to carry 4,000 lb (1814.4 kg) of underwing ordnance. The prototype, powered by 960-hp (715.9 kW) Allison V-1710-11/15 engines driving inward-rotating propellers, was brought out of secrecy for an 11 February 1939 transcontinental speed dash, crossing the US in 7 hrs 2 min with two refuelling stops, but was lost when it undershot the runway at Mitchell Field, NY.

Thirteen YP-38 service-test airframes followed and demonstrated promise, powered by two 1,150-hp (857.6-kW) V-1710-27/29 engines with outward-rotating propellers. One XP-38A was built for experiments with a pressurised cockpit. Armament on these pre-production Lightnings was one 37-mm Oldsmobile cannon, two 0.5-in (12.7-mm) machine-guns and two 0.3-in (7.62-mm) machine-guns).

P-38B and P-38C proposals failed to produce actual hardware and the first production order was for 35 P-38Ds followed by 210 P-38Es with the smaller 20-mm Hispano nose cannon. The P-38D introduced self-sealing fuel tanks and armour protection, and was in service with the 27th Pursuit Squadron, 1st Pursuit Group, Selfridge Field, Michigan, by October 1941, just before US entry into the war. P-38Es served with 12 squadrons and some fought in the Aleutians.

One of the classic aircraft shapes of the war, the Lockheed P-38 defied designers who thought that competitive speed performance could only be derived from single-engined aircraft. It was quickly dubbed the 'Fork-tail devil'.

A British order for 143 Lightning Mk Is failed to satisfy RAF needs (as they were delivered without turbochargers), and most of these airframes reverted to the newly-renamed US Army Air Forces (USAAF) as trainers, called P-322s. The Lightning Mk II also had a short career wearing British roundels and, again, was not fully successful even though American pilots were finding the Lightning fully competitive with the Mitsubishi Zero and Messerschmitt Bf 109.

Some 527 improved P-38F fighters, 20 completed as F-4A photo-reconnaissance craft, were followed by 1,082 P-38Gs, including 181 converted to F-5A and 200 to F-5B photo-planes. On 12 April 1943, P-38Gs led by Captain Thomas G. Lanphier intercepted and shot down the Mitsubishi G4M carrying Admiral Isoroku Yamamoto, the master strategist of Pearl Harbor and Midway. A total of 601

Lockheed P-38

This P-38F of the 347th Fighter Group, New Caledonia, is seen on detachment to the 13th AAF, Guadalcanal in February 1943.

P-38J of the 338th Fighter Squadron, 55th Fighter Group at Nuthampstead, England. It was used for long-range bomber escort duties during the spring of 1944.

heavier P-38Hs, 128 of them converted to F-5C reconnaissance standard, fought mainly in Europe among the 87 USAAF squadrons which operated Lightnings.

The only major change in the Lightning during its long production life took place with the P-38J, when the intakes under the engines were enlarged to house core-type intercoolers, the curved windscreen was replaced by a flat panel, and the boom-mounted radiators were enlarged. The P-38J powered by 1,425-hp (1062.6 kW) V-1710-89/91 engines entered combat in August 1943 carrying droptanks which stretched its range to 2,300 miles (3701 km), making possible long-distance penetration flights into Hitler's 'Fortress Europe'.

The first bomber-escort missions to Berlin were flown by P-38s which, at the extreme of range, finally seemed to have met their match in the nimble Focke-Wulf Fw 190. In the Pacific, P-38s remained at the front-line of battle as the island-hopping campaign progressed. The P-38L variant, produced in greatest numbers (3,923), including 113 built by Vultee in Nashville, Tennessee, was powered by 1,600-hp (1193.1-kW) V-1710-111/113 engines and proved especially effective in the Pacific, as did its F-5G reconnaissance version. A few became TP-38L aircraft with tandem seating for training purposes configured so awkwardly that the rear-seat instructor had to keep his head bent-down throughout the mission.

By adopting the twin-boom layout the P-38 could mount a nose full of guns with no heavy interrupter equipment. Viewed from the front the Lightning exhibited a small cross-sectional area, giving low drag for a twin. This is a P-38L, the most numerous version.

The mysterious-looking, all-black P-38M was a converted P-38L model with ASH radar for the night-fighting mission, its tandem seat arrangement made more practical with a raised hood and roomier cockpit for the second crewman. No clear record exists on how many P-38Ms were converted, but four are thought to have gone into combat in the Philippines and several were noted in occupied postwar Japan. Numerous P-38 airframes survived the end of their operational life with US forces in 1948 to serve in foreign air arms, notably in Latin America. Given the importance of the type, it is saddening that fewer than a dozen P-38s exist today, an airworthy example being the sole surviving P-38M night-fighter (44-53097) once operated by the Honduras air force and now part of the Champlin Fighter Museum in Mesa, Arizona.

Combat

No event in the voluminous annals of the Lightning at war meant more to its participant than Lieutenant Stanley A. Long's success with the war's first air-to-air kill by a P-38. On 4 August 1942 in the freezing, gruelling, long-distance war in the Aleutians 'where single-engine fighters just didn't have the staying power,' Long in a winterised P-38E (41-2007) of the 54th Fighter Squadron, 343rd Fighter Group joined his flight leader Lieutenant Kenneth Ambrose to intercept a pair of heavily-armed Kawanishi H6K4 Type 97 flying-boats. The men were on a maximum-endurance mission about 1,000 miles (1609 km) from their base at Unmak. Weary but undaunted, they attacked. Ambrose took the left Kawanishi and missed with his first burst of cannon fire. Long hit both aircraft, pulled away, followed them toward a fog bank, and began shooting

Lockheed P-38

Wearing invasion stripes is this P-38J of the 401st Fighter Squadron, 370th Fighter Group based at Florennes in Belgium in November 1944.

again from maximum distance of about 450 yards (410m). He had to make a third pass to see his shells breaking up the pilot's cabin of the flying-boat, tearing into its flight deck and hull. The big craft trembled, veered out of control, and plunged into Nazan Bay. Ambrose downed the second Kawanishi before it could escape into fog. The toughness of the P-38 was 'critical' to the success of this long-range intercept in poor weather and, recalls Long, 'the P-38 was an exceptionally stable firing platform'. Several days later, P-38s shot down a Focke-Wulf Fw 200 Condor near Iceland, the first American kill against the Luftwaffe.

In the Pacific, where range and durability were the *sine qua non*, Major Richard Ira Bong of the 49th Fighter Group became the top-scoring American ace of all time with 40 air-to-air victories. Major Thomas McGuire was runner-up with 38 Japanese kills. Both these P-38 pilots won the Medal of Honor. Major Charles H. MacDonald of the 475th Fighter Group began his victory string in New Guinea, flew a P-38L nicknamed 'Putt Putt Maru', and downed 27 Japanese aircraft by war's end. In all theatres, the P-38 proved itself again and again. Fittingly, an F-5 photo-reconnaissance variant became the first Allied aircraft to land in Japan after the surrender.

Specification

P-38L

Type: single-seat fighter

Powerplant: two 1,600-hp (1193.1-kW) Allison V-1710-111/113G30 liquid-cooled 12-cylinder Vee piston engines driving three-blade, outward-rotating propellers

Performance: maximum speed 414 mph (666.3 km/h) at 25,000 ft (7620 m); climb to 20,000 ft (6096 m) in 7 minutes; service ceiling 44,000 ft (13411 m); normal range 450 miles (724 km); maximum range 2,600 miles (4184 km)

Weights: empty 12,800 lb (5806.1 kg); maximum take-off 21,600 lb (9797.8 kg)

Dimensions: span 52 ft 0 in (15.85 m); length 37 ft 10 in (11.53 m); height 9 ft 10 in (3.00 m); wing area 327.5 sq ft (30.42 m²)

Armament: one 20-mm cannon and four 0.5-in (12.7-mm) machine-guns, plus provision for two 2,000-lb (907-kg) or two 1,600-lb (726-kg) bombs and 10 5-in (127-mm) rocket projectiles under wings

Perhaps the strangest of the Lightning variants was the P-38M night fighter, which added radar aerials in a nose pod and under the wings, and a second raised cockpit for the radar operator. These saw brief service in the final fighting in the Pacific.

Lockheed P-38J Lightning cutaway drawing key

1. Starboard navigation light
2. Wingtip trailing edge strake
3. Landing light (underwing) location
4. Starboard aileron
5. Aileron control rod/quadrant
6. Wing outer spar
7. Aileron tab drum
8. Aileron tab control pulleys
9. Aileron tab control rod
10. Aileron trim tab
11. Fixed tab
12. Tab cable access
13. Flap extension/retraction cables
14. Control pulleys
15. Flap outer carriage
16. Fowler-type flap (extended)
17. Control access panel
18. Wing spar transition
19. Outer section leading-edge fuel tanks (P-38J-5 and subsequent) capacity 46 Imp gal (208 litres) each
20. Engine bearer/bulkhead upper attachment
21. Firewall
22. Triangulated tubular engine bearer supports
23. Polished mirror surface panel (undercarriage visual check)
24. Cantilever engine bearer
25. Intake fairing
26. Accessories cooling intake
27. Oil radiator (outer sections) and intercooler (centre section) tripleintake
28. Spinner
29. Curtiss-Electric three-blade (left) handed propeller
30. Four machine gun barrels
31. Cannon barrel
32. Camera-gun aperture
33. Nose panel
34. Bulkhead
35. Machine gun blast tubes
36. Four 0.5-in (12.7-mm) machine guns
37. Cannon flexible hose hydraulic charger
38. Chatellerault-feed cannon magazine (150 rounds)
39. Machine gun firing solenoid
40. Cannon ammunition feed chute
41. Nose armament cowling clips
42. Case ejection chute (port lower machine gun)
43. Ammunition box and feed chute (port lower machine gun)
44. Case ejection chute (port upper machine gun)
45. Ammunition box and feed chute (port upper machine gun)
46. Radio antenna
47. Ejection chute exit (shrouded when item 52 attached)
48. Nosewheel door
49. Nosewheel shimmy damper assembly and reservoir
50. Torque links
51. Towing eye
52. Type M10 triple-tube 4.5-in (11.4-cm) rocket-launcher
53. Rearward-retracting nosewheel
54. Alloy spokes cover plate
55. Fork
56. Rocket-launcher forward attachment (to 63)
57. Nosewheel lower drag struts
58. Nosewheel oleo leg
59. Nosewheel pin access

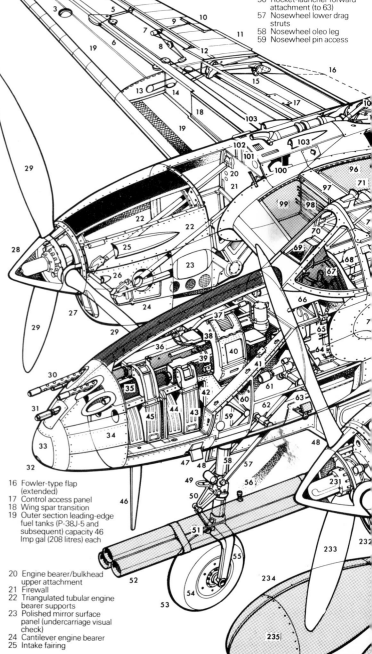

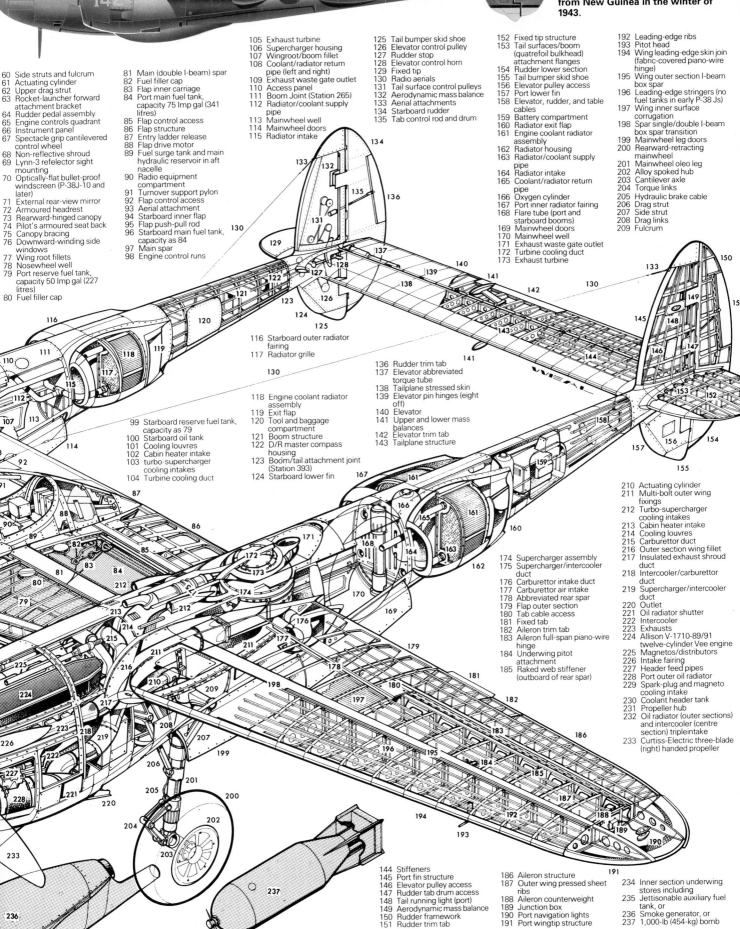

P-38s fought with distinction in both Europe and the Pacific. This P-38J flew with the 432nd FS, 475th FG from New Guinea in the winter of 1943.

60 Side struts and fulcrum
61 Actuating cylinder
62 Upper drag strut
63 Rocket-launcher forward attachment bracket
64 Rudder pedal assembly
65 Engine controls quadrant
66 Instrument panel
67 Spectacle grip cantilevered control wheel
68 Non-reflective shroud
69 Lynn-3 reflector sight mounting
70 Optically-flat bullet-proof windscreen (P-38J-10 and later)
71 External rear-view mirror
72 Armoured headrest
73 Rearward-hinged canopy
74 Pilot's armoured seat back
75 Canopy bracing
76 Downward-winding side windows
77 Wing root fillets
78 Nosewheel well
79 Port reserve fuel tank, capacity 50 Imp gal (227 litres)
80 Fuel filler cap

81 Main (double I-beam) spar
82 Fuel filler cap
83 Flap inner carriage
84 Port main fuel tank, capacity 75 Imp gal (341 litres)
85 Flap control access
86 Flap structure
87 Entry ladder release
88 Flap drive motor
89 Fuel surge tank and main hydraulic reservoir in aft nacelle
90 Radio equipment compartment
91 Turnover support pylon
92 Flap control access
93 Aerial attachment
94 Starboard inner flap
95 Flap push-pull rod
96 Starboard main fuel tank, capacity as 84
97 Main spar
98 Engine control runs

105 Exhaust turbine
106 Supercharger housing
107 Wingroot/boom fillet
108 Coolant/radiator return pipe (left and right)
109 Exhaust waste gate outlet
110 Access panel
111 Boom Joint (Station 265)
112 Radiator/coolant supply pipe
113 Mainwheel well
114 Mainwheel doors
115 Radiator intake

116 Starboard outer radiator fairing
117 Radiator grille

118 Engine coolant radiator assembly
119 Exit flap
120 Tool and baggage compartment
121 Boom structure
122 D/R master compass housing
123 Boom/tail attachment joint (Station 393)
124 Starboard lower fin

125 Tail bumper skid shoe
126 Elevator control pulley
127 Rudder stop
128 Elevator control horn
129 Fixed tip
130 Radio aerials
131 Tail surface control pulleys
132 Aerodynamic mass balance
133 Aerial attachments
134 Starboard rudder
135 Tab control rod and drum

136 Rudder trim tab
137 Elevator abbreviated torque tube
138 Tailplane stressed skin
139 Elevator pin hinges (eight off)
140 Elevator
141 Upper and lower mass balances
142 Elevator trim tab
143 Tailplane structure

144 Stiffeners
145 Port fin structure
146 Elevator pulley access
147 Rudder tab drum access
148 Tail running light (port)
149 Aerodynamic mass balance
150 Rudder framework
151 Rudder trim tab

152 Fixed tip structure
153 Tail surfaces/boom (quatrefoil bulkhead) attachment flanges
154 Rudder lower section
155 Tail bumper skid shoe
156 Elevator pulley access
157 Port lower fin
158 Elevator, rudder, and table cables
159 Battery compartment
160 Radiator exit flap
161 Engine coolant radiator assembly
162 Radiator housing
163 Radiator/coolant supply pipe
164 Radiator intake
165 Coolant/radiator return pipe
166 Oxygen cylinder
167 Port inner radiator fairing
168 Flare tube (port and starboard booms)
169 Mainwheel doors
170 Mainwheel well
171 Exhaust waste gate outlet
172 Turbine cooling duct
173 Exhaust turbine

174 Supercharger assembly
175 Supercharger/intercooler duct
176 Carburettor intake duct
177 Carburettor air intake
178 Abbreviated rear spar
179 Flap outer section
180 Tab cable access
181 Fixed tab
182 Aileron trim tab
183 Aileron full-span piano-wire hinge
184 Underwing pitot attachment
185 Raked web stiffener (outboard of rear spar)

186 Aileron structure
187 Outer wing pressed sheet ribs
188 Aileron counterweight
189 Junction box
190 Port navigation lights
191 Port wingtip structure

192 Leading-edge ribs
193 Pitot head
194 Wing leading-edge skin join (fabric-covered piano-wire hinge)
195 Wing outer section I-beam box spar
196 Leading-edge stringers (no fuel tanks in early P-38 Js)
197 Wing inner surface corrugation
198 Spar single/double I-beam box spar transition
199 Mainwheel leg doors
200 Rearward-retracting mainwheel
201 Mainwheel oleo leg
202 Alloy spoked hub
203 Cantilever axle
204 Torque links
205 Hydraulic brake cable
206 Drag strut
207 Side strut
208 Drag links
209 Fulcrum

210 Actuating cylinder
211 Multi-bolt outer wing fixings
212 Turbo-supercharger cooling intakes
213 Cabin heater intake
214 Cooling louvres
215 Carburettor duct
216 Outer section wing fillet
217 Insulated exhaust shroud duct
218 Intercooler/carburettor duct
219 Supercharger/intercooler duct
220 Outlet
221 Oil radiator shutter
222 Intercooler
223 Exhausts
224 Allison V-1710-89/91 twelve-cylinder Vee engine
225 Magnetos/distributors
226 Intake fairing
227 Header feed pipes
228 Port outer oil radiator
229 Spark-plug and magneto cooling intake
230 Coolant header tank
231 Propeller hub
232 Oil radiator (outer sections) and intercooler (centre section) tripleintake
233 Curtiss-Electric three-blade (right) handed propeller

234 Inner section underwing stores including
235 Jettisonable auxiliary fuel tank, or
236 Smoke generator, or
237 1,000-lb (454-kg) bomb

99 Starboard reserve fuel tank, capacity as 79
100 Starboard oil tank
101 Cooling louvres
102 Cabin heater intake
103 turbo-supercharger cooling intakes
104 Turbine cooling duct

Representative of the thousands of P-38s which served with the USAAF in Europe during World War II, this aircraft was a P-38J-15 assigned to the 55th Squadron, 20th Fighter Group based at Kingscliffe, Northamptonshire between August 1943 and October 1945. This group was tasked with both escort and ground attack duties, and became known as the 'Loco Group' for its prowess at destroying enemy trains. The gun armament of one cannon and four machine-guns was augmented in the ground attack role by bombs or rocket projectiles.

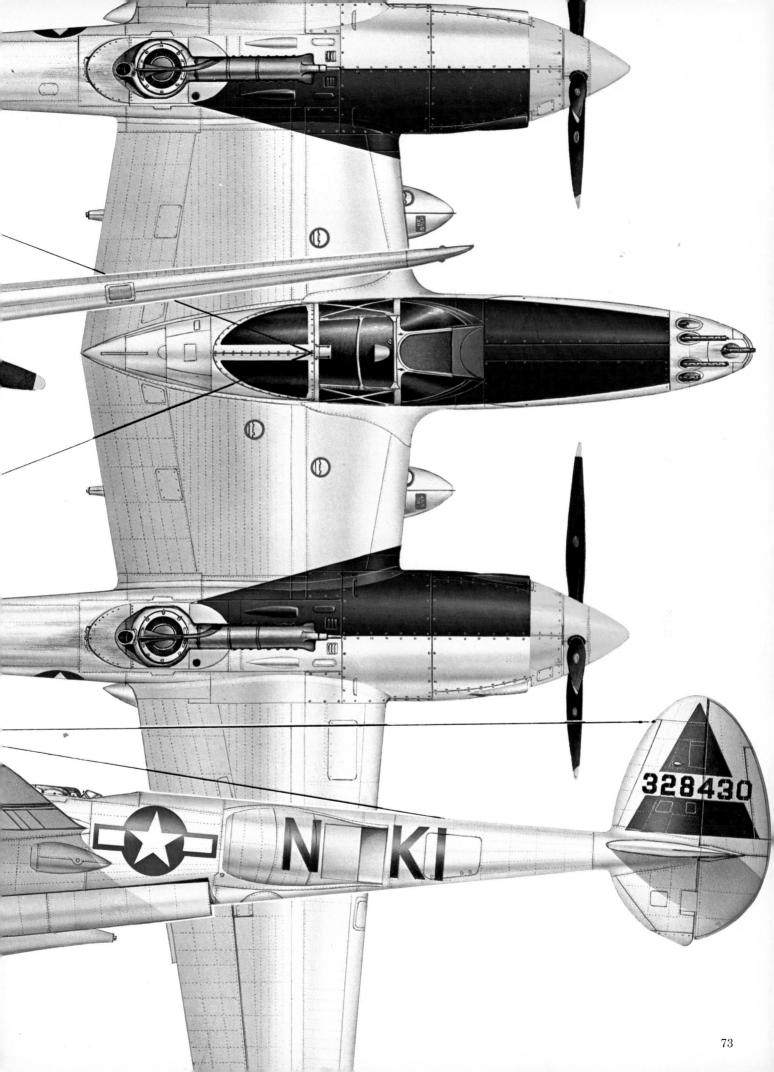

328430

N KI

Many Lightnings were built for the dedicated photo-reconnaissance role. The blue camouflage and camera-equipped nose identifies the nearest aircraft as one of these, in this case an F-5B. This variant was descended from the P-38J fighter, one of which flies behind to provide a comparison.

The Whirlwind Strikes

Although its industry was turning out aircraft for the Allies fighting in Europe and North Africa, the United States was ill-prepared for t war that lay ahead. For the most part the Army pursuit squadrons relied on the P-3(and P-40.

The bomb-ravaged cities of war-torn Europe could not have seemed further away when the men and women of Hawaii awoke to a beautiful Sunday morning, yet within hours the very heart would be ripped out of not just the islands but the nation itself. The date was 7 December 1941, the place Pearl Harbor. Two waves of carrier-based Japanese bombers wrought havoc on the moorings of the Pacific Fleet, leaving flaming hulks of once-proud ships in their wake. More bombers turned their attention to Hickam, Bellows and Wheeler Fields, aided by strafing fighters. All three were heavily hit, losing 64 aircraft to the attackers. The United States was now at war.

In the two years leading to war, the United States had made little progress in the fighter field, despite the monumental air battles being fought daily in the skies of Europe and North Africa. Remaining neutral, the United States provided friendly yet restricted support to the United Kingdom as it stood alone during the early years. The aviation industry in turn was building warplanes for the fight in Europe, initially for

Above: Despite its radical innovations such as large-calibre hub-firing cannon, tricycle undercarriage and mid-mounted engine, the P-39 was not a great success with the US forces. Most served as fighter trainers after an inauspicious few months in the front line.

Below: While never achieving greatness of any kind, the Curtiss P-40 Warhawk was built in large numbers and gave sterling service in all theatres. Outclassed by most of the opposition in the air, it was sturdier than most and fought many famous battles.

It was the Republic P-47 which eventually provided the USAAF with a world-beating single-engined fighter, combining speed with power. In air-to-air combat its brute strength overcame all comers, while it added a new dimension of air-to-ground capability.

France and then more importantly for the UK. Large numbers of Curtiss P-40s were produced for the RAF, as were P-39s. Earlier types such as the P-36 were built for France, but were switched to the RAF (as the Mohawk) after the fall of France in 1940. Critics blamed these exports for holding back the US forces, but they were later to lead directly to providing the United States with the finest all-round fighter of the war, the P-51 Mustang.

Slow production

Fighter production for home consumption did not rise greatly with the outbreak of war in Europe, nor with the constant rise of Japanese power in the Pacific. The P-39 and P-40 were introduced to service shortly before the outbreak of war, and while they represented a useful increase in capability compared with the severely outclassed P-35 and P-36, they were no match for the A6M Reisen. It was almost as though the US fighter community was closing its eyes to the rumblings across the oceans. Perhaps the most significant event was the renaming of the USAAC in June 1941 to the United States Army Air Force.

Pearl Harbor shattered the blinkered complacency as comprehensively as a hammer blow, and an awful realisation filled the minds of politicians and military commanders alike. Having spent two years keeping out of 'Europe's war', the United States could no longer sit on the fence and let its industry prosper at the expense of Britain and France – it now had to get its hands dirty, both in Europe and the Pacific.

With regard to fighter aviation, Pearl Harbor had shown that the USAAF was virtually impotent against a well-orchestrated, mass attack of the kind witnessed almost daily in Europe. The devastation wrought by the Japanese was massive, and it gave them a clear breathing space to expand and consolidate their stranglehold on the Pacific region. The complete lack of effective defence against the onslaught was largely due to two factors. Firstly there was no real warning of the impending attack. Fighters based in defence of the islands were on four-hour readiness. No action alert had been posted, only one for possible terrorist attacks which meant they had to be guarded by armed troops. Ironically this fact made the carnage on the ground easier for the Japanese, as the aircraft were parked close together to facilitate the guards' job.

Brave defence

Despite the low readiness, a few aircraft made it into the air to attack the bombers. Mostly P-40s, these claimed ten brave victories, but showed the second fundamental weakness: US aircraft were no real match for the Japanese carrier aircraft. This fact was born out again in the next few days over the Philippines, where Japanese bombers attacked the bastion of US Pacific power, decimating the airfields while losing only a handful of aircraft to the outclassed defenders. Within two days US fighter defences were down to a force of 30, a mixture of P-40s and P-35s.

These opening attacks against Pearl Harbor and the Philippines heralded a massive offensive throughout the Pacific region, which swept the Japanese through an unbelievable amount of territory in rapid time. To be fair to the Americans, the British had an equally bad time during these opening assaults, but this was due largely to the fact that the prime equipment was fully tied-up fighting in Europe and Africa. On its entry into the war, the United States would also see Europe as the main priority, and the Pacific war became one of containment.

To fight this new battle in Europe, the USAAF would need a lot of fighters, and a lot of good fighters. The gauntlet was down to the aviation industry to produce huge quantities of high quality machines, initially Lockheed P-38s and Republic P-47s, but before they could become available in sufficient numbers, the USAAF would have to turn elsewhere. For its initial operations in Europe, it turned to Britain and the superb Spitfire.

Gearing up for war, the Curtiss P-40 featured prominently in the USAAC's plans of the 1939-1941 period, being perceived as the main fighter. The early variants were basically the P-36 with the Allison V-1710 engine, but this powerplant later gave way to the far better Rolls-Royce Merlin.

Bell P-39 Airacobra

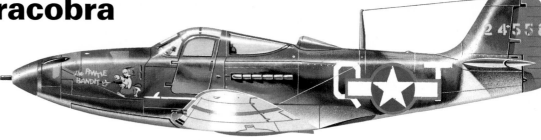

This is a P-39L flown by the 93rd Fighter Squadron, 81st Fighter Group. The unit was based in Tunisia in 1943, and used the P-39 mainly for ground attack duties.

History and notes

The P-39 introduced a major wartime manufacturer of USAAF fighters, the Bell Aircraft Corporation of Buffalo, New York, founded in 1935 by Lawrence D. Bell with a team of designers recruited from the defunct Detroit Aircraft firm. First flown 6 April 1938, the Bell P-39 Airacobra, outwardly conventional in appearance, was unique in having its powerplant located behind the pilot. It was also the first US Army single-seat fighter with retractable tricycle landing gear and heavy, nose-mounted cannon. The decision to mount an American Armament Corporation T9 37-mm cannon in the propeller hub, together with two synchronized and cowl-mounted 0.5-in (12.7-mm) Browning machine-guns, meant that the 1,200-hp (894.8-kW) Allison V-1710 inline engine had to be positioned within the fuselage above the rear half of the low-set monoplane wing, its propeller driven by an extension shaft which passed beneath the cockpit floor. This unorthodox but reliable arrangement, combined with a side-door for entry/exit to and from the raised, braced-canopy cockpit, was maintained throughout the long production run of 9,589 Airacobras (8,914 with USAAF funding), but advances elsewhere made the P-39 a second-rank fighter aircraft as early as war's outset. Ultimately, nearly half the production run (4,779 aircraft) went via Lend-Lease to the Soviet Union which only later reached the point of operating fighters as advanced as those of other major combatants.

Modifications

Following evaluation of the sole XP-39 (38-326) at Wright Field, Ohio, the US Army ordered 13 service-test YP-39s (40-27/39), while the prototype was returned to the manufacturer to be rebuilt as the XP-39B with fairing doors for its mainwheel units, a lowered canopy, two additional 0.3-in (7.62-mm) nose machine-guns and other modifications. When a 10 August 1939 contract for further production was awarded, the 20 airframes on order initially received the new designation P-45, but were quickly reclassified as P-39Cs. These were equipped with bullet-resistant windscreens and self-sealing fuel tanks. The first major production variant, of which 923 were ordered in fiscal 1940-41, was the P-39D, which received two further 0.3-in (7.62-mm) guns (four now being mounted in the wings) and had provision for a 500-lb (227-kg) bomb or a 75-US gal (283.9-litre) centreline drop tank. It was this P-39D variant which won an April 1941 British order for 675 Airacobra Mk I fighters for the Royal Air Force, these differing in having armament of one 20-mm nose cannon and six 0.303-in (7.7-mm) machine-guns.

Except for the 14 pre-production specimens, the P-39 lacked a turbocharger and this (not its unusual engine layout) was the principle reason why the Bell fighter never contended on equal terms with Mitsubishi, Supermarine and North American products as a front-line combat craft. Group Captain Christopher Clarkson, who flew the P-39D at Buffalo, recalls recommending the Airacobra Mk I to the RAF 'with some trepidation'. Only about 65 Airacobras in fact saw service with No. 601 Squadron, the RAF's sole operator of the type whose inadequate climb and poor high-altitude performance led to its replacement by Supermarine Spitfires in March 1942. The type suffered other difficulties, including severe vibration, and mal-

Bell P-39D Airacobra cutaway drawing key

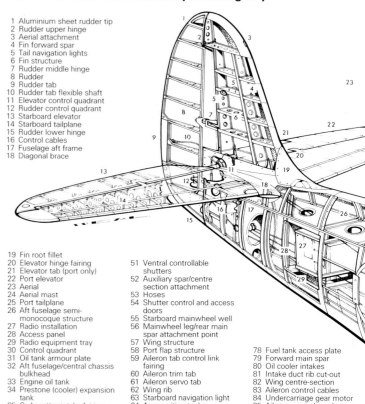

1 Aluminium sheet rudder tip
2 Rudder upper hinge
3 Aerial attachment
4 Fin forward spar
5 Tail navigation lights
6 Fin structure
7 Rudder middle hinge
8 Rudder
9 Rudder tab
10 Rudder tab flexible shaft
11 Elevator control quadrant
12 Rudder control quadrant
13 Starboard elevator
14 Starboard tailplane
15 Rudder lower hinge
16 Control cables
17 Fuselage aft frame
18 Diagonal brace

19 Fin root fillet
20 Elevator hinge fairing
21 Elevator tab (port only)
22 Port elevator
23 Aerial
24 Aerial mast
25 Port tailplane
26 Aft fuselage semi-monocoque structure
27 Radio installation
28 Access panel
29 Radio equipment tray
30 Control quadrant
31 Oil tank armour plate
32 Aft fuselage/central chassis bulkhead
33 Engine oil tank
34 Prestone (cooler) expansion tank
35 Carburettor intake fairing
36 Carburettor intake shutter housing
37 Engine accessories
38 Central chassis web
39 Frame
40 Starboard longitudinal fuselage beam
41 Exhaust stubs
42 Allison V-1710-35 Vee 12-cylinder engine

51 Ventral controllable shutters
52 Auxiliary spar/centre section attachment
53 Hoses
54 Shutter control and access doors
55 Starboard mainwheel well
56 Mainwheel leg/rear main spar attachment point
57 Wing structure
58 Port flap structure
59 Aileron tab control link fairing
60 Aileron trim tab
61 Aileron servo tab
62 Wing rib
63 Starboard navigation light
64 Ammunition tanks
65 Two 0.3-in (7.62-mm) wing machine guns
66 Inboard gun ammunition feed chute
67 Machine gun barrels

78 Fuel tank access plate
79 Forward main spar
80 Oil cooler intakes
81 Intake duct rib cut-out
82 Wing centre-section
83 Aileron control cables
84 Undercarriage gear motor
85 Aileron control quadrant
86 Undercarriage emergency handcrank

The sole Bell XP-39 certainly looked more potent than the P-35 and P-36 that swelled the pursuit squadrons at the time of its first flight in 1938, but by 1941 it was severely outclassed as a fighter. Nevertheless, the Soviet Union turned it into a success story.

43 Engine compartment decking
44 Aft-vision glazing
45 Crash turnover bulkhead
46 Turnover bulkhead armour plate
47 Auxiliary air intake
48 Ventral Prestone (cooler) radiator
49 Rear main spar-centre section attachment
50 Cylindrical oil radiator

68 Mainwheel door fairing
69 Starboard mainwheel
70 Axle
71 Mainwheel fork
72 Torque links
73 Mainwheel oleo leg
74 Wing fuel cells (6)
75 Fuel filler cap
76 Mainwheel retraction spindle
77 Fuel tank gauge capacity plate

87 Coolant radiator/oil temperature shutter controls
88 Sutton harness
89 Pilot's seat
90 Armoured glass turnover bulkhead frame
91 Cockpit entry doors
92 Internal rear-view mirror

Bell P-39

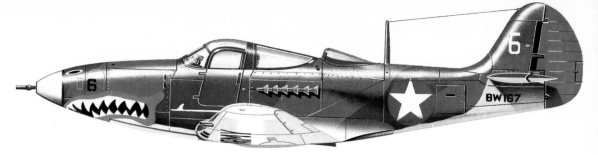

The RAF-style serial denotes this Airacobra as a P-400, this designation applied to aircraft destined for the UK but requisitioned for USAAF use after Pearl Harbor. This example flew with the 67th FS, 35th FG in New Caledonia, 1942.

function of the radio, located in a compartment behind the engine. At New Guinea and Guadalcanal, ex-British Airacobras, designated P-400 by the USAAF, could not cope with the Mitsubishi Zero. In the Pacific and in Europe, the P-39 was quickly removed from the air-to-air combat arena and relegated to other duties. A few were field-modified to become TP-39F and RP-39Q two-seat familiarisation trainers.

The three XP-39E airframes (41-19501/19502 and 42-71464) were testbeds with 1,510-hp (1126-kW) Allison V-1710-47 engines, laminar-flow wings and taller vertical tails. These characteristics were embodied in a wholly separate fighter which became the Bell P-63 Kingcobra and which only resembled the P-39 series externally.

Very minor changes, of propeller and engine variant, distinguished the P-39F, P-39J, P-39K, P-39L and P-39M fighters, many of which were retained in the USA for training duties. Together with a few P-39Ds, and P-39N and P-39Q versions were built in significant numbers for the Soviet Union, most being delivered by USAAF pilots via Alaska. The P-39Q carried the same nose armament as other USAAF machines, but the four wing 0.3-in (7.62-mm) machine-guns were replaced by two 0.5-in (12.7-mm) machine-guns in underwing fairings. From the P-39Q-21-BE block onward, a four-

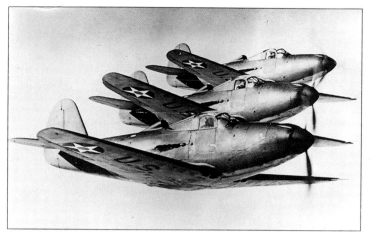

The Airacobra saw initial service with the USAAF as a fighter, the number swelled by some aircraft diverted from the RAF as the P-400. Brief service was seen in Europe and the Pacific, but combat experience was unhappy, and the type was relegated to training.

---

93 Gunsight
94 Armoured glass windscreen
95 Steel plate armour overlap
96 Instrument panel frame
97 Control column
98 Control column yoke/drive shaft
99 Nosewheel retraction chain coupling
100 Rudder pedal assembly
101 Fuselage machine gun ammunition tank
102 Nosewheel drive motor
103 Nosewheel retraction strut forged 'A'-frame attachments
104 Retraction screw
105 Nosewheel doors

106 Link assembly
107 Access plate
108 Nosewheel well
109 Drive shaft
110 Cannon aft support frame
111 37-mm M4 cannon breech
112 Circular endless belt-type cannon magazine (30 rounds)
113 Cockpit forward armoured plate
114 Two 0.5-in (12.7-mm) fuselage machine guns
115 Flap links

116 Aileron tab actuating link
117 Aileron control
118 Aileron trim tab
119 Aileron servo tab
120 Wing skinning
121 Port navigation light
122 Pitot tube
123 Ammunition feed chute access
124 Gun charge cable access
125 Wing gun service access
126 Machine gun barrels
127 Aileron and tab control pulleys

128 Fuel tank filler cap
129 Reduction gear oil tank
130 Machine gun blast tubes
131 Machine gun ports
132 Reduction gearbox frontal armour
133 Three-blade Curtiss Electric constant-speed propeller
134 Spinner

145 Ventral stores, options including auxiliary fuel tank, or:
146 Two-man life raft

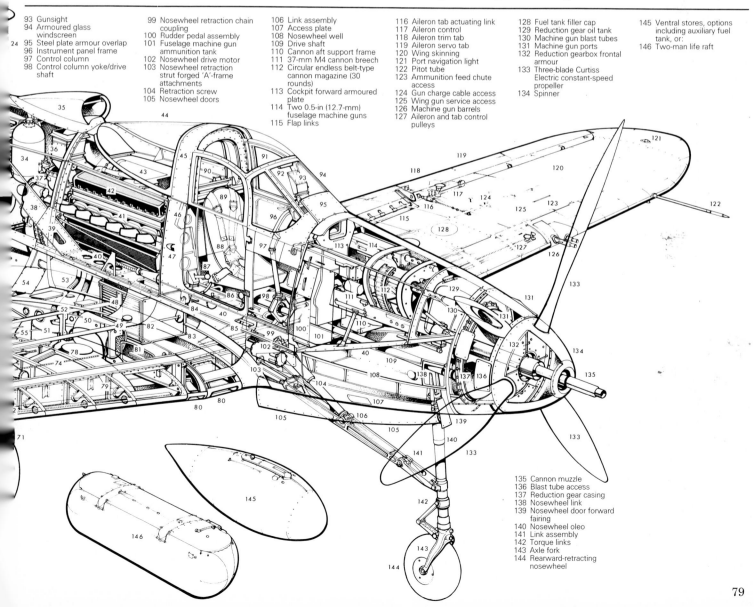

135 Cannon muzzle
136 Blast tube access
137 Reduction gear casing
138 Nosewheel link
139 Nosewheel door forward fairing
140 Nosewheel oleo
141 Link assembly
142 Torque links
143 Axle fork
144 Rearward-retracting nosewheel

blade propeller was fitted. Further production of Airacobras under the new designation P-76 was planned in 1942 but did not materialise.

The US Navy had tested a tailwheel landing-gear variant as the XFL-1 Airabonita and acquired seven P-39s for use as target drones under the designation F2L-1K.

P-39s also saw service in Portugal and with the Free French and Italian Co-belligerent air arms. Some ex-Soviet examples may have reached North Korea in the late 1940s. Though it served worldwide, the P-39 Airacobra never felt the touch of greatness, inspired few poets or songsters, and handily missed becoming legend. Only a handful survive today, including a preserved machine at the Air Force Museum, Dayton, Ohio. A P-39D (41-6951) and a P-39F (41-7215) in Queensland, Australia, are currently being salvaged by enthusiasts who hope to return at least one example of this unheralded fighter to flying status.

Specification
P-39M
Type: single-seat fighter
Powerplant: one 1,200-hp (894.8-kW) Allison V-1710-83 liquid-cooled 12-cylinder Vee piston engine driving a three-blade Curtiss propeller
Performance: maximum speed 386 mph (621.2 km/h) at 9,500 ft (2896 m); cruising speed 200 mph (321.9 km/h); service ceiling 36,000 ft (10973 m); range 650 miles (1046 km)
Weights: empty 5,610 lb (2544.7 kg); maximum take-off 8,400 lb (3810.2 kg)
Dimensions: span 34 ft 0 in (10.36 m); length 30 ft 2 in (9.19 m); height 11 ft 10 in (3.61 m); wing area 213 sq ft (19.79 m^2)
Armament: one 37-mm T9 cannon, two 0.5-in (12.7-mm) machine-guns and four 0.3-in (7.62-mm) machine-guns, plus provision for one 500-lb (227-kg) bomb

Curtiss P-40 Warhawk

History and notes

The Curtiss P-40 Warhawk, seemingly quite advanced as a low-wing monoplane fighter in a pre-war world, was obsolescent when the USA entered World War II. About 13,800 airframes were manufactured (12,043 with USAAF funding) making the P-40 third most numerous of American fighters, behind the Thunderbolt and Mustang.

The P-40 began life as a P-36 redesigned with the Allison V-1710 liquid-cooled inline engine, offering better aerodynamics, more power and better fuel consumption than air-cooled radial engines of similar output. The Allison powerplant, however, was ineffective at altitude and, with other fighter designs showing more promise, was not deemed worth improving through retrofit of a turbocharger. Thus, above 15,000 ft (4572 m) the P-40 was inferior to just about all Axis fighters. Still, the P-40 fought in every theatre and is remembered with fondness as a tough and reliable mount, able to absorb and inflict punishment, and always effective in the air-to-ground role.

Above: Curtiss P-40s of the 8th Pursuit Group line up for the camera, the propeller spinner colours denoting the individual squadrons. Altitude performance remained the major problem with this fighter, although it retained the beautiful handling of the P-36.

Below: First of the large-scale production versions of the Warhawk was the P-40E, which introduced the standard fighter armament fit of six 0.5-in (12.7-mm) machine-guns. A centreline rack allowed the carriage of bombs, a practice widely used in the deserts of North Africa.

Curtiss P-40

Curtiss P-40 of the 55th Fighter Squadron, 20th Pursuit Group based at March Field, California in 1941.

Hawk 81A-2 flown by Charles Older, 3rd Squadron 'Hell's Angels', American Volunteer Group, Kunming, China in the spring of 1942. The 'Flying Tigers' were by far and away the most famous P-40 users.

The sole XP-40 (38-10) was first flown in late 1938 and was actually the tenth production P-36A airframe re-engined with the 1,000-hp (745.7-kW) Allison V-1710-19 powerplant. After being awarded a May 1939 contract for production which was then the largest ever issued by the US Army, the prototype was modified by having its coolant radiator moved from under the rear fuselage to the nose, and the essential configuration of the P-40 series was then established. As production of P-40 and P-40B machines progressed, the latter introducing both armour protection for the pilot, and self-sealing fuel tanks, hundreds of export machines known as Tomahawk Mks I, IA, IB and II, were sold to the UK's Royal Air Force, some 100 being diverted to China for use by the American Volunteer Group, the 'Flying Tigers'. RAF machines carried 0.303-in (7.7-mm) Browning wing machine-guns instead of the 0.3-in (7.62-mm) guns employed on American airframes. The RAF would eventually use Tomahawks with Nos 2, 13, 26, 94, 112, 171, 239, 250, 368, 400, 403 and 414 Squadrons. Some Tomahawk Mk II aircraft were shipped to the Soviet Union after having American machine-guns re-installed. P-40Bs were among the first American casualties at Pearl Harbor and Clark Field, Philippines. Second Lieutenant George S. Welch of the 47th Pursuit Squadron went aloft in a P-40B during the Pearl Harbor raid to shoot four Japanese aircraft out of the skies, later ending the war with 16 aerial victories.

Increased production

Improved self-sealing fuel tanks were introduced beginning in 1941 with the first P-40C (41-13328), of which 193 were delivered to the USAAF. The P-40D model with 1,150-hp (857.6-kW) Allison V-1710-39 engine was used only in token numbers by the USAAF, but 560 reached the RAF as the Kittyhawk Mk I. The P-40E, of which 2,320 were built for the USAAF and several hundred for the RAF as the Kittyhawk Mk IA, introduced standard armament of six wing 0.5-in (12.7-mm) machine-guns, an increased gross weight of 8,840 lb (4009.8 kg) and fuel capacity of 201 US gal (760.9 litres). The P-40E also had a centreline fitting permitting it to carry a 500-lb (227-kg) bomb or other ordnance up to 700 lb (317.5 kg) in place of the tank. In China the P-40E replaced P-40Bs with the American Volunteer Group, which accounted for 286 Japanese aircraft with the loss of but eight pilots in air-to-air combat. It was flown by Robert H. Neale, top-scoring AVG ace with 16 aerial victories. By 1943, P-40Es and Kittyhawk Mk IAs were fighting in the Pacific, North Africa and Sicily. P-40Es were also flown by Canadian, New Zealand and South African pilots.

Despite its beautifully-crafted fuselage and canopy, the XP-40Q could not achieve the performance of the Mustang or Thunderbolt. Curtiss made many attempts to improve the basic design, but despite its inherent poor performance, nearly 14,000 Warhawks were built.

A milestone in the P-40's career came in 1941 when a British-built Rolls-Royce Merlin 28 engine (soon to be manufactured in the US as the Packard V-1650) was installed in the sole XP-40F (40-360). The Merlin was rated at 1,120-hp (835.2-kW) at 18,500 ft (5639 m), and permitted a maximum speed of 373 mph (600.3 km/h). The production P-40F, powered by the Packard-built Merlin V-1650-1, had a gross weight of nearly 10,000 lb (4536 kg). Some 1,311 were ordered by the USAAF which now introduced the widely-known Warhawk nickname, although the same variant was called Kittyhawk Mk II in RAF service.

The only P-40G (39-221) was a P-40 modified to carry what eventually became standard armament, six 0.5-in (12.7-mm) guns. The P-40J was a proposal to improve the performance of the Allison V-1710 powerplant with a turbocharger but, as noted earlier, was not proceeded with. The XP-40K was a modified airframe in the P-40K series although not a prototype for the P-40K model. Development of Allison-powered Warhawks continued despite the superiority of the Merlin, and the P-40K had the 1,200-hp (894.8-kW) Allison V-1710-73 and eventually employed both the extended fuselage and taller fin which distinguished late-model P-40s.

A 'stripped' variant of the Packard V-1650 Merlin-powered Warhawk was introduced as the P-40L. The P-40L had two of the usual six 0.5-in (12.7-mm) guns removed and incorporated weight-saving changes. Though 700 were delivered to the USAAF, the hoped-for improvement in performance for short-range combat was exceed-

Hawk 81A-2 flown by Henry Geselbracht of the 2nd Squadron, American Volunteer Group, flying from Toungoo in February 1942. The AVG's Hawks flew with Chinese insignia.

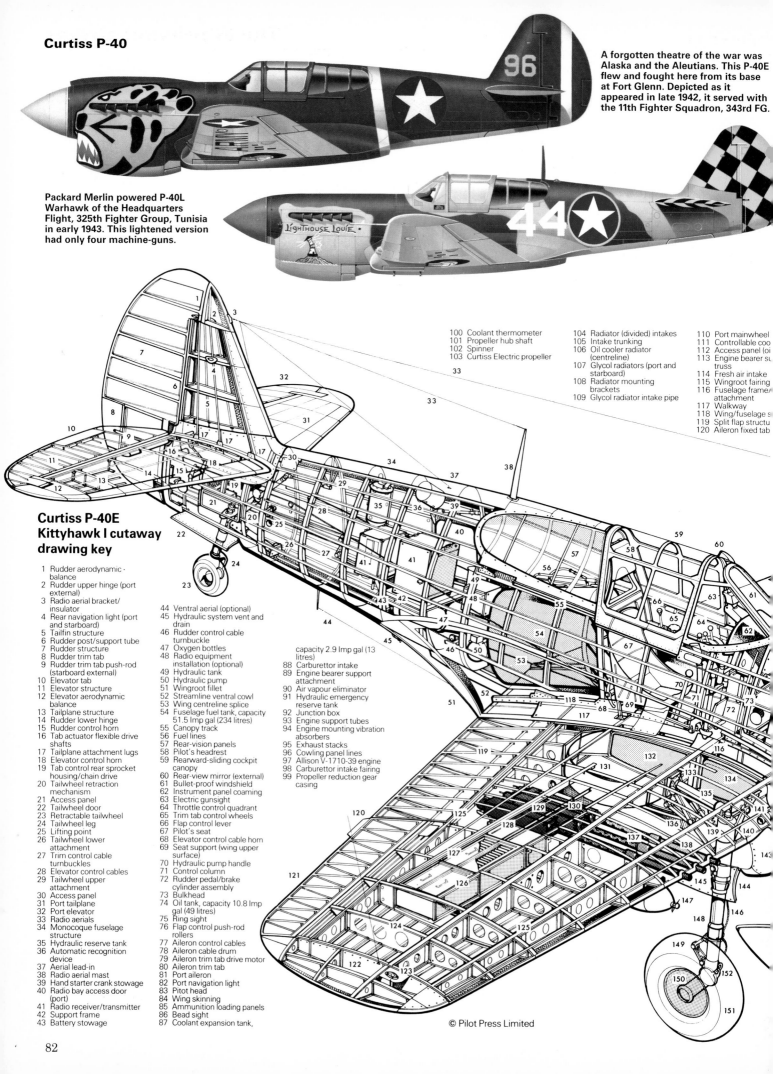

Curtiss P-40

A forgotten theatre of the war was Alaska and the Aleutians. This P-40E flew and fought here from its base at Fort Glenn. Depicted as it appeared in late 1942, it served with the 11th Fighter Squadron, 343rd FG.

Packard Merlin powered P-40L Warhawk of the Headquarters Flight, 325th Fighter Group, Tunisia in early 1943. This lightened version had only four machine-guns.

Curtiss P-40E Kittyhawk I cutaway drawing key

1 Rudder aerodynamic · balance
2 Rudder upper hinge (port external)
3 Radio aerial bracket/insulator
4 Rear navigation light (port and starboard)
5 Tailfin structure
6 Rudder post/support tube
7 Rudder structure
8 Rudder trim tab
9 Rudder trim tab push-rod (starboard external)
10 Elevator tab
11 Elevator structure
12 Elevator aerodynamic balance
13 Tailplane structure
14 Rudder lower hinge
15 Rudder control horn
16 Tab actuator flexible drive shafts
17 Tailplane attachment lugs
18 Elevator control horn
19 Tab control rear sprocket housing/chain drive
20 Tailwheel retraction mechanism
21 Access panel
22 Tailwheel door
23 Retractable tailwheel
24 Tailwheel leg
25 Lifting point
26 Tailwheel lower attachment
27 Trim control cable turnbuckles
28 Elevator control cables
29 Tailwheel upper attachment
30 Access panel
31 Port tailplane
32 Port elevator
33 Radio aerials
34 Monocoque fuselage structure
35 Hydraulic reserve tank
36 Automatic recognition device
37 Aerial lead-in
38 Radio aerial mast
39 Hand starter crank stowage
40 Radio bay access door (port)
41 Radio receiver/transmitter
42 Support frame
43 Battery stowage
44 Ventral aerial (optional)
45 Hydraulic system vent and drain
46 Rudder control cable turnbuckle
47 Oxygen bottles
48 Radio equipment installation (optional)
49 Hydraulic tank
50 Hydraulic pump
51 Wingroot fillet
52 Streamline ventral cowl
53 Wing centreline splice
54 Fuselage fuel tank, capacity 51.5 Imp gal (234 litres)
55 Canopy track
56 Fuel lines
57 Rear-vision panels
58 Pilot's headrest
59 Rearward-sliding cockpit canopy
60 Rear-view mirror (external)
61 Bullet-proof windshield
62 Instrument panel coaming
63 Electric gunsight
64 Throttle control quadrant
65 Trim tab control wheels
66 Flap control lever
67 Pilot's seat
68 Elevator control cable horn
69 Seat support (wing upper surface)
70 Hydraulic pump handle
71 Control column
72 Rudder pedal/brake cylinder assembly
73 Bulkhead
74 Oil tank, capacity 10.8 Imp gal (49 litres)
75 Ring sight
76 Flap control push-rod rollers
77 Aileron control cables
78 Aileron cable drum
79 Aileron trim tab drive motor
80 Aileron trim tab
81 Port aileron
82 Port navigation light
83 Pitot head
84 Wing skinning
85 Ammunition loading panels
86 Bead sight
87 Coolant expansion tank, capacity 2.9 Imp gal (13 litres)
88 Carburettor intake
89 Engine bearer support attachment
90 Air vapour eliminator
91 Hydraulic emergency reserve tank
92 Junction box
93 Engine support tubes
94 Engine mounting vibration absorbers
95 Exhaust stacks
96 Cowling panel lines
97 Allison V-1710-39 engine
98 Carburettor intake fairing
99 Propeller reduction gear casing
100 Coolant thermometer
101 Propeller hub shaft
102 Spinner
103 Curtiss Electric propeller
104 Radiator (divided) intakes
105 Intake trunking
106 Oil cooler radiator (centreline)
107 Glycol radiators (port and starboard)
108 Radiator mounting brackets
109 Glycol radiator intake pipe
110 Port mainwheel
111 Controllable coo[
112 Access panel (oi[
113 Engine bearer su[truss
114 Fresh air intake
115 Wingroot fairing
116 Fuselage frame[attachment
117 Walkway
118 Wing/fuselage s[
119 Split flap structu[
120 Aileron fixed tab[

© Pilot Press Limited

82

Curtiss P-40s of the 16th Fighter Squadron, 51st Fighter Group line up prior to take-off at an air base in China. This theatre saw the lowest level of opposition in terms of aircraft capability, allowing the Warhawks to be more successful in air-to-air fighting than in other theatres.

ingly marginal. Most P-40Ls had the extended fuselage configuration typical of late Warhawks.

The P-40M, known as the Kittyhawk Mks III and IV in RAF service, reverted to the 1,200-hp (894.8-kW) Allison V-1710-81, a more advanced model of the familiar powerplant intended for improved performance at higher altitude. A total of 600 was built and, apart from the USAAF, the P-40M served with South African Air Force squadrons.

The P-40N, also called Kittyhawk Mk IV by the RAF, was the most numerous variant of this famous fighter, no fewer than 5,219 being built by three Curtiss plants. The weight-saving effort begun with the P-40L model was continued, though most P-40Ns were eventually built with the full armament of six 0.5-in (12.7-mm) guns. Late P-40Ns had the 1,200-hp (894.8-kW) Allison V-1710-99 and a few were converted to two-seat TP-40N trainers. The P-40N, many of which reached the Soviet Union, had new radio and oxygen equipment and flame-damping exhausts.

The XP-40Q, three of which were converted from P-40Ks and a P-40N, and powered by the 1,425-hp (1062.6-kW) Allison V-1710-121, had clipped wingtips, four-blade propeller, and bubble canopy. The XP-40Q may also have been the most beautiful fighter ever built but despite significant improvement in performance it was still no match for the Thunderbolt and Mustang, and was not mass-produced. The final designation in this series, P-40R, went to some 300 P-40F and P-40L airframes completed with Allison engines during a shortage of Merlins.

Despite sheer numbers and considerable press coverage (P-40s with the AVG and elsewhere were often depicted wearing shark's teeth) the P-40 remains in history a second-rank fighter, one flown by as many victims as heroes, a classic in some respects but never, at any time, a candidate for greatness. A number of flyable P-40s can still be seen at air shows in the USA and Europe.

Specification
P-40N

Type: single-seat fighter
Powerplant: one 1,200-hp (894.8-kW) Allison V-1710-81 liquid-cooled 12-cylinder Vee piston engine driving a three-blade propeller
Performance: maximum speed 343 mph (552 km/h) at 15,000 ft (4572 m); initial climb rate about 2,800 ft (853 m) per minute; climb to 14,000 ft (4267 m) in 6.7 minutes; service ceiling 31,000 ft (9449 m); range with auxiliary fuel at 10,000 ft (3048 m) 1,080 miles (1738 km)
Weights: empty 6,200 lb (2812.3 kg); maximum take-off 8,850 lb (4014.4 kg)
Dimensions: span 37 ft 4 in (11.38 m); length 33 ft 4 in (10.16 m); height 12 ft 4 in (3.76 m); wing area 236 sq ft (21.92 m²)
Armament: six 0.5-in (12.7-mm) fixed forward-firing machine-guns, plus provision for up to 1,500 lb (680.4 kg) of bombs

tarboard aileron
tarboard wingtip
onstruction
tarboard navigation light
ving rib
Multi (7)-spar wing
tructure
board gun ammunition
ox (235 rounds)
entre gun ammunition
ox (235 rounds)
utboard gun ammunition
ox (235 rounds)
hree 0.50-in (12.7-mm)
1-2 Browning machine
uns
mmunition feed chute

131 Starboard wheel well
132 Wing centre-section main fuel tank, capacity 42.1 Imp gal (191 litres)
133 Undercarriage attachment
134 Wing centre-section reserve fuel tank, capacity 29.2 Imp gal (133 litres)
135 Retraction cylinder
136 Retraction arm/links
137 Machine gun barrel forward support collars
138 Blast tubes
139 Bevel gear
140 Undercarriage side support strut
141 Gun warm air
142 500-lb (227-kg) bomb (ventral stores)
143 Undercarriage oleo leg fairing

144 Undercarriage fairing door
145 Machine gun ports
146 Hydraulic brake line
147 One (or two) underwing 40-lb (18-kg) bomb(s)
148 Oleo leg
149 Torque links
150 Axle
151 30-in (76.2-mm) diameter smooth-contour mainwheel tyre
152 Tow ring/jack point
153 Ventral auxiliary tank, capacity 43.3 Imp gal (197 litre)
154 Vent line
155 Sway brace pads
156 External fuel line
157 Shackle assembly
158 Filler neck
159 Alternative ventral 250-lb (113.5-kg) bomb with:
160 Extended percussion fuse

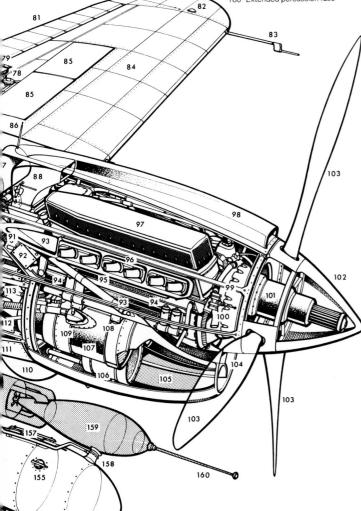

Seversky P-41

History and notes

The P-41 designation marked another step by Seversky and its chief designer Alexander Kartveli toward the ultimate radial-engine fighter achievement which would see fruition as the Thunderbolt. The sole XP-41 (36-430) may not have contributed so much directly toward fighter progress, being clearly a design of the pre-war era before fighter development began to move more rapidly. The machine had begun life on the Farmingdale production line as the final Seversky P-35. First flown in March 1939, the XP-41 was outwardly almost identical to the P-35 and was powered by the same 1,200-hp (894.8-kW) Pratt & Whitney R-1830-39 Twin Wasp radial, with a two-stage two-speed supercharger.

Little historical record has survived regarding the flight testing of the XP-41. Fairchild Republic historian Theron Rinehart wishes that his predecessor company had 'set more documents aside for us to peruse' on this one-of-a-kind machine. From outward appearance, it is evident that the XP-41 influenced the P-43 Lancer, the unbuilt P-44 Rocket and the P-47 Thunderbolt. But almost no details exist on the XP-41 itself, not even the final disposition of the airframe. Apparently, the XP-41 was evaluated at Wright Field and, by war's outset, scrapped. By then, the Sever-

sky firm was moving on to greater things with a new name, Republic.

Specification
XP-41

Type: single-seat fighter
Powerplant: one 1,200-hp (894.8kW) Pratt & Whitney R-1830-39 Twin Wasp turbocharged air-cooled 14-cylinder radial piston engine driving a three-blade propeller

Performance: maximum speed 323 mph (519.8 km/h) at 14,300 ft (4359 m); initial climb rate 2,635 ft (803 m) per minute; service ceiling 23,000 ft (7010 m); range 490 miles (789 km)
Weights: empty 5,390 lb (2444.9 kg); maximum take-off 7,000 lb (3175.2 kg)
Dimensions: span 36 ft 0 in (10.97 m); length 27 ft 0 in (8.23 m); height 12 ft 5 in (3.78 m); wing area

220 sq ft (20.44 m^2)
Armament: one 0.3-in (7.62-mm) and one 0.5-in (12.7-mm) fixed forward-firing machine-guns

The single XP-41 was very similar to the P-35, featuring a neater inward-retracting main undercarriage. Obviously obsolete at the time of its construction, it did however provide one more stepping stone to the classic Thunderbolt.

Curtiss P-42

History and notes

The Curtiss XP-42, a conversion of a P-36A Mohawk airframe (38-4), was employed as a testbed at Wright Field, Ohio, beginning in March 1939 to determine whether streamlining could reduce drag in a radial-powered fighter and make it competitive with more advanced fighters employing inline engines. This concept was seen as an alternative to adapting the P-36A airframe to an inline powerplant, as had been done with the prototype P-40 Warhawk. Delivered to the Army in March 1939, the XP-42 was powered by a 1,050-hp (783-kW) Pratt & Whitney R-1830-31 Twin Wasp radial enclosed by a bullet-shaped, sheet-metal cowling extended forward to culminate in a large, pointed spinner. An airscoop below the spinner provided cooling air, while smaller intakes above the engine provided air to the carburettor. It was immediately clear that this sleek, long-nosed configuration offered none of the advantages of the inline engine employed not only by the P-40 but also by such types as the Messerschmitt Bf 109 and North American Mustang. The aerodynamic nose shape provided almost no reduction in drag, and cooling problems proved almost insurmountable. While the XP-42 was marginally faster than the open-cowl P-36A, its performance did not compare favourably with the P-40 or with other, newer fighters of the immediate pre-war period.

A variety of nose configurations was tried on the XP-42, altering its fuselage length with each change, but none vindicated the enclosed radial engine and Curtiss's produc-

tion facilities, in the event, were taken up with the inline-powered P-40. When hostilities began, the XP-42 had been ruled out as a possible production aircraft but continued to aid in research. In 1942, the XP-42 tested an all-flying stabilizer, similar to the stabilator found on modern jets. The XP-42 had begun flying in natural metal finish and was camouflaged during one of its minor rebuilds. The airframe, which contributed knowledge to designers and engineers, was eventually taken out of service as other wartime priorities beckoned. Curtiss would continue to explore new fighter ideas with XP-46, XP-60 and

XF-87, but the company's predominant role in the fighter field was fast becoming history.

Specification
XP-42

Type: single-seat fighter
Powerplant: one 1,050-hp (783-kW) Pratt & Whitney R-1830-31 Twin Wasp air-cooled 14-cylinder radial piston engine driving a three-blade propeller
Performance: maximum speed 315 mph (506.9 km/h) at 15,000 ft (4572 m); initial climb rate about 2,800 ft (853 m) per minute; service ceiling about 31,000 ft (9449 m);

range about 600 miles (966 km)
Weights: empty 4,818 lb (2185.4 kg); maximum take-off 6,260 lb (2839.5 kg)
Dimensions: span 37 ft 4 in (11.38 m); length 30 ft 7 in (9.32 m); height 12 ft 0 in (3.66 m); wing area about 235 sq ft (21.83 m^2)
Armament: none

As with the PW-8/P-1/P-6 series, Curtiss produced a myriad of experimental fighters based on the P-36/P-40 series. The XP-42 tested cowled radial engines with a variety of configurations, but they showed no worthwhile increase in performance and a lot of cooling problems.

Republic P-43 Lancer

History and notes

The Republic P-43 Lancer was designer Alexander Kartveli's follow-up to the P-35 and XP-41, and was built by the Farmingdale, Long Island, manufacturer which in October 1939 changed its name from Seversky to Republic. Kartveli had made an attempt to put a streamlined cowl around a radial engine, in the fashion of the Curtiss XP-42, using the experimental company Model AP-4. The concept was stymied by cooling problems and Kartveli's P-43 was a company Model AP-4 with a return to traditional radial-engine configuration. Though this meant accepting the drag imposed by a broad open cowl, Kartveli hoped to compensate with an otherwise clean aerodynamic design and brute power. This worked moderately well with the P-43 Lancer and would achieve real success with the Thunderbolt to follow.

Powered by a 1,200-hp (894.8-kW) Pratt & Whitney R-1830-35 Twin Wasp radial, the P-43 began flying in 1939 and offered some improvement in performance over the Seversky P-35 and Curtiss P-36 then in use. The US Army placed a 12 May 1939 contract for 13 service-test YP-43 airframes. Meanwhile, studies aimed at finding a more powerful engine resulted in Republic's proposal for the R-2180-powered P-44 Rocket. In September 1940, the planned purchases of the latter machine were redirected to the P-43 Lancer as a stopgap measure while the P-44 was cancelled and the Farmingdale line was tooled-up in anticipation of the P-47 Thunderbolt.

The 13 service-test YP-43s were followed by 54 production P-43s with R-1830-47 engines, 80 P-43As with the R-1830-49 ordered in lieu of the P-44, and 125 P-43A-1s with the R-1830-57. The 272 airframes served eminently forgettable careers with the US Army 1st Pursuit Group and other units, being used in 1940 to

simulate the enemy in war games. Some 150 machines were converted to P-43B standard for the reconnaissance role with cameras, and a further two airframes were converted to P-43C, also a reconnaissance variant. Even as a photoplane, the Republic P-43 Lancer never saw significant action with US

Further refinement by Seversky/Republic's Alex Kartveli led to the P-43 Lancer, procured in small numbers. Although showing a small improvement over the P-35 and P-36, it led a wholly undistinguished career with the fighter units.

forces. Some appear to have been delivered to India. About 60 P-43s reached the Chinese Nationalist air force and saw combat against Japanese forces.

Specification
P-43A

Type: single-seat fighter
Powerplant: one 1,200-hp (894.8-kW) Pratt & Whitney R-1830-49 Twin Wasp air-cooled 14-cylinder radial piston engine driving a three-blade propeller
Performance: maximum speed 355 mph (571.3 km/h) at 20,000 ft

(6096 m); initial climb rate about 2,700 ft (823 m) per minute; service ceiling 26,000 ft (7925 m); range 800 miles (1287 km)
Weights: empty 5,730 lb (2599.1 kg); maximum take-off 7,800 lb (3538.1 kg)
Dimensions: span 36 ft 0 in (10.97 m); length 28 ft 6 in (8.67 m); height 14 ft 0 in (4.27 m); wing area 224 sq ft (20.81 m²)
Armament: two cowl 0.3-in (7.62-mm) and two wing 0.5-in (12.7-mm) fixed forward-firing machine-guns, plus provision for six 20-lb (9.07-kg) or two 200-lb (90.7-kg) bombs

Republic P-44 Rocket

History and notes

The Republic P-44 Rocket was a false start at improving upon the P-43 Lancer, a step in the right direction which reached fruition with the P-47 Thunderbolt. Ordered into production in September 1940 but cancelled almost immediately, the P-44 would have been powered by a 1,400-hp (1044-kW) Pratt & Whitney R-2180-1 radial. Because it would have been but a marginal improvement over the P-43 and could not match the performance expected of the P-47, the P-44 remains a sidelight in history.

The P-44-1, or company Model AP-4J, was the recipient of an order for 80 airframes which was called off almost as soon as it was issued. It appears that difficulties in obtaining the R-2180-1 powerplant rendered it uneconomical for a short production run and 80 P-43A Lancers were built instead to keep the Farmingdale line open. The P-44-2 or company Model AP-4L, to which the US Army acquired design rights only, was intended for the 2,000-hp (1491.4-kW) Pratt & Whitney R-2800-7 Double Wasp, virtually identical to the R-2800-17 installed in the prototype

XP-47B Thunderbolt. Though metal was cut on neither P-44 variant, the design work contributed markedly to the P-47 which followed.

Specification
P-44-1

Type: single-seat fighter
Powerplant: (planned) one 1,400-hp (1044-kW) Pratt & Whitney R-2180-1 air-cooled radial piston engine driving a three-blade propeller
Performance: (estimated) maximum speed 386 mph

(621.2 km/h) at 15,000 ft (4572 m); initial climb rate 2,900 ft (883.9 m) per minute; service ceiling 26,000 ft (7925 m); range 800 miles (1287 km)
Weights: (estimated) empty 5,900 lb (2676.2 kg); maximum take-off 8,330 lb (3778.5 kg)
Dimensions: (planned) span 36 ft 0 in (10.97 m); length 28 ft 4 in (8.64 m); height 14 ft 0 in (4.27 m); wing area 224 sq ft (20.81 m²)
Armament: (planned) two cowl 0.3-in (7.62-mm) and two wing 0.5-in (12.7-mm) fixed forward-firing machine-guns, plus provision for a 400-lb (181.4-kg) bomb-load

Bell P-45

History and notes

The P-45 designation was briefly assigned to a variant of the Bell Airacobra, 80 of which (40-2971/3050) were ordered by the US Army on 10 August 1939. These would have had bulletproof windshields and, a ubiquitous lesson from early fighting in various conflicts on the eve of World War II, self-sealing fuel tanks. Before production had proceeded very far, these airframes were redesignated P-39C although the final 60 were actually completed as P-39Ds.

Specification
P-45

Type: single-seat fighter
Powerplant: one 1,150-hp (857.6-kW) Allison V-1710-35 liquid-cooled 12-cylinder Vee piston engine driving a three-blade propeller
Performance: maximum speed 379 mph (609.9 km/h) at 9,500 ft (2896 m); cruising speed 200 mph (321.9 km/h); initial climb rate about 2,600 ft (792 m) per minute; service ceiling 32,000 ft (9754 m); range 650 miles (1046 km)
Weights: empty 5,610 lb

(2544.7 kg); maximum take-off 7,180 lb (3256.8 kg)
Dimensions: span 34 ft 0 in (10.36 m); length 30 ft 2 in (9.19 m); height 11 ft 10 in (3.61 m); wing area 213 sq ft (19.79 m²)
Armament: one 37-mm T9 cannon and six 0.3-in (7.62-mm) fixed forward-firing machine-guns, plus provision for one 500-lb (227-kg) bomb

Curtiss P-46

History and notes

The XP-46 of 1939 was a late attempt by Curtiss to capitalize on lessons from early fighting in Europe and to develop a fighter powered by an inline engine which could succeed the P-40 Warhawk on production lines. The lack-lustre performance of the Curtiss XP-37 and XP-42 designs was yet to become fully apparent on 29 September 1939, when this most promising of the three Curtiss designs was ordered in prototype form. The US Army ordered one XP-46 (40-3053) and one XP-46A (40-3054), the latter without armament to expedite the testing programme. Both were powered by the 1,150-hp (857.6-kW) Allison V-1710-39 inline engine, which promised to be readily available if production materialized, being the powerplant for the P-40D already on factory lines. The XP-46A flew first on 15 February 1941 and both machines were being tested by the time of Pearl Harbor.

The XP-46 and XP-46A had moderately good performance except for their limited range of 325 miles (523 km). They were heavier and costlier than the P-40D, however, and seemed to lack 'stretching' potential for further development. The two airframes were markedly different from each other in detail, especially in cockpit layout, the XP-46 being viewed by pilots as cramped and uncomfortable, a 'sweatbox'. Clearly the two machines added knowledge, but a production order eluded them.

Specification
XP-46A

Type: single-seat fighter
Powerplant: one 1,150-hp (857.6-kW) Allison V-1710-39 liquid-cooled 12-cylinder Vee piston engine driving a three-bladed propeller
Performance: maximum speed 355 mph (571.3 km/h) at 12,200 ft (3719 m); initial climb rate about 3,000 ft (914 m) per minute; climb to 12,200 ft (3719 m) in 5 minutes; service ceiling 29,500 ft (8992 m); range 325 miles (523 km)

Weights: empty 5,625 lb (2551.5 kg); maximum take-off 7,322 lb (3321.3 kg)
Dimensions: span 34 ft 4 in (10.46 m); length 30 ft 2 in (9.19 m); height 13 ft 0 in (3.96 m); wing area 208 sq ft (19.32 m²)
Armament: none

Yet another abortive Curtiss fighter design, the XP-46 was considerably cleaned up compared with the P-40 it was intended to replace. However, as with many other types, its performance increase was marginal, resigning it to only two airframes being completed.

Bristol Beaufighter

History and notes

In the wake of the Munich Agreement of 1938, when UK Prime Minister Neville Chamberlain returned to the UK waving a 'piece of paper' (peace pact) that he believed had resolved the Czech-German crisis, promising "peace in our time", the British aircraft industry gained a short breathing space in which to do its utmost to strengthen the Royal Air Force. The need for a heavily-armed fighter, suitable for the long-range escort or night fighter roles, was a significant gap in its inventory. This requirement was placed high on the list of priorities and Roy Fedden and Leslie Firse of the Bristol Aircraft Company proposed a compromise design to fill this need.

The wings, tail unit and landing gear of the in-production Bristol Beaufort were to be united by a new fuselage and to be powered by two of the company's Hercules sleeve-valve radial engines in wing-mounted nacelles. The draft proposal, submitted to the Air Ministry in October 1938, was adopted with such alacrity that the first prototype was in the air just under nine months later, on 17 July 1939. Known to Bristol as the Type 156, but far better known as the Beaufighter, it proved sufficiently important to the RAF that the British production totalled 5,562 aircraft.

In view of the large number built there were several variants, and of these the Beaufighter Mk VIF was the only version to find short-term service with the US Army Air Force. This occurred in the Mediterranean theatre during 1942-3, at a period when the USAAF was desperately in need of night fighter aircraft. In an interservice arrangement between the RAF and USAAF, the 12th Air Force gained for its 1st Tactical Air Command sufficient Beaufighter Mk VIFs to equip four squadrons. These saw extensive service during the German withdrawal from North Africa, especially in providing night air cover during the army landings at Anzio and Salerno.

Specification
Beaufighter Mk VIF

Type: two-seat night/long-range fighter
Powerplant: two 1,670-hp (1245-kW) Bristol Hercules radial piston engines
Performance: maximum speed 333 mph (536 km/h) at 15,600 ft (4755 m); maximum cruising speed 276 mph (444 km/h) at 15,000 ft (4570 m); service ceiling 26,500 ft (8075 m); range, internal fuel 1,480 miles (2382 km)
Weights: empty 14,600 lb (6622 kg); maximum take-off 21,600 lb (9798 kg)
Dimensions: span 57 ft 10 in (17.63 m); length 41 ft 8 in (12.70 m); height 15 ft 10 in (4.83 m); wing area 503 sq ft (46.73 m²)

Bristol Beaufighter Mk VIF of the 416th Night Fighter Squadron, serving on Corsica in 1943-44.

The Bristol Beaufighter was the RAF's standard night fighter before Mosquitoes appeared in large numbers, and several were supplied to the USAAF under Reverse Lend-Lease agreements. These were Mk VIFs, equipped with airborne intercept radar in a lengthened nose.

Supermarine Spitfire

History and notes

One of those aircraft (such as the Douglas DC-3 and North American P-51 Mustang) which is so well known to aviation enthusiasts that it requires no description, the Supermarine Spitfire served in comparatively small numbers with the US Army Air Force during World War II. Its first use was by those gallant American pilots who decided to come to the aid of the 'little guy' being bullied by Hitler's Luftwaffe. They volunteered initially in numbers adequate for the Royal Air Force to establish in 1940 No. 71 'Eagle' Squadron at Church Fenton. Operational with Hawker Hurricanes in February 1941, this squadron was soon in the thick of battle and on 20 August of that year received its first Spitfire Mk IIAs. Subsequently Nos 121 and 133 'Eagle' squadrons were formed with American pilots. In September 1942 all three squadrons were transferred to the US 8th Air Force in the UK, as the 4th Pursuit Group's Nos 334th, 335th and 336th Squadrons respectively. Spitfire Mks IIA, VA and VB aircraft had been used by all three 'Eagle' squadrons, but No. 133 was the only one also to use the more advanced Spitfire Mk IX.

In addition to this use by American pilots in the RAF, many Spitfires saw service with the USAAF, acquired under a process known as 'Reverse Lend-Lease', and in numbers that appear to be most inaccurately recorded, varying between 350 and 600 according to source. Spitfire Mks VA/VBs served for a brief period with the 31st and 52nd Fighter Groups in the UK before embarking to take part in Operation 'Torch', the invasion of North Africa. Following this action these Groups continued to serve there until 1944, equipped with the tropicalised Spitfire Mk VC. The Spitfire Mk VA/VB were the types most extensively used by the 8th Air Force but with a shortage of photo-reconnaissance aircraft, 21 camera-equipped and unarmed Spitfire Mk XIs were supplied from 7 January 1944 to its 14th Photographic Squadron of the 7th Group. Soon after, adequate numbers of US-built aircraft became available, and surviving Spitfires of all units were returned to the RAF.

Spitfire Mk Vs were the first fighter equipment of the USAAF in Europe, bridging the gap before more potent US equipment could be delivered. This 307th FS, 31st FG aircraft was presented to the USAAF by a Peruvian citizen, hence the name 'Lima Challenger'.

Specification

Spitfire Mk VB

Type: single-seat fighter
Powerplant: one 1,470-hp (1096-kW) Rolls-Royce Merlin 45 Vee piston engine
Performance: maximum speed 369 mph (594 km/h) at 19,500 ft (5945 m); cruising speed 270 mph (435 km/h) at 5,000 ft (1525 m); initial climb rate 4,750 ft (1450 m) per minute; service ceiling 36,200 ft (11035 m); range 395 miles (636 km)
Weights: empty 5,050 lb (2291 kg); maximum take-off 6,650 lb (3016 kg)

Supermarine Spitfire Mk VB of the 334th Fighter Squadron in September 1942. This unit had previously been the famous No 71 (Eagle) Sqn of the RAF formed from US volunteers.

Dimensions: span 32 ft 2 in (9.8 m); length 29 ft 11 in (9.12 m); height 9 ft 11 in (3.02 m); wing area 231 sq ft (21.46 m²)
Armament: four 0.303-in (7.7-mm) machine-guns and two-in (20-mm) Hispano cannon

Supermarine Spitfire Mk VIII of the 308th Fighter Squadron, 31st Fighter Group serving in Italy in 1944.

Republic P-47 Thunderbolt

History and notes

The P-47 designation was originally assigned to a fighter never built, a lightweight craft designed by Republic's Alexander Kartveli around the 1,150-hp (857.6-kW) Allison V-1710-39 12-cylinder Vee inline engine and armed with but two 0.5-in (12.7-mm) machine-guns. Seen as the logical follow-up to the P-43 Lancer and P-44 Rocket, this lightweight design was abandoned after encompassing the P-47 and P-47A designations. Kartveli then turned to the huge 2,000-hp (1491.4-kW) Pratt & Whitney R-2800 Double Wasp 18-cylinder two-row radial with turbocharger, to design the largest and heaviest single-engine fighter at that time built. The XP-47B Thunderbolt (40-3051), first flown 6 May 1941 with Lowery Brabham at the controls, was also prototype for the most numerous American fighter ever manufactured, an impressive 15,683 airframes being constructed over the period 1941-5 by Republic at Farmingdale, New York, and Evansville, Indiana, and under licence by Curtiss at Buffalo, New York. The P-47 was also the most heavily-armed American fighter with its eight 0.5-in (12.7-mm) wing-mounted guns.

A misconception about the P-47 involves its unofficial nickname. It was called 'Jug' not because it was a juggernaut (though indeed it was) but because its cavernous fuselage resembled a moonshiner's whisky jug. C. Hart Miller, Republic's director for military contracts and a test pilot, thought up the official title Thunderbolt. The first production P-47B (41-5895) began flying about June 1941, the same month when the US Army Air Corps (USAAC) officially became the US Army Air Forces (USAAF). Orders soon followed for 171 production P-47B machines with flush canopies and an upper fuselage that peaked in a sharp spine, inspiring the term 'razorback'. The similar P-47C (602 built) retained the 'razorback' configuration, as did early P-47Ds, but had a 10.5-in (2.67-cm) fuselage extension to relocate the centre of gravity, as well as other minor changes.

Initially, only Thunderbolts built by Republic in Evansville were to be designated P-47D, but this was soon changed, those from Evansville being P-47D-RA and those from Farmingdale P-47D-RE. (Identical airframes built by Curtiss in Buffalo retained the distinct P-47G designation). No fewer than 12,065 P-47D models were built. By early 1943, the first P-47Ds had arrived with combat units in England. After crashes and delays occasioned by corrosion problems incurred during their trans-Atlantic journey in leaking protective cocoons, Thunderbolts were sent into battle, beginning one of the great sagas of American fighter aviation.

The sole XP-47E (41-6065) had been taken from the P-47B line and completed as an unarmed testbed for a pressurised cabin, evaluated at Wright Field in 1943-4, modified, and eventually fitted with a 2,300-hp (1715.1-kW) R-2800-59. The only XP-47F (41-5938), also from the P-47B model line, was a shortlived test ship with increased-span laminar-flow wing. The XP-47F crashed 14 October 1943, killing pilot Captain A. McAdams. At least two Curtiss-built P-47Gs were converted to two-seat trainers as the TP-47G. Another P-47G was evaluated at Wright Field with ski landing gear.

While Thunderbolts fought from Europe to New Guinea, pro-

This Evansville-built P-47D was one of the last 'razorback' aircraft. Assigned to the Pacific theatre, it flew with the 19th FS, 318th FG based on Saipan in the summer of 1944. The 'razorback' produced a 20° blind spot at the rear.

Below: There can be few greater expressions of brute power in aviation than the Thunderbolt. Unpopular at first, Kartveli's monster showed such performance and firepower that its brutish handling was quickly forgotten by ex-Spitfire pilots in Europe. These are early 'razorback' P-47s.

Republic P-47

Republic P-47D of the 352nd Fighter Squadron, 353rd FG at Raydon, England in July 1944. This unit pioneered the use of the P-47 in dive-bombing attacks.

grammes intended to improve the basic fighting airframe continued. Two XP-47H testbeds (42-23297/8) flew with the 2,500-hp (1864.3-kW) Chrysler XI-2220-11 inverted-Vee inline engine. They were the only Thunderbolts with liquid-cooled powerplants, although the programme was so long delayed that meaningful data were not available even by war's end. The XP-47J (43-46952) was a testbed for the R-2800-59 with an engine cooling fan system and other modifications which enabled it to reach the then phenomenal level-flight speed of 504 mph (811.1 km/h) at 34,300 ft (10485 m). Its improved power system was never used operationally. The out-of-sequence P-47K designation pertains to the first airframe (42-8702) evaluated with the bubble canopy used operationally from the P-47D-25 sub-variant onwards. The sole XP-47L (42-76614) also evaluated the bubble hood which was to fundamentally alter appearance and visibility in not just the Thunderbolt but the Hawker Typhoon (originator of the concept) and P-51 Mustang as well.

Faster and further

The P-47M Thunderbolt, of which only 133 were built and used in combat in Europe, was an interim improvement on the P-47D model, powered by the 2,100-hp (1566-kW) R-2800-57 series. The slightly improved performance of the P-47M caused it to be pressed into service in 1944 to counter the menace of the German V-1 'buzz bomb' which earlier Thunderbolts were unable to catch. P-47Ms were also pitted with success against Me 262 jet fighters.

The P-47N was a nearly new aircraft design with a longer-span wing of new configuration which for the first time carried fuel and which culminated in clipped wingtips. The P-47N was produced expressly for operations in the Pacific theatre where range was a principle concern, and the 'wet' wings permitted a fuel capacity of 1,266 US gal (4792.3 litres), extending range to no less than 2,350 miles (3782 km). A total of 1,667 P-47N airframes rolled off the Farmingdale line, while a further 149 came from Evansville. Features of the P-47N included the R-2800-77 engine, enlarged ailerons and square-tipped wings for rapid roll, and zero-length rocket-launchers.

The Republic P-47 Thunderbolt was instrumental in the Allied victory and served well past 1950 in Air National Guard (ANG) units, and the type was also used in post-war years by more nations than may ever be accurately counted. Bolivia, Brazil, Chile, China, Colombia, the Dominican Republic, Ecuador, France, Honduras, Iran, Italy, Mexico, Nicaragua, Peru, Turkey, the UK, Venezuela and Yugoslavia all belong on the roster. Numerous airworthy Thunderbolts survive today and are frequently seen at 'warbird' convocations in the USA and elsewhere.

Combat

When P-47C Thunderbolts joined the USAAF 4th Fighter Group at Debden, England, in January 1943, pilots accustomed to the Spitfire considered the 'Jug' overheavy, unresponsive and unmanoeuvrable. Radio chatter was drowned out by noise from the engine's ignition. "A discomforting transition," said Major Donald Blakeslee, who shot down a Focke-Wulf Fw 190 on 15 April 1943 in the first kill by a Thunderbolt. Early teething problems were overcome and the 56th Fighter Group at Halesworth, England, under Colonel Hubert Zemke soon proved that the Thunderbolt combined toughness with enormous firepower and gave a good account of itself. Leadership, an aggressive fighting spirit, and plain tenacity produced American aces in Europe, but never easily. As Colonel Roderick MacDowall of the 78th Fighter Group put it:

"The Germans had the advantage of fighting over home ground.

Though our machine-guns worked at long range, their cannons did too. The odds were evened by us having the P-47 with superior performance above 20,000 feet [6096 m] and incredible dive acceleration which enabled us to catch up with any German who used the standard technique of breaking off an engagement by going into a half-roll and diving."

Once Luftwaffe pilots learned that diving to escape a P-47 was tantamount to suicide, they developed a corkscrew climb manoeuvre to break an engagement, unaware that Curtiss paddle-blade propellers enhanced the Thunderbolt's climb rate, leaving Bf 109s and Fw 190s highly vulnerable. Lieutenant Colonel Francis S. Gabreski with 28 air-to-air kills and Major Robert S. Johnson with 27, the top-scoring US aces in Europe, both flew P-47s. From D-Day to VE-Day in Europe, the P-47 Thunderbolt proved its air-to-ground prowess by accounting for 86,000 railway wagons, 9,000 locomotives, 6,000 tanks and armoured vehicles, and 68,000 trucks. According to one figure, Thunderbolts in air combat shot down no fewer than 3,916 enemy aircraft.

In the Pacific, white-tailed 'razorback' P-47Ds of the 348th Fighter Group under Lieutenant Colonel Neel Kearby matched the best the Japanese had. On 11 October 1943 near Wewak, Kearby, at the controls of a P-47D-2-RA (42-8145) nicknamed 'Firey Ginger', Lieutenant Kearby shot down six Japanese fighters in a gruelling engagement at the limits of fuel and endurance, proving the Thunderbolt's staying power and stability as a gun platform and he won the Medal of Honor. With 22 kills, Kearby was top ace in the Pacific when shot down and killed five months later. P-47C and P-47D fighters fought throughout the Pacific, and the advanced P-47N was hurled against Japan toward war's end, operating with units like the 318th Fighter Group at Ie Shima. On a few instances, P-47Ns escorted B-29 bombers over Japan.

Not everything about the Thunderbolt was perfect. Its take-off run was unduly long. It was never really certain to turn inside the agile Fw 190 at any altitude. The cockpit design, however, was exceedingly comfortable, 'like being in a lounge chair,' says Major M. P. Curphey who transitioned from the P-38 Lightning to the P-47D with the 357th Fighter Group in Europe. Curphey flew a P-47D-25-RE (42-27401) nicknamed 'Alice Yardum', and scored four air-to-air kills.

The contribution of the P-47 to the Allied effort in Europe cannot be overestimated. Heavily-armed and fast in level flight, dive and climb, the P-47 was superb in ground attack and a tricky air-to-air opponent. These aircraft are of the 82nd FS, 78th FG at Duxford, England.

Republic P-47

Republic P-47D of the 366th FS, 358th FG at Toul in France during the winter of 1944.

"With its stability and heavy armament, the P-47D would get you out of a scrape as long as you didn't let the other guy lure you into a close-quarters manoeuvring contest. I saw an Fw 190 sucker a guy into a turning match when the guy should have simply broken away and re-engaged – something you could often do with a fuel advantage over the other fellow, even when he was close to home. This guy got killed by that Fw 190 because he forgot that the Thunderbolt, although manoeuvrable, wasn't at its best in a dogfight."

P-47 Thunderbolts served with no fewer than 42 American fighter groups in combat zones. In the Royal Air Force, they served with Nos 5, 30, 34, 42, 60, 79, 81, 113, 121, 131, 134, 135, 146, 258, 261 and 615 Squadrons. One Brazilian fighter group, the 1 Grupo de Caca, operated P-47Ds in Europe. A sole Mexican fighter group, the 201 Escuadron, flew P-47Ds against Japan. Seven Free French groups flew the P-47D. Lead-Lease Thunderbolts also fought in small numbers for the Soviet Union.

Specification

P-47D

Type: single-seat fighter

Powerplant: one 2,535-hp (1890.3-kW) Pratt & Whitney R-2800-59W Double Wasp air-cooled 18-cylinder radial piston engine driving a four-blade propeller

Performance: maximum speed (clean) 433 mph (696.8 km/h); initial climb rate 3,200 ft (975 m) per minute; service ceiling 41,000 ft (12497 m); range with three drop tanks 1,900 miles (3060 km)

Weights: empty 9,950 lb (4513.3 kg); maximum take-off 17,500 lb (7938.0 kg)

Dimensions: span 40 ft 9½ in (12.43 m); length 36 ft 1¾in (11.02 m); height 14 ft 8 in (4.47 m); wing area 300 sq ft (27.87 m²)

Armament: eight 0.5-in (12.7-mm) fixed forward-firing machine-guns, plus provision for a maximum external load of 2,500 lb (1134 kg) including bombs, napalm or eight rockets

Thunderbolts also served with distinction in the Mediterranean and Pacific theatres, proving again their prowess in ground attack and air-to-air fighting. Difficult to taxi on account of its long nose, ground crew were often employed in directing pilots.

Republic P-47D-10 Thunderbolt cutaway drawing key

1 Rudder upper hinge
2 Aerial attachment
3 Fin flanged ribs
4 Rudder post/fin aft spar
5 Fin front spar
6 Rudder trim tab worm and screw actuating mechanism (chain driven)
7 Rudder centre hinge
8 Rudder trim tab
9 Rudder structure
10 Tail navigation light
11 Elevator fixed tab
12 Elevator trim tab
13 Starboard elevator structure
14 Elevator outboard hinge
15 Elevator torque tube
16 Elevator trim tab worm and screw actuating mechanism
17 Chain drive
18 Starboard tailplane
19 Tail jacking point
20 Rudder control cables
21 Elevator control rod and linkage
22 Fin spar/fuselage attachment points
23 Port elevator
24 Aerial
25 Port tailplane structure (two spars and flanged ribs)
26 Tailwheel retraction worm gear

27 Tailwheel anti-shimmy damper
28 Tailwheel oleo
29 Tailwheel doors
30 Retractable and steerable tailwheel
31 Tailwheel fork
32 Tailwheel mount and pivot
33 Rudder cables
34 Rudder and elevator trim control cables
35 Lifting tube
36 Elevator rod linkage
37 Semi-monocoque all-metal fuselage construction
38 Fuselage dorsal 'razorback' profile

39 Aerial lead-in
40 Fuselage stringers
41 Supercharger air filter
42 Supercharger
43 Turbine casing
44 Turbosupercharger compartment air vent

45 Turbosupercharger exhaust hood fairing (stainless steel)
46 Outlet louvres
47 Intercooler exhaust doors (port and starboard)
48 Exhaust pipes
49 Cooling air ducts
50 Intercooler unit (cooling and supercharged air)
51 Radio transmitter and receiver packs (Detrola)
52 Canopy track
53 Elevator rod linkage
54 Aerial mast
55 Formation light

56 Rearward-vision frame cut-out and glazing
57 Oxygen bottles
58 Supercharged and cooling air pipe (supercharger to carburettor) port
59 Elevator linkage
60 Supercharged and cooling air pipe (supercharger to carburettor) starboard
61 Central duct (to intercooler unit)
62 Wingroot air louvres
63 Wingroot fillet
64 Auxiliary fuel tank (100 US gal/379 litres)
65 Auxiliary fuel filler point

PILOT PRESS COPYRIGHT DRAWING

66 Rudder cable turnbuckle
67 Cockpit floor support
68 Seat adjustment lever
69 Pilot's seat
70 Canopy emergency release (port and starboard)
71 Trim tab controls
72 Back and head armour
73 Headrest
74 Rearward-sliding canopy
75 Rear-view mirror fairing
76 'Vee' windshields with central pillar
77 Internal bulletproof glass screen
78 Gunsight
79 Engine control quadrant (cockpit port wall)
80 Control column
81 Rudder pedals
82 Oxygen regulator

Fastest of the regular Thunderbolts was the 'hot-rod' P-47M, developed hastily to meet the threat of V-1 flying bombs. This aircraft served with the 63rd FS, 56th FG, with its own special brand of colour scheme introduced for the P-47M.

83 Underfloor elevator control quadrant
84 Rudder cable linkage
85 Wing rear spar/fuselage attachment (tapered bolts/bushings)
86 Wing supporting lower bulkhead section
87 Main fuel tank (205 US gal/776 litres)
88 Fuselage forward structure
89 Stainless steel/Alclad firewall bulkhead
90 Cowl flap valve
91 Main fuel filler point
92 Anti-freeze fluid tank
93 Hydraulic reservoir
94 Aileron control rod
95 Aileron trim tab control cables
96 Aileron hinge access panels
97 Aileron and tab control linkage

98 Aileron trim tab (port wing only)
99 Frise-type aileron
100 Wing rear (No. 2) spar
101 Port navigation light
102 Pitot head
103 Wing front (No. 1) spar
104 Wing stressed skin
105 Four-gun ammunition troughs (individual bays)
106 Staggered gun barrels
107 Removable panel
108 Inter-spar gun bay access panel
109 Forward gunsight bead
110 Oil feed pipes
111 Oil tank (28.6 US gal/108 litres)
112 Hydraulic pressure line
113 Engine upper bearers
114 Engine control correlating cam
115 Eclipse pump (anti-icing)
116 Fuel level transmitter
117 Generator
118 Battery junction box
119 Storage battery
120 Exhaust collector ring
121 Cowl flap actuating cylinder

122 Exhaust outlets to collector ring
123 Cowl flaps
124 Supercharged and cooling air ducts to carburettor (port and starboard)
125 Exhaust upper outlets
126 Cowling frame
127 Pratt & Whitney R-2800-59 18-cylinder twin-row engine
128 Cowling nose panel
129 Magnetos
130 Propeller governor
131 Propeller hub
132 Reduction gear casing
133 Spinner
134 Propeller cuffs
135 Four-blade Curtiss constant-speed electric propeller
136 Oil cooler intakes (port and starboard)
137 Supercharger intercooler (central) air intake
138 Ducting
139 Oil cooler feed pipes
140 Starboard oil cooler
141 Engine lower bearers
142 Oil cooler exhaust variable shutter
143 Fixed deflector
144 Excess exhaust gas gate

145 Belly stores/weapons shackles
146 Metal auxiliary drop tank (75 US gal/284 litres)
147 Inboard mainwheel well door
148 Mainwheel well door actuating cylinder
149 Camera gun port
150 Cabin air-conditioning intake (starboard wing only)
151 Wingroot fairing
152 Wing front spar/fuselage attachment (tapered bolts/bushings)
153 Wing inboard rib mainwheel well recess
154 Wing front (No. 1) spar
155 Undercarriage pivot point
156 Hydraulic retraction cylinder
157 Auxiliary (undercarriage mounting) wing spar
158 Gun bay warm air flexible duct
159 Wing rear (No. 2) spar
160 Landing flap inboard hinge
161 Auxiliary (No. 3) wing spar inboard section (flap mounting)
162 NACA slotted trailing-edge landing flaps

163 Landing flap centre hinge
164 Landing flap hydraulic cylinder
165 Four 0.5-in (12.7-mm) Browning machine guns
166 Inter-spar gun bay inboard rib
167 Ammunition feed chutes
168 Individual ammunition troughs
169 Underwing stores/weapons pylon
170 Landing flap outboard hinge
171 Flap door
172 Landing flap profile
173 Aileron fixed tab (starboard wing only)
174 Frise-type aileron structure
175 Aileron hinge/steel forging spar attachments
176 Auxiliary (No. 3) wing spar outboard section (aileron mounting)
177 Multi-cellular wing construction
178 Wing outboard ribs
179 Wingtip structure
180 Starboard navigation light

181 Leading-edge rib sections
182 Bomb shackles
183 500-lb (227-kg) M43 demolition bomb
184 Undercarriage leg fairing (overlapping upper section)
185 Mainwheel fairing (lower section)
186 Wheel fork
187 Starboard mainwheel
188 Brake lines
189 Landing gear air-oil shock strut
190 Machine gun barrel blast tubes
191 Staggered gun barrels
192 Rocket-launcher slide bar
193 Centre strap
194 Front mount (attached below front spar between inboard pair of guns)
195 Deflector arms
196 Triple-tube 4.5-in (11.5-cm) rocket-launcher (Type M10)
197 Front retaining band
198 4.5-in (11.5-cm) M8 rocket projectile

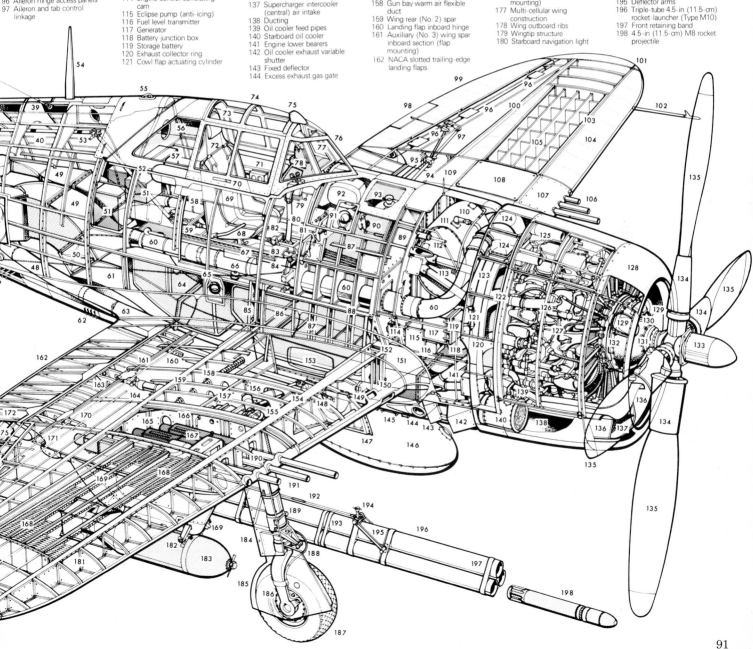

RABBIT

Fighter-bomber par excellence, the P-47D could carry large bombs or rockets under the wing for ground attack duties, with a centreline fuel tank to extend its range. This particular aircraft flew with the 527th Fighter Squadron (today the USAF Europe 'Aggressor' unit) of the 86th Fighter Group. This was one of the leading units in the Mediterranean theatre, having fought its way through North Africa, Sicily and Italy. During 1944 it received the Thunderbolt, and was used not only for hounding German forces in Italy from its main base at Pisa, but also for escorting B-24 bombers on long range missions as far as Berlin itself.

War in Europe

With the nation embroiled in war, the aviation industry produced a string of unsuccessful fighter prototypes. However, one aircraft from this period was to stand head and shoulders above the rest: the P-51 Mustang.

With Europe seen as the principal theatre of operations, it came as no surprise when the USAAF sent the majority of its aircraft to England to begin combat operations against the Luftwaffe. However, the build-up of forces took some considerable time, and it was not until 25 June 1942 that the first combat sortie was flown. Earlier 13 B-24s had flown from Egypt to bomb the oil complex at Ploesti on 11 June, these being the first US bombs to fall on Europe.

On the other side of the globe, the American Volunteer Group had been established under Brigadier-General Claire L. Chennault. This famous band of men soon racked up impressive tallies against the Japanese in China, flying various early P-40 models. They paved the way for a major US fighter effort in the China-Burma-India theatre which would last until the end of the war. North Africa was another theatre in which US fighters were to be employed. Of lesser importance to the overall strategy, these were mostly Curtiss P-40s, although the P-47 and P-38 would later take prominence as the Luftwaffe was driven back into Italy.

Back in Europe, the bomber build-up continued. Initially this consisted of A-20 mediums, with the first of the B-17 heavies arriving in July. Fighters were left at home, personnel transferring to RAF-supplied Spitfires to form the initial escort component of the 8th Air Force. Certainly these Spitfires were better than the P-39s and P-40s then in service with USAAF units, and they provided adequate cover until more potent equipment arrived from the US. During early bombing missions, most fighter cover came from the experienced squadrons of the RAF itself, these raids

Right: The arrival of the P-47 Thunderbolt in Europe heralded the start of air superiority for the US forces. Although lacking the range to escort bombers throughout their entire mission, P-47s kept them clear of trouble for most of the transit.

Below: Oft-maligned due to its inferior altitude performance, the early Allison-engined Mustangs were in fact superb low-level fighters. Right from the start the P-51 proved a winner, and it was quickly issued to fighter units in the front line. These aircraft are seen in India, destined for China.

being largely confined to short-range coastal attacks until the USAAF's confidence increased.

Thunderbolt in service

As the USAAF entered 1943, it was still without adequate fighter cover; the first P-47s were not used operationally until 4 May. Designed as an interceptor, the mighty Thunderbolt was impressed into service as an escort. It performed well, covering the bomber forces for much of their transit but unable to cover the longer missions during the final attack. By the end of July, P-47s

When the USAAF arrived in Europe, such was the state of US fighters that it relied heavily on the Spitfire until sufficient P-47s could be delivered. Many US volunteers had previously flown the type with the RAF's 'Eagle' squadrons and were well-versed in European operations.

were carrying drop tanks, this important innovation allowing the fighters to range further.

Despite the considerable successes of the P-47s, and the veritable wall of defensive fire thrown up by the bomber formations, there were appalling losses. Tactical mistakes led to occasions where bombers were left unprotected, and the Luftwaffe took full advantage: Schweinfurt is still an emotive word among ex-aircrew of the USAAF.

By the end of October losses were huge, and the need for escort fighters that could cover the entire raid was painfully obvious.

Mass operations over Europe were largely suspended pending a solution to the problem. This was partially offset by the arrival in-theatre of the P-38 in October 1943. This could at least cover the long-range missions, but did not have much fuel for combat over the target, and was generally inferior in close dogfighting to the Bf 109 and Fw 190.

A solution was at hand in the shape of the North American P-51 Mustang. The story of how the Mustang came to be built to a British order for P-40s from Curtiss' subcontractor is well known, and at last the success of the type silenced the critics who had

cast doubt over US industry supplying Europe with fighters during the early period of the war. Blessed with superb performance, the Mustang could outfly any aircraft extant and, with its highly-advanced and efficient wing, could carry out very long-range escort missions.

First deliveries to Europe went to the tactical 9th Air Force, but these machines were soon employed escorting heavies to Germany. With the debut of the P-51, the USAAF experienced a considerable turn of fortune, which would last for most of the remainder of the conflict.

Douglas P-48

History and notes

The XP-48 tells a familiar story: that aeroplanes which never flew often intrigue the imagination as much as those which did. The Douglas Aircraft Company in Santa Monica, California, with legendary designers like Edward Heineman and Jack Northrop undertook engineering efforts which produced some of the finest warplanes of a global conflict still ahead, but fighter aviation was not the company's forte.

The XP-48, its designation skewed out of time sequence, properly belongs to the pre-war period when air racers excited the hopes of Army planners. It would have been a misfit in the wartime struggle when armour, ordnance and fuel needs produced successful fighters having nothing in common with the slim, trim speedsters of the 1930s' National Air Races. 'What if?' is an appropriate epitaph for the short-lived XP-48, or company Model 312.

The XP-48 was conceived in 1939 as an ultra-lightweight, high-altitude pursuit ship to have been powered by a 525-hp (391.5-kW) Ranger SGV-770 inline engine. A small, sleek, low-wing tricycle-gear craft, it was to have reached 525 mph (844.9 km/h), a speed never attained in the real world even by later, more advanced, combat machines. The XP-48 looked like, and would have been, a fast aeroplane with little pragmatic application. And even then, the prediction for top speed must have been wildly optimistic. The XP-48 would not have possessed the range or load-carrying capability for any mission other than, perhaps, local point-defense of an airbase. US Army air chief General H. 'Hap' Arnold is rumoured to have felt that the concept was 'frivolous' when other priorities beckoned. In 1940, the Army cancelled the proposal before a serial number was assigned or metal cut.

Specification
XP-48

Type: single-seat fighter
Powerplant: (planned) one 525-hp (391.5-kW) Ranger SGV-770 air-cooled 12-cylinder inverted-Vee piston engine
Performance: (estimated) maximum speed 525 mph (844.9 km/h); other performance characteristics never determined
Weights: (estimated) empty 2,675 lb (1213.4 kg); maximum take-off 3,400 lb (1542.2 kg)
Dimensions: span 32 ft 0 in (9.75 m); length 21 ft 9 in (6.63 m); height 9 ft 0 in (2.74 m); wing area 92 sq ft (8.55 m²)
Armament: (planned) one 0.3-in (7.62-mm) and one 0.5-in (12.7-mm) fixed forward-firing machine-guns

Lockheed P-49

History and notes

The Lockheed XP-49, its designation seemingly out of sequence in that it was a conception of pre-war years, was designed in 1939 with the ambitious goal of attaining 473 mph (761.2 km/h) in level flight at 15,000 ft (4572 m). The XP-49 would have been a veritable flying arsenal in its day as it was to be armed with two 20-mm cannon and four 0.5-in (12.7-mm) machine-guns. It was rigorously and exhaustively tested at Burbank, California, and Wright Field, Ohio, and the XP-49 was denied production status because of an engine substitution and the appearance of the Thunderbolt and Mustang.

The XP-49 was an outgrowth of the P-38 Lightning but in most respects was an entirely new design by the Lockheed-Burbank fighter team

Bearing a close resemblance to the P-38, the P-49 was a high-performance warplane with good fighting qualities. The requirement for this long-range aircraft never materialised as the P-51D proved a superior escort fighter when fitted with drop tanks.

under H. L. Hibbard and Clarence (Kelly) Johnson. Ordered by the US Army on 3 August 1939 to meet a twin-engine fighter requirement (which also produced the Grumman XP-50) the sole XP-49 (40-3055) was expected to attain unprecedented performance by mating the Lightning's familiar twin-boom layout with two 2,300-hp (1715.1-kW) Pratt & Whitney X-1800 24-cylinder inline engines.

When plans to develop the powerplant proved too ambitious, twin 1,350-hp (1006.7-kW) Continental XIV-1430-1 engines had to be substituted, reducing speed to a still-impressive 458 mph (737.1 km/h), although this was reached because the test ship lacked the added weight of protective armour which would have been fitted on a production variant. "We still felt we had a winner," says a Lockheed engineer. "We had a roomy, pressurised cabin, good handling characteristics and, eventually, good manoeuvrability." US Army planners saw the XP-49 as a possible 'convoy fighter' able to escort bombers on deep penetration raids. It might have been accorded higher priority had England been lost as a base from which to mount the air assault on the Third Reich.

The XP-49 first flew 11 November 1942 at Burbank, apparently with Milo Burcham at the controls. When it became necessary to increase the vertical fin area to improve yaw characteristics, the result was an unusual set of markings: Army directives called for 13 alternating red and white horizontal stripes on the rudder, symbolic of the original 13 American colonies. When the tail was heightened, painters simply added non-regulation extra stripes.

At Burbank, the XP-49 survived a crash-landing caused by hydraulic failure, was repaired, and was ferried to Wright Field, Ohio, on 25 June 1943. Though it was a clear improvement over the P-38, able to "fly rings around the Lightning" in the words of one pilot, minor but troublesome fuel leakage problems led to XP-49 tests being discontinued and the airframe being scrapped, just when Mustangs with long-range drop tanks were appearing over Berlin. The 'convoy fighter' concept was studied later with the Lockheed XP-58 but never produced an operational aircraft.

Specification
XP-49

Type: single-seat fighter
Powerplant: two 1,350-hp (1006.7-kW) Continental XIV-1430-1 liquid-cooled 12-cylinder inverted-Vee piston engines driving three-blade outward rotating propellers
Performance: maximum speed 458 mph (737.1 km/h) at 20,000 ft (6096 m); initial climb rate 3,300 ft (1006 m) per minute; service ceiling 40,000 ft (12192 m); range 800 miles (1287 km)
Weights: empty 15,475 lb (7019.5 kg); maximum take-off 18,750 lb (8505.0 kg)
Dimensions: span 52 ft 0 in (15.85 m); length 40 ft 1 in (12.22 m); height 9 ft 9½ in (2.98 m); wing area 327.5 sq ft (30.42 m²)
Armament: two 20-mm cannon and four 0.5-in (12.7-mm) fixed forward-firing nose machine-guns planned but not installed

Grumman P-50

History and notes

The Grumman XP-50 was a one-off landplane fighter from the Grumman Aircraft Engineering Corporation of Bethpage, Long Island, better known for its generations of US Navy carrier-based aircraft. The XP-50 was an offshoot of the unsuccessful US Navy XF5F-1 Skyrocket shipboard fighter of 1938. Ordered on 3 August 1939 together with the Lockheed XP-49, the XP-50 was an unattractive, low-wing, tricycle-gear twin-radial fighter. The sole example (39-2517, widely reported in error as serial 40-3057) was powered by two supercharged 1,200-hp (894.8-kW) Wright R-1820-67/69 9-cylinder radials with outward-rotating Curtiss constant-speed propellers. It was first flown 18 February 1941 (not 14 May as usually reported) by company test pilot Robert Hall.

The XP-50 was far from a success, and illustrates the folly of building only one prototype of an experimental fighter. Even worse, in its brief life the XP-50 seems to have generated more historical inaccuracies than any other fighter type. One report says that the airframe was eventually written off after suffering serious damage. Most published reports indicate that the XP-50 crashed and was lost on its maiden flight. Neither is true. In March 1941, the XP-50's right gear collapsed during a skid on an icy runway, but the fighter was repaired and was flying again by May. It was on 14 May that the aircraft was lost, but only after accumulating more than 20 hours of flying time. The right engine turbo-compressor exploded and damaged the hydraulic system, preventing retraction of the

Grumman was committed almost totally to Navy fighter production during the war, but did find time to produce the XP-50 version of the Navy's XF5F-1. This is the XF5F during its unsuccessful flight test programme.

main landing gear or lowering of the nose wheel. Pilot Bob Hall bailed out successfully and the XP-50 plunged into Smithtown Bay of Long Island Sound. It remains at the bottom of the Sound today, only the turbine compressor wheel having been recovered.

All of Grumman's facilities were earmarked for production of US Navy carrier fighters and a USAAF contemplated order of 36 production P-50s would have required building a new factory. The US Army liked the twin-engine fighter concept and manufacture by another firm was considered, but nothing was done about it. Though the XP-50 had given excellent performance, superior to competitors of its time, the project had to be abandoned. Grumman would return to the US Army with another twin-engine design, the XP-65, but because of the premature loss of the only airframe, the XP-50 never achieved the potential it seemed to promise.

Specification
XP-50
Type: single-seat fighter
Powerplant: two 1,200-hp (894.8-kW) Wright R-1820-67/69 air-cooled 9-cylinder radial piston engines driving three-blade Curtiss constant-speed propellers
Performance: maximum speed 360 mph (579.3 km/h) at 20,000 ft (6096 m); initial climb rate 3,000 ft (914 m) per minute; service ceiling 35,000 ft (10668 m); range 490 miles (789 km)
Weights: empty 8,307 lb (3768.1 kg); maximum take-off 10,558 lb (4789.1 kg)
Dimensions: span 42 ft 0 in (12.80 m); length 38 ft 11 in (11.86 m); height 11 ft 5½ in (3.49 m); wing area 303.5 sq ft (28.20 m²)
Armament: two 0.5-in (12.7-mm) machine-guns and two 20-mm cannon in fixed forward-firing nose position planned but not installed

North American P-51 Mustang

History and notes

The P-51 Mustang, arguably the greatest American fighter of all time and among the greatest from any nation, was not requested by the US Army. It began as the company NA-73X (civil registry NX 19998), designed and assembled with remarkable haste in the mid-1940s by a company, North American Aviation of Los Angeles, that had never before made a fighter. North American, established in 1934 and presided over by J. H. 'Dutch' Kindelberger, was contacted by the British Purchasing Commission in 1940 as a potential new supplier of the Curtiss P-40. Company designers Raymond Rice and Edgar Schmued, the latter a veteran of service with Messerschmitt and Fokker, wanted instead to create a new fighter powered by the 1,150-hp (857.6-kW) Allison V-1710-39 inline engine used in the P-40. The coolant section for the powerplant would be located behind and below the pilot, a configuration tried on the prototype P-40 but not on subsequent production machines, and tried again on the Curtiss XP-46. The designers' decision turned out to be half right since a later engine change would be needed to assure the Mustang's greatness. The British agreed on the proviso that the NA-73 fighter be completed within 120 days. Kindelberger's fighter team actually conceived, designed and constructed the prototype in 102 days and had to wait three weeks longer for Allison to deliver an engine. Test pilot Vance Breese took the unpainted, unmarked NA-73X aloft on its maiden flight on 26 October 1940.

It is unbelievable to think that the P-51 was largely overlooked by US planners during its early life, being built entirely to RAF orders. Nevertheless, the two XP-51s supplied to the USAAF quickly established it as a world-beater.

The P-51A as built for the USAAF featured only four 0.50-in machine guns. This example was flown by Colonel Philip Cochran, commanding officer of the 1st Air Commando, Burma 1944.

North American P-51

The first US variant was simply designated P-51. Built for the RAF as the Mustang Mk IA with four 20-mm cannon, several were repossessed for the USAAF. This one served with the 154th FS in Tunisia and Sicily in 1943.

On 29 May 1940, the UK ordered 320 of the yet-unflown NA-73 fighters under an arrangement which called for two examples to be given to the USAAF without cost as the XP-51. Much, much later, USAAF chief of staff General H. H. 'Hap' Arnold would acknowledge that it had been an extraordinary error not to have entered the fighter into American squadron service immediately. The first production RAF Mustang Mk I (AG345) flew within a year of the prototype and the second (AG346) was first to arrive in the United Kingdom, in November 1941. Though the two XP-51s (41-38/39) were soon flying in US markings, American planners preoccupied with the Lightning and Thunderbolt paid not nearly enough attention to the new design – although, in fact, rather more than has been generally suggested.

Major improvements

The Mustang was a low-wing single-seater, a sleek, all-metal, stressed-skin fighter not unlike the Messerschmitt Bf 109 but much larger and considerably more advanced. It was one of the first fighters to employ a laminar-flow wing which had its maximum thickness well aft and resulted in greatly reduced drag. It differed from nearly all fighters of its time in having square-cut tips to both wing and tail surfaces. The liquid-cooled engine with the radiator far back under the rear fuselage, as noted, further reduced drag. The big fighter reached 382 mph (614.8 km/h), a speed not then possible even for the smaller, sleeker Spitfire which carried half as much fuel.

The RAF Mustang Mk I flew its first combat mission on 27 July 1942 and, three weeks later, flew close support for the Dieppe landings. Despite the fighter's superb potential, the limitations of its Allison engine relegated the RAF's 620 Mustang Mk I and Mk 1As to ground-attack and reconnaissance duties. Meanwhile, still moving with undue caution, the USAAF ordered 150 P-51s armed with four 20-mm wing cannon; 310 P-51As were then ordered, with 1,200-hp (894.8-kW) V-1710-81 engine, four wing 0.5-in (12.7-mm) machine-guns and underwing racks for two 500-lb (227-kg) bombs or two 150-US gal (567.8-litre) drop tanks.

In England, the dramatic step which would assure the Mustang's place in history occurred when Rolls-Royce proposed installing the Merlin engine in this excellent airframe. Thought was given to locating the engine behind the cockpit in the manner of the Bell P-39 Airacobra, but a more conventional layout was decided upon. Four RAF Mustangs (AL963, AL975, AM203 and AM208) were equipped with Merlins and four-blade propellers and performed so well, exceeding 400 mph (643.7 km/h), that North American began plans for

P-51 variants powered by the 1,520-hp (1133.5-kW) licence-built Merlin 61, the Packard V-1650-3.

The USAAF ordered 500 Allison-powered A-36 aircraft, identical to the P-51A but for dive brakes which overstressed the airframe and had to be wired inoperative. The A-36A was never really wanted for the attack role but was used as a device to keep production going while the merits of the basic design were still being argued. To confuse things further, the A-36A was known initially as the Apache and later as the Invader until the Mustang name stuck. The aeroplanes were moderately successful in Sicily and southern Italy, and claimed their share of Luftwaffe victims in air-to-air combat despite the 'attack' appellation.

Some P-51s were converted for the photo-reconnaissance role as F-6As. Finally, a Merlin-powered variant, the XP-51B, took to the air on 30 November 1942 with Bob Chilton at the controls. The US Army had ordered 2,200 P-51Bs before that maiden flight. A bit more cantankerous than earlier Mustangs, reliable but not as easy to fly, the P-51B retained a flush pattern framed canopy as did the P-51C, armed with six 0.5-in (12.7-mm) guns. Most Mustangs were to come from North American's Inglewood, California, facility but the P-51C, reflecting wartime expansion of the aircraft industry, was produced at the firm's Dallas, Texas, plant.

England to Berlin

The P-51D variant first ordered in 1943 introduced the bubble canopy and a dorsal fin to correct stability problems. In later P-51Ds, an 85-US gal (321.8-litre) fuel cell was added behind the pilot's seat, bringing total fuel capacity to the point where the P-51D could range all the way from England to Berlin, as it did by March 1944 with Lieutenant Colonel Donald L. Blakeslee's 4th Fighter Group. The long-range fighters weaving above massed formations of B-17 and B-24 bombers greatly complicated the Third Reich's air defence burden and, once drop tanks were discarded, could fight on equal or better terms with anything belonging to the Luftwaffe. By 1944, early P-51Bs were operating in Burma, and later machines would range against the Japanese homeland from Ie Shima and Iwo Jima. But it was in Europe where the type excelled. First Lieutenant Urban L. Drew of the 361st Fighter Group illustrated this by shooting down two Messerschmitt Me 262 jet fighters.

Following F-6B and F-6C variants of flush-canopy Mustangs, good results were obtained with the bubble-canopy F-6D tactical reconnaissance craft, 136 of which were converted from P-51D standard at Dallas with hatches for oblique and vertical cameras in the rear fuselage and additional radio (including D/F) gear. Though

The P-51A returned to machine-gun armament, employing four of the universal 0.5-in (12.7-mm) weapons. The early Mustangs exhibited classic lines, the engine installation being a masterpiece of streamlining. This is the second P-51A off the Inglewood production lines.

North American P-51

P-51B Mustang of the 355th Fighter Squadron, 354th Fighter Group, 9th Air Force. The unit was based in England in late 1943.

the earlier Malcolm hood which improved visibility on the Mustang Mk II and Mk III was also employed by the USAAF, the bubble canopy became the accepted feature and a few so-equipped P-51Ds operated in British service as the Mustang Mk IV. One hundred P-51D airframes were assembled in Australia by Commonwealth, and 226 more were manufactured there. Ten USAAF machines were converted to two-seat trainers as the TP-51D.

Minimising weight

The P-51E designation was not used. Three XP-51F airframes (43-43332/43334) came from Inglewood as the first lightweight Mustang, with the V-1650-7 Merlin but with major internal redesign which lowered maximum take-off weight to 9,060 lb (4109.6 kg) and introduced new wing and landing-gear features. One of these (FR409) reached the RAF as the Mustang Mk V. Two further lightweight Mustang test ships, designated XP-51G (43-43335/43336) were powered by the 1,500-hp (1118.6-kW) Rolls Royce Merlin 145 with an unusual Rotol five-blade propeller. The XP-51G grossed a mere 8,765 lb (3975.8 kg) and reached a top speed of 468 mph (753.2 km/h) in level flight. One (FR410) was flown by the RAF. These efforts to lower the Mustang's weight culminated in the taller-tailed production P-51H, 555 of which were built. The P-51H had a shorter bubble canopy, a four-blade Aeroproducts propeller, and an increase in overall length to 33 ft 4 in (10.16 m). One (KN987) was evaluated in the UK. The P-51H did get into combat in World War II, a few flying missions from the Philippines before VJ-Day.

Two experimental XP-51Js (44-76027/76028) were similar to the lightweight XP-51F but for the 1,500-hp (1118.6-kW) Allison V-1710-119. The P-51K was the Dallas-built production equivalent of Inglewood's P-51D, differing only in having an Aeroprop propeller, and 1,500 were delivered during the war years, 163 performing the reconnaissance role as the F-6K. The P-51L was a production

machine cancelled at the war's end and the sole P-51M (45-11743) was another lightweight variant powered by a 1,400-hp (1044-kW) V-1650-9A.

The P-51 was essential to wartime victory. About 40 USAAF fighter groups and 31 RAF squadrons operated the type. The P-51 was also among the most widely-used of post-war fighters. As aviation writer Bill Gunston points out, it would be easier to list those nations which never operated the Mustang than those which did. The P-51D fought in Israel's war for independence and in China on both sides, an example being on display today in a Beijing museum. The Korean War of 1950-3 brought the type back into combat in US markings, Mustangs serving the USAF and Air National Guard to the end of the 1950s. Hundreds of flyable examples remain in the world today. The first USAAF machine, XP-51 41-38, was prudently saved for the US Air Force Museum at Dayton, Ohio.

Fitting the Merlin engine to the Mustang produced the best all-round fighter of the war, and it came to be the aircraft most feared by the Luftwaffe. With drop tanks the P-51B could easily reach Berlin with enough fuel for 20 minutes' combat.

Left: The P-51D was the most numerous and best-known of the Mustang variants, differing primarily from the preceding aircraft by having a cut-down rear fuselage and 'teardrop' canopy. This provided a considerable improvement in all-round view. In all 6,502 P-51Ds were built at Inglewood and 1,454 at Dallas.

'Shangri-La' was one of the best-known Mustangs, being the P-51B flown by Captain Don S. Gentile. Flying with the 336th FS, 4th FG from Debden in England, Gentile scored 16½ of his 21.8 confirmed kills with this aircraft between February and April 1944.

North American P-51

Combat

Geoffrey Page, a celebrated Royal Air Force fighter pilot who flew most types during 1940-3, recalls a friend being jumped by two Bf 109s over the English Channel while flying the Allison-powered, flush-canopy Mustang Mk I.

"He was near the end of a mission and the Germans must have expected that he was down to absolute fuel minimums. That, coupled with the advantages of altitude and surprise, must have made them overconfident. He had petrol remaining and he whipped that Mustang around in the tightest snap-turn I've ever seen. It took him 30 seconds to hose down one Messerschmitt and chase the other off."

Page remains loyal to the Hurricane but found the Mustang, even in its early form, a solid fighter. Its fuel-carrying potential was not always a blessing, however.

"Getting a fully-loaded Mustang off the ground on a long-range mission was one bear of a job," says former First Lieutenant David Jones of the USAAF 4th Fighter Group. The P-51D loaded with maximum fuel, including drop tanks, tipped the scales at 11,600 lb (5261.8 kg) and "could scarcely be handled until you'd burned a initial amount of that fuel away," says Jones. The high risk of take-off on a maximum escort mission to Berlin is dramatised in a key crash scene in Len Deighton's novel *Goodbye Mickey Mouse*. Jones and Deighton, members of Mustang International, a private group devoted to P-51 history and preservation today, agree that, however beautiful, the aircraft was difficult to get going and suffered from serious lateral stability problems. "The pilot had to be constantly alert to the need for opposite rudder to prevent a skid or sideslip which could throw the P-51 into a spin." A dorsal fin corrected this tendency but reduced manoeuvrability in combat. "But when you'd pickled off the drop tanks," says Jones, "you were on equal terms with the other guy. The Mustang could manoeuvre with and outgun even the latest models of the Focke-Wulf Fw 190. With a teardrop-shaped canopy, you had super visibility and could spot the other guy first." Lieutenant Urban Drew, air ace and killer of Messerschmitt Me 262 jets, flew both the P-51D and the later P-47N. Drew says that he greatly preferred the P-51D and wished that more had been available in the Pacific, where he flew after his European successes.

Best armament

Colonel Hubert A. (Hub) Zemke, the only man to command P-38, P-47 and P-51 fighter groups in Europe, considered the P-51D the best air-to-air fighter of the three below 25,000 ft (7620 m) and found its armament adequate, although he preferred the Thunderbolt for its ruggedness, its eight 0.5-in (12.7-mm) guns (compared with six on the P-51D) and its better performance at higher altitude. Captain Henry Lawrence of the all-black 332nd Fighter Group had only the P-39 to compare with the P-51D and considered the Mustang "as fine a flying machine as men could make, most of the bugs worked out of it by late in the war." On 24 March 1945, escorting bombers to Berlin, Lawrence joined the ranks of pilots who have shot down Me 262 jet fighters.

A lengthening of the fuselage and (in most aircraft) a heightening of the fin distinguished the last major production variant of the Mustang, the P-51H. It was a lightened version stemming from the P-51F and G prototypes, and it saw small-scale use in World War II in the Far East.

North American P-51 Mustang cutaway key

1. Plastic (Phenol fibre) rudder trim tab
2. Rudder frame (fabric covered)
3. Rudder balance
4. Fin front spar
5. Fin structure
6. Access panel
7. Rudder trim-tab actuating drum
8. Rudder trim-tab control link
9. Rear navigation light
10. Rudder metal bottom section
11. Elevator plywood trim tab
12. Starboard elevator frame
13. Elevator balance weight
14. Starboard tailplane structure
15. Reinforced bracket (rear steering stresses)
16. Rudder operating horn forging
17. Elevator operating horns
18. Tab control turnbuckles
19. Fin front spar/fuselage attachment
20. Port elevator tab
21. Fabric-covered elevator
22. Starboard balance weight
23. Port tailplane
24. Tab control drum
25. Fin root fairing
26. Elevator cables
27. Tab control access panels
28. Tailwheel steering mechanism
29. Tailwheel
30. Tailwheel leg assembly
31. Forward-retracting steerable tailwheel
32. Tailwheel doors
33. Lifting tube
34. Fuselage aft bulkhead/break point
35. Fuselage break point
36. Control cable pulley brackets
37. Fuselage frames
38. Oxygen bottles
39. Cooling-air exit flap actuating mechanism
40. Rudder cables
41. Fuselage lower longeron
42. Rear tunnel
43. Cooling-air exit flap
44. Coolant radiator assembly
45. Radio and equipment shelf
46. Power supply pack
47. Fuselage upper longeron
48. Radio bay aft bulkhead (plywood)
49. Fuselage stringers
50. SCR-695 radio transmitter-receiver (on upper sliding shelf)
51. Whip aerial
52. Junction box
53. Cockpit aft glazing
54. Canopy track
55. SCR-552 radio transmitter-receiver
56. Battery installation
57. Radiator/supercharger coolant pipes
58. Radiator forward air duct
59. Coolant header tank/radiator pipe
60. Coolant radiator ventral access cover
61. Oil-cooler air inlet door
62. Oil radiator
63. Oil pipes
64. Flap control linkage
65. Wing rear spar/fuselage attachment bracket
66. Crash pylon structure
67. Aileron control linkage
68. Hydraulic hand pump
69. Radio control boxes
70. Pilot's seat
71. Seat suspension frame
72. Pilot's head/back armour
73. Rearward-sliding clear-vision canopy
74. External rear-view mirror
75. Ring and bead gunsight
76. Bullet-proof windshield
77. Gyro gunsight
78. Engine controls
79. Signal-pistol discharge tube
80. Circuit-breaker panel
81. Oxygen regulator
82. Pilot's footrest and seat mounting bracket
83. Control linkage
84. Rudder pedal
85. Tailwheel lock control
86. Wing centre-section
87. Hydraulic reservoir
88. Port wing fuel tank filler point
89. Port Browning 0.5-in guns
90. Ammunition feed chutes
91. Gun-bay access door (raised)
92. Ammunition box troughs
93. Aileron control cables
94. Flap lower skin (Alclad)
95. Aileron profile (internal aerodynamic balance diaphragm)
96. Aileron control drum and mounting bracket
97. Aileron trim-tab control drum
98. Aileron plastic (Phenol fibre trim tab)
99. Port aileron assembly
100. Wing skinning
101. Outer section sub-assembly
102. Port navigation light
103. Port wingtip
104. Leading-edge skin
105. Landing lamp
106. Weapons/stores pylon
107. 500 lb (227 kg) bomb
108. Gun ports
109. Gun barrels
110. Detachable cowling panels
111. Firewall/integral armour
112. Oil tank
113. Oil pipes
114. Upper longeron/engine mount attachment
115. Oil-tank metal retaining straps
116. Carburettor
117. Engine bearer assembly
118. Cowling panel frames
119. Engine aftercooler
120. Engine leads
121. 1,520 hp Packard V-1650 (R-R Merlin) twelve-cylinder liquid-cooled engine
122. External fairing panel
123. Stub exhausts
124. Magneto
125. Coolant pipes
126. Cowling forward frame
127. Coolant header tank
128. Armour plate
129. Propeller hub
130. Spinner
131. Hamilton Standard Hydromatic propeller
132. Carburettor air intake, integral with (133)
133. Engine-mount front-frame assembly
134. Intake trunk
135. Engine-mount reinforcing tie
136. Hand-crank starter
137. Carburettor trunk vibration-absorbing connection
138. Wing centre-section front bulkhead
139. Wing centre-section end rib
140. Starboard mainwheel well
141. Wing front spar/fuselage attachment bracket
142. Ventral air intake (radiator and oil cooler)
143. Starboard wing fuel tank
144. Fuel filler point
145. Mainwheel leg mount/pivot
146. Mainwheel leg rib cut-outs
147. Main gear fairing doors
148. Auxiliary fuel tank (plastic/pressed-paper composition 90 gal/409 litres)
149. Auxiliary fuel tank (metal 62.5 gal/284 litres)
150. 27-in smooth-contour mainwheel
151. Axle fork
152. Towing lugs
153. Landing-gear fairing
154. Main-gear shock strut
155. Blast tubes

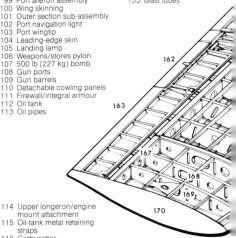

North American P-51

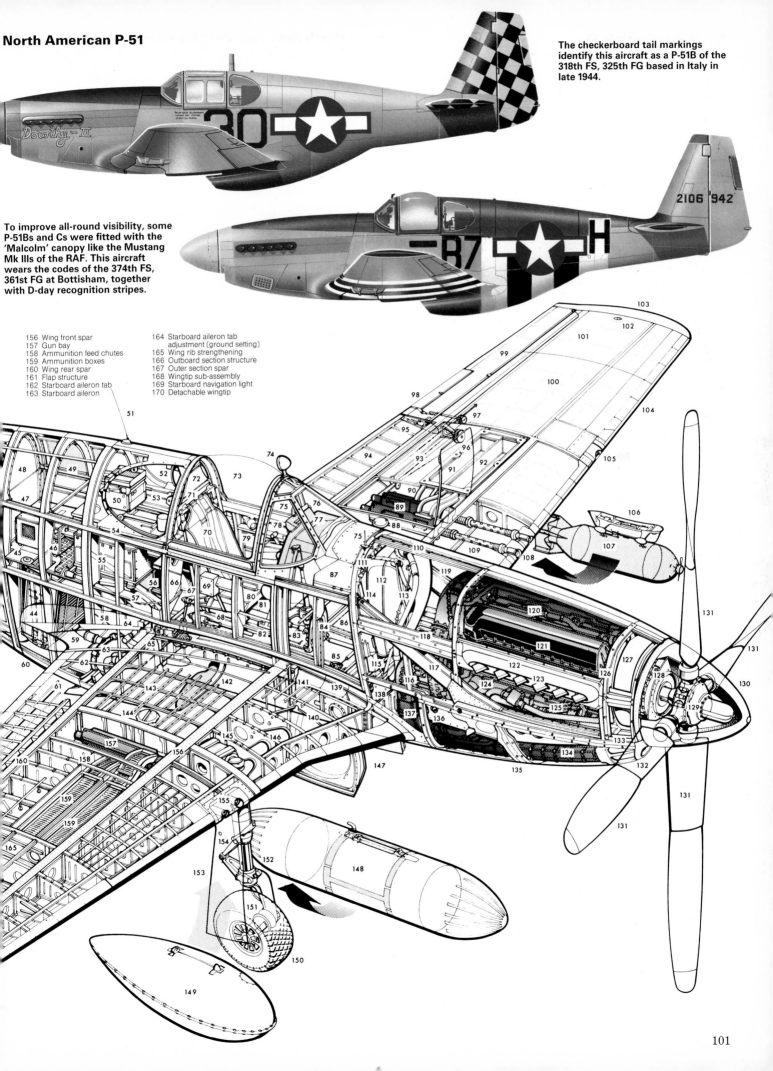

The checkerboard tail markings identify this aircraft as a P-51B of the 318th FS, 325th FG based in Italy in late 1944.

To improve all-round visibility, some P-51Bs and Cs were fitted with the 'Malcolm' canopy like the Mustang Mk IIIs of the RAF. This aircraft wears the codes of the 374th FS, 361st FG at Bottisham, together with D-day recognition stripes.

156 Wing front spar
157 Gun bay
158 Ammunition feed chutes
159 Ammunition boxes
160 Wing rear spar
161 Flap structure
162 Starboard aileron tab
163 Starboard aileron
164 Starboard aileron tab adjustment (ground setting)
165 Wing rib strengthening
166 Outboard section structure
167 Outer section spar
168 Wingtip sub-assembly
169 Starboard navigation light
170 Detachable wingtip

North American P-51

Typical of the many P-51Ds that fought in Europe during the last year of the war is this Mustang of the 375th Fighter Squadron, 361st Fighter Group, based at Little Walden in England. The Group later moved to France and Belgium, based at St. Dizier and Chievres before returning to England at the end of hostilities. The aircraft carries the 62.5 gallon underwing tanks that gave it enough range to support bombers across most of Germany and has the underwing racks that enabled the Mustang to carry rocket projectiles for use in the ground attack role. The six wing guns were standard on this variant.

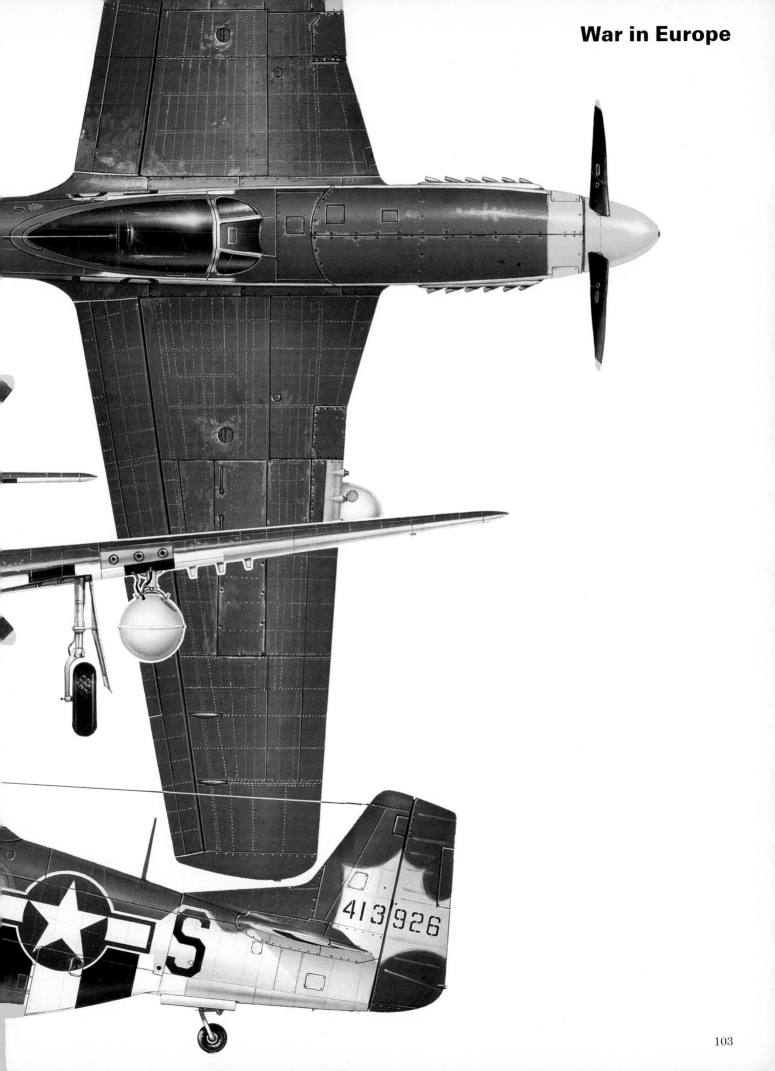

A flight of 375th FS, 361st FG aircraft over England display three different Mustang variants. First and third in the formation are early production P-51Ds lacking the dorsal fin, second is a full-production P-51D with the fin, and behind is a P-51B with the original cockpit and raised back. From its first mission on 21 January 1944 to its last on 20 April 1945, the Group claimed 226 enemy aircraft destroyed in the air and 105 on the ground for the loss of 81 P-47s and P-51s.

By the time of the Korean war the Mustang had been redesignated the F-51. The D-variant went to war in a big way, employed on both fighter and ground attack duties. The type scored 12 confirmed air-to-air victories during the conflict, and destroyed 7 aircraft on the ground.

Though the lightweight P-51H did see limited combat in the Pacific, contrary to most published reports, the best Japanese fighters were no longer available as competitors by late 1945. Postwar tests showed the P-51H faster and more manoeuvrable than the Mitsubishi A6M5 Zero in all performance regimes. The P-51H had been relegated to second-line duties by 1950, however, and it was the more popular P-51D which went to war in Korea. The Mustang's 0.5-in (12.7-mm) guns and 5-in (127-mm) high-velocity aircraft rockets (HVAR) were of marginal effectiveness against North Korean T-34 tanks, but in the air with remarkable ease P-51Ds cleared the skies of North Korean Yakovlev fighters. Major Dean Hess, who instructed Republic of Korea Air Force (ROKAF) pilots in the P-51D, said that "the Mustang was remarkably easy for an inexperienced pilot to learn how to fly."

On 7 November 1950, Captain Howard Tanner of the 36th Fighter-Bomber Squadron at Kimpo AB, Korea, was flying a 'sweep' near the Yalu River when three MiG-15 jet fighters tore into his formation of F-51D Mustangs (as the P-51D had been redesignated on 1 June 1948). A fourth MiG locked onto Tanner and began firing from too far out. Tanner was able to turn inside the MiG, pull lead, and

striking the newer, faster jet. Surprised by the Americans' aggressiveness, the MiGs pulled away, but then re-engaged. Tanner and his wingmen scored further hits on MiGs without themselves sustaining damage, although they could not confirm any certain kills. This was early evidence of the coming Chinese entry into the Korean War, a conflict to be waged by another North American product, the F-86 Sabre.

Specification

P-51D

Type: single-seat fighter
Powerplant: one 1,590-hp (1185.7-kW) Packard V-1650-7 Merlin liquid-cooled 12-cylinder Vee piston engine driving a four-blade Hamilton Standard propeller
Performance: maximum speed (clean) 448 mph (721.0 km/h); initial climb rate 3,475 ft (1059 m) per minute; operating radius with maximum fuel 1,300 miles (2092 km)
Weights: empty 7,125 lb (3231.9 kg); maximum take-off 11,600 lb (5261.8 kg)
Dimensions: span 37 ft 0½ in (11.29 m); length 32 ft 3 in (9.83 m); height 13 ft 8 in (4.17 m); wing area 235 sq ft (21.83 m²)
Armament: six 0.5-in (12.7-mm) fixed forward-firing machine-guns, plus provision for two 500-lb (227-kg) bombs, eight rockets or other under-wing ordnance in place of drop tanks

Bell P-52

History and notes
The first pusher design with a USAAF fighter designation, the Bell XP-52 was first in a series of creations by men who worked in secret, experimenting and innovating, to produce unusual warplanes in heavily-guarded design shops as American planners struggled to catch up with Axis advances. Never built, unlike other pusher fighters which took to the air under top security from remote Californian deserts (Vultee XP-54, Curtiss XP-55 and Northrop XP-56), the XP-52 would have been a heavily-armed twin-boom pusher with various combat applications. Its 1,200-hp (894.8-kW) Continental XIV-1430-5 powerplant, driving

contra-rotating Curtiss propellers, would have been mounted behind the cockpit with engine-cooling air taken from an opening in the nose and fed around the pilot's enclosure. In the point-defence interceptor role, the XP-52 would have reached 20,000 ft (6096 m) in just over six minutes.

The development of such unorthodox fighter designs enjoyed high priority in 1941, when the XP-52 was ordered, and the design was cancelled only because Bell was also working on a more powerful prop-pusher, the XP-59 (a totally different design from the P-59 Airacomet jet fighter). Lawrence Bell's fighter team at Buffalo, New York, had several original proposals in the

works and, in the end, others showed greater promise than the XP-52. It is intriguing to form a mental picture of this twin-boomed speedster, of which no engineering drawings appear to have survived. Barring some new 'find' by historians, however, the XP-52 is likely to remain among the lesser-known of fighters that 'might have been'.

Specification
XP-52
Type: single-seat fighter
Powerplant: (planned) one 1,200-hp (894.8-kW) Continental XIV-1430-5 12-cylinder double-bank inverted-Vee liquid-cooled piston engine driving a Hamilton

Standard contra-rotating propeller unit
Performance: (estimated) maximum speed 435 mph (700.0 km/h); climb to 20,000 ft (6096 m) in 6.3 minutes; service ceiling 40,000 ft (12193 m); range 960 miles (1545 km)
Weights: (estimated) empty 6,480 lb (2939.3 kg); maximum take-off 8,200 lb (3719.5 kg)
Dimensions: (planned) span 35 ft 0 in (10.67 m); length 34 ft 0 in (10.36 m); height 9 ft 3 in (2.82 m); wing area 233 sq ft (71 m²)
Armament: (planned) two 20-mm cannon and six 0.5-in (12.7-mm) machine-guns in a fixed forward-firing installation

Curtiss P-53

History and notes

The Curtiss XP-53 would have been virtually identical to the company's experimental XP-46 but for an engine change to the 1,200-hp (894.8-kW) Continental XIV-1430 inline engine, the same powerplant chosen for the pusher Bell XP-52. The XP-53 reflected continuing efforts by the Curtiss team to remain competitive and to develop a replacement for the P-40. Two prototypes were ordered in 1940, and some reports indicate that one airframe was virtually completed but was cannibalised for other projects before it could fly. On balance, it seems more accurate to class the XP-53 as 14th among the pursuit/fighter designs in the USAAF series which were never built, along with P-11, P-14, P-18, P-19, P-27, P-28, P-32, P-33, P-34, P-44, P-45, P-48 and P-52. No photograph of a mock-up or partially or fully completed airframe exists.

It was the choice of a relatively un-successful engine, at the wrong time, which doomed the XP-53. In December 1940, apparently based on recommendations by Major Thomas Hitchcock, US Army attaché in London, the US Army informed manufacturers that it was looking for a major fighter type powered by a licence-built Rolls-Royce Merlin. This was the decision which resulted in the Merlin-powered Mustang (and one variant of the later Curtiss XP-60), but it was also the death knell for the XP-53 project which had been cancelled by mid-1941.

Specification
XP-53

Type: single-seat fighter
Powerplant: (planned) one 1,200-hp (894.8-kW) Continental XIV-1430-3 12-cylinder double-bank inverted-Vee liquid-cooled piston engine driving a four-blade propeller
Performance: (estimated) maximum speed 430 mph (692.0 km/h) at 15,000 ft (4572 m); other performance characteristics never determined
Weights: (estimated) empty 7,650 lb (3470.0 kg); maximum take-off 10,603 lb (4809.5 kg)
Dimensions: (planned) span 41 ft 5 in (12.62 m); length 35 ft 3 in (10.74 m); height 12 ft 1 in (3.78 m); wing area 275 sq ft (25.55 m²)
Armament: (planned) eight 0.5-in (12.7-mm) fixed forward-firing machine-guns

Vultee P-54

History and notes

The Vultee XP-54 or company Model 84, apart from being a twin-boom pusher, stood out for its sheer size, which made it by far the largest USAAF single-engine fighter of its time. The result of later thinking than the Bell XP-52 of similar layout, the twin-boom, single-seat, tricycle-gear XP-54 was ordered in late 1941 together with the closely-related Curtiss XP-55 and Northrop XP-56. It was conceived for the 1,850-hp (1379.5-kW) Pratt & Whitney X-1800-A4G engine with contra-rotating propellers, and early can-cellation of the powerplant reduced the type's performance and production prospects from the start. At the very time when the smaller but similarly-configured Swedish Saab J21 was taking shape, destined for widespread operational use, the XP-54 was prevented by an engine change from reaching its planned top speed of 510 mph (820.7 km/h) and would not see squadron service.

Two prototypes (41-1210/1211) were built with minor structural dif-ferences, the first flown 15 January 1943 with the alternate 2,300-hp (1715.1-kW) Lycoming XH-2470, the first product by this manufacturer to power a USAAF fighter. The plan to install contra-rotating propellers was dropped.

Armed with two 37-mm cannon and two 0.5-in (12.7-mm) machine-guns, the XP-54 was equipped with a nose section that could be tilted upward to 'lob' its low-velocity cannon shells at their target, while its machine-guns remained in depressed position. Another novel feature was a powered lift which raised the pilot into his cockpit 8 ft (2.44 m) off the ground. In an emer-gency bail-out, the pilot's seat slid downward, a hinged panel protect-ing him from being hurled back into the pusher propeller. It is unclear whether protection from the forward airstream was adequate, but the arrangement was prophetic: it

The Vultee P-54 showed considerable potential, mainly on account of its high speed and awesome firepower. The nose section could be tilted to offset the drop of the low-velocity 37-mm cannon shells, but this feature did not function adequately.

Nicknamed the 'Swoose Goose', the P-54 was a large aircraft but extremely slender. Sitting high off the ground, the pilot was winched into the cockpit from below.

would not appear again until the US Navy Douglas F-10 (F3D) Skyknight fighter of the 1950s.

The camouflaged first XP-54 (41-1210) made 86 flights before being ferried to Wright Field, Ohio, on 28 October 1943 where only limited further tests took place. The natural-metal second XP-54 (41-1211) flew only once on a test hop from the manufacturer's plant at Downey, California, to nearby Nor-ton Field. Though the XP-54 showed awesome potential, the programme was discontinued after the tilting nose-gun section, dismantled from the airframe, was evaluated at Eglin Field, Florida. By late 1943, the time of innovation with propeller-driven fighters was nearing a close.

A further development of the XP-54 design, the XP-68 Tornado, was cancelled before construction could begin.

Specification
XP-54

Type: single-seat fighter
Powerplant: one 2,300-hp (1715.1-kW) Lycoming XH-2470-1 24-cylinder liquid-cooled H-type piston engine driving a pusher four-blade propeller
Performance: maximum speed 403 mph (648.5 km/h) at 12,000 ft (3658 m); initial climb rate 2,300 ft (701 m) per minute; climb to 26,000 ft (7925 m) in 17.3 minutes; service ceiling 37,000 ft (11278 m); range 500 miles (805 km)
Weights: empty 15,262 lb (6922.8 kg); maximum take-off 19,335 lb (8770.4 kg)
Dimensions: span 53 ft 10 in (16.41 m); length 54 ft 9 in (16.69 m); height 13 ft 0 in (3.96 m); wing area 456 sq ft (42.36 m²)
Armament: two 37-mm cannon and two 0.5-in (12.7-mm) machine-guns in a forward-firing installation

Curtiss P-55

History and notes

The Curtiss XP-55 Ascender is perhaps best known of the three pusher fighters built for a 1941 competition in response to US Army 'Request for Data R40-C' dated 20 February 1940 (the others being the Vultee XP-54 and Northrop XP-56). A flying wing in most respects, albeit with a small fuselage and a canard foreplane (with only the horizontal portion of this surface forward of the wing), the XP-55 went through numerous design changes at Curtiss's St Louis, Missouri, plant and, like its competitors, was long-delayed getting into the air although it eventually carried out a test programme which involved four airframes.

Curtiss built a full-scale flying testbed, the company Model CW-24B, powered by an 850-hp (633.8-kW) Menasco C65-5 engine. The fabric-covered CW-24B went to a new US Army test site, the ultra-secret airfield at Muroc Dry Lake, California, for 1942 tests. These revealed serious stability problems which were only partly resolved by moving its vertical fins farther out from their initial mid-way position on the swept-back wing.

The full-sized XP-55 fighter was ordered in fiscal year 1942, based on the proven 1,475-hp (1099.9-kW) Allison V-1710-F23R engine being used for the first time as a pusher. The XP-55 used a single rotation, three-bladed propeller instead of the co-axial, contra-rotating type which had been planned and which was, in fact, employed with the parallel Northrop XP-56.

The first of three XP-55 aircraft (42-78845/78847) was delivered on 13 July 1943 and underwent early flights at Scott Field, Illinois. It was found that excessive speed was required in the take-off run before the nose-mounted elevator could become effective. Before this problem could be addressed, the first machine was lost during spin tests at St Louis on 15 November 1943, the pilot parachuting to safety.

The novel XP-55 Ascender featured swept-back wings and a small foreplane, but was never to achieve the desired stability for a production fighter. The performance on the Allison V-1710 engine was not remarkable and the intended four machine-gun armament was considered too light.

The second XP-55 was flown in St Louis on 9 January 1944. The third followed on 25 April 1944 and, soon after, went to Eglin Field, Florida, for tests of its nose-mounted 0.5-in (12.7-mm) machine-guns. The XP-55 had the advantage of being constructed largely from non-strategic materials and for a time a jet version, the company Model CW-24C, was contemplated. But lingering problems, including generally poor stability, remained unsolved when the third XP-55 was returned to Wright Field, Ohio, for further tests continuing into 1945.

On 27 May 1945, at a Wright Field air show and bond rally attracting a crowd of more than 100,000, the third XP-55 took off to give a public flying display. Captain William C. Glascow flew across the field leading five other fighters in formation. Glascow made one roll before the crowd, began another, and suddenly dived into the ground inverted. The pilot was thrown from the wreckage but suffered mortal injuries, while a nearby motorist was also killed.

Few aircraft contributed more to advancing technology while remaining trouble-plagued and failing to reach production. The second XP-55 has survived and is among numerous historically valuable airframes held by the Smithsonian Institue's National Air and Space Museum in Washington D.C.

Specification
XP-55

Type: single-seat fighter
Powerplant: one 1,475-hp (1099.9-kW) Allison V-1710-F23R liquid-cooled 12-cylinder Vee piston engine driving a three-blade pusher propeller
Performance: maximum speed 390 mph (627.6 km/h) at 19,300 ft (5883 m); climb to 20,000 ft (6096 m) in 7.1 minutes; service ceiling 34,600 ft (10546 m); range 490 miles (789 km)
Weights: empty 6,354 lb (2882.2 kg); maximum take-off 7,330 lb (3324.2 kg)
Dimensions: span 44 ft 6 in (13.56 m); length 29 ft 7 in (9.02 m); height 10 ft 0 in (3.05 m); wing area 235 sq ft (21.83 m²)
Armament: four 0.5-in (12.7-mm) nose-mounted fixed forward-firing machine-guns

Northrop P-56

History and notes

The Northrop XP-56, informally called Black Bullet, was third of the pusher fighters conceived in 1940 (together with the Vultee XP-54 and Curtiss XP-55). First flown on 6 September 1943 in secrecy at Muroc Dry Lake, California, with John Myers as pilot, the XP-56 was the only one of the three designs to actually employ contra-rotating propellers. It was also the first true flying wing tested by the US Army and the first of many flying wing designs to come from Northrop's facility at Hawthorne, California.

The US Army ordered two XP-56 airframes (41-786 and 42-38353) and, after initially considering other powerplants, had them built with

One of Northrop's many flying-wing designs, the P-56 'Black Bullet' sported a contra-rotating propeller to alleviate torque problems. Handling was adequate, but the long-span wings and novel arrangement made it unmanoeuvrable and unsuitable as a fighter.

Northrop P-56

the 2,000-hp (1491.4-kW) Pratt & Whitney R-2800-9 air-cooled radial. The aircraft flew well despite its revolutionary configuration, but proved unable to manoeuvre effectively in a dogfight situation. The unpressurised cockpit was positioned immediately ahead of the engine and posed interesting problems to any pilot thinking of bailing out with two three-blade Curtiss Electric contra-rotating airscrews behind him.

After the all-silver first XP-56 was wrecked in a mishap which injured Myers, the camouflaged second ship flew on 23 March 1944 at Hawthorne with Harry Crosby at the controls. This machine had a greatly enlarged dorsal vertical stabiliser (not actually a rudder, since steering was done from blown-air jets at the wingtips) to improve yaw tendencies. The machine proved underpowered and, because it was nose-heavy, difficult to handle during the take-off roll. Though it typifies an era of adventure and secrecy in the parched expanses of the Californian desert involving undaunted test pilots with the 'right stuff', and ending the predominance of Wright Field, Ohio, as the USAAF's test centre, the XP-56 was always a test ship, one which contributed knowledge but would never have reached squadron service. The second machine is held by

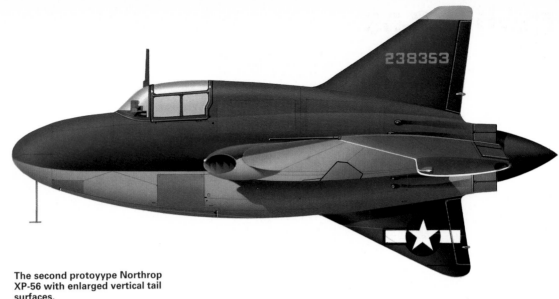

the National Air and Space Museum, and a group of aviation enthusiasts are working to restore it.

Specification
XP-56

Type: single-seat fighter
Powerplant: one 2,000-hp (1491.4-kW) Pratt & Whitney R-2800-9 air-cooled 18-cylinder radial piston engine driving two three-blade Curtiss Electric contra-

The second protoyype Northrop XP-56 with enlarged vertical tail surfaces.

rotating propellers
Performance: maximum speed 465 mph (748.3 km/h) at 25,000 ft (7620 m); climb to 20,000 ft (6096 m) in 7.2 min; service ceiling 33,800 ft (10302 m); range 660 miles (1062 km)
Weights: empty 8,700 lb (3946.3 kg); maximum take-off 12,143 lb (5508.1 kg)
Dimensions: span 43 ft 7 in (13.28 m); length 27 ft 7 in (8.41 m);

height 11 ft 0 in (3.35 m); wing area 307 sq ft (28.52 m²)
Armament: two 20-mm cannon and four 0.5-in (12.7-mm) machine-guns planned but not installed

To cure some longitudinal stability problems, the second XP-56 had a large fin added. Actual steering was provided by jets powered by the engine, the exhausts for which are clearly visible on the wingtips.

Tucker P-57

History and notes

The XP-57, unbuilt and the only fighter design ever submitted by Tucker Aviation Company of Detroit (a short-lived builder of luxury automobiles), owes its origin to USAAF efforts in 1940 to get away from radical aircraft and develop a simple machine. The XP-57 was intended to be highly manoeuvrable and lightweight. It was to have made extensive use of wood in its construction, in addition to metal, to exploit the ready availability of non-strategic materials. Proposed to

General H. H. 'Hap' Arnold in May 1940, the XP-57 was almost immediately doomed by its builder's financial difficulties.

A remarkably small craft with a fuselage of aluminium-covered steel tubing and plywood wings, the XP-57 was to be powered by the 720-hp (536.9-kW) Miller L-510-1 in-line engine, the only USAAF powerplant from a firm which lasted little longer than Tucker. In the manner of the Bell P-39 Airacobra, the engine would have been driven via an extension shaft to pass between

the pilot's legs. The design was cancelled at an early stage and it is believed that no comprehensive drawings were produced.

Specification
XP-57

Type: single-seat fighter
Powerplant: (planned) one 720-hp (536.9-kW) Miller L-510-1 8-cylinder inline engine driving a two-blade propeller
Performance: (estimated) maximum speed 308 mph (495.7 km/h) at sea level; climb to

18,000 ft (5486 m) in 11.0 minutes; service ceiling 20,000 ft (6096 m); range 960 miles (1545 km)
Weights: (estimated) empty 1,920 lb (870.9 kg); maximum take-off 3,000 lb (1360.8 kg)
Dimensions: (planned) span 28 ft 5 in (8.66 m); length 26 ft 7 in (8.10 m); height about 8 ft 0 in (2.44 m); wing area 120 sq ft (11.15 m²)
Armament: (planned) one 20-mm cannon and one 0.5-in (12.7-mm) machine-gun in a fixed forward-firing installation

Wartime Developments

With war around the world at fever pitch, American industry responds with its full might to produce thousands of aircraft to fight and eventually win the raging battles.

Few decades saw as much advance in engineering as the 1940s, these developments spurred of course by the massive war effort conducted by participant nations. In the field of fighter aviation, no nation could rival the United States for the rapidity and enormity of its development. When it entered the decade, the US forces were woefully ill-equipped in terms of numbers, and the aircraft they did possess were decidedly obsolete. By the war's end they were the best-equipped nation in the world, and they were already well-advanced on the road to an all-jet tactical air force.

If ever there were a watershed in this upturn of fortune, it was the moment the North American P-51 Mustang first entered service. Finally here was an aircraft that was the best in the world, and above all it was American (one must allow most patriotic Americans to forget that it was the British Merlin engine that turned it from a very good low-level fighter into a superlative all-round warplane). From the moment it entered service in Europe it was the machine to have, sweeping all before it in a display of power, endurance and agility.

Naturally the talents of the Mustang were required by many commanders, but initial deliveries were split between the 'strategic'

8th Air Force and the 'tactical' 9th, both in England. The need for these fighters was paramount, for the forces massing in Britain were preparing for 'Overlord', the invasion of Normandy. When the landings eventually took place in June 1944, the air war erupted into a furious battle that spread out across northern Europe. With a similar spreading of operational areas in the Pacific theatre, the need for greater numbers of fighters grew daily.

Combining with the technological developments achieved in the United States, the Army Air Force was also to benefit greatly from the swiftness with which the giant US industrial machine was turned from commercial to military matters. Within a short time the factories were turning out hundreds upon hundreds of aircraft, centred upon the four aircraft types that would carry the Allies to victory, namely B-17, B-24, P-47 and P-51.

Back at the front the fighters were now in-

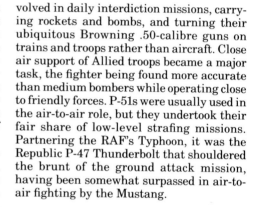

After the initial Normandy landings, the fighters followed behind the front line as the ground forces advanced. In early 1945 the fighters took up station on fields vacated by Luftwaffe aircraft perhaps hours before. Behind these 356th FG P-47s are abandoned Ju 88 night fighters.

volved in daily interdiction missions, carrying rockets and bombs, and turning their ubiquitous Browning .50-calibre guns on trains and troops rather than aircraft. Close air support of Allied troops became a major task, the fighter being found more accurate than medium bombers while operating close to friendly forces. P-51s were usually used in the air-to-air role, but they undertook their fair share of low-level strafing missions. Partnering the RAF's Typhoon, it was the Republic P-47 Thunderbolt that shouldered the brunt of the ground attack mission, having been somewhat surpassed in air-to-air fighting by the Mustang.

The final battles

Of course as the 8th Air Force stepped up its bombing effort against Germany, the P-51 was heavily used to escort the bombers, due to the type's extraordinary range capability. Until the last days of war the Luftwaffe was far from dead, and there were some memorable battles between Mustangs and Bf 109s. During the last months of the war the 'long-nose' Fw 190D rose to challenge the P-51 for air superiority, and had the Me 262 jet been fielded in numbers, allied pilots would have been in real trouble.

However, shortages of fuel, strategic materials and, above all, experienced pilots began to take their toll on the Luftwaffe's ability to defend, faced at the same time with ever-growing numbers of Allied aircraft crewed by well-trained and highly-motivated airmen. Despite notable counter-offensives, German forces and their air cover were rolled back towards the heart of the Reich, and the Allied fighters followed, snapping at the heels of the retreating forces. Such was the rapidity of some of the advances that Allied fighters, desperately trying to keep up with the ground echelons they were protecting, moved in to airfields vacated only hours before by Luftwaffe machines. During the last weeks of war there was little of any value for the USAAF to do: with the RAF they had crushed the Luftwaffe under an avalanche of bombs and firepower.

Remaining essentially a naval/marine assault battle until towards the end, US forces had island-hopped their way from the Guadal canal and New Guinea to the islands

Even with excellent fighters in mass production, the US industry embarked on a major development effort to find better aircraft. Few companies expended more energy than Curtiss, who tested many prototypes. This YP-60E is just one of many P-60 experimental variants.

Above: Night fighting had to a large extent been dominated by the RAF and Luftwaffe, but with the arrival of the Northrop P-61 the USAAF entered the field in a big way. By this time however, the mighty Black Widow had little to do in Europe.

surrounding Japan. By the time the Marianas had been reached it was time for the USAAF to step in with its fleet of B-29 bombers. From here the destruction of Japan could be undertaken. Once again the P-51 was instrumental in protecting bombers during their raids, but the Japanese defences were weak despite being fanatically motivated. P-51s made a big difference in the final attacks, being able to operate from the island of Iwo Jima, captured after a particularly bloody struggle.

A world away from Europe, the war in the Pacific reached a climax during the last months, and the USAAF became more and more involved. In China and Burma the P-51 Mustang arrived to relieve the hard-pressed P-40s long after it had made its debut against the Luftwaffe.

Lockheed P-58 Chain Lightning

History and notes

The Lockheed XP-58 Chain Lightning resulted from a US Army contract, of 27 April 1943, which tasked Lockheed to build 'one (1) airplane, pursuit, fighter, two-engine, two-place, known as the XP-58, complete and conforming to the contractor's specifications'. The big, twin-boom XP-58 'convoy fighter' followed in the tradition of the P-38 Lightning and experimental XP-49 but had almost nothing in common with them – not dimensions, not components, not performance. The XP-58 owed its origin to Colonel Elliot Roosevelt, son of the President, who almost alone created the notion that a brute-sized, awesomely-armed escort fighter was needed. Roosevelt, however, really wanted Howard Hughes, not Lockheed, to build it.

The first of two XP-58s (41-2670/2671) began taxi tests in 1943 and took to the air very belatedly on D-Day, 6 June 1944. The second airframe was never fully completed but was trucked in parts to the super-secret test centre at Muroc Dry Lake, California. By the time Howard Hughes' competing machine, the XF-11 reconnaissance craft, flew in 1946, the 'convoy fighter' idea had been dropped and the sole flyable XP-58 was a relic, abandoned to the elements after being moved to Wright Field, Ohio.

Its first flight was a 50-minute shakedown which took the XP-58 from the manufacturer's Burbank plant to Muroc. From 6 June to 8 September 1944, Lockheed pilots put

19.3 hours on the airframe. On 22 October 1944, it was ferried to Wright Field where it performed well in tests but, because of the cost of continuing a marginal programme with a 'one-off' machine, even with a second for spare parts, the programme was terminated in 1945. Derelict at Wright Field as late as January 1946, the Chain Lightning was scrapped in 1947.

Specification
XP-58

Type: two-seat fighter
Powerplant: two 2,100-hp (1566-kW) Allison V-3420-11 turbocharged liquid-cooled 24-cylinder inline piston engines driving four-blade propellers
Performance: maximum speed 436 mph (701.7 km/h) at 25,000 ft

The only flying example of the XP-58 Chain Lightning. Its performance and handling never matched that of its illustrious forebear, although it would have featured impressive firepower.

(7620 m); initial climb rate 2,660 ft (811 m) per minute; estimated service ceiling 40,000 ft (12192 m); estimated range 3,000 miles (4828 km)
Weights: empty about 20,000 lb (9072.0 kg); maximum take-off 39,200 lb (17781.1 kg)
Dimensions: span 70 ft 0 in (21.34 m); length 49 ft 5 in (15.06 m); height 12 ft 0 in (3.66 m); wing area 600 sq ft (55.74 m²)
Armament: four 37-mm fixed

A misguided attempt to provide a 'convoy fighter', the XP-58 was never to seriously challenge enemy fighters. Only one example of this monster was built, by which time the concept had been dropped, the P-51 with drop tanks performing the escort mission adequately.

forward-firing cannon and four 0.5-in (12.7-mm) machine-guns in two turrets planned but not installed

Bell P-59 Airacomet

History and notes

The XP-59 designation was initially assigned to the Bell company Model 16, a twin-boom, propeller-driven pusher fighter developed from the firm's unbuilt XP-52. The fighter would have been powered by a 2,000-hp (1491.4-kW) Pratt & Whitney R-2800 engine driving six-blade Hamilton Standard dual-rotation contra-rotating propellers. Futuristic in appearance, with a bullet-shaped nose including cockpit, the aircraft was, nonetheless, a holdover from the past. When the project was cancelled at an early stage, re-issuing the XP-59 appellation seemed a prudent way to guard the secrecy of one of the most hush-hush projects of the war, the Bell P-59 Airacomet, the first American jet fighter. Roughly contemporary with the Heinkel He 178 and Gloster E.28/39 but flown only after the later Messerschmitt Me 262 and Gloster Meteor, the P-59 Airacomet was to be an American vehicle for the British Whittle jet engine.

Because the UK was so far ahead of the USA in gas turbine development, the UK supplied the General Electric Company with specifications of what became the 2,000-lb (907.2-kg) thrust I-16 powerplant, later redesignated J31-GE-5. On 5 September 1941, Bell was tasked to build the XP-59A airframe, the company Model 27. The first of three XP-59As (42-108784/108786) was trucked in secrecy to Muroc Dry Lake, California, draped in tarpaulin with a fake propeller affixed to conceal its revolutionary power

source. First flight of the XP-59A was achieved on 1 October 1942 with Bell's chief test pilot, Robert M. Stanley, at the controls. The first military flight was by Brigadier General Laurence C. Craigie on 2 October 1942.

The twin-jet, mid-wing, tricycle-gear XP-59A offered only modest improvement in performance over the best propeller-driven fighters of

the early 1940s, but USAAF planners recognized that jet power was the wave of the future. Following three test craft which had been powered by British-built engines designated I-A, 13 service-test YP-59As (42-108771/108783) flew with the I-16. Production orders followed for 20 P-59A aircraft (44-22609/22628). The XP-59B was originally to have been a single-

Sitting on the bed of Muroc Dry Lake, this example of the P-59 shows the simple installation of the two J35 engines. Some numbers were built but they showed little improvement over piston-engine fighters. Nevertheless, the experience with jet aircraft was highly valuable.

Bell P-59

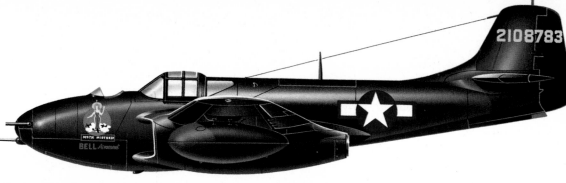

Bell YP-59A Airacomet of the 412th Fighter Group. Note the open second cockpit.

engine variant but the 30 P-59Bs completed (44-22629/22658) of 80 originally ordered retained the twin-jet layout with but minor changes. A sole YP-59A (42-108773), in 'trade' for a Gloster Meteor flown by the USAAF, was shipped to the British test centre at Farnborough, given RAF serial RJ362/G, and evaluated only briefly. The US Navy designation XF2L-1 is sometimes quoted for machines tested at NATC Patuxent River, Maryland, and the three P-59Bs in Navy markings (44-22651, 44-22657/22658) did acquire

bureau numbers (64100, 64108/64109) but the P-59B nomenclature was retained.

All production had been completed by the end of the war and many Airacomets were assigned to the USAAF's 412th Fighter Group for use as drones or controllers, some aircraft having a second open cockpit in the nose for an observer. In fact, it was in this unique open cockpit that Lawrence Bell made his first ride in a jet aircraft. No P-59, however, ever reached fully operational status or saw combat.

Though none is flyable, several P-59 Airacomet airframes remain in existence today. A lesser-known example is a P-59B (44-22656) preserved indoors at the Harold Warp Pioneer Village Museum in Minden, Nebraska.

Specification
P-59B

Type: single-seat jet fighter
Powerplant: two 2,000-lb (907.2-kg) thrust General Electric I-16 (J31-GE-5) centrifugal-flow turbojet engines

Performance: maximum speed 409 mph (658.2 km/h); cruising speed 375 mph (603.5 km/h); service ceiling 46,200 ft (14082 m); range 400 miles (644 km)
Weights: empty 8,165 lb (3703.6 kg); maximum take-off 13,700 lb (6214.3 kg)
Dimensions: span 45 ft 6 in (13.87 m); length 38 ft 1½ in (11.62 m); height 12 ft 0 in (3.66 m); wing area 385.8 sq ft (35.84 m²)
Armament: one 37-mm M4 cannon and three 0.5-in (12.7-mm) machine-guns in nose

Curtiss P-60

History and notes

The P-60 designation applies to a family of widely different Curtiss fighters, each reflecting the urgency of the builder's unsuccessful effort to develop a P-40 replacement. Though only four airframes carried out the P-60 programme, no fewer than nine designations were involved: XP-60, XP-60A, YP-60A, P-60A, XP-60B, XP-60C, XP-60D, XP-60E and YP-60E. The programme ran from early 1941 to December 1944 and was Curtiss's last gasp in the propeller-driven fighter field, an ambitious but unfocused effort which involved several engines, propellers, and canopy configurations.

The XP-60 (42-79245) was a low-wing, conventional-gear fighter developed from the uncompleted XP-53 but powered by a 1,300-hp (969.4-kW) Packard V-1560-1 licence-built Merlin, belatedly determined by the USAAF to be the best engine available in 1941. This airframe flew on 18 September 1941. With all Merlin-related resources soon committed to the P-51 Mustang programme, the USAAF then decided to employ the ubiquitous 1,425-hp (1062.6-kW) Allison V-1710-75 in planned production-model P-60s. On 31 October 1941, 1,950 such fighters were ordered. Soon, however, it became evident that Curtiss' Buffalo, New York, plant could be more usefully employed building P-47G Thunderbolts and the contract was cancelled. Three XP-60A airframes were tested with the Allison powerplant before being re-engined. The proposed YP-60A, which would have had a 2,000-hp (1491.4-kW) Pratt & Whitney R-2800-10 radial, was another variation which did not result in a finished airframe. The XP-60B was to have been the original machine with a shift from Merlin to Allison power but apparently this change was never made.

The XP-60C, converted in 1943 from one of the three Allison test ships, employed the R-2800 radial. This was the sole example tested

with Curtiss Electric contra-rotating propellers. The XP-60D was the original machine retaining its Merlin but with enlarged tail surfaces and other minor changes. The XP-60E was another R-2800 radial-powered variant. Last in the series was the YP-60E, another conversion, again R-2800 radial-powered but now uncamouflaged and with bubble canopy, the result being formidable competition to the Curtiss P-40Q for the claim of most beautiful fighter ever built.

In November 1942, the US Army ordered 500 Pratt & Whitney-powered P-60 fighters but the production contract was soon set aside in favour of other priorities. The P-60 programme ended by mid-1944, the last airframe being scrapped on 22 December 1944.

Specification
XP-60C

Type: single-seat fighter
Powerplant: one 2,000-hp (1491.4-kW) Pratt & Whitney R-2800-53 air-cooled 18-cylinder radial piston engine driving a six-

blade Curtiss Electric contra-rotating propeller unit.
Performance: maximum speed 386 mph (621.2 km/h) at sea level; climb to 10,000 ft (3048 m) in 3.7 minutes; service ceiling 36,000 ft (10972 m); range 615 miles (990 km)
Weights: empty 8,698 lb (3945.4 kg); maximum take-off 10,525 lb (4774.1 kg)
Dimensions: span 41 ft 4 in (12.60 m); length 34 ft 1 in (10.39 m); height 15 ft 0 in (4.57 m); wing area 275 sq ft (25.55 m²)
Armament: none

One of the many P-60 variants was the XP-60A with an Allison V-1710 engine driving a four-blade propeller. Only four airframes were involved in the P-60 programme, but there were nine different variants.

Below: The original XP-60 was a fighter designed to incorporate the superb Rolls-Royce Merlin engine. Although a large order was placed, this was cancelled in favour of the Mustang (for the engine) and the P-47 (for Curtiss' production capability).

Northrop P-61 Black Widow

History and notes

The Northrop P-61 Black Widow was the first US aircraft intended from the outset as a night-fighter. Earlier night-fighting craft, some equipped with primitive air intercept (AI) radar, were conversions of existing types like the Douglas A-20 Havoc, actually designed for the ground attack role. The effectiveness of Luftwaffe night bombing raids during the Battle of Britain had signalled the need for a dedicated night-fighter with better AI radar. In December 1941 the USAAF ordered the P-61 in an ambitious effort to combine the SCR-720 AI radar with a massive, heavily-armed, twin-boom airframe no smaller than many medium bombers. The P-61 was also the first modern project undertaken by the firm headed by Jack K. Northrop after his departure from Douglas. The programme resulted in flight of the first of two prototype XP-61s (41-19509/19510) at Hawthorne, California, on 26 May 1942 with Vance Breese at the controls. The first machine was configured rather differently from production craft to follow, and it was apparent from the start that the basic design was complex and trouble-plagued: nose radar and a dorsal barbette for four 20-mm cannon were to cause diverse aerodynamic and functional problems. The three-seat arrangement for pilot, navigator/gunner (in a stepped cockpit with unimpeded vision) and rear gunner, although roomy and comfortable, was not easy to get used to. Wing flying surfaces, eventually to include elaborate meshed airbrakes, had to be constantly re-evaluated and redesigned. The USAAF was so anxious to get the P-61 Black Widow into service that 13 service-test YP-61s (41-18876/18888) were built and production commenced while these problems were addressed. The gun barbette caused tail buffeting so serious that it was deleted after the first 37 out of 80 P-61 and 120 P-61A production machines (42-5485/5634 and 42-39348/39397) were built.

Delays and development problems continued after March 1944 when the first examples of the brutish, all-black P-61 were delivered to the 481st Night Fighter Group at Orlando, Florida. A total of 450 P-61B aircraft (42-39398/39757 and 43-8231-8320) with minor im-

provements and powered by twin 2,000-hp 1491.4-kW) Pratt & Whitney R-2800-65 Double Wasp radials, had been ordered in January 1943. The first 200 P-61Bs were delivered without the dorsal gun barbette until further tests resolved the tail buffeting tendency and a different version of this armament was restored from machine no. 201 onward. In the event, it was to develop that the P-61 was most effective in the air combat role using the traditional measure of manoeuvring to bring fixed, forward-firing guns to bear on target.

P-61s were more widely used in Europe and the Pacific than is often recognised and, despite teething problems, the type was a joy to fly. 'We could hurl it all over the sky just like a lightweight fighter,' said one pilot. On 6 July 1944 the type scored its first air-to-air victory, accounting for a Mitsubishi G4M bomber. It is understood that three USAAF pilots became aces in the P-61, although some of their kills were scored while flying other types. In Europe, five night-fighter squadrons were in service by war's end and, although the night bombing threat had long since dissipated, the P-61 proved effective against several Luftwaffe fighter types. The Black Widow also accounted for nine German V-1 'buzz bombs'.

Some 41 P-61C models (43-8321/8361) with improved systems and Curtiss Electric paddle-blade hollow steel propellers were delivered before 476 further examples were cancelled at war's end. The XP-61D designation was applied to two machines re-engined with turbocharged R-2800-77 engines. Two XP-61E fighters were rebuilt with slimmer crew nacelles, four 0.5-in (12.7-mm) nose machine-guns in lieu of nose radar, and the pilot and navigator positioned in tandem under a bubble canopy – this being the essential configuration of a distinct reconnaissance aircraft to follow. The XP-61F

An early production Northrop P-61A-1 'Jap-Batty' of the 6th Night Fighter Squadron based at East Field, Saipan in the Marianas during the summer of 1944.

An early production P-61 displays the four-gun dorsal barbette fitted to the first 37 aircraft (and from #201, onwards) and the fuselage side aerials for the SCR-720 airborne intercept radar. The olive drab camouflage gave way to all-over black as the war progressed.

Northrop P-61

'Moonlight Serenade' was a Northrop P-61B-1 of the 550th Night Fighter Squadron based at Tacloban on Leyte in the Philippines during June 1945.

was a planned modification never completed. The post-war P-61G designation was assigned to several Black Widows converted for weather reconnaissance duties. Twelve P-61A airframes were briefly used for training duties with the US Marine Corps as the F2T-1N.

Derived from the Black Widow and based upon the XP-61E configuration was the F-15 Reporter photo-reconnaissance aircraft, the first two examples of which were converted from an XP-61E and P-61C respectively. The F-15 was certainly the most graceful twin-boom aircraft ever built. A total of 36 F-15As (43-59300/59335) built from partially completed P-61C airframes served with the USAF until 1952, being redesignated RF-61C in 1948. Several museum examples of the P-61 Black Widow have survived, including a beautiful machine belonging to the National Air and Space Museum in Washington, D.C.

Specification

P-61B

Type: three-seat night-fighter

Powerplant: two 2,000-hp (1491.4-kW) Pratt & Whitney R-2800-65 Double Wasp air-cooled 18-cylinder radial piston engines driving four-blade Aeroproducts propellers

Performance: maximum speed 366 mph (589 km/h) at 20,000 ft (6096 m); initial climb rate 2,090 ft (637 m) per minute; climb to 20,000 ft (6096 m) in 6.8 minutes; service ceiling 40,000 ft (12192 m); range 1,350 miles (2172 km)

Weights: empty 23,450 lb (10636.9 kg); maximum take-off 36,200 lb (16420.3 kg)

Despite its enormous size the Black Widow was a manoeuvrable and enjoyable aircraft to fly, and was good at the night fighting role. By the time it got into service there was little night fighting to do, and virtually none of the bombers it was designed to tackle.

Dimensions: span 66 ft 0¾ in (20.14 m); length 49 ft 7 in (15.11 m); height 14 ft 8 in (4.47m); wing area 662.36 sq ft (61.53 m²)

Armament: four 20-mm M2 fixed forward-firing cannon and two or four 20-mm cannon or 0.5-in (12.7-mm) machine-guns in dorsal barbette on some aircraft, plus 6,400 lb (2903 kg) of external fuel or ordnance

Curtiss P-62

History and notes

The Curtiss XP-62 was the final propeller-driven fighter built by its manufacturer and the second largest single-seat fighter of orthodox layout developed during World War II, its dimensions being exceeded only by the Boeing XF8B naval fighter. The XP-62 was ordered by the USAAF on 27 June 1941 as a vehicle for the 2,300-hp (1715.1-kW) Wright R-3350 radial engine. Initial plans called for delivery of one XP-62 and one XP-62A and later for 100 production P-62 fighters, but it was clear almost from the beginning that the design was overweight, underpowered, and an uneconomical alternative to continued Curtiss production of the P-47G Thunderbolt. Because it would be an effective testbed for dual-rotation propellers and a pressurized cabin, it was decided on 18 July 1942 to proceed with a sole airframe, the remaining machines on order being cancelled.

Development of the XP-62's cabin pressurisation system was delayed and the aircraft did not fly until early 1944. By then even the XP-62's value as a test ship was marginal and the programme was terminated after a few hours' flying time. Though the unbuilt XP-71 and the jet XF-87 still lay ahead, the great days of Curtiss as a leading fighter manufacturer were now to become history.

Specification

XP-62

Type: single-seat fighter

Powerplant: one 2,300-hp (1715.1-kW) Wright R-3350-17 Cyclone air-cooled 18-cylinder twin-row radial engine driving a six-blade dual-rotation propeller unit

Performance: (estimated) maximum speed 448 mph (721.0 km/h) at 27,000 ft (8230 m); initial climb rate 2,000 ft (610 m) per minute; service ceiling 35,700 ft (10881 m); range 710 miles (1143 km)

Weights: empty 11,773 lb (5340.2 kg); maximum take-off 14,660 lb (6649.8 kg)

Dimensions: span 53 ft 8 in (16.36 m); length 39 ft 6 in (12.04 m); height 16 ft 3 in (4.95 m); wing area 420 sq ft (39.02 m²)

Armament: none

Although appearances can be deceptive, it seemed obvious that the Curtiss XP-62 fighter would be too heavy and underpowered to gain production orders. The single example completed was only ever used as a test-bed for pressurised cabins and contra-rotating propellers.

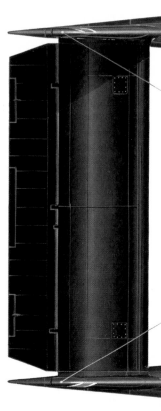

Two turreted P-61Bs make their way across the Pacific Ocean from their base on Saipan in the Marianas island group. As the standard Army Air Force night fighter, no less than 10 squadrons flew the Widow in this theatre.

This illustration shows one of the most famous Black Widows of the Pacific theatre. Built as a P-61B-1-NO, 'Times a'wastin' was one of only two of the first 200 P-61Bs to retain the dorsal four-gun turret, this not being revived until Block 15 when buffeting problems associated with the guns were cured. Visible in the front view are the four wing pylons (here carrying tanks) which distinguished this variant from the earlier P-61A, which only had two. Other improvements were a slightly longer nose and Curtiss Electric propellers with broader, more efficient blades.

403

Bell P-63 Kingcobra

History and notes

The Bell P-63 Kingcobra was a wholly new fighter design using the essential layout of the P-39 Airacobra and introducing the laminar-flow wing and taller tail tested on the XP-39E. The USAAF ordered two XP-63 prototypes (41-19511/19512) in June 1941, powered by the 1,325-hp (988.1-kW) Allison V-1710-47 engine located behind the pilot and driven by an extension shaft. The first machine flew on 7 December 1942 but was lost in an accident a few weeks later. The XP-63A (42-78015) was originally conceived as a Merlin engine testbed under the designation XP-63B but became, instead, a third prototype powered by a 1,325-hp (988.1-kW) Allison V-1710-93. The XP-63A was actually the fastest Kingcobra built, attaining 426 mph (685.6 km/h) on military power at 20,000 ft (6096 m), but air combat was not to be the type's forte: the Kingcobra was envisaged for the ground-attack role and for export, primarily to the Soviet Union.

The production P-63A, 1,825 of which were built in numerous sub-variants with minor changes in armament, armour and ordnance, was followed in 1943 by the P-63C with an 1,800-hp (1342.3-kW) Allison V-1710-117 engine with water injection. One P-63A (42-68937) was tested by the UK's Royal Air Force as the Kingcobra Mk I (FR 408). The first P-63C (42-70886) introduced a distinctive small ventral fin intended to improve lateral stability characteristics. The sole P-63D (43-11718) was configured with a bubble canopy and increased wing span. The first P-63E (43-11720) with minor changes was followed by 12 further examples before contracts for 2,930 were cancelled at war's end. One P-63F (43-11719) introduced the V-1710-135 powerplant and, while a second was cancelled, survived to be H. L. Pemberton's mount in the 1947 Cleveland Air Races with civil registration NX1719.

Ferried to the USSR via Alaska and Iran, the P-63 Kingcobra proved a potent attack craft and tank-buster. P-63s also served with Free French forces. The relatively few aircraft retained by the USAAF were used primarily for training and none is thought to have seen combat.

In 1945 and afterwards, P-63 Kingcobras were used as flying targets, painted bright red, piloted, and shot at by other fighters using frangible bullets. These 'robot' RP-63A and RP-63G aircraft were insulated with a protective covering of duralumin alloy, bulletproof windscreen and canopy glass, a steel grill over the engine air intake, steel guards for the exhaust stacks, and thick-walled, hollow propellers. When a hit was scored by an attacking aircraft, a red light blinked to confirm impact, causing one RP-63A (42-69654) to be nicknamed 'Pinball'. For more than 25 years an RP-63G (45-57295) has been on outdoor display at Lackland AFB, Texas. This unique piloted target was redesignated QF-63G in 1948, although the Q prefix usually denotes an unmanned drone.

The sole XP-63H was converted from a P-63E to test new internal systems. Two P-63s without specific designations were modified to test the V-shaped tail configuration more familiarly associated with the Beechcraft Bonanza. A sole P-63 was rebuilt with swept back wings and test-flown by the US Navy, known as the L-39.

Though total Kingcobra production was a respectable 3,362 airframes, 2,456 being delivered to the Soviets, the type must be included among the second rank of wartime fighters – and remembered as Bell's last great success in the fighter field.

Specification
P-63A

Type: single-seat fighter
Powerplant: one 1,325-hp (988.1-kW) Allison V-1710-93 liquid-cooled 12-cylinder Vee piston engine driving a four-blade propeller
Performance: maximum speed 410 mph (659.8 km/h) at 25,000 ft (7620 m); cruising speed 378 mph (608.3 km/h); service ceiling 43,000 ft (13106 m); range 450 miles (724 km)
Weights: empty 6,375 lb (2891.7 kg); maximum take-off 10,500 lb (4762.8 kg)
Dimensions: span 38 ft 4 in (11.68 m); length 32 ft 8 in (9.96 m); height 12 ft 7 in (3.84 m); wing area 248 sq ft (23.04 m²)
Armament: one 37-mm cannon and four (two wing-mounted and two nose-mounted) fixed forward-firing 0.5-in (12.7-mm) machine-guns, plus up to three 522-lb (237-kg) bombs

'Pin Ball' was one of the Bell RP-63A Kingcobras used as manned targets. The pilot was protected by armour and special frangible bullets were used.

The vast majority of the P-63 Kingcobras built were not for USAAF consumption, but for Lend-Lease supply. The main recipient was the Soviet Union, and it was tailored for the ground attack role following the successes in this regime of the P-39 Airacobra.

North American P-64

History and notes

The P-64 designation falls out of chronological order and belongs to a North American product the USAAC never intended to use. The company Model NA-50A, ordered by Siam on 30 December 1939, was little more than a single-seat pursuit ship patterned after the Harvard trainer and developed from the NA-50 used by Peru. The six examples of this strictly export craft were built at Inglewood and painted in Siamese markings, and were *en route* to Siam when the US Army confiscated them, removed the armament, and assigned them to training duties at Luke Field, Arizona. A widely-published report that the Siam-bound aircraft were caught at Pearl Harbor during the 7 December 1941 Japanese attack is inaccurate: the NA-50As were apparently embargoed in October 1940 and a camouflaged example in USAAF markings was noted at Luke as early as 16 September 1941.

Never really a fighter in USAAF service, the six P-64s were essentially base 'hacks' and possibly never received American serial numbers. A privately-owned survivor in civil registry as N840 was airworthy in the US as recently as 1975.

North American P-64 of an advanced training unit, circa 1941.

Specification
P-64

Type: single-seat trainer
Powerplant: one 870-hp

(648.8-kW) Wright R-1820-77 air-cooled 9-cylinder radial piston engine driving a three-blade propeller
Performance: maximum speed 270 mph (434.5 km/h) at 8,700 ft (2652 m); initial climb rate 1,200 ft (366 m) per minute; service ceiling 14,000 ft (4267 m); range 860 miles (1384 km)
Weights: empty 4,660 lb (2113.8 kg); maximum take-off 5,990 lb (2717.1 kg)
Dimensions: span 37 ft 3 in (11.35 m); length 27 ft 0 in (8.23 m); height 9 ft 0 in (2.74 m); wing area 228 sq ft (21.18 m²)
Armament: none

The side view of the P-64 shows its obvious derivation from the T-6 trainer, being little more than a single-seat fighter version for export. Six were embargoed on the outbreak of war and impressed into use, mainly for communications.

Grumman P-65

History and notes
The Grumman XP-65 twin-engine fighter design stemmed partly from the developments which culminated in the loss of the sole XP-50 and partly from the fascination with large 'convoy fighters' at the eve of World War II. Known as the company Model 51, the XP-65 was essentially a land-based variant of the aircraft which became the US Navy F7F Tigercat, but it was well into the planning stage long before the F7F appeared. To have been powered by twin 1,700-hp (1267.7-kW), Pratt & Whitney R-2800-22W Double Wasp radials, the XP-65 would have lacked the folding wings, carrier deck landing gear and second crew member of the Tigercat and, especially if available years earlier, would have been an outstanding performer, ideal for long-

range escort missions over Europe. On 16 January 1942, in a rush of decisions made just after Pearl Harbor and because Grumman was needed to manufacture naval types, the XP-65 was cancelled.

It is not true, as has been reported, that the US Army tested an F7F Tigercat at Wright Field, Ohio, and found the craft unsuited for its use. In fact, the F7F did not fly until December 1943, long after the USAAF's decision had been made, and none ever went to Wright at all. The premature cancellation of the XP-65, however, seems in retrospect to have been a mistake. The aircraft would have outperformed all other twin-engine fighters then under contemplation (XP-49, XP-58, Hughes XF-11) and could have been available much sooner. Further, the USAAF needed another air-cooled

fighter, the P-47 Thunderbolt being the only type employed in numbers during the war. The project could have been shifted to another builder, such as Vultee or Vought, where Charles Lindbergh was investigating the performance of twin-engine fighter designs.

Because of its early cancellation, only powerplant engineering drawings of the XP-65 were completed. These contributed to the development of the Tigercat, if not to what could have been among the most promising of US Army fighters.

Specification
XP-65

Type: single-seat fighter
Powerplant: (planned) two 1,700-hp (1267.7-kW) Pratt &

Whitney R-2800-22W Double Wasp air-cooled 18-cylinder radial piston engines driving three-blade Hamilton Standard propellers
Performance: (estimated) maximum speed 429 mph (690.4 km/h) at 19,200 ft (5852 m); cruising speed 222 mph (357.3 km/h); initial climb rate 4,530 ft (1381 m) per minute; service ceiling 40,700 ft (12405 m); range 825 miles (1397 km)
Weights: (estimated) empty 15,943 lb (7231.7 kg); maximum take-off 21,425 lb (9718.4 kg)
Dimensions: (planned) span 52 ft 6 in (16.00 m); length 46 ft 5 in (14.15 m); height 15 ft 2 in (4.62 m); wing area 455 sq ft (42.27 m²)
Armament: four 20-mm cannon and four 0.5-in (12.7-mm) machine-guns in a fixed forward-firing installation

Vultee P-66 Vanguard

History and notes
No fighter came into USAAF livery more indirectly, had as much international 'flavour' or, in the end, failed so utterly as the Vultee P-66 Vanguard, which was known as the manufacturer's Model 48 long before acquiring its fighter designation. Ordered by Sweden, tested by the UK, used in the defence of the western USA, and blooded in Chinese markings, the P-66 will most be remembered as a collection of wrecked relics cluttering a hangar in Karachi.

Vultee's design team under Richard Palmer conceived the Model 48 in 1938 as an all-metal, low-wing monoplane fighter with retractable landing gear and a unique, flush-fitting cowl over its 1,200-hp (894.8-kW) Pratt & Whitney R-1830 radial engine. The low-drag cowl design, fitted on the same engine in the Curtiss XP-42, posed cooling problems and, although tested on the fourth airframe by Vance Breese in 1939, was discarded in favour of conventional, open-air cooling. The production prototype of the Vultee Model 48C, as it became known, flew in

September 1940 and 144 airframes were ordered by Sweden with the Flygvapen designation J10. Though one Vanguard flew with Swedish markings, the 1940 embargo on US sales to Stockholm prevented delivery, and these machines acquired US serials 42-6832/6975. In anticipation of acquisition by the UK, 100 Royal Air Force serials (BW208/BW307) were assigned but only three machines (BW208/BW210) flew bearing these serials. The yet-unfinished production run of 144 machines was again diverted, 15 Vanguards being assigned to USAAF operational training units on the American west coast including the 14th Pursuit Group at NAS Oakland, California, and 129 being earmarked for China. The Chinese P-66 Vanguards were shipped by sea to Karachi in US markings for re-assembly and onward ferrying to Chengtu, China. Some were lost *en route*, others crashed during early trial flights from Karachi airfield where they were kept for a time in the aerodrome's massive hangar. Says technician Sam Timson: "Some of them rotted there."

The P-66 should have been more than a match for the Nakajima Ki-43 fighters Japan would throw against it in the south-west China theatre. Formidably armed with no fewer than four 0.3-in (7.62-mm) and four 0.5-in (12.7-mm) machine-guns, the Vanguard was manoeuvrable and had good endurance. But Chinese pilots, trained in the tricycle-gear Bell P-39, found it difficult to land this unforgiving 'tail dragger', and pranged many in trial hops at Karachi. Hydraulic problems and swollen rubber seals hampered P-66s already weathered by their long sea voyage. As few as 79 aircraft of the intended 129 actually reached Chengtu, these being assigned nonsequential Chinese serials in the P-13002/P-26886 range. Worse, in a confusing 21 November 1943 air battle, Chinese pilots shot down one Japanese Ki-43 but also despatched two friendly P-66s!

Flying the P-66 in combat from Fengwaushan airfield near Chengtu was an experience, but scarcely a favourable one for beleaguered Chinese airmen. In a crosswind on

the ground, the wide 13 ft (3.96 m) landing gear track of the P-66 almost invited a catastrophic ground loop. Aloft, the craft handled well and was comfortable, but was unstable in a high-speed dive and had poor spin/stall characteristics. Many P-66s were caught on the ground by Japanese strafing and the Vanguard took longer than most types to scramble into the air. A few Chinese pilots scored air-to-air kills, but the Vanguards were retired from service by late 1943. Some were crated and may have ended in the hands of Chinese Communist operators.

No P-66 airframe is known to have survived.

Specification
P-66

Type: single-seat fighter
Powerplant: one 1,200-hp (894.8-kW) Pratt & Whitney R-1830-S3C4-G Twin Wasp air-cooled 14-cylinder radial piston engine driving a Hamilton Standard 23E50 three-blade hydromatic propeller
Performance: maximum speed

Vultee P-66

340 mph (547.2 km/h) at 15,000 ft
(4572 m); climb to 17,000 ft (5182 m)
in 9.2 minutes; service ceiling
28,200 ft (8595 m); range 850 miles
(1360 km)
Weights: empty 5,235 lb
(2374.6 kg); maximum take-off
7,400 lb (3356.6 kg)
Dimensions: span 35 ft 10 in
(10.92 m); length 28 ft 5 in (8.66 m);
height level 13 ft 0 in (3.96 m) and
at rest 10 ft 0 in (3.05 in); wing area
197 sq ft (18.30 m²)
Armament: four 0.5-in (12.7-mm)
Colt synchronized cowl machine-
guns and four 0.3-in (7.62-mm)
Colt wing machine-guns, all
forward-firing

The P-66 Vanguard was an
interesting fighter which offered
high performance and heavy
armament. Unfortunately it suffered
from several aerodynamic vices
which made it tricky to fly. Those of
the USAAF flew mainly on fighter
training duties.

McDonnell P-67

History and notes

The XP-67 'Bomber Destroyer' or
'Moonbat' emanated from a little-
known St Louis, Missouri, firm
established by James S. McDonnell
in 1939. Though there existed strong
interest in twin-engine fighters in
the immediate pre-war period and
although the McDonnell Aircraft
Company would later make an in-
delible mark on history with just
such craft, the XP-67 was hampered
by so many delays and tribulations
that, when it flew on 6 January 1944,
it had been bypassed by history.

The original design for an engine,
located behind the pilot, driving a
pair of pusher propellers through
right-angle extension shafts was re-

The heavily-armed P-67 was
designed as a bomber-destroyer, the
twin-propeller layout allowing the
intended carriage of six 37-mm
cannon in the nose. A supreme
example of fuselage/wing/nacelle
blending, only one example of the
XP-67 was finished.

jected by the US Army at the very
time in 1940 when it was ordering
three not dissimilar and wholly unsuccessful machines (Vultee XP-54,
Curtiss XP-55, Northrop XP-56).
McDonnell engineers redesigned a
more conventional twin-engine
fighter powered by twin 1,150-hp
(857.6-kW) Continental XI-1430-
17/19 engines with augmentor
stacks providing additional thrust
beyond that afforded by the four-
blade propeller. The sleek engine
nacelles blended smoothly into the
wings, as did the fuselage shape at
the wing roots, thus posing minimal
drag although not providing additional lift. The company received a
go-ahead on 22 May 1941 to build
two XP-67s (42-11677/11678).

Rolled out at St Louis 29 November 1943 more than a year after the
builder had originally hoped to fly it,
the XP-67 was plagued with engine
problems and, once, by a ground fire
which nearly destroyed the airframe. In its early 1944 flight tests,
the machine handled well but every

measure of its performance fell short
of expectations. It had been intended
that the engines would each provide
1,400-hp (1044-kW) and that a speed
of 448 mph (721 km/h) at 20,000 ft
(6096 m) could be attained. Actual
top speed was 405 mph (651.8 km/h).

Ferried to Wright Field, Ohio, the
XP-67 was undergoing an official US
Army Air Force's evaluation on 6
September 1944 when the right
engine caught fire. The pilot landed
safely but the blaze engulfed the
XP-67. A plan to complete the
second prototype with an unusual
four-engine configuration consisting
of two 1,695-hp (1264-kW) Packard
V-1650 licence-built Rolls-Royce
Merlins and two unspecified
2,300-lb (1043.3-kg) thrust jet
engines proved too ambitious and
the project had to be shelved. Available earlier, the XP-67 might not
have been needed to destroy
bombers but could have escorted
Fortresses and Liberators to Berlin.
It was not the first time that an aircraft type with some promise was

denied production status partly
because of the loss of the only prototype.

Specification
XP-67

Type: single-seat fighter
Powerplant: two 1,150-hp (857.6-
kW) Continental XI-1430-17/19
liquid-cooled 12-cylinder inverted-
Vee piston engines driving four-
blade propellers
Performance: maximum speed
405 mph (651.8 km/h) at 20,000 ft
(6096 m); initial climb rate 2,100 ft
(640 m) per minute; service ceiling
37,000 ft (11278 m); range 2,100
miles (3380 km)
Weights: empty 16,395 lb
(7436.8 kg); maximum take-off
23,115 lb (10,485.0 kg)
Dimensions: span 55 ft 0 in
(16.76 m); length 42 ft 0 in)
(12.80 m); height 14 ft 9 in (4.50 m);
wing area 414 sq ft (38.46 m²)
Armament: six 37-mm fixed
forward-firing cannon planned but
not installed

Vultee P-68

History and notes

The Vultee XP-68 Tornado was to have coupled the airframe of the twin-boom, pusher XP-54 with one of the more formidable engines designed during the war years, the 2,500-hp (1864.6-kW) Wright R-2160 inline powerplant with no fewer than 42 cylinders arrayed in six rows and displacing 2,160 cu in (35.396 litres) to drive large, hollow-steel contra-rotating propellers. The same power source was also in-

tended for the unbuilt Republic XP-69. Had it been built, possibly at Vultee's Nashville, Tennessee, factory which already had P-38 Lightning experience, the XP-68 would surely have been a monster of a fighter aircraft and might have been heavily armed with 37-mm and 20-mm cannon. The XP-68 was briefly on order by the USAAF in 1941 but, partly because of development problems with the engine, was cancelled before details could be

finalized. The specifications which follow are largely presumptive.

Specification
XP-68

Type: single-seat fighter
Powerplant: (planned) one 2,500-hp (1864.6-kW) Wright R-2160 liquid-cooled 42-cylinder six-row inline piston engine driving contra-rotating propellers
Performance: (presumed) maximum speed 450 mph

(724.2 km/h) at 20,000 ft (6096 m); initial climb rate 4,000 ft (1219 m) per minute; service ceiling 46,000 ft (14021 m); range 1,200 miles (1931 km)
Weights: (estimated) empty 15,250 lb (6917.4 kg); maximum take-off 20,000 lb (9072 kg)
Dimensions: (presumed) span 53 ft 10 in (16.41 m); length 54 ft 9 in (16.69 m); height 13 ft 0 in (3.96 m); wing area 456 sq ft (42.36 m²)
Armament: never determined

Republic P-69

History and notes

The Republic XP-69 was conceived around the same huge 2,500-hp (1864.6-kW) Wright R-2160 engine as the Vultee XP-68 Tornado, but would have been a conventional fighter of rather graceful lines. Its development seems to have progressed slightly further than that of its Vultee counterpart. The USAAF ordered two examples of the XP-69, or company Model AP-18, in July 1941. Engineering work was undertaken by Alexander Kartveli's design team in Farmingdale at about the same time the team began work on a 'Super Thunderbolt', to become the XP-72. The latter seems to have

had priority, although a three-quarter scale mock-up of the XP-69 was completed by May 1942. The mock-up suggested an exceedingly clean aerodynamic shape but with the pilot essentially blind, having only lateral vision. It remains unclear whether it was intended that the pilot should see forward using a periscope, a Republic concept which was to recur often as late as the XF-103, or whether a windscreen was simply deleted from the scale model.

The engine would have been mounted amidships with a bulged under-fuselage cowling scoop and, in the manner of the Bell P-39 Aira-

cobra, would have been connected to nose contra-rotating propellers via an extension shaft passing beneath the pilot's feet.

Difficulties with the engine, coupled with the significantly greater promise of the XP-72, doomed the unbuilt XP-69.

Specification
XP-69

Type: single-seat fighter
Powerplant: (planned) one 2,500-hp (1864.6-kW) Wright R-2160 liquid-cooled 42-cylinder six-row inline piston engine driving contra-rotating propellers
Performance: (estimated)

maximum speed 450 mph (724.2 km/h) at 35,000 ft (10668 m); initial climb rate 3,000 ft (914 m) per minute; climb to 35,000 ft (10668 m) in 20.0 minutes; service ceiling 48,900 ft (14905 m); range 1,800 miles (2896 km)
Weights: (estimated) empty 15,595 lb (7073.9 kg); maximum take-off 26,164 lb (11868.0 kg)
Dimensions: (planned) span 51 ft 8 in (15.75 m); length 51 ft 6 in (15.70 m); height 17 ft 3 in (5.26 m); wing area 505 sq ft (46.91 m²)
Armament: (planned) two 37-mm cannon and four 0.5-in (12.7-mm) machine-guns in a fixed forward-firing installation

Douglas P-70

History and notes

The Douglas P-70 night-fighter, a converted A-20 Havoc light bomber, fits in time sequence ahead of the Northrop P-61 Black Widow, being an interim solution to the need for a night interceptor during the P-61's development. The first P-70 (39-735) was a conversion of the prototype A-20 fitted with two 1,600-hp (1193.1-kW) Pratt & Whitney R-2600-11 radial engines, a 'solid' nose containing British-designed air intercept (AI) radar and an underfuselage gun pack with four 20-mm cannon. The UK's Royal Air Force had enjoyed modest success employing the Havoc as a night-fighter, and the USAAF hoped to do likewise. The prototype was followed by 59 P-70s, converted from A-20 standard, 13 P-70A-1s converted from A-20C standard with six nose 0.5-in (12.7-mm) machine-guns encircling the AI radar, and 26 P-70A-2s converted from A-20G standard. The sole P-70B was another A-20 conversion with the six-gun armament in blisters on the sides of the fuselage, and the designation P-70B-2 went to A-20Gs and A-20Js used as night-fighter trainers.

Throughout the P-70 programme, various attempts were made to refine and develop the night-fighting capability of the 205 airframes involved. The sole P-70B, however, was the only machine equipped with fully-working SCR-720 centimetric AI radar of the type later used on the P-61 Black Widow, and early radars on other P-70s were less effective. The 6th Fighter Squadron in the South-West Pacific, though it achieved some successes, found its P-70s unable to climb rapidly enough for real effectiveness and only a few kills were scored at

The USAAF's first US-built night fighter was based on the A-20 medium bomber, and consequently always suffered from lack of performance. The original P-70 featured a British radar in a solid nose, with a ventral cannon tray. Most served on training duties.

Guadalcanal and New Guinea. The 418th, 419th and 421st Night Fighter Squadrons arrived in the South-West Pacific in late 1943 and fought briefly with P-70s before converting to other types. During their period with P-70s, however, pilots of the 418th were so dissatisfied that they requested and obtained P-38H Lightnings with jury-rigged SCR-540 AI radar, long before the P-38M night-fighter was developed. Most P-70 airframes were kept in

P-70B-2s were used as trainers for potential night fighter crews, these being standard A-20G Havocs equipped with SCR-720 radar. Most crews progressed from these to P-61 Black Widows, a better performing and sweeter-handling night fighter.

the USA for training duties but, in any event, hundreds of pilots learned about night-fighting through their experience with the type. Colonel Carroll Smith, who became a top US night-fighter ace, flew the P-70 before shifting to the P-61 Black Widow.

Specification
XP-70

Type: two-seat night-fighter
Powerplant: two 1,600-hp (1193.1-kW) Pratt & Whitney R-2600-11 air-cooled 14-cylinder radial piston engines driving three-

blade propellers
Performance: maximum speed 338 mph (543.9 km/h) at 14,000 ft (4267 m); initial climb rate 2,910 ft (887 m) per minute; service ceiling 28,250 ft (8611 m); range 1,090 miles (1754 km)
Weights: empty 15,730 lb (7135.1 kg); maximum take-off 19,750 lb (8958.6 kg)
Dimensions: span 61 ft 4 in (18.69 m); length 47 ft 7 in (14.50 m); height 18 ft 1 in (5.51 m); wing area 465 sq ft (43.20 m²)
Armament: four 20-mm forward-firing cannon in a forward-firing ventral gun pack

Enter the Jet Age

With some manufacturers still toying with piston-engined designs, the first-generation jets are set to sweep the fighter squadrons, led by the remarkable Lockheed P-80.

Perhaps fittingly, it was the United States Army Air Forces which ended the war, the two atomic fission weapons dropped on Hiroshima and Nagasaki bringing the Japanese to their senses before further needless blood was spilled during what would have been a fierce, protracted but nevertheless inevitable invasion of the Japanese homeland.

The USAAF's war had been won by the giant industrial infrastructure back home, the American factories churning out thousand upon thousand of warplanes without

disturbance from bombing or ground action. The vast reserve of youth had been more than willing to undergo the high standard of training necessary to man the large fleets, these growing ever larger as those of their enemies grew smaller. With the war's end, the need for these fleets was taken away overnight, and a massive demobilisation took place.

This matched any force reduction seen after World War I. After the end of war the USAAF level of 2,200,000 personnel fell to just 303,000 by early 1947. Nevertheless,

the US air forces were not committing quite the same mistakes as they had made after World War I, for they were restructuring for the future.

On an organisational basis the USAAF formed itself into major Commands during late 1945 and 1946, these having direct descendants today. Most important were the

Changing the guard: a pair of the new Lockheed F-80 Shooting Star fighters formate with the type they are replacing, the Republic F-47 Thunderbolt. Taken over the Alps, the date of this photograph is 1947.

The F-84 Thunderjet was a more capable warplane than the F-80, employing an axial-flow turbojet rather than the centrifugal powerplants favoured by other early jets. It had a long career as a fighter-bomber, yet never shone in the air-to-air role.

creation of the continental US Commands in March 1946, these being Strategic Air Command, Tactical Air Command and Air Defense Command. Finally, on 18 September 1947 the air forces achieved their goal of gaining autonomy from the Army, thus becoming the United States Air Force.

The war had been fought, lost and won with a wide variety of aircraft which for the most part had two things in common: straight wings and piston engines. The US was quick to realise that things would change rapidly in the years following World War II, and that jet engines and swept wings would rule the roost.

Jet propulsion was just one of three wartime advances that would affect post-war military aviation, the others being the guided missile and radar. Of course research into jet engines had been going on throughout the war, especially in the UK and Germany. The first US attempt was the Bell P-59 Airacomet, but this offered few performance advances over existing fighters. More successful was the Lockheed P-80, this fighter beginning to replace piston-engined fighters in 1947.

Of course the superb Mustang continued in service for many years after the arrival of jets, its tremendous capabilities representing the pinnacle of piston-engined fighter design and keeping it in the forefront of tactical airpower into the 1950s. Yet it was a last stand, for newer and better jets were following hard on the heels of the P-80, the F-84 Thunderjet becoming the second jet in service.

Even before the war's end, tensions were beginning to show themselves between East and West, these continuing to grow through the Berlin crisis until war broke out again, this time in Korea. Here two of the other great wartime advances would be called into play to help US fighters gain the upper hand: the swept-back wing and fighter radar.

Left: Mustangs remained long after the war's end, although their tasks turned towards ground attack as jets became available for the air superiority. These P-51Ds are seen on Iwo Jima during the final assault on Japan.

Below: Hastily developed, at least four P-80s reached Italy and England before the end of the war in Europe, but due to technical difficulties it was some time before they entered service in numbers.

123

Curtiss P-71

History and notes

The unbuilt Curtiss XP-71 is another result of USAAF interest in heavy, long-range fighters prevalent on the eve of World War II. Had it been completed, the XP-71 would have been larger than a B-25 Mitchell medium bomber with nearly twice the bomber's wing area. It would have been able to 'convoy' heavy bombers to their targets even if bases in England had been unavailable. Based upon two turbocharged 3,450 hp (2572.7-kW) Pratt & Whitney R-4360-13 Wasp Major pusher radials, the three-man XP-71 might, indeed, have been the biggest fighter ever built anywhere. It was also the fighter first intended to use a 75-mm cannon, as well as two 37-mm cannon.

Ordered by the USAAF in November 1941, before it became clear that England would hold and that Curtiss's production lines would be better used for other types, the XP-71 was cancelled in early 1942 before construction could begin.

Specification
XP-71

Type: three-seat escort fighter
Powerplant: (planned) two turbocharged 3,450-hp (2572.7-kW) Pratt & Whitney R-4360-13 Wasp Major air-cooled 28-cylinder radial piston engines driving a six-blade contra-rotating propeller unit
Performance: (estimated) maximum speed 428 mph (688.8 km/h) at sea level; initial climb rate 2,600 ft (792 m) per minute; climb to 25,000 ft (7620 m) in 12.5 minutes; service ceiling 40,000 ft (12192 m); range 3,000 miles (4828 km)
Weights: (estimated) empty 31,060 lb (14088.8 kg); maximum take-off 46,951 lb (21297.0 kg)
Dimensions: (planned) span 82 ft 0 in (24.99 m); length 61 ft 10 in (18.85 m); height 19 ft 0 in (5,79 m); wing area 902 sq ft (83.80 m²)
Armament: one 75-mm and two 37-mm fixed forward-firing cannon

---

Republic P-72

History and notes

The Republic XP-72 was based upon the P-47 airframe and was designed by Alexander Kartveli's fighter team as a 'Super Thunderbolt' around the 3,000-hp (2237.1-kW) Pratt & Whitney R-4360 Wasp Major radial engine. The powerplant was, simply, the most powerful

Basically a P-47 airframe wrapped around a massive radial engine, the XP-72 was designed as a fast and fast-climbing interceptor to match German flying bombs. Its unofficial top speed of nearly 500 mph made it probably the fastest piston-engined aircraft ever.

piston engine to reach production in any country during World War II. Intended primarily to be faster than the Thunderbolt, the XP-72 was viewed in part as a remedy for the Third Reich's high-speed V-1 buzz bomb. The USAAF planned to use the fighter to intercept buzz bombs, taking advantage of its ability to reach 20,000 ft (6096 m) in just under five minutes. An armament of six 0.5-in (12.7-mm) guns would have been carried.

The first of two examples (43-6598) flew at Farmingdale on 2 February 1944 using a large four-bladed propeller. The name of the pilot is not recorded, but C. Hart Miller was active in Republic flight test at the time. The second XP-72 (43-6599) flew in July 1944 with the intended Aeroproducts six-bladed contra-rotating propeller. The second aircraft, however, was lost on an early flight.

With priority shifted to long-range escort fighters, this promising interceptor was not needed. The other XP-72 airframe is thought to have been scrapped at Wright Field around VJ-Day.

Specification
XP-72

Type: single-seat fighter
Powerplant: one 3,000-hp (2237.1-kW) Pratt & Whitney R-4360-13 Wasp Major air-cooled 28-cylinder radial piston engine driving an Aeroproducts six-bladed contra-rotating propeller unit
Performance: maximum speed 490 mph (788.6 km/h) at 25,000 ft (7620 m); initial climb rate 3,100 ft (945 m) per minute; climb to 20,000 ft (6096 m) in 5 minutes; service ceiling 42,000 ft (12,802 m); range 1,200 miles (1931 km)
Weights: empty 10,965 lb (4973.7 kg); maximum take-off 14,750 lb (6690.6 kg)
Dimensions: span 40 ft 11⅞ in (12.49 m); length 36 ft 7¹³⁄₁₆ in (11.17 m); height 14 ft 6 in (4.42 m); wing area 300 sq ft (27.87 m²)
Armament: six 0.5-in (12.7-mm) fixed forward-firing machine-guns, plus provision for two 1,000-lb (453.6-kg) bombs under the wings

P-73
The P-73 designation was not assigned by the USAAF.

P-74
The P-74 designation was not assigned by the USAAF.

Fisher P-75 Eagle

History and notes
The XP-75 Eagle fighter manufactured by Fisher Body Division of General Motors, built to a 1942 USAAF specification for a single-seat fighter with a high rate of climb, was in fact an 'oddball' assortment of parts from existing production aircraft. The builder's wish for an appealing designation number is said to account for the USAAF's failure to allocate the P-73 and P-74 appellations. Fisher's design team under Don Berlin, formerly with Curtiss, reckoned that components of other machines could be combined

with the 2,885-hp (2151.3-kW) Allison V-3420-23 engine at greatly reduced cost, the result being a fighter easy to manufacture in a short time to cope with the war's urgent demands. The first of two prototype XP-75s (43-46950 and 44-32162), which flew on 17 November 1943, was built with P-51 Mustang outer wing panels, F4U Corsair landing gear, and A-24 Dauntless empennage. Production of 2,500 machines was authorised before it became apparent that this hybrid was not going to work.

There followed a contract for six production XP-75As which had bubble canopy rather than the braced hood on earlier machines.

The XP-75As introduced a number of changes brought about by a shift in primary mission from the interceptor to the escort-fighter role. The XP-75As also had more components designed and built new from the outset. By the time the first XP-75A (44-44550) flew in September 1944, it was clear that the type was a disappointment and that, in any event, the escort role was being carried out more effectively by the P-51 Mustang. Eventually, three Eagles were lost in crashes, two of

Redesign and the introduction of many more parts built as new resulted in the XP-75A escort fighter, but this fared little better than its predecessor, unable to compare with the Mustang which was in service before the XP-75A first flew. Six were built.

them fatal, and on 27 October 1944 the USAAF cancelled the programme so abruptly that the sixth and final XP-75A never flew. One immaculate XP-75A (44-44553) has survived in a non-flying condition and is displayed in the Air Force Museum at Dayton, Ohio.

Specification
XP-75A

Type: single-seat long-range escort fighter
Powerplant: one 2,885-hp (2151.3-kW) Allison V-3420-23 liquid-cooled 24-cylinder banked-Vee piston engine driving a six-bladed contra-rotating propeller unit
Performance: maximum speed about 400 mph (643.7 km/h) at sea level; cruising speed 310 mph (498.9 km/h); service ceiling 36,000 ft (10973 m); range 3,000 miles (4828 km)
Weights: empty 11,495 lb (5214.1 kg); maximum take-off 18,210 lb (8260.1 kg)
Dimensions: span 49 ft 4 in (15.04 m); length 40 ft 5 in (12.32 m); height 15 ft 6 in (4.72 m); wing area 347 sq ft (32.24 m²)

With Mustang wings, Corsair undercarriage and Dauntless tail, the Fisher XP-75 interceptor was a bizarre contraption, powered by a centrally-mounted V-3420 engine. Not surprisingly, it was a dismal failure.

Armament: 10×0.5-in (12.7-mm) forward-firing machine-guns (six in wings and four in fuselage), plus provision for two 500-lb (227-kg) bombs on racks beneath the wing centre section

Bell P-76

History and notes
The P-76 designation was assigned on 24 February 1942 to a variant of the Bell P-39 Airacobra, 4,000 of which were to be manufactured in Bell's Atlanta, Georgia, plant. Like other variants of the low-wing, tricycle-gear fighter, the P-76 would have been powered by a 1,325-hp (988.1-kW) Allison V-1710-47 piston engine

located behind the pilot and driving the propeller via an extension shaft. It is unclear whether the P-76 would have been precisely identical with, or merely similar to, the P-39M. In any event, production of Airacobra variants was kept in Buffalo, to free the Atlanta plant for licence manufacture of B-29 bombers, and the P-76 production scheme was cancelled on 20 May 1942. The specifications given are provisional.

Specification
P-76

Type: single-seat fighter
Powerplant: one 1,325-hp (988.1-kW) Allison V-1710-47 liquid-cooled 12-cylinder Vee piston engine driving a three-bladed Curtiss propeller
Performance: maximum speed 386 mph (621.2 km/h) at 9,500 ft (2896 m); cruising speed 200 mph (321.9 km/h); service ceiling 36,000 ft (10973 m); range 650

miles (1046 km)
Weights: empty 5,610 lb (2544.7 kg); maximum take-off 8,400 lb (3810.2 kg)
Dimensions: span 34 ft 0 in (10.36 m); length 30 ft 2 in (9.19 m); height 11 ft 10 in (3.61 m); wing area 213 sq ft (19.79 m²)
Armament: one 37-mm T9 cannon, two 0.5-in (12.7-mm) machine-guns and four 0.3-in (7.62-mm) machine-guns (all forward-firing), plus provision for one 500-lb (227-kg) bomb

Bell P-77

Bell P-77 lightweight fighter.

History and notes

The Bell XP-77, an all-wood lightweight fighter made from Sitka spruce, patterned after racers of the 1930s, and intended to operate from grass runways, was an astonishingly attractive machine. Yet when the first of two XP-77s (43-34915/34916) flew on 1 April 1944 at Niagara Falls, New York, with Jack Woolams at the controls, it was not unfitting that the date was April Fools' Day.

Initially, the idea of a small, cheap, all-wood fighter built with few strategic materials had held high appeal. In early 1941, Larry Bell's upstate New York fighter team had begun work on a plane at first called the 'Tri-4', shorthand for an informal USAAF requirement for '400 hp, 4,000 lbs, 400 mph'. On 16 May 1942, the USAAF ordered 25 'Tri-4' aircraft. Delays, technical problems with subcontracting on plywood construction, and disappointing wind-tunnel tests caused the manufacturer to suggest by early 1943 that the number of machines on order be reduced to six. In May 1943, the USAAF pared this figure to two, seeing the XP-77 as

having no operational utility but as useful in lightweight fighter research.

Beginning in July 1944, the second XP-77 was tested at Eglin Field, Florida. Spin problems led to a crash of this aircraft on 2 October 1944, which the pilot survived.

The programme did not. Plagued by noise and vibration, an unexpectedly long take-off run, and general performance 'inferior to the present fighter aircraft employed by the USAAF' (according to a report of the time), the XP-77 was killed by administrative fiat on 2 December 1944. The prototype went to Wright Field, then back to Eglin, then to Wright again. It was seen at postwar displays wearing spurious markings and its final disposition is

unknown. Described in a wartime promotional release as 'an engine with a saddle on it', this effort ended up being another of the many 1941-5 programmes which failed to produce an operational aircraft.

Specification
XP-77

Type: single-seat fighter
Powerplant: one 520-hp (387.8-kW) Ranger XV-770-7 air-cooled 12-cylinder inverted Vee piston engine driving a two-blade propeller
Performance: maximum speed 330 mph (531.1 km/h); initial climb rate 3,600 ft (1097 m) per minute; service ceiling 30,100 ft (9174 m); range 550 miles (885 km)

Weights: empty 2,855 lb (1295 kg); maximum take-off 4,029 lb (1827.6 kg)
Dimensions: span 27 ft 6 in (8.38 m); length 22 ft 10½ in (6.97 m); height 8 ft 2¼ in (2.5 m); wing area 100 sq ft (9.29 m²)
Armament: two 0.5-in (12.7-mm) fixed forward-firing machine-guns, plus provision for one bomb or other ordnance up to 300 lb (136.1 kg) in weight

Powered by a Ranger engine and built almost entirely of non-strategic materials, the XP-77 was a novel attempt to provide a mass-produced fighter. Such was the position of the US industry that materials were never a problem. The fighter did not reach adequate performance.

North American P-78

History and notes

The XP-78 designation was briefly applied to the re-engined North American P-51 Mustang with 1,300-hp (969.4-kW) Packard V-1650-3 inline engine, precisely the merger of airframe and powerplant which brought the Mustang to

greatness. Before any were actually built, the aircraft was redesignated P-51B.

Specification
P-78

Type: single-seat fighter

Powerplant: one 1,300-hp (969.4-kW) Packard V-1650-3 Merlin liquid-cooled 12-cylinder Vee piston engine driving a four-blade propeller
Performance: maximum speed 414 mph (666.3 km/h) at 20,000 ft (6096 m); initial climb rate 3,200 ft (975 m) per minute; service ceiling 41,000 ft (12497 m); range 2,000

miles (3218 km)
Weights: empty 7,028 lb (3187.9 kg); normal loaded 10,548 lb (4784.6 kg)
Dimensions: span 37 ft 0 in (11.28 m); length 32 ft 3 in (9.83 m); height 13 ft 8 in (4.17 m); wing area 235 sq ft (21.83 m²)
Armament: six 0.5-in (12.7-mm) fixed forward-firing machine-guns

Northrop P-79

History and notes

The XP-79 designation was assigned at first to a Northrop flying-wing fighter of all-magnesium construc-

tion with a prone position for the pilot, powered by one 2,000-lb (907.2-kg) thrust Aerojet rocket

engine. As early as January 1943, it was foreseen that this rocket-propelled craft would attain 518 mph (833.6 km/h) at 40,000 ft (12192 m). After development of the rocket powerplant was delayed to the extent that two prototypes had to be cancelled, Northrop built the sole

XP-79B 'Flying Ram' (43-52437), propelled by two 2,000-lb (907.2-kg) thrust Westinghouse axial-flow turbojets eventually designated J30. Combining Northrop's ongoing work in the flying-wing field with a twin tail, the XP-79B was intended to succeed in battle in a unique

Perhaps the most radical of Northrop's flying-wing designs, the XP-79B was intended to ram enemy fighters, slicing off vital parts with its strengthened leading edge. This jet-powered project did not get beyond its first flight.

fashion: although not a suicide aircraft, it was designed to slice off portions of enemy aircraft with the sturdily-built leading edge of its wing. In addition, an armament of four 0.5-in (12.7-mm) machine-guns would have been installed on a production version.

In early taxi tests at Muroc Dry Lake, California, the XP-79B encountered various problems, including frequent tyre blowouts. On 12 September 1945, Northrop test pilot Harry Crosby took the craft aloft for its tragic first and only flight. After narrowly missing a fire truck which inadvertently blocked his runway, Crosby made a seemingly normal take-off. He made a sweeping circle over onwatchers at 10,000 ft (3048 m), and, on a second pass, went into a stall. The XP-79B plunged into a nose-down spin and Crosby attempted to parachute to safety. He was struck by a portion of the aircraft and his parachute never opened. Though the airframe was too badly burned for an accident investigation, it is believed that a trim tab failure caused the violent manoeuvre which resulted in Crosby's death.

The true purpose of the XP-79B, to ram enemy aircraft, had not been

disclosed when its construction was originally authorised. The flying-wing fighter might have showed promise with a different purpose, such as point defence, and the choice of turbojet power was a clear sign of things to come. But with World War II at an end and the US Army Air Forces about to become an independent US Air Force, the future was to belong to conventional, jet-powered fighter aircraft.

Specification
XP-79B

Type: single-seat fighter
Powerplant: two 2,000-lb (907.2-kg) thrust Westinghouse J30 axial-flow turbojet engines
Performance: maximum speed 547 mph (880.3 km/h) at 20,000 ft (6096 m); cruising speed 480 mph (772.5 km/h); initial climb rate 4,000 ft (1219 m) per minute;

service ceiling 40,000 ft (12192 m); range 993 miles (1598 km)
Weights: empty 6,250 lb (2835 kg); maximum take-off 8,669 lb (3932.3 kg)
Dimensions: span 38 ft 0 in (11.58 m); length 14 ft 0 in (4.27 m); height 7 ft 0 in (2.13 m); wing area 278 sq ft (25.83 m²)
Armament: four 0.5-in (12.7-mm) machine-guns planned but not installed

Lockheed F-80 Shooting Star

History and notes

The F-80, known as the P-80 until the newly independent US Air Force (USAF) adopted the F for fighter designation on 1 June 1948, was the first genuinely successful American jet fighter and could, in fact, have been available earlier. Clarence L. (Kelly) Johnson's Lockheed design team at Burbank, California, had proposed a jet fighter in 1939, only to have its L-133 design quashed by lack of an engine and by bureaucratic indifference. Pressured by wartime exigencies, the USAAF in 1943 asked Johnson to produce the XP-80, a low-wing, tricycle-gear, conventional single-seat jet fighter, in just 180 days! Put together ahead of this demanding schedule in a scant 143 days, the prototype XP-80 (44-83020), nicknamed 'Lulu Belle', was powered by a 3,000-lb (1360.8-kg) thrust de Havilland-built Goblin centrifugal-flow turbojet engine.

The spinach-green XP-80 made its first flight on 8 January 1944 with Milo Burcham at its controls. Testing was undertaken on a crash basis at Muroc Dry Lake, California. By VE-Day, two P-80s were in Italy readying for combat, two had reached England, and in all no fewer than 16 examples were flying. Early P-80 accidents claimed the lives of Burcham on 20 October 1944 and of America's top ace, Major Richard I. Bong on 6 August 1945, but the programme was in all an exceedingly successful one and an improved engine was to make it more so. Developed from British technology by General Electric but manufactured by Allison, the 4,000-lb (1814.4-kg) thrust J33-A-11, 5,200-lb (2352.7-kg) thrust J33-A-19 and 5,400-lb (2449.4-kg) thrust J33-A-25 centrifugal-flow turbojet

The P-80B introduced a thinner aerofoil section wing, which improved high speed performance marginally. In early fighting in Korea the advantages of jet fighters were plainly seen, as F-80s cleared the skies of North Korean Yaks and Lavochkins with ease.

powered the similar P-80A, P-80B and P-80C variants of the Lockheed Shooting Star.

The designation F-14A was assigned to the photo-reconnaissance version of the Lockheed fighter (F for 'foto' being changed to R for reconnaissance in 1948) which developed into the RF-80A and RF-80C, and demonstrated its mettle as an intelligence-gathering

Lockheed P-80A of the 412th Fighter Group in 1946, the first unit to equip on the type.

Lockheed F-80

Lockheed F-80C Shooting Star of the 36th Fighter-Bomber Squadron, 8th F-B Wing, serving in Korea in 1949.

platform during the 1950-3 Korean War. The designation P-80R was used for an ultra-streamlined, one-off racing aircraft which set a speed record in the late 1940s but was otherwise less than a full success.

Various 'odd mod' Shooting Stars were typical of the post-war spirit of innovation, but never received their own designations. One P-80A (44-84995) was fitted with an experimental, revolving gun mount while another P-80A had four 20-mm cannon in place of the six 0.5-in (12.7-mm) machine-guns normally carried. A P-80A (44-85042) was used to test two 20-in (50.8-cm) ramjet engines on the wingtips and another (44-85214) was flown with larger ramjets 30-in (76.2-mm) in diameter. An F-80C was literally dragged through the sky by a B-29 bomber in a towing experiment. It was a time of experimentation, but none of these ideas led anywhere.

By the late 1940s, a dozen squadrons throughout the USA and Alaska operated the F-80. Various speed and distance records demonstrated the fighter's potential. On 22 January 1946, Colonel William H. Councill flew a P-80A (44-85123) coast to coast in 4 hours 13 minutes, averaging 580.9 mph (934.8 km/h) for the 2,435.8 miles (3919.9 km) between Long Beach, California and La Guardia, New Jersey. On 19 June 1947, Colonel Albert Boyd flew the sole P-80R (44-85200), nicknamed 'Racey', to a new world speed record of 623.8 mph (1003.88 km/h) at Muroc Dry Lake, California. In 1949, wartime ace Colonel David Schilling began mass ferry flights of fighters across the Atlantic using the F-80, a range-stretching exercise he would later employ to full potential with the Republic F-84.

When President Truman committed United States forces to battle in Korea on 25 June 1950, F-80s such as those of the 49th Fighter Bomber Group at Misawa AB, Japan, were abruptly hurled into combat. F-80s rapidly cleared the skies of the propeller-driven clunkers of the North Korean air force. But when the Chinese entered the war in November 1950, the Lockheed fighter was quickly outclassed by their new jet fighter, the MiG-15. In history's first jet-versus-jet action on 8 November 1950, First Lieutenant Russell Brown, flying an F-80C (49-737), was credited with a MiG-15 kill. For the remainder of the war, however, the F-80 was relegated to the air-to-ground role, in which it performed yeoman service.

There are persistent reports that the Communist side obtained a flyable F-80 during the war and used it to harass US aircraft.

F-80s were used by the US Navy under the designation TV-3 (originally TO-1) in the training role. The two-seat trainer variant, initially called TF-80C but legendary as the T-33 (US Navy TV-2), was to become more numerous than the fighter upon which it was based. The essential F-80 design was also developed into the F-94 all-weather interceptor which, for a brief period, was known as the YF-97.

By 27 July 1953 when the Korean conflict ended, the principal F-80C variant was clearly a second-line fighter, but it had made a mark. In Korea, F-80s flew 98,515 combat sorties, shot down 37 enemy aircraft including six MiG-15s, dropped 33,266 US tons (30,179 tonnes) of bombs and launched 80,935 air-to-ground rocket projectiles. Total F-80 losses from enemy action numbered 143, including 14 destroyed by MiG-15s, 113 claimed by ground fire, and 16 lost to unknown causes. F-80 Shooting Stars, which had once served with no fewer than 13 fighter groups (the group designation being replaced by the wing in 1951), served with Air National Guard squadrons until at least October 1955.

F-80s were provided as part of US military assistance to Latin America and served with the air forces of Brazil, Chile, Colombia, Ecuador, Peru and Uruguay. Numerous museum examples of the F-80 remain on public view today. Total production of fighter versions was 1,714.

Left: Displaying the classically simple lines of the Shooting Star is this trio of F-80Bs. In addition to the thin wing, this version had an uprated engine and increased armour protection compared with the original production version. 240 F-80Bs were built, and many F-80As were raised to this standard.

Above: The sleek shape of the P-80 made a considerable change from the propeller-driven fighters it succeeded. In just a short time after the end of World War II it had become obsolete as a fighter, but the experience gained was invaluable to the new generation of jet pilots. This is a P-80A.

A flight of bomb-armed F-80Cs head for communist positions in Korea during the fighting. Although credited with the first US MiG-15 kill, and displaying a good kill-loss ratio, the F-80 was outclassed in air-to-air fighting and was mainly used in the ground-pounding role.

Specification

F-80C

Type: single-seat fighter
Powerplant: one 5,400-lb (2449.4-kg) thrust Allison J33-A-35 axial-flow turbojet engine
Performance: maximum speed 594 mph (955.9 km/h) at sea level; service ceiling 46,800 ft (14265 m); range 825 miles (1328 km)

The modified nose shape shows this aircraft to be an RF-80A tactical reconnaissance platform. Some RF-80s (FP-80 prior to 1948) were converted from F-80 fighters.

Weights: empty 8,420 lb (3819.3 kg); maximum take-off 16,856 lb (7645.9 kg)
Dimensions: span 38 ft 9 in (11.81 m); length 34 ft 5 in (10.49 m); height 11 ft 3 in (3.43 m); wing area 237.6 sq ft (22.07 m²)
Armament: six 0.5-in (12.7-mm) fixed forward-firing nose machine-guns, plus provision for two 1,000-lb (454-kg) bombs and eight underwing rockets

Consolidated Vultee F-81

History and notes

The Consolidated Vultee XP-81 (its newly-merged builder soon to be better known as Convair) was the first American aircraft powered by a turboprop engine. Ordered by the USAAF on 11 February 1944, the XP-81 was intended as a long-range escort fighter using compound power, with one 1,650-shp (1230.4-kW) General Electric TG-100 turbo-prop and one 3,750-lb (1701-kg) thrust Allison I-40 jet engine, eventually designated J33-A-5. When delays with the turboprop powerplant were encountered, the prototype XP-81 (44-91000) was flown on 11 February 1945 with a Packard V-1650-7 Merlin installed temporarily in the nose. The first flight with the intended turboprop engine followed on 21 December 1945 and, to the astonishment of pilots and observers, the turboprop provided no advantage in performance over the Merlin! A second XP-81 flew in early 1946 to join the first machine in exploring the poten-

tial for this unusual powerplant, but several factors (war's end, the disappointing results with the TG-100, and the evident superiority of pure jet designs) resulted in cancellation of an order for 13 YP-81 service-test aircraft.

Both XF-81 airframes have survived, albeit in poor condition, and are today derelict on a test range at Edwards AFB, California, known until 1949 simply as Muroc Dry Lake.

Specification

XP-81

Type: single-seat fighter
Powerplant: one 1,650-shp (1230.4-kW) General Electric

Like other manufacturers elsewhere, Convair found the turboprop to offer no performance increase compared with piston engines, despite its early promise. Only two XF-81s were built and used mainly for turboprop research purposes.

TG-100 (XT-31) turboprop engine driving a four-bladed propeller, plus one 3,750-lb (1701-kg) thrust Allison I-40 (J33-A-5) turbojet engine
Performance: maximum speed 507 mph (815.9 km/h) at 20,000 ft (6096 m); cruising speed 275 mph (442.6 km/h); initial climb rate 4,600 ft (1402 m) per minute; service ceiling 35,500 ft (10820 m); range 2,500 miles (4023 km)
Weights: empty 12,755 lb (5785.7 kg); maximum take-off about 28,000 lb (12700.8 kg)
Dimensions: span 50 ft 6 in (15.39 m); length 44 ft 10 in (13.67 m); height 14 ft 0 in (4.27 m); wing area 425 sq ft (39.48 m²)
Armament: six 0.5-in (12.7-mm) machine-guns or six 20-mm cannon planned but not installed, plus provision for up to 3,200 lb (1451.5 kg) of underwing bombs or rockets

North American F-82 Twin Mustang

History and notes

The North American F-82 Twin Mustang was not, as is often stated, two P-51 aircraft joined to a single wing. Rather, the F-82 was a wholly new design, ultimately to be powered by twin 1,600-hp (1193.1-kW) Allison V-1710-143/145 piston engines, using the twin-boom configuration to achieve long range and good endurance. Conceived as early as 1943 for the Pacific war where pilots often spent six to eight hours in their cockpits on maximum-distance missions, the two-man F-82 was intended to provide a navigator who, although not equipped with full flight controls, could also 'spell' the pilot for brief periods. The two booms or 'fuselages', although resembling those of the P-51, were in fact entirely new structures. The pilot was located on the port side of the aircraft.

The first of two XP-82 aircraft (44-83887/83888) first flew on 15 April 1945 powered by Merlin engines.

The P-82B was the first production version, developed for long-range fighter missions in the Pacific theatre, but only 20 had been completed at the war's end. Denied a viable mission in the post-war Air Force, the type was re-roled as a night fighter.

These were followed by the sole XP-82A, which introduced the Allison powerplant. Testing of the three prototypes led to a USAAF order for 500 Merlin-powered P-82B fighters, but only 20 had been built when the war ended. Two of this number were converted as night-fighters designated P-82C and P-82D, with SCR-720 and APS-4 radar respectively. Successful trials with the night-fighters led to orders for 100 F-82E escort fighters, 100 F-82F night-fighters with SCR 720 radar, and 50 F-82G night-fighters with APS-4 radar. The last version to enter service was the F-82H, a winterised variant for service in Alaska. By the end of 1949, the Twin Mustang was in wide operational use, its night-fighter variants having replaced the Northrop F-61 Black Widow.

F-82 Twin Mustangs were operated by the US 5th Air Force headquartered in Japan, and were hurled into the Korean hostilities when fighting began on 25 June 1950. The first air-to-air kill of the war was scored on 27 June 1950 by Lieutenant William Hudson (pilot) and Lieutenant Carl Fraser (radar observer) in an all-black F-82G (46-382) of the 68th Fighter (All Weather) Squadron when the pair shot down a North Korean Yakovlev Yak-7U. The 339th Fighter (All Weather) Squadron also achieved a victory that day when Major James Little, piloting another F-82G (46-392), shot down a Yak-9. The Twin Mustang's combat career in Korea lasted only a period of weeks (the older F-51 Mustang was to play a more important part in fighting on that peninsula) but the aircraft un-

North American F-82G Twin Mustang of the 4th Fighter (All-Weather) Squadron based on Okinawa. The tail badge depicts Fuujin, the Okinawan God of Wind.

questionably made a valuable contribution in both the air-to-air and air-to-ground roles. Total production was 275 aircraft.

A number of non-flying F-82 airframes are on display in the USA today, one being an F-82G (46-262) at Lackland Air Force Base, Texas, home of the USAF's basic enlisted training centre.

Specification

F-82G

Type: two-seat fighter
Powerplant: two 1,600-hp (1193.1-kW) Allison V-1710-143/145 liquid-cooled 12-cylinder Vee piston engines driving four-bladed propellers
Performance: maximum speed 461 mph (741.9 km/h) at 21,000 ft (6401 m); initial climb rate 3,770 ft (1149 m) per minute; service ceiling 38,900 ft (11857 m); range 2,240 miles (3605 km)
Weights: empty 15,997 lb (7256.2 kg); maximum take-off 25,591 lb (11608.1 kg)
Dimensions: span 51 ft 3 in (15.62 m); length 42 ft 5 in (12.93 m); height 13 ft 10 in (4.22 m); wing area 408 sq ft (37.9 m²)
Armament: six 0.5-in (12.7-mm) fixed forward-firing wing machine-guns, plus provision for up to four 1,000 lb (454-kg) bombs or four auxiliary fuel tanks on underwing racks

An F-82G cruises over Korea during the first weeks of the Korean war, displaying the SCR-20 airborne interception radar it used for the night fighter role.

Bell F-83

History and notes

The XP-83 was the final contribution by the Bell firm to the US Air Force fighter series. On 24 March 1944, with the war in Europe signalling the need for a long-range escort fighter and the P-51 Mustang not yet proven in this role, the USAAF tasked the builder of the first American jet aircraft to build a larger, longer-legged jet fighter. Bell assigned engineer Charles Rhodes to 'bring along' the bulky XP-83, powered by two 3,600-lb (1633-kg) thrust General Electric I-40 (later J33-GE-5) turbojets. The craft was to be armed with six 0.5-in (12.7-mm) Browning nose machine-guns.

First flown on 25 February 1945, apparently by company test pilot Jack Woolams, the first XP-83 (44-84990) proved underpowered and unstable. The close proximity of the two low-slung powerplants caused hot exhaust gases to buckle the tailplane unless, during run-ups, fire trucks were used to play streams of water over the rear fuselage!

The second XP-83 (44-84991) was completed with a slightly different bubble canopy and extended nose to accommodate six 0.6-in (15.2-mm) guns, the increase in barrel diameter being based on anticipated firepower needs for the planned amphibious invasion of Japan. This airframe was used in gunnery tests at Wright Field, Ohio.

Modified tailpipes, angled outwards, resolved the heat/buckling problem. Wind tunnel tests showed than an 18-in (45.7-mm) extension of the vertical tail would assure stability, though it is not clear whether this modification was actually made.

Except with respect to range, which was a formidable 2,200 miles (3540 km) with underwing droptanks, the Bell XP-83 seemed to offer no improvement over the Lockheed F-80 Shooting Star then in production. For the post-war fighter-escort role, the newly independent USAF turned to the North American F-82 Twin Mustang. The redesignated XF-83 soldiered on as a flying testbed for new technology.

The first machine was assigned to a ramjet engine test programme. A hatch was cut in the belly to provide entry into the aft fuselage and an engineer's station, 'blind' except for a small port-side window, was created behind the pilot. Experimental ramjets were slung under the wings. The intent was for the XF-83 to serve as a proving vehicle for ramjet power, once aloft flying with the ramjets alone. In the later

1940s, similar tests were conducted with F-51s, F-80s and other types although no practical application was ever found.

On 4 September 1947, just as this test programme had begun, a ramjet caught fire and flames spread to the wing. Pilot Chalmers 'Slick' Goodlin and engineer Charles Fay, without benefit of ejection seats, bailed out safely. The Bell XF-83, which never received a popular name, had made its last flight.

Specification
XP-83

Type: single-seat long-range escort fighter
Powerplant: two 3,600-lb (1633-kg) thrust General Electric I-40 (J33-GE-5) turbojet engines
Performance: maximum speed 522 mph (840.1 km/h) at 15,660 ft

First flying some months before the end of World War II, the Bell XP-83 experienced several major problems during its development. Designed for long-range escort missions, it was ousted by the piston-engined P-51 and P-82.

(4773 m); initial climb rate 7,000 ft (2134 m) per minute; service ceiling 45,000 ft (13716 m); range 1,580 miles (2543 km) increased to 2,200 miles (3540 km) with droptanks
Weights: empty 14,105 lb (6398 kg); normal take-off 24,090 lb (10927.2 kg); maximum take-off 27,500 lb (12474 kg)
Dimensions: span 53 ft 0 in (16.15 m); length 45 ft 0 in (13.72 m); height 14 ft 0 in (4.27 m); wing area 431 sq ft (40.04 m²)
Armament: six 0.5-in (12.7-mm) fixed forward-firing nose machine-guns

---

Republic F-84 Thunderjet, Thunderstreak and Thunderflash

History and notes

The F-84 Thunderjet/Thunderstreak/Thunderflash series resulted from Republic's design team under Alexander Kartveli bucking the tide again. Just as Kartveli had chosen a radial engine while everybody else was turning to inline powerplants, thus creating the P-47 Thunderbolt, his engineers selected an axial-flow turbojet for the F-84 when all other American designs (Bell P-59, Lockheed F-80, Grumman F9F) had centrifugal-flow turbine powerplants. Initially planned as nothing more than a jet-powered Thunderbolt, the prototype XP-84 (45-59475) was a wholly new design when rolled out at Farmingdale, Long Island, in February 1945. Powered by a 4,000-lb (1814.4-kg) thrust Allison TG-180 (soon developed into the J35 series), the clean, straight-wing, tricycle-gear fighter was trucked to Muroc Dry Lake, California, and flown by Major Wallace Lein on 28 February 1946. A second machine set a US national speed record of 611 mph (983.3 km/h) in August 1946 and Republic proceeded with construction of 16 armed YP-84As (45-59482/59497). The last of these was eventually built as the first of 226 P-84Bs, armed with six 0.5-in (12.7-mm) M3 machine-guns and placed into service with the 14th Fighter Group, Dow Field, Maine, in November 1947. The F-84B, as the type was redesignated on 11 June 1948, was not an easy craft to handle but was popular with pilots from the beginning.

The F-84C, of which 191 were built, employed the J35-A-13 engine and entered service with the 33rd Fighter Group at Kirtland AFB, New Mexico, in 1948. The F-84D variant followed, with upgraded 5,000-lb (2268-kg) thrust J35-A-17D, structural changes, and improved cockpit layout; 154 examples of the F-84D rolled off the Farmingdale line, and this was the first Thunderjet to deploy overseas, going to Korea with the 27th Fighter Escort Group in 1950.

The definitive F-84E model, slated to fight in Korea and to achieve long-distance operational deployments as fighters began to spread their legs across oceans, had a 12-in (30.5-cm) longer fuselage giving more fuel capacity and more cockpit space, pylons under the wings for two 1,000-lb (454-kg) bombs, and other changes including a Sperry radar-ranging gunsight. Retractable jet assisted take-off (JATO) racks were added to the underside of the rear fuselage, making it possible to raise maximum take-off weight to 24,000 lb (10886.4 kg) and to carry an impressive load of rocket and bomb ordnance; 743 were built, including about 100 for France and other

Republic F-84E Thunderjet of the 9th FBS, 49th FBW, based at K-2 in Korea in late 1951. All of the Wing's aircraft carried the star under the cockpit to commemorate the unit's first MiG kill on 19th September.

Republic F-84

Like their P-47 predecessors, straight-wing F-84s exhibited great qualities of strength and weapons carrying ability, making them much more attractive for the fighter-bomber role than for pure air-to-air work. This F-84G was assigned to nuclear weapons tests at Indian Springs, Nevada.

The F-84G was the final Thunderjet model, featuring an autopilot to make long-distance flights easier, inflight refuelling probe and nuclear capability. Thunderjets even saw service with Strategic Air Command as fighter escorts.

NATO countries. This was to become the principal fighter-bomber of the 1950-3 Korean conflict, commencing its combat role with the 27th Fighter Escort Group at Taegu on 6 December 1950. F-84Es of the 116th Fighter Bomber Group in May 1952 became the first warplanes ever to be refuelled aloft on combat missions, using wingtip-mounted probes to couple with Boeing KB-29M tankers. Although not a match for the MiG-15 in air combat, the F-84E did account for some MiG kills.

Essentially a new aircraft was the F-84F, originally known as the YF-96A, flown in prototype form (49-2430) on 3 June 1950 with wing and tail surfaces swept back at 38.5 degrees and a 7,220-lb (3275-kg) thrust Wright J65-W-3 turbojet, an American-built version of the British Armstrong Siddeley Sapphire. Installing this engine required major redesign of the fuselage, one of the more obvious changes being a short steel-framed canopy which opened on two hinged side arms and a third at the rear to swing up and back in a level attitude. Given the name Thunderstreak, the first service-test YF-84F (51-1344) flew on 14 February 1951. Initially, the F-84F suffered from a high-g stall pitch-up tendency severe enough to rip the wings off the airframe. Improvement was achieved by introducing a horizontal tail with a single powered 'slab' surface although the F-84F continued to face manoeuvrability restrictions throughout much of its service life and was always regarded as a fighter-bomber rather than an air-to-air combat craft. Despite this, with no other fighter type readily available, the F-84F entered service with the Strategic Air Command's 506th Strategic Fighter Wing at Dow AFB, Maine, in January 1954 and (together with some straight-wing F-84 aircraft) was for many years intended as an escort fighter for deep penetrations into the Soviet Union. After long delays, the Tactical Air Command's first F-84Fs went into service with the 405th Fighter-Bomber Wing at Langley AFB, Virginia, on 12 May 1954. Some 2,348 F-84Fs were delivered, including 852 manufactured by General Motors in Kansas City. Though it was to become a

principal arm of the NATO nations and a widely employed fighter in USAF and Air National Guard service, delays prevented the F-84F from entering combat in Korea and its first action under fire was with French forces in Suez in 1956.

The second service-test YF-84F (51-1345) was tested with wing-root air inlets and pointed nose, a configuration once intended for the fighter variant but used only for the RF-84F Thunderflash reconnaissance machine, whose nose was encumbered by six cameras, defensive armament of four 0.5-in (12.7-mm) machine-guns being mounted in the upper part of the inlet ducts. The YRF-84F prototype (51-11828) was ready at Edwards AFB, California, by July 1952, but structural difficulties and engine delays kept the RF-84F from entering service with the 363rd Tactical Reconnaissance Wing at Shaw AFB, South Carolina, until March 1954. A total of 715 aircraft in the RF-84F series was built, of which 386 were supplied to NATO operators.

The F-84G designation, if out of sequence, applies to the final straight-wing Thunderjet, powered by the 5,600-lb (2540.2-kg) thrust Allison J35-A-29. The F-84G incorporated systems which made it the first fighter able to deliver tactical nuclear weapons. It introduced the multi-framed canopy which was fitted retroactively to many earlier straight-wing F-84s. With a flying boom refuelling receptacle in the port wing, the F-84G joined early variants in the long-range SAC escort role. F-84Gs also fought in the air-to-ground war in Korea with the 49th Fighter Bomber Group at Taegu and other units. No fewer than 3,025 F-84Gs were built, of which 1,900 went to NATO nations.

Two experimental XF-84Hs (51-17059 and 51-17060), originally designated XF-106 according to some sources, were built to test-fly supersonic propellers. A huge, three-blade propeller was driven by a large 5,850-hp (4362.3-kW) Allison coupled turboprop. At an aircraft speed of 670 mph (1078.2 km/h), the propeller blades emitted 900 sonic booms per minute! Production of the prop-driven Thunderstreak was never seriously contemplated, but it provided extensive scientific knowledge. The second example is on outdoor display today at Meadows Field, Bakersfield, California.

Two YF-84J Thunderstreaks (51-11708/11709) with 7,200-lb (3265.9-kg) thrust General Electric J73 engines, were tested at Edwards AFB in the mid-1950s with favourable results but production prospects were, by then, pre-empted by the higher performing 'century series' of fighters. The RF-84K designation, originally

Above: With its all-swept flying surfaces and more powerful engine, the F-84F bore little resemblance to earlier variants. Thunderstreaks were still tailored mainly to the fighter-bomber role, although they were more adept at air-to-air fighting than the straight-wing Thunderjets.

Below: Intended mainly as research aircraft, the two XF-84Hs were rebuilt with a powerful turboprop driving a supersonic propeller. As well as looking bizarre, they made their mark by being two of the noisiest aircraft ever.

Republic F-84

Republic F-84F Thunderstreak of the 91st Fighter Squadron, RAF Bentwaters. F-84Fs served in USAFE mainly for the strike role, armed with tactical nuclear bombs among other weapons.

GRF-84F, was given to 25 Thunderflash reconnaissance machines which, after earlier tests with F-84E and YF-84F airframes, were carried operationally by Convair B-36 bombers in the fighter conveyor (FICON) programme. The 91st Strategic Reconnaissance Squadron at Fairchild AFB, Washington D.C., flew these parasite fighters with GRB-36D mother ships.

Straight-wing F-84Es served with Air National Guard units well into the 1950s and sweptwing F-84Fs were in ANG service as late as 1971. Both were tested with zero-length launchers, being launched from the ground by rocket boosters, in an unusual early programme to develop zero-runway take-off capability. Both variants equipped the USAF's *Thunderbirds* flight demonstration team. Examples of these aircraft are beginning to appear in civil registry in the USA today. Total production was 6,789 aircraft.

Combat

Though pilots liked it, they never spoke of flying the F-84 as a joy. It was a rigorous, demanding task. The F-84 series, like the same builder's P-47 Thunderbolt, was characterised by weapons-carrying ability, ruggedness, the capacity to absorb punishment, and not a few problems ranging from maintenance headaches to yaw and stall handling difficulties. Though a few F-84Ds reached the Korean combat theatre, their J35-A-17D engines required replacement every 45 flying hours and they were 'down' more than 'up'. On the ground, the wide landing gear of the F-84 provided ease of handling but foreign object damage (FOD) was an especially pesky problem for the temperamental J35. F-84Es and F-84Gs flown by USAF and activated Air National Guard units in Korea became the bomb- and rocket-haulers of the war, ranging through mountain passes to attack trains, convoys and other targets. A fully-laden F-84E, even with JATO boost, was not an easy aircraft to get off the ground and more than one Thunderjet 'went in' at runway's end carrying 500-lb (227-kg) bombs or 5-in (127-mm) high-velocity aircraft rockets (HVAR). F-84s were involved in every major air operation in all but the first months of the three-year Korean War, including raids on the Yalu River dams in the summer of 1952 which cut off the supply of hydro-electric power to North Korea. But pilots found the F-84 a fair-weather friend, with virtually no usefulness in bad weather. Korea's howling blizzards kept more Thunderjets down than did enemy AA fire. The straight-wing F-84 was never a match for the MiG-15 and

18 were shot down in air battles in 'MiG Alley' along the Yalu, although nine MiGs fells before Thunderjets' guns. There were occasional high moments, as when First Lieutenant Arthur Oligher and Captain Harry Underwood of the 136th Fighter Bomber Group shared credit for a MiG-15 in July 1951.

During the 1956 Suez crisis, with the UK and France supporting Israel against Soviet-backed Egypt, the French sent two squadrons of sweptwing F-84Fs to war, one operating from Israel's Lydda Airfield. F-84Fs are reported to have destroyed 20 Ilyushin Il-28 bombers on the ground and one in the air in November 1956 and to have emerged from the Suez fighting with the loss of only one plane and pilot. F-84Fs were employed by Turkey in fighting over Cyprus in the 1970s.

The F-84 was an effective 'mud mover' and one which pilots decorated gaudily, even if they never sang its praises without some concern for the sheer difficulty of flying the type. The F-84F was far more forgiving than straight-wing Thunderjets and must be awarded a ranking position in history. The tradition of big, tough Republic fighters was to continue in the 1960s with the F-105 Thunderchief.

Specification

F-84F

Type: single-seat fighter-bomber
Powerplant: one 7,220 lb (3275-kg) thrust Wright J65-W-3 Sapphire turbojet engine
Performance: maximum speed 695 mph (1118.5 km/h) at sea level and 658 mph (1058.9 km/h) at 20,000 ft (6096 m); initial climb rate 8,200 ft (2499.4 m) per minute; service ceiling 46,000 ft (14021 m); combat radius with two droptanks 810 miles (1304 km)
Weights: empty 13,830 lb (6273.3 kg); maximum take-off 28,000 lb (12700.8 kg)
Dimensions: span 33 ft 7¼ in (10.24 m); length 43 ft 4¾ in (13.23 m); height 14 ft 4¾ in (4.39 m); wing area 325 sq ft (30.19 m²)
Armament: six 0.5-in (12.7-mm) fixed forward-firing Browning M3 machine-guns, plus provision for 6,000 lb (2721.6 kg) of external ordnance including US tactical nuclear weapons

The F-84 served on Air National Guard units until the start of the 1970s. These F-84Fs proudly wear three-tone tactical camouflage, serving with the 179th Tactical Fighter Group at Elmendorf AFB, Alaska.

Republic F-84

This illustration depicts a Republic F-84F of one of the later production blocks, these aircraft having an all-moving slab tailplane. It has also been field-modified with a brake parachute in the rear of the ventral underfin compartment. The striking markings are those of the 78th Tactical Fighter Squadron 'Bushmasters', component squadron of the 81st TFW at RAF Bentwaters/Woodbridge. Today the ground attack role carried out so well by the F-84 is still performed from the same bases by the 81st, their current equipment being the Fairchild A-10.

26675

FS·675

KOREA Jet Age Air War

Less than five years after Hiroshima and Nagasaki, the US Air Force was back at war in Korea. The air war was to reach a climax in the duel between two classic protagonists: the MiG-15 and Sabre.

With East-West relations worsening by the day, following the end of World War II, it was inevitable that the relative calm would be shattered. Despite the ferocity of the battle that lay ahead, it was probably fortunate that the fuse broke in the Korean peninsula rather than Europe. At around 6.00 am on 25 June 1950, North Korean troops stormed across the 38th parallel and swept through South Korean defences. Six hours later, plans were being laid in Far East Air Forces headquarters to control the evacuation of US personnel, this involving the use of North American F-82G Twin Mustang aircraft.

By the next morning, General Douglas MacArthur was Commander of the United Nations forces that would fight the communist aggressors, and as the major part of that UN effort, the United States found itself at war again. This time it did not have a monopoly on nuclear weapons, as the Soviets possessed a bomb, and the spectre of the newly-formed Chinese republic loomed large over Korea. FEAF had F-80 and F-82 fighters under its control, and these were in action by 27 June, gaining easy victories over the North Korean Yak-9 and Ilyushin Il-10 warplanes.

Throughout the war the bomber assets re-mained propeller-powered, the Douglas B-26 Invader and Boeing B-29 handling the bulk of bombing and reconnaissance missions. Nevertheless, from the start the USAF had jets in-theatre in the shape of F-80s, although the North American F-51 Mustangs of the Air National Guard came to be very important to the ground attack effort.

Enter the Chinese

The first months were easy for the fighters, with only sporadic attacks by the untrained and uncoordinated North Korean crews to contend with. This changed dramatically on 1 November when the Chinese entered the fray, sending their MiG-15s across the Yalu river for the first time. On 17 December, Lt Russell J. Brown of the 51st FIW scored the first jet-versus-jet victory of history flying his F-80C, two days after the North American F-86 Sabre had arrived in-theatre.

The MiG-15 had come as a considerable shock to the UN forces, its swept wing allowing it to outperform easily the F-80s put up against it, and even out-turning and out-climbing the famous Sabre. The initial Sabre effort was short-lived, for by January 1951 their bases were being overrun on the

ground by North Korean forces. They retired to Japan to await a change in events, having already proved that the Sabre could defeat the MiGs by superior tactics.

On the ground a reversal allowed the Sabres to return to Korea in March and they began a systematic destruction of the Chinese MiG force. With Soviet backing, the Chinese were not to be put off, sending out huge formations of MiGs to battle with the hopelessly outnumbered Sabres. Hopeless was not quite the word, for the US pilots were often World War II veterans with far more experience than their young Chinese counterparts, and tallies rose steadily for the Sabre pilots. In mid-December 1951 the Chinese stopped their campaign to rest for a while, this period ending in May 1952 when they set out again with renewed vengeance and under the direction of newly-installed GCI radar.

Many pilots were Soviet, and the MiG pilots became more competent adversaries. The US countered this by offering a reward to any pilot who defected to the South com-

'El Diablo' was a North American F-86E Sabre assigned to the 335th Fighter Squadron, Kimpo, spring 1952. The mount of Captain Chuck Owens, the aircraft displayed the squadron's victory tallies. Note the open leading-edge slats.

Operating under top cover provided by Sabres, straight-wing Thunderjets performed much of the ground attack mission, where groundfire was their biggest danger. This aircraft is an F-84G from the 69th Fighter-Bomber Squadron.

plete with his MiG. Fearing international embarrassment, it is believed the Soviet Union pulled its pilots from the fight immediately (one North Korean was later to defect). By the start of 1953 the Chinese were beginning to think of a truce, but with the more capable F-86F in its inventory, the USAF was going in for the kill. June, July and August turned into a 'turkey shoot' for the Sabre pilots, who were again facing inexperienced communists in aircraft that had lost their performance advantage over the earlier models of F-86.

With Sabres keeping the MiGs busy, UN attack aircraft were free to pound the North Korean ground forces, and this sealed the fate of the war. Kill figures have been subject to much confusion, but around 800 MiG-15s were downed by Sabres for the loss of around 80 US machines. The contribution of the Sabre can be measured by the fact that the next highest-scoring UN type was the B-29 bomber with around 30 kills! Down in the weeds the F-80 and F-84 had proved themselves as good ground-attack aircraft, but they could not operate without effective top cover from Sabres. At night the F-94 Starfire had made a name for itself as a radar-equipped jet fighter, and this avenue was to point the way forward for the fighter aircraft.

Without doubt the Sabre will go down into history as one of the most important fighters ever. Yet in some ways it was a less capable performer than the MiG-15. What made the difference was the training and tactics of the pilots, something that was to be a considerable debating point during the next US shooting war in Vietnam. Although the clear-air eyeball dogfighting of Korea is still important to this day, the advent of effective fighter radar would add another dimension to the future air battle.

Lockheed P-80Cs were the first fighters in the Korean theatre, and scored several kills against North Korean prop-driven aircraft. Although a handful of MiG-kills were recorded, the P-80 was generally no match for the MiG-15.

McDonnell F-85 Goblin

History and notes

The McDonnell XF-85 Goblin was the only USAF aircraft ever conceived from the outset as a 'parasite' fighter to be carried aboard bombers, in the same manner by which the converted Republic RF-84K Thunderflash was employed operationally for a time. Designed by Herman D. Barkey, the XF-85 was to be stowed in the number one or four bomb bay of the B-36 intercontinental bomber. Over target, it would be dropped free to protect the B-36 from enemy interceptors.

Because of its unusual task, the XF-85 Goblin was a unique design. It had 36-degree swept wings which folded upward from the root for storage inside its mother ship. It had an odd-looking, X-shaped tail, although flight controls were conventional. Equipped with a probe or 'skyhook' designed to engage a trapeze lowered by the bomber (a process much like threading a needle) the XF-85 was powered by a 3,000-lb (1360.8-kg) thrust Westinghouse J34-WE-12 turbojet engine.

In 1947, indoor tests were begun to evaluate the mating arrangement between the Goblin and a mock-up of a B-36 fuselage. On 9 November 1947 the first of two XF-85s (46-523/524) was disassembled at the manufacturer's St Louis plant and flown aboard a C-97 transport to Moffett Field, California, for wind-tunnel tests. While being positioned in the tunnel, the aircraft fell 40 ft (12.2 m), was badly damaged, and had to be returned to St Louis, being replaced

Two XF-85 Goblins were built, this example surviving to be placed on display in the US Air Force Museum at Wright-Patterson AFB, Ohio. Not surprisingly, in view of its short fuselage and complicated tail arrangement, the XF-85 had stability problems.

at Moffett by the second machine. On 5 June 1948, this second XF-85 was transported to Muroc AFB, California, and, with no B-36 airframe available for evaluation of the parasite fighter concept, experiments began using an EB-29B Superfortress (44-84111). Ed Schoch, a former US Navy F6F Hellcat pilot with four air combat kills in the Pacific war, was the only man ever to fly the XF-85. His first attempt nearly killed him. On 23 August 1948, Schoch was attempting to re-engage the bomber's trapeze when he slammed into it, shattering his canopy, ripping his helmet off, and knocking him unconscious. Schoch recovered in time to make a shaky landing on the XF-85's underside skid in the Muroc desert, damaging the plane.

The second flight on 14 October 1948, resulted in a normal mid-air drop and subsequent hook-up. Three more times, however, struggling to manoeuvre the tricky Goblin, Schoch was forced to make belly landings in the desert rather than regain his link-up with the Superfortress.

On 8 April 1949, the original XF-85 made its first and only flight. In budget-lean 1949, the XF-85 pro-

gramme was quietly terminated, although the Strategic Air Command eventually became interested in the parasite fighter concept when it became possible to carry an RF-84K aboard a B-36. The first XF-85 is on display at the Air Force Museum in Dayton, Ohio, while the second is at the Strategic Air Command Museum in Omaha, Nebraska, displayed in highly inaccurate markings with a spurious tail number.

Specification
XF-85
Type: single-seat fighter
Powerplant: one 3,000-lb

(1360.8-kg) thrust Westinghouse J34-WE-22 turbojet engine
Performance: maximum speed 648 mph (1042.8 km/h) at sea level and 573 mph (922.1 km/h) at 40,000 ft (12192 m); initial climb rate 12,500 ft (3810 m) per minute; service ceiling 48,200 ft (14691 m); combat radius 32 minutes at cruising speed at 40,000 ft (12192 m)
Weights: empty 3,984 lb (1807.1 kg); maximum take-off 5,600 lb (2540.2 kg)
Dimensions: span 21 ft 0 in (6.4 m); length 21 ft 0 in (6.4 m); height (wings folded) 11 ft 0 in (3.35 m); wing area 100.52 sq ft (9.34 m²)
Armament: none installed

North American F-86 Sabre

History and notes

The North American F-86 Sabre, best-recalled for prevailing over the MiG-15 in Korea but used by numerous air forces, owes its creation to a project authorised in 1943 by company president J. H. 'Dutch' Kindelberger and taken up by a design team under J. Lee Atwood and Ray Rice. By late 1944, the company was at work on its model NA-134, which would emerge as the US Navy's FJ-1 Fury, a conventional jet fighter with a straight, thin wing set low on the fuselage and a straight-through flow of air from nose inlet to jet exhaust. This design, powered by a 4,000-lb (1814.4-kg) thrust Allison TG-180, soon to be known as the J35, offered little advantage over the identically powered Republic XP-84. Soon, however, with L. P.

Greene taking over North American's design effort, German research on sweptback wings was exploited and Kindelberger made a bold policy decision. Rather than merely proceed with an already good design, the company went for the revolutionary swept wing. The Soviet Union was taking the same course with the MiG-15, which flew in 1947, although British fighters well into the 1950s would be handicapped by the straight-wing configuration.

First flight

The first of three XP-86 prototypes (45-59597/59599) was rolled out 8 August 1947, powered by the J35-C-3 engine (developed by General Electric but manufactured first by the Chevrolet Division and later the Allison Division of General Motors). On 1 October 1947, the first flight was made by company test pilot George Welch, last encountered in this narrative flying a Curtiss P-40 at Pearl Harbor. The prototype exceeded the speed of sound in a dive for the first time on 26 April 1948 and was formally delivered to the USAF on 30 November 1948. An initial order for 33 F-86As (47-605/637) powered by the more advanced 5,000-lb (2268-kg) thrust General Electric J47-GE-3 turbojet resulted in the first flight of an F-86A on 20 May 1948. The first operational F-86As were delivered in March 1949 to the 9th Fighter Squadron, part of the 1st Fighter Group, at March AFB, California. The name Sabre was adopted on 4 March 1949 (the F-86 has never officially been named Sabrejet). Much later in their service lives, some F-86As were converted as DF-86A drone-control and RF-86A reconnaissance craft.

The F-86B designation was briefly assigned to a minor variant among the 554 airframes eventually delivered in the F-86A series.

The North American company was in the forefront of technological advances in the late 1940s, its swept-wing Sabre revolutionising the fighter world and its B-45 Tornado being the USAF's first jet bomber. The Sabre is the first prototype, designated XP-86 at the time. In the background is the second prototype XB-45.

The F-86C designation was temporarily assigned to a significantly different aircraft which was redesignated YF-93A.

The F-86D was a radar-guided, rocket-armed all-weather fighter intended for ground-controlled intercept (GCI) of Soviet bombers penetrating North American airspace. Briefly known as YF-95A, the first of two YF-86D service-test aircraft (50-577/578) was flown on 22 December 1949 by Welch, and though no radar was yet available it had the giant nose radome and chin inlet beneath, which would characterise the series. There were delays and difficulties in the development of the interceptor, powered by 7,650-lb (3470-kg) thrust (with afterburning) General Electric J47-GE-13, equipped with APS-6 radar and Hughes fire-control system, and armed with 24 2.75-in (69.85-mm) folding-fin aircraft rockets (FFAR) in a retractable nose tray. The first operational F-86D was delivered on 5 March 1951. On 19 November 1952, Captain J. Slade Nash piloted an F-86D (51-2495) to a world air speed record of 699.9 mph (1126.35 km/h) in a sea-level dash at Salton Sea, California. Some 2,504 of the F-86D interceptors were delivered and served with the USAF's Air Defense Command (ADC) and units in Europe, as well as in the Air National Guard (ANG) and the air forces of Denmark, Japan and South Korea.

Improved day-fighter

The F-86E was an improved day-fighter Sabre with an 'all-flying tail'. The tailplane became a primary control surface, the elevators merely increasing its effect, and artificial feel was added for the first time in a production fighter. The first F-86E flew in 1950, was operationally employed by the USAF, and became the basis for production of a series of Sabres built under licence by Canadair Limited in Montreal. The six variants of Canadair Sabre totalling 655 airframes for Canada, Germany, South Africa and Colombia are outside the scope of this work. The only Canadair machines assigned a USAF designation were the 120 F-86E-6(CAN) airframes built with US funding, many of which served with the UK's Royal Air Force. In the mid-1980s, however, numbers of Canadair-built Sabres were arriving in the USA for conversion to QF-86 target drones at the US Navy Missile Test Center, Point Mugu, California.

The first example of the F-86F model (51-2850) was flown 19 March 1952 by George Smith. The F-86F was initially built in Los Angeles as previous North American machines had been but, given

A pair of F-86Es launch on an air-to-air mission. In Korea the Sabre ruled supreme, but was slightly inferior in performance respects to the MiG-15. Well-trained pilots flying far better tactics more than redressed the balance.

the urgency of the Korean War, a second production line was established at the firm's former Curtiss plant in Columbus, Ohio. The F-86F had a new wing leading edge extended 6 in (0.152 cm) at the root and 3 in (0.076 cm) at the tip, with small boundary layer fences introduced for the first time. This '6-3' wing improved the Sabre's manoeuvrability at high altitude, and the F-86F was rushed to Korea where earlier F-86A and F-86E machines were regarded, by some, as less agile than the MiG-15. By the time the 1950-3 Korean War reached its peak, all three Sabre fighter wings on the peninsula had converted to the F-86F model, 2,540 of which were manufactured. Two F-86Fs were converted as two-seat TF-86F trainer prototypes. An RF-86F reconnaissance variant was originated in Japan. In the 1980s, a number of QF-86F drones were serving the US Navy at Point Mugu. It would be impossible to list every country which eventually obtained used F-86F airframes (Tunisia being an example of how far afield the type went) but among early major users were South Africa, Korea and Japan. In 1984, Korea was considering converting its high-hour F-86F airframes into pilotless flying bombs.

The designation F-86G was briefly applied to a variant of the all-weather interceptor powered by the J47-GE-33 and eventually delivered as an F-86D.

What gave both the MiG-15 and F-86 their tremendous performance was the adoption of the swept-wing, which overcame many of the compression problems associated with high transonic flight. German wartime research had led the field in this arena, and North American had made full use of captured German data.

A major change in the Sabre airframe was marked when the first of two service-test YF-86H aircraft (52-1975/1976) was flown on 30 April 1953 by Joseph Lynch. The production F-86H, built in Columbus, introduced the 9,300-lb (4218.5-kg) thrust General Electric J73-GE-3 turbojet and was intended to be armed with four 20-mm cannon, although the first 116 of 473 built retained the six 0.5-in (12.7-mm) machine-guns of all other American day-fighter Sabres. Never exported, the re-engined F-86H arrived too late for combat in Korea but was widely used by USAF and ANG units. A few have been converted to QF-86H target drones for the US Navy at China Lake, California.

Canadian Sabres

The F-86J appellation went to a converted F-86A (49-1069) powered by the 7,275-lb (3300-kg) thrust Avro Orenda turbojet, which was used on most Canadian-built Sabres but no other USAF machines.

The two service-test YF-86K Sabres (52-3630 and 52-3804), the first flown on 15 July 1954 by Ray Morris and both converted from F-86D standard, introduced a version of the radar-equipped, all-weather interceptor armed with four 20-mm cannon instead of FFAR rockets. The F-86K, the first production example of which

An F-86E rests on the pierced-steel planking that typified Korean airfields during the conflict. Although the MiG-15 carried large-calibre cannon armament, the six 0.5-in (12.7-mm) machine-guns of the Sabre were far more accurate and had better convergence.

(53-8273) was introduced to service in 1955, was intended primarily for export to NATO allies. Of 341 built, 221 were assembled from knockdown kits by Fiat in Italy. Italy and West Germany were principal F-86K operators.

The F-86L was a conversion of the F-86D and a further development of the all-weather interceptor, being refitted with 2 ft (0.61 m) wider wings and data-link capability for the Semi-Automatic Ground Environment (SAGE) system. Some 981 were converted for service with the USAF's Air Defense Command and a few reached Thailand and other users.

The US Navy's straight-wing FJ-1 Fury was followed in service by the FJ-2, FJ-3 and FJ-4, all sweptwing, navalised Sabres. On 18 September 1962 when the US system for designating military aircraft was changed, the FJ-3 and FJ-4 Fury acquired the new F-1 designation. By that time, however, their service career was nearly over. A Sabre variant was also manufactured by Commonwealth in Australia.

Of the 7,000 plus Sabres built, only two had a second seat for training duties. Designated TF-86F, these were converted F-86Fs with a lengthened forward fuselage to accommodate the extra seat. Two nose guns were retained, as was the provision for two underwing pylons. The type received the company designation NA.304, but the scheme was abandoned due to the ease with which pilots transferred to the fighter from existing trainer types.

Until the arrival in service of more modern types, the F-86D 'Sabre Dog' was the mainstay of Air Defense Command during the early 1950s, its radar giving it a limited measure of all-weather capability in the interceptor role. Like most interceptors it was fast, an example capturing the world speed record in 1952. Its engine featured rudimentary afterburning. The lower pair of this cavorting quartet show the leading edge slats to advantage.

North American F-86

Designed as an interceptor rather than clear-air dogfighter, the F-86D 'Dogship' featured a radar in a nose radome for the interception of bombers. Gun armament was dispensed with in favour of a retractable pack of 24 unguided missiles.

Well over 7,300 Sabres were manufactured, 6,874 with USAF designations and serial numbers, and the Sabre remains in such widespread service that it probably faces more battles before its career is concluded. The battles that will always be remembered, however, were fought at the northern extreme of a narrow Asian peninsula where American pilots were forbidden from crossing the river to strike the enemy's airbases in China.

Combat

When China entered the Korean War in November 1950, its MiG-15s based on the Manchurian side of the Yalu River quickly established supremacy over the F-51s, F-80s and F9F Panthers in the combat zone. On 8 November 1950, the 4th Fighter-Interceptor Wing was despatched from Dover AFB, Delaware and, taking its F-86A Sabres across the Pacific by sea, began combat operations at Seoul's Kimpo AB on 17 December. Their first mission drew blood. Flying at 32,000 ft (9754 m) at a speed of 472 mph (759.6 km/h), Lieutenant Colonel Bruce Hinton of the wing's 336th Fighter Squadron in an F-86A (49-1236), callsign BAKER Lead, began the classic ploy that would continue throughout the war, the fighter sweep along the Yalu where the Americans deliberately placed themselves in position to be engaged by the MiGs. At that point, incredible as it seems with today's intelligence-gathering methods, Hinton and his wingmen had no information about the armament or manoeuvrability of the MiG-15. When the MiGs took the bait, Hinton ordered BAKER Flight to jettison wingtanks. Hinton pulled into a turning MiG-15, watched the Chinese pilot discard his wingtanks, and used the advantage of the F-86A's superior acceleration in a dive to close rapidly. Though his F-86A was redlined at (restricted to) Mach 0.95, Hinton was at almost the speed of sound when he fired a short burst of 0.5-in (12.7-mm) fire. The Chinese fighter broke up in pieces and the F-86 had its first kill.

The F-86A, F-86E and F-86F used in Korean combat are usually reported to have been at a manoeuvring disadvantage with the MiG-15 and to have prevailed only because of superior pilot skill. It is true that many American fighter pilots were World War II veterans. Most, however, believe that their airframe, too, was superior. This is especially so with regard to the F-86F with the '6-3' wing and, most importantly, the only radar-ranging gunsight on any fighter in the war. Captain Manuel 'Pete' Fernandez spoke highly of the gunsight and of the Sabre's stability at high angles of attack. On 10 May 1953, Fernandez, of the 334th Fighter-Interceptor Squadron, flying an F-86F (51-2857), callsign JOHN DOG Lead, found himself in a furious manoeuvring situation at medium altitude where the MiG-15 supposedly had the greatest advantage. Outnumbered and in a critical fuel situation, Fernandez was able to turn inside his opponents each time they closed in. He found the Sabre's 0.5-in

North American F-86E Sabre cutaway drawing key

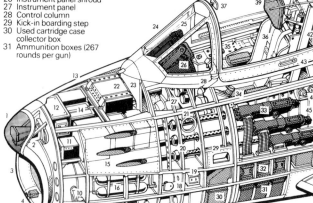

1 Radome
2 Radar antenna
3 Engine air intake
4 Gun camera
5 Nosewheel leg doors
6 Nose undercarriage leg strut
7 Nosewheel
8 Torque scissor links
9 Steering control valve
10 Nose undercarriage pivot fixing
11 Sight amplifier
12 Radio and electronics equipment bay
13 Electronics bay access panel
14 Battery
15 Gun muzzle blast troughs
16 Oxygen bottles
17 Nosewheel bay door
18 Oxygen servicing point
19 Canopy switches
20 Machine-gun barrel mountings
21 Hydraulic system test connections
22 Radio transmitter
23 Cockpit armoured bulkhead
24 Windscreen panels
25 A-1CM radar gunsight
26 Instrument panel shroud
27 Instrument panel
28 Control column
29 Kick-in boarding step
30 Used cartridge case collector box
31 Ammunition boxes (267 rounds per gun)
32 Ammunition feed chutes
33 0.5-in (12.7-mm) Colt-Browning machine-guns
34 Engine throttle
35 Starboard side console panel
36 North American ejection seat
37 Rear view mirror
38 Sliding cockpit canopy cover
39 Ejection seat headrest
40 ADF sense aerials
41 Pilot's back armour
42 Ejection seat guide rails
43 Canopy handle
44 Cockpit pressure valves
45 Armoured side panels
46 Tailplane trim actuator
47 Fuselage/front spar main frame
48 Forward fuselage fuel tank (total internal fuel capacity 434.4 US gal/1644 litres)
49 Fuselage lower longeron
50 Intake trunking
51 Rear radio and electronics bay

(12.7-mm) machine-guns more accurate at greater range than the MiG's 23-mm and 37-mm cannon, although other pilots tended to berate the fifty-caliber round's low hitting power. When 10 F-86Fs were refitted with four 20-mm cannon and sent to Korea under Project GUNVAL, the American cannon also proved farther-reaching and more accurate than the MiG's weapons, although posing maintenance problems not encountered with the machine-guns. Fernandez, who finished as the war's third-ranking ace with 14 MiG kills, was adamant about the Sabre's overall superiority and was by no means alone.

Although the F-86 is often reported to have achieved a remarkable 12-to-1 kill ratio over the MiG-15, revised analysis makes the actual figure roughly 7-to-1, still so extraordinary as to be unmatched in any other air campaign in history. F-86s shot down 792 MiG-15s while sustaining 78 air-to-air losses. The UK's future Air Marshal John Nichol shot down a MiG-15 while flying an F-86 on a USAF exchange tour. Of 40 American aces in Korea, 39 flew the F-86. The ranking aces were Captain Joseph D. McConnell Jr with 16 kills and Major James Jabara with 15. The final air-to-air kill of the war was an Ilyushin Il-12 transport downed on 27 July 1953 by Captain Ralph S. Parr, flying an F-86F (51-12959).

Specification

F-86F

Type: single-seat fighter

Powerplant: one 5,910 lb (2680.8-kg) thrust General Electric J47-GE-27 turbojet engine

Performance: maximum speed 695 mph (1118.5 km/h) at 40,000 ft (12192 m); initial climb rate (clean) 9,300 ft (2835 m) per minute; service ceiling 48,000 ft (14630 m); range with droptanks 1,270 miles (2044 km)

Weights: empty 10,890 lb (4939.7 kg); maximum take-off 20,357 lb (9233.9 kg)

Dimensions: span 37 ft 1⅖ (11.31 m) (later increased); length 37 ft 6½ in (11.44 m); height 14 ft 8¾ in (4.50 m); wing area 288 sq ft (26.76 m²)

Armament: six 0.5-in (12.7-mm) fixed forward-firing machine-guns, plus provision for two 1,000-lb (454-kg) bombs or various other bombs, rockets or other ordnance with or without two 200-US gal (757.1-litre) tanks

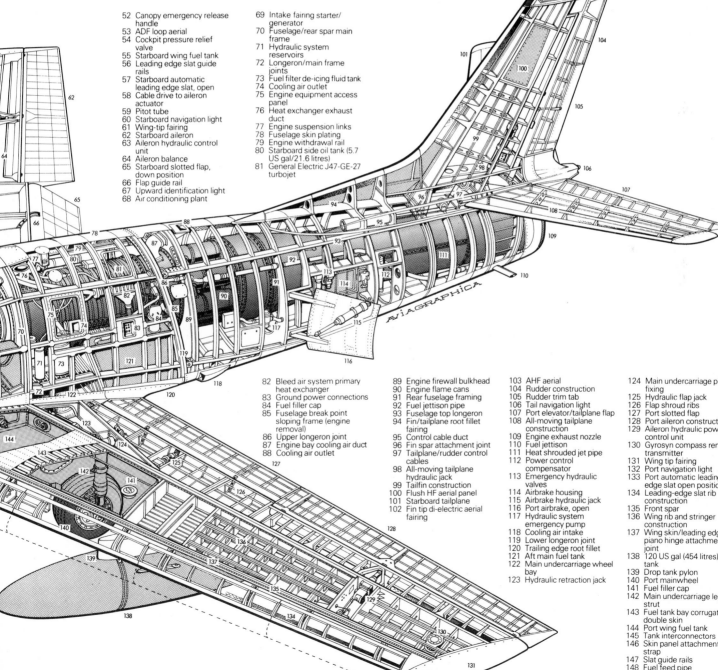

52 Canopy emergency release handle
53 ADF loop aerial
54 Cockpit pressure relief valve
55 Starboard wing fuel tank
56 Leading edge slat guide rails
57 Starboard automatic leading edge slat, open
58 Cable drive to aileron actuator
59 Pitot tube
60 Starboard navigation light
61 Wing-tip fairing
62 Starboard aileron
63 Aileron hydraulic control unit
64 Aileron balance
65 Starboard slotted flap, down position
66 Flap guide rail
67 Upward identification light
68 Air conditioning plant
69 Intake fairing starter/generator
70 Fuselage/rear spar main frame
71 Hydraulic system reservoirs
72 Longeron/main frame joints
73 Fuel filter de-icing fluid tank
74 Cooling air outlet
75 Engine equipment access panel
76 Heat exchanger exhaust duct
77 Engine suspension links
78 Fuselage skin plating
79 Engine withdrawal rail
80 Starboard side oil tank (5.7 US gal/21.6 litres)
81 General Electric J47-GE-27 turbojet

82 Bleed air system primary heat exchanger
83 Ground power connections
84 Fuel filler cap
85 Fuselage break point sloping frame (engine removal)
86 Upper longeron joint
87 Engine bay cooling air duct
88 Cooling air outlet
89 Engine firewall bulkhead
90 Engine flame cans
91 Rear fuselage framing
92 Fuel jettison pipe
93 Fuselage top longeron
94 Fin/tailplane root fillet fairing
95 Control cable duct
96 Fin spar attachment joint
97 Tailplane/rudder control cables
98 All-moving tailplane hydraulic jack
99 Tailfin construction
100 Flush HF aerial panel
101 Starboard tailplane
102 Fin tip di-electric aerial fairing
103 AHF aerial
104 Rudder construction
105 Rudder trim tab
106 Tail navigation light
107 Port elevator/tailplane flap
108 All-moving tailplane construction
109 Engine exhaust nozzle
110 Fuel jettison
111 Heat shrouded jet pipe
112 Power control compensator
113 Emergency hydraulic valves
114 Airbrake housing
115 Airbrake hydraulic jack
116 Port airbrake, open
117 Hydraulic system emergency pump
118 Cooling air intake
119 Lower longeron joint
120 Trailing edge root fillet
121 Aft main fuel tank
122 Main undercarriage wheel bay
123 Hydraulic retraction jack
124 Main undercarriage pivot fixing
125 Hydraulic flap jack
126 Flap shroud ribs
127 Port slotted flap
128 Port aileron construction
129 Aileron hydraulic power control unit
130 Gyrosyn compass remote transmitter
131 Wing tip fairing
132 Port navigation light
133 Port automatic leading-edge slat open position
134 Leading-edge slat rib construction
135 Front spar
136 Wing rib and stringer construction
137 Wing skin/leading edge piano hinge attachment joint
138 120 US gal (454 litres) drop tank
139 Drop tank pylon
140 Port mainwheel
141 Fuel filler cap
142 Main undercarriage leg strut
143 Fuel tank bay corrugated double skin
144 Port wing fuel tank
145 Tank interconnectors
146 Skin panel attachment joint strap
147 Slat guide rails
148 Fuel feed pipe
149 Aileron cable drive

North American F-86

'Dottie' was a North American F-86F-30-NA Sabre flown by Captain D. R. Hall during the Korean War. The aircraft carries the markings of the 336th Fighter-Interceptor Squadron, 4th Fighter-Interceptor Wing, based at K-14, the air base at Kimpo north-west of Seoul. The yellow wing and fuselage bands were an ordered identification mark applied to all Sabres of the Far East Air Forces, a step taken to avoid any confusion with the swept-wing MiG-15s of the Chinese and North Korean forces.

Dottie

U.S. AIR FORCE
24701

FU-701

Curtiss F-87 Blackhawk

History and notes

The Curtiss XF-87 Blackhawk fighter was an eye-catching and truly graceful all-black aircraft which attracted plenty of attention in flights over the California desert. The XF-87 resulted from studies by the manufacturer in a last-ditch effort to compete in the jet era. Curtiss had obtained tentative approval to build a twin-jet ground-attack aircraft, the XA-43. On 21 November 1945, this project was redirected towards completion of the Blackhawk fighter, a huge, mid-wing, four-engine craft with a two-man crew in side-by-side seating and with impressive fuel capacity. Powered by four 3,000-lb (1360.8-kg) thrust Westinghouse XJ34-WE-7 turbojets, the sole XF-87 (46-522) was belatedly flown at Muroc Dry Lake, California, on 1 March 1948 following long delays in its development and shipment from the company's plant (later sold to North American) in Columbus, Ohio.

The XF-87 proved to be underpowered. In the expectation that a different powerplant arrangement would make the Blackhawk more competitive, the twin-engine scheme was resurrected. On 10 June 1948, the USAF awarded a contract to Curtiss for 57 production F-87As to be powered by two 6,000-lb (2721.6-kg) thrust each General Electric J47-GE-7 engines. A further order was placed for 30 RF-87A reconnaissance aircraft.

The F-87 Blackhawk or company model CW-29A would have been fit-

The attractive Blackhawk was mainly notable for being Curtiss' last fighter for the US Air Force. Its potential as an all-weather fighter and reconnaissance platform was undermined by lack of power and company troubles.

ted with an extraordinary nose turret developed by the Glenn L. Martin Company which revolved in a 60-degree arc enabling four 20-mm guns to be fired at any angle from zero to 90 degrees from the centreline.

Though the Blackhawk was able to overcome teething troubles in flight tests and seemed to offer promise as an all-weather intercep-

tor, it was the misfortune of this beautiful aircraft that Curtiss was suffering from management difficulties and Northrop was developing an interceptor with solid potential, the F-89 Scorpion. On 18 October 1948, the USAF cancelled the F-87 Blackhawk programme in favour of the F-89. A second prototype which would have evaluated the twin J47 installation was never completed. It was to be the last Curtiss fighter.

Specification
XF-87

Type: two-seat all-weather interceptor

Powerplant: four 3,000-lb (1360.8-kg) thrust Westinghouse XJ-34-WE-7 turbojet engines
Performance: maximum speed 600 mph (965.6 km/h) at sea level; climb to 35,000 ft (10668 m) in 13.8 minutes; service ceiling 41,000 ft (12497 m); range 1,000 miles (1609 km)
Weights: empty 25,930 lb (11761.8 kg); maximum take-off 49,900 lb (22634.6 kg)
Dimensions: span 60 ft 0 in (18.29 m); length 62 ft 10 in (19.15 m); height 20 ft 0 in (6,1 m); wing area 600 sq ft (55.74 m^2)
Armament: four 20-mm cannon in flexible Martin nose turret planned but not installed

McDonnell F-88

History and notes

The McDonnell XF-88 was developed (together with the Lockheed XF-90 and North American YF-93A) to meet a 1946 USAAF requirement for a long-range turbojet fighter that could be used in a penetration or escort role. McDonnell, which had not gained a production order for its XP-67 but was emerging as a builder of straight-wing US Navy fighters, put Herman Barkey's design team to work on the 35-degree sweepback, low-wing, twin-jet XF-88. Designed around two 3,000-lb (1360.8-kg) thrust Westinghouse J34-WE-13 turbojets positioned amidships in the fuselage (hint of Voodoos and Phantoms to come), the first of two XF-88s (46-525/526) flew on 29 October 1948. As had been the case with other fighters employing the same powerplant, the sleek XF-88 turned in disappointing performance and the second machine was re-engined with two 3,600-lb (1633-kg) afterburning thrust Westinghouse J34-WE-15s, acquiring the new designation XF-88A. This increased the fighter's speed from 631 mph (1015.5 km/h) to 706 mph (1136.2 km/h) at 20,000 ft

(6096 m), but the XF-88A's overall performance was still viewed as less than satisfactory. Further, with the Soviet Union's detonation of its first atomic bomb in 1949, the USAF's priority shifted to all-weather interceptors and the penetration mission was de-emphasised. In 1950, after 210 flying hours, the programme was shelved and the XF-88 and XF-88A were placed in storage.

With the outbreak of Korean fighting on 25 June 1950, the XF-88A was returned to flight status as a prototype for a new fighter, to become the F-101 Voodoo.

The XF-88 prototype was also resurrected, as a testbed for the 5,600-shp (4175.9-kW) Allison XT38A turboprop powerplant. Redesignated XF-88B, it flew in this three-engine configuration on 14 April

1953. Exhaustive tests were conducted, first for the USAF and later for the National Advisory Committee for Aeronautics (NACA), evaluating a variety of high-speed propellers and propeller hub configurations. The data compiled from this composite power arrangement was invaluable, and the XF-88B had the distinction of being the final propeller-driven fighter in the USAF designation series. The jet/prop combination did not seem practical enough to warrant a production order, however, and by 1956 the XF-88A and XF-88B were again withdrawn from flight status. The XF-88A sat in forlorn condition in a junkyard at Langley AFB, Virginia, for many years, apparently after being rejected as a possible 'gate guardian', and both were eventually scrapped. The basic design would reappear in the F-101 Voodoo and an unbuilt variant, the XF-109.

Specification
XF-88A

Type: single-seat penetration fighter
Powerplant: two 3,600-lb (1633-kg) afterburning thrust Westinghouse J34-WE-15 turbojet engines
Performance: maximum speed 706 mph (1136.2 km/h) at 20,000 ft (6096 m); initial climb rate 8,000 ft (2438 m) per minute; service ceiling 39,400 ft (12009 m); range 1,737 miles (2793 km)
Weights: empty 12,140 lb (5506.7 kg); maximum take-off 18,500 lb (8391.6 kg)
Dimensions: span 39 ft 8 in (12.09 m); length 54 ft 2 in (16.51 m); height 17 ft 3 in (5,26 m); wing area 350 sq ft (32.52 m^2)
Armament: six 20-mm fixed forward-firing nose cannon

The XF-88 was designed for the penetration/escort fighter role, and was consequently planned for speed. With the disappointing J34 engine this was not forthcoming, and the XF-88 remained in prototype form only. The XF-88A was to form the basis of the more successful F-101 Voodoo family.

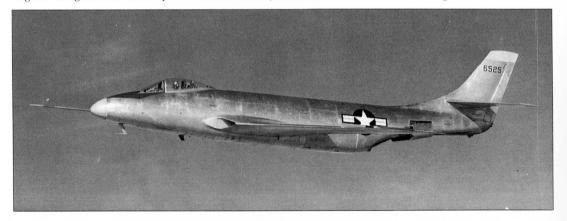

Northrop F-89 Scorpion

History and notes

The Northrop F-89 Scorpion, for many years an integral part of the defence of North America, was the USAF's first two-seat all-weather jet fighter. Two prototypes were ordered in December 1946 and the first, the XF-89 (46-678), was flown on 16 August 1948 at Muroc by Fred Bretcher. The F-89 had a shoulder-mounted straight wing and twin 7,200-lb (3265.9-kg) afterburning thrust Allison J35-A-35 turbojet engines mounted side-by-side beneath the tandem cockpit for pilot and radar observer (RO). A big, sturdy machine not usually regarded as very pretty, the production F-89 started out with fixed wingtip tanks, nose air intercept (AI) radar and six 20-mm M24 nose cannon.

Though the all-black XF-89 or company model N-24 was lost in a crash on 22 February 1950, the second aircraft (46-679) was then flying as the XF-89A, or N-49, in natural metal finish with a more pointed nose and lengthened fuselage. Deliveries of the production F-89A or company N-35 began in July 1950, this early variant being powered by two 5,100-lb (2313.4-kg) thrust Allison J33-A-21A engines which, with afterburners, developed 6,800-lb (3084.5-kg) thrust each. The F-89A began to reach Air Defense Command (ADC) squadrons in mid-1951 at a time when the threat of a Soviet bomber force assaulting North America was taken very seriously. Much later in their careers, some of the 18 F-89A airframes were transferred to the Air Research and Development Command (ARDC) to serve as DF-89A missile and drone directors.

Internal equipment changes from the 19th airframe led to the F-89B, which had a Lear autopilot and instrument landing system (ILS); 30

Northrop F-89D Scorpion of the 64th Fighter Interceptor Squadron, Elmendorf AFB, Alaska.

The major Scorpion production model was the F-89D, which accounted for well over half the total. Entering service in 1954, it was the first to feature the unguided rocket packs in huge wingtip pods that also contained fuel to increase range.

were built and some later served as DF-89Bs.

The 164 F-89C aircraft introduced new internal systems and used several variants of the Allison turbojet engine. A major change in the Scorpion's armament was ushered in with the service-test YF-89D (49-2463), actually a converted F-89B model, and the 682 production F-89Ds, or N-68s, which followed. A wingtip installation containing 104 2.75-in (69.85-mm) folding-fin aircraft rockets (FFAR), plus fuel, enabled the F-89D to bracket an area the size of a football field with the lethal, unguided projectiles. F-89Ds became operational with ADC units in Alaska in 1954 and many later served with the Reserve (AFRES) and Air National Guard (ANG).

The sole YF-89E (50-752), or N-71, a converted F-89C model, was a testbed for two 6,000-lb (2721.6-kg) thrust Allison YJ71-A-3 engines. The F-89F designation went to a production version which was cancelled. The F-89G was also a Scor-

pion variant which never progressed beyond the design stage.

Final production Scorpion was the F-89H, or N-138, of which 156 were manufactured. The fixed wingtip tanks of the F-89H were reconfigured to accommodate three Hughes Falcon air-to-air missiles in addition to 21 FFARs. The F-89J variant, or N-160, was a conversion from the F-89D equipped to carry two Douglas MB-1 Genie unguided rockets with nuclear warheads plus four underwing Falcons. The wingtip rocket pods were replaced by fuel tanks.

Scorpions were eventually replaced by Convair F-102s in the air-defence role. Some remained in ANG service well into the 1960s. An F-89J (52-1911) is on display at the Air Force Museum in Dayton, Ohio. Total production was 1,050 aircraft.

Specification
F-89D

Type: two-seat all-weather interceptor

At the time of the F-89's conception, the long-range bomber threat was not that great, but by the time of its period in service, the threat was taken very seriously. Scorpions were the main US weapon against attack, serving in the interceptor role until replaced by F-102s. These are F-89Js.

Powerplant: two 7,200-lb (3265.9-kg) afterburning thrust Allison J-35-A-35, -33A, -41 or -47 turbojet engines
Performance: maximum speed 636 mph (1023.5 km/h) at 10,600 ft (3231 m); initial climb rate 7,700 ft (2347 m) per minute; service ceiling 49,200 ft (14996 m); range 2,600 miles (4184 km)
Weights: empty 25,194 lb (11428 kg); maximum take-off 42,241 lb (19160.5 kg)
Dimensions: span 59 ft 8 in (18.19 m); length 53 ft 10 in (16.41 m); height 17 ft 7 in (5.36 m); wing area 562 sq ft (52.21 m²)
Armament: 104×2.75-in (69.85-mm) folding-fin aircraft rockets (FFAR) in wingtip pods

Lockheed F-90

History and notes

The Lockheed XF-90 was built to meet a USAF requirement for a long-range penetration fighter (along with the McDonnell XF-88 and North American YF-93A). Developed by Clarence L. (Kelly) Johnson's Lockheed fighter team, known in later years as the 'Skunk Works', the XF-90 combined swept-wing technology with the experience gained in producing the straight-wing F-80 Shooting Star. It was intended as an almost-all-purpose fighter, capable of handling the ground-attack role in addition to its prime task of escorting bombers deep into Soviet airspace. The two prototypes (46-687/688) were to be tested in a fly-off competition with the McDonnell and North American designs.

Actually, the XF-90 evolved over two years and resulted from 65 different designs created by Johnson's engineers. These included butterfly-

tailed aircraft, three-engine aircraft, 'W' winged designs and, finally, the big, tough craft that was chosen. The final XF-90 had 0.5-in (12.7-mm) rivets in the wings and weighed as much as a DC-3. Its powerplants, sadly, were twin 3,100-lb (1406.2-kg) thrust Westinghouse J34-WE-11 turbojets, the same engines which simply offered too little 'push' to so many fighter designs of the period. Still, the XF-90 reached 665 mph (1070.2 km/h) at 32,100 ft (9784 m) in level flight and could easily be pushed through the sound barrier in a shallow dive. Throughout April and May 1950, the air above Muroc Dry Lake, California, exploded in sonic booms as Lockheed test pilot Tony LeVier put the XF-90 through

An elegant, yet sturdy fighter, the XF-90 showed some family likeness to the P-80/F-94 series which preceded it. It was built to the same escort fighter specification as the XF-88, and consequently also suffered from inadequate engines and changes in military policy.

high-speed dive tests. LeVier dived the XF-90 to Mach 1.12 on 17 May 1950.

The XF-90 stalled at 127 mph (204.4 km/h), making it no easy machine to control on the approach. Its take-off performance enabled it to clear a 50-ft (15.24-m) obstacle in 8,625 ft (2629 m) without the rocket-assisted take-off (RATO) units used in some tests, hardly a spectacular getaway from the ground. In the 1949 fly-off, the XF-88 came in first, the XF-90 second, and the YF-93A third, but by then the results were academic. With the September 1949 detonation of the Soviet Union's first nuclear weapon, the USAF penetration-fighter concept died

A nuclear fate befell the second XF-90 which was rigged with instruments on the ground and destroyed in the 1952 atomic bomb tests at Frenchman's Flat, Nevada. Lockheed records indicate that the first XF-90 was shipped in 1953 to a National Advisory Committee for Aeronautics (NACA) laboratory in Cleveland, Ohio. Apparently, it was eventually broken up in tests at that NACA facility.

Specification

XF-90

Type: single-seat long-range penetration fighter
Powerplant: two 3,100-lb (1406.2-kg) thrust Westinghouse J34-WE-11 turbojet engines; afterburning on second airframe only
Performance: maximum speed 665 mph (1070.2 km/h) at 32,100 ft (9784 m); initial climb rate 8,100 ft (2469 m) per minute; service ceiling 39,000 ft (11887 m); range 2,300 miles (3701 km)
Weights: empty 18,520 lb (8400.7 kg); maximum take-off 27,200 lb (12337.9 kg)
Dimensions: span 40 ft 0 in (12.19 m); length 56 ft 2 in (17.12 m); height 15 ft 9 in (4.8 m); wing area 345 sq ft (32.05 m²)
Armament: six 20-mm fixed forward-firing cannon beneath engine inlets planned but not installed

Republic F-91 Thunderceptor

History and notes

The Republic XF-91 Thunderceptor, ordered in 1946, was by far the fastest US Air Force fighter of its time. It was also one of the most innovative of the many experimental aircraft of the late 1940s and early 1950s. With a mid-wing configuration and conventional fuselage design almost identical with that of the F-84F Thunderstreak, the XF-91 was built to test the use of rocket power to boost a jet fighter in combat. In addition to a 5,200-lb (2358.7-kg) afterburning thrust General Electric J47-GE-3 turbojet, the two XF-91s (46-680/681) each employed

four 1,500-lb (680.4-kg) thrust Reaction Motors XLRII-RM-9 rocket motors mounted two-each above and below the jet exhaust. With all five powerplants burning, the XF-91 was supersonic in level flight, attaining 1,126 mph (1812.1 km/h).

The first XF-91 made its initial flight on 9 May 1949 on jet power alone. By late 1949, evaluation of the rocket boost powerplant began. But the rocket engines were not the only unusual feature of the Thunderceptor. Its 35-degree swept wing could

The prototype Republic XF-91 shows the bulky engine installation comprising one jet and four rocket motors.

be adjusted to vary the incidence to the most effective angle for take-off, cruise and landing. And the wing planform was of inverse taper (the only time this concept was tried on a USAF fighter) with the thickest and widest portion of the wing at the tip instead of the root. This provided greater lift outboard and reduced the tendency of the wingtip to stall at low speeds. Because the wing was

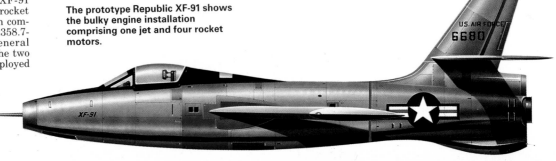

too thin inboard to accommodate the tandem bogie-type main landing gear, the undercarriage retracted outward to fit into the thickened tips.

The first XF-91 was refitted with a nose radome housing APS-6 radar above the engine intake, in the same manner as the F-86D Sabre. The second machine was retrofitted with a V-shaped butterfly tail and tested with this configuration after it was determined, in 1951, that the XF-91 would not be placed into production. This second airframe was eventu-

ally destroyed while the first has been retained by the Air Force Museum in Dayton, Ohio. Republic pilots of the period felt that the XF-91 was one of the truly outstanding fighters of its day, even if the jet-rocket combination may have been impracticable for operational use, and believed that the airplane should have reached squadron service.

Specification
XF-91

Type: single-seat fighter/research

aircraft
Powerplant: one 5,200-lb (2358.7-kg) afterburning thrust General Electric J47-GE-3 turbojet engine and four 1,500-lb (680.4-kg) thrust Reaction Motors XLRII-RM-9 rocket motors
Performance: maximum speed 1,126 mph (1812.1 km/h) or Mach 1.71 at 50,000 ft (15240 m); climb to 50,000 ft (15240 m) in 5.5 minutes; service ceiling 46,000 ft (14021 m); range about 1,000 miles (1609 km)
Weights: empty 15,853 lb

In addition to its mixed powerplant, the Thunderceptor also had a remarkable wing. Not only could the incidence be varied for take-off and landing, but it was also thicker and wider nearer the tip.

(7190.9 kg); maximum take-off 23,807 lb (10798.9 kg)
Dimensions: span 31 ft 3 in (9.53 m); length 43 ft 3 in (13.18 m); height 18 ft 8 in (5.69 m); wing area 320 sq ft (29.73 m²)
Armament: none

Convair F-92

History and notes
The Convair XF-92A (46-682), which made its first flight on 8 June 1948, was not the aircraft originally assigned the F-92 designation but a hybrid, hastily-built machine designed solely to test the delta wing planform.

The US Air Force had obtained wartime German data on the delta wing from its leading proponent, Dr Alexander Lippisch. The XF-92 designation originally went to a Convair design with delta wing and V-shaped butterfly tail powered by no fewer than six 2,000-lb (907.2-kg) thrust liquid-fuel rocket engines plus a 1,560-lb (707.6-kg) thrust Westinghouse J30-WE-1 turbojet as backup. This would have been a very fast point-defence interceptor with exceedingly limited range and duration. To flight-test its wing planform, Convair built its model 7002, hastily assembled partly from components of other aircraft. This was a remarkably simple airplane with latticed canopy cover, nose air inlet, and through-flow arrangement for its 5,200-lb (2358.7-kg) thrust Allison J33-A-23 turbojet. Its delta wing was swept 60 degrees. When the fully-fledged rocket-powered XF-92 design was cancelled because of its

obviously limited military application, the model 7002 was redesignated XF-92A. Since it had been intended only as a flying mock-up for the cancelled machine, the XF-92A was never a candidate for a production order, though it performed valuable, if unintended, service as a testbed for the company's F-102 interceptor.

The XF-92A originally flew without afterburning. During continuing tests at Edwards AFB (as the Muroc Dry Lake base was renamed) it was re-engined and its fuselage lengthened to provide reheat for the new 7,500-lb (3402-kg) afterburning thrust Allison J33-A-29. At the same time, the natural-metal XF-92A was painted gloss white.

Always a research aircraft rather than a fighter, the XF-92A was turned over to NACA for tests before its flight career ended in 1953. By

that time, work was well advanced on the operational delta-wing craft to follow, the F-102.

Specification
XF-92A

Type: single-seat fighter/research aircraft
Powerplant: one 7,500-lb (3402-kg) afterburning thrust Allison J33-A-29 turbojet engine
Performance: maximum speed

590 mph (949.5 km/h) at sea level; initial climb rate 5,000 ft (1524 m) per minute; service ceiling 46,000 ft (14021 m); range 360 miles (579 km)
Weights: empty 8,500 lb (3855.6 kg); maximum take-off 15,000 lb (6804 kg)
Dimensions: span 31 ft 3 in (9.53 m); length 42 ft 5 in (12.93 m); height 17 ft 8 in (5.38 m); wing area 230 sq ft (21.37 m²)
Armament: none

The Convair XF-92A was never intended to serve as a fighter, and was more at home in the 'X' series. Utilising German data, the design was the principal test vehicle for the delta wing concept, and was instrumental in the design of the F-102, F-106 and B-58 service aircraft.

The 'Century' Series

As the dust settled over Korea, the US aviation industry was embarking on an exciting period of aircraft development, the shining light of which were the 'Century' series fighters.

Just as World War II had shaped the combat aircraft of the immediate post-war period, so the Korean war had a profound effect on the fighters of the 1950s and 1960s. Later the Vietnam and Arab-Israeli wars would similarly shape the fighters of the 1970s and 1980s. Air war in Korea had been fought at high speed, and although there was still much dogfighting to be done, the designers erroneously felt that this speed was the most important attribute for a future fighter. In the ultimate expression of this design philosophy, the F-104, the error was finally made glaringly obvious, and a return to manoeuvrability followed.

In addition to the higher speeds of combat, two other major changes were afoot, both of which had surfaced towards the end of World War II and had become major facets of fighter aviation in Korea. Firstly the airborne radar was becoming an important part of the interceptor's equipment, allowing it to make kills in all weathers and under a fair degree of autonomy. F-94s and F-82 Twin Mustangs had made kills in

Korea directed entirely by radar, and developments in this direction, and of air-to-air missiles, would assume great importance in the 1950s as the Cold War heated up. Secondly the fighter had been burdened with the additional role of ground-attack, even superb fighters such as the Sabre having to do their share of 'mud-moving' when required. Thus dual-role versatility was also to feature in the future design of fighters.

'Century' glamour

Korea had seen the introduction into service of the radar-equipped F-94, and numerically this had been followed by some variations on aircraft then in service (F-95, F-96 and F-97) followed by two anti-aircraft missiles (F-98 and F-99). Consequently, the next major aircraft type was the F-100, and this was to be followed by five aircraft in the '100' series that would be of major importance to the US Air Force. Together they became known as the 'Century' fighters, and attained a glamour and mystique that

matched their exciting attributes.

Originally known as the Sabre 45, the F-100 was later called Super Sabre, and in many ways this reflected its design. The use of an afterburner and sharply swept wings gave the 'Hun' sustained supersonic performance, taking the US Air Force into another era of fighter aviation. Still armed principally with guns, it was later given Sidewinder missile capability and became the standard, air defence day fighter. As more capable types came on strength, it increased its share of the fighter-bomber role, and in this was to gain fame as the bread-and-butter attack aircraft in South Vietnam.

Following the 'Hun' was the McDonnell Voodoo, conceived as an SAC escort fighter but reworked as a missile-equipped inter-

Further development of the F-80/T-33 family led to the F-94, with radar in the nose and two crew, but performance of the early variants was disappointing. Nevertheless, the type did reach Korea and scored some kills. This F-94B served with the 68th FIS at Itazuke in Japan during 1952.

Much emphasis was placed during the late 1950s on all-weather interceptors, the bomber threat being perceived as the main danger to the United States. Originating in a Strategic Air Command requirement, the F-101 Voodoo served in large numbers as a long-range bomber-destroyer.

ceptor. Convair's F-102 Delta Dart was another interceptor, this time employing high performance to catch Soviet bombers before they could penetrate US airspace and deliver their weapons. The 'Deuce' represented another conceptual step, being considered as part of an overall weapon system employing ground radars and the like. Both F-101 and F-102 dispensed with gun armament totally, relying in the main on the newly-developed Hughes Falcon missile.

Both the Lockheed F-104 and Republic F-105 were direct results of Korean experience, being conceived as answers to the shortcomings of fighters and fighter-bombers respectively. The F-104 failed in US service, despite its designer 'Kelly' Johnson visiting front-line units in Korea to find out exactly what they would like in a fighter. Speed was their universal answer, but as

The next truly important fighter following the F-86 was the F-100 Super Sabre. Although suffering initially from roll coupling problems, it went on to become the universal day fighter/fighter-bomber for the USAF.

has been noted earlier, this was not to prove the case in later years. Only when it was reworked as a fast fighter-bomber for export did the Starfighter achieve its phenomenal success. The Thunderchief, on the other hand, addressed the disadvantages of the F-84, emerging as a rugged, no-nonsense attack bomber that was also no slouch at air-to-air fighting.

Convair's F-106 Delta Dart was the last successful 'Century' fighter, replacing the F-102 as the prime USAF interceptor, a role in which it continued for nearly 30 years. Others in the series were an exciting F-100 follow-on (F-107) and radical fighter projects

Research from the XF-92A programme led to the F-102 interceptor which, when it was redesigned to incorporate area-rule, became a stalwart of the US air defence network. Its prowess in the air superiority role was unchallenged for many years.

(F-103 and F-108).

Whatever the merits of each individual member, the 'Century' series represented a dramatic advance in fighter technology, firmly placing the genre in the supersonic arena. While Korea had provided the initial spur for this rapid development, it was the tense Cold War between East and West that provided the ongoing encouragement. Designed for war against Soviet bombers in the far north or Warsaw Pact ground forces on the plains of West Germany, most of these aircraft were to see combat in a much dirtier environment, the steamy jungles and limestone mountains of South East Asia.

North American F-93

History and notes

The North American YF-93A, developed from the F-86 Sabre and originally designated F-86C, eventually became the third design in the penetration fighter competition with the McDonnell XF-88 and Lockheed XF-90. The YF-93A was a bigger, bulkier Sabre: the nose inlet of the F-86 design was replaced with side-mounted inlets and the fuselage was widened to house a 6,250-lb (2835-kg) thrust Pratt & Whitney turbojet. The result was a larger, heavier machine with longer range and greater load-carrying capacity than the Sabre. On 9 June 1948, the USAF ordered 118 F-93s, but the order was cancelled a year later. The YF-93A lost its second chance to attain production status when it emerged a poor third in the penetration fighter contest which, as it turned out, did not result in any production contract anyway.

The first of the two YF-93As (48-316 and 48-317), also known as the company NA-157, was first flown on 24 January 1950 by George Welch. The two machines underwent various modifications during evaluation, including changes in the shape of their lateral air inlets. After the USAF was no longer a potential buyer, the two airframes were turned over to the National Advisory Committee for Aeronautics (NACA), where they were employed in various tests until eventually being retired and scrapped.

Specification

YF-93A

Type: single-seat long-range penetration fighter
Powerplant: one 6,250-lb (2835-kg) thrust Pratt & Whitney J48-P-1 turbojet engine
Performance: maximum speed 708 mph (1139.4 km/h) at sea level and 622 mph (1001 km/h) at 35,000 ft (10668 m); initial climb rate with afterburning 11,960 ft (3645 m) per minute; service ceiling 46,800 ft (14265 m); range 1,967 miles (3165 km)
Weights: empty 14,035 lb (6366.3 kg); maximum take-off 26,516 lb (12027.7 kg)
Dimensions: span 38 ft 9 in (11.81 m); length 44 ft 1 in (13.44 m); height 15 ft 8 in (4.78 m); wing area 306 sq ft (28.43 m²)
Armament: none

The F-93 was twice offered to the US Air Force, both times without result. Drawing heavily upon the F-86 design, it incorporated a radar in a redesigned nose, the engine inlets moving to the lateral position. The beefier fuselage housed a J48 turbojet.

Lockheed F-94 Starfire

History and notes

The Lockheed F-94 became perhaps the best-known all-weather interceptor of the 1950s, teaming up with the F-86D and F-89 in the defence of North America. This conventional, low-wing, two-seat tandem interceptor was the culmination of the F-80/T-33 series. The first service-test YF-94 (48-356) had, in fact, begun life as a TF-80C and had become the first T-33 (and would, much later, serve as prototype for the F-94A and F-94B models). In its incarnation as a YF-94, this machine first flew on 16 April 1949 piloted by Tony LeVier. The first production F-94A (49-2479) flew on 16 September 1949 and the type was rushed into squadron service with the Air Defense Command (ADC) by December 1949.

The first production F-94B (50-805) introduced only minor changes, including a Sperry Zero-reader flight director. The F-94A and F-94B models carried APG-33 radar in the nose and the unimpressive armament of four 0.5-in (12.7-mm) machine-guns. One machine was fitted with additional wing guns in trials which proved unsuccessful. The engine afterburner, intended to boost combat

Lockheed F-94B of the 319th Fighter Interceptor Squadron, serving in Korea.

speed and added to the Allison J33-A-33 engine of 6,000-lb (2721.6-kg) thrust, guzzled fuel voraciously and produced disappointing performance. The F-94 was barely capable of 600 mph (965.6 km/h), the same speed as the F-80.

F-94A and F-94B aircraft served with about two dozen ADC squadrons in the USA and Alaska. By 1952, F-94Bs had reached the Korean combat theatre. On 30 January 1953, an F-94B crewed by Captain Ben Fithian and Second Lieutenant Sam R. Lyons blasted a Soviet-built Lavochkin La-9 fighter out of Korean skies. Fithian and Lyons became the first airmen in history to destroy an opposing aircraft solely on instruments. Later, F-94Bs were credited with four MiG kills, sustaining no losses.

Significant changes were introduced with the YF-94C interceptor, the first example of which (50-955) was briefly known as the YF-97A. To defend the US against Soviet bomber attack, Lockheed developed the F-94C, the only variant named Starfire, with a new engine in the form of the Pratt & Whitney J48-P-5 of 6,350-lb (2880.4-kg) dry and 8,750-lb (3969.0-kg) afterburing thrusts. Rocket armament was 24 2.75-in (69.85-mm) Mighty Mouse folding-fin aircraft rockets (FFAR). The missiles were at first carried in the nose of the aircraft and were later transferred to mid-wing pods.

With the advent of the J48 engine, Lockheed was able to redesign the entire aircraft for higher Mach numbers. The F-94C accordingly had a new wing, thinner than before but much stronger, a rede-

signed fuselage, larger inlets and a much longer rear section, stepped cockpits and a swept tailplane for control at Mach 0.92.

The purpose of the aircraft, of course, was to intercept and destroy Soviet bombers approaching targets in North America. The Air Defense Command kept F-94Cs on three-minute alert, the aircrews in flight garb in ready rooms at the runway's end. During ground control intercept (GCI) exercises, the F-94C crew would receive transmissions from ground stations reporting the speed, altitude and direction of their target, and would be vectored to within visual distance when possible. Since the aircraft's radar had a range of only 20 miles (32 km) or less, it was of marginal utility except when commencing an actual firing pass, at which time the radar observer attempted to 'lock on'. Actual firing of the 24 rockets in the nose shook the F-94C violently and blinded both crew members in exhaust smoke. The F-94C was capable virtually of stopping itself in mid-air by firing this ordnance and, like the F-89 Scorpion, could 'blanket' an area the size of a football field with projectiles.

The F-94D, a proposed single-seat interceptor, was never built. By the time the F-94C had reached full service, it was already close to the end of its brief career, which concluded in Air National Guard

Initially the F-94C Starfire carried its 24 Mighty Mouse rockets in the nose, arranged in a circle around the radar, but an undesirable side effect was to blind the crew temporarily.

Lockheed F-94

Serving with Air Defense Command in the mid-1950s, the Lockheed F-94C Starfire guarding North American cities was the final variation on a theme begun with 'Kelly' Johnson's wartime XP-80 fighter. As seen at the 1954 gunnery meet at Yuma, Arizona (later to become the biennial 'William Tell' competition), this F-94C-1-LO wears the distinctive markings of the 84th Fighter Interceptor Squadron.

To make use of the extra power of the J48 engine, the F-94C was redesigned with a longer fuselage and thinner wings, resulting in considerably better performance. The rockets were moved to wing pods to minimise the blinding problem.

squadrons in the mid-1950s. Lockheed had manufactured two F-94s, 110 F-94As, 357 F-94Bs and 387 F-94Cs, a total of 856 airframes. No flying examples are left today, but several museum pieces have survived including the prototype YF-94 (48-356) on display at Lackland AFB, Texas.

Specification
F-94C

Type: two-seat all-weather interceptor
Powerplant: one 8,750-lb (3969-kg) afterburning thrust Pratt & Whitney J48-P-5 turbojet engine
Performance: maximum speed 585 mph (941.4 km/h) at 22,000 ft (6706 m); initial climb rate 7,980 ft (2432 m) per minute; service ceiling 51,400 ft (15667 m); range 1,200 miles (1931 km)
Weights: empty 12,700 lb (5760.7 kg); maximum take-off 24,200 lb (10977.1 kg)
Dimensions: span 42 ft 5 in (12.93 m); length 44 ft 6 in (13.56 m); height 14 ft 11 in (4.55 m); wing area 338 sq ft (31.40 m²)
Armament: 24 2.75 in (69.85-mm) Mighty Mouse air-to-air rocket projectiles (48 with wing launchers)

North American F-95

History and notes

The F-95 designation was assigned initially to the radar-equipped, all-weather interceptor version of the North American F-86 Sabre. The first two YF-95A airframes (50-577/578) were hastily assembled in 1949 with the nose configuration but not the radar of production aircraft. The two YF-95As also lacked the missile armament and afterburner of the production machine, being equipped instead with an extremely crude external reheat device at the exhaust for the 5,425-lb (2460-kg) thrust General Electric J47-GE-17 turbojet engine. By the time the first of these machines had been completed and made its first flight on 22 December 1949 with company test pilot Joseph Lynch at the controls, it had been redesignated F-86D. Subsequent production machines were the F-86D, F-86K and F-86L.

Specification
YF-95A

Type: single-seat all-weather interceptor
Powerplant: one 7,500-lb (3402-kg) thrust with afterburning General Electric J47-GE-17 turbojet engine
Performance: maximum speed 707 mph (1137.8 km/h) at sea level; initial climb rate 10,000 ft (3048 m) per minute; service ceiling 54,600 ft (16642 m); range 835 miles (1344 km)
Weights: empty 12,470 lb (5656.4 kg); maximum take-off 17,100 lb (7756.6 kg)
Dimensions: span 37 ft 1 in (11.30 m); length 40 ft 4 in (12.29 m); height 15 ft 0 in (4.57 m); wing area 288 sq ft (27.76 m²)
Armament: 24×2.75-in (69.85-mm) folding-fin aircraft rockets (FFAR) intended for production aircraft

Republic F-96

History and notes

The F-96 designation was initially assigned to the swept-wing version of the Republic F-84 Thunderjet. The first airframe in the series (49-2430) was known as YF-96A while it was taking shape at Republic's Farmingdale, Long Island, plant. By the time the aircraft made its first flight on 3 June 1950, it had been redesignated F-84F. It was revealed to the public under the latter designation on 16 January 1951. Subsequent production and service-test machines with the swept wing were the F-84F, RF-84F, XF-84H, YF-84J and RF-84K.

Specification
YF-96A

Type: single-seat fighter-bomber
Powerplant: one 7,220-lb (3275.0-kg) thrust Wright J65-W-3 Sapphire turbojet engine
Performance: maximum speed 695 mph (1118.5 km/h) at sea level and 658 mph (1058.9 km/h) at 20,000 ft (6096 m); initial climb rate 8,200 ft (2499 m) per minute; service ceiling 46,000 ft (14021 m); combat radius with two drop tanks 810 miles (1304 km)
Weights: empty 13,830 lb (6273.3 kg); maximum take-off 28,000 lb (12700.8 kg)
Dimensions: span 33 ft 7¼ in (10.24 m); length 43 ft 4¾ in (13.23 m); height 14 ft 4¾ in (4.39 m); wing area 325 sq ft (30.19 m²)
Armament: six 0.5-in (12.7-mm) fixed forward-firing machine-guns, plus provision for 6,000 lb (2721.6 kg) of external ordnance

Lockheed F-97

History and notes

The F-97 designation was assigned in 1949 to the interceptor which became the all rocket-armed Lockheed Starfire. The first unarmed service-test airframe (50-955) was designated YF-97A while under construction at Lockheed's Burbank facility, and during this period a production order was placed for 108 F-97A interceptors. By the time the test aircraft flew in 1950 with Tony LeVier at the controls, it had been redesignated YF-94C. The production machines were completed among the 387 F-94C interceptors manufactured.

Specification
YF-97A

Type: two-seat all-weather interceptor
Powerplant: one 6,350-lb (2880.4-kg) thrust Pratt & Whitney J48-P-5 turbojet engine; afterburning added to production aircraft
Performance: maximum speed 585 mph (941.4 km/h) at 22,000 ft (6706 m); initial climb rate 7,980 ft (2432 m) per minute; service ceiling 51,400 ft (15667 m); range 1,200 miles (1931 km)
Weights: empty 12,700 lb (5760.7 kg); maximum take-off 24,200 lb (10977.1 kg)
Dimensions: span 42 ft 5 in (12.93 m); length 44 ft 6 in (13.56 m); height 14 ft 11 in (4.55 m); wing area 338 sq ft (31.4 m²)
Armament: none installed on service test aircraft

Hughes F-98

History and notes

The XF-98 designation for an 'unmanned fighter' was assigned in 1947 to the project which resulted in the Hughes Falcon, the world's first operational air-to-air guided missile. Before the first Falcon was completed, a decision made in 1950 changed its designation to GAR-1. Eventually, an entire family of semi-active radar homing (SARH) missiles appeared under the Falcon name and in 1962 the designation of the missile was changed to AIM-4.

Hughes GAR-1 (AIM-4) Falcon radar-guided air-to-air missile.

Specification
XF-98

Type: air-to-air semi-active radar-homing missile
Powerplant: solid-fuel rocket motor
Performance: maximum speed 2,130 mph (3427.8 km/h) or Mach 3.23; range 5 miles (8.04 km)
Weight: launch 110 lb (49.9 kg)
Dimensions: fin span 1 ft 8 in (508 mm); length 6 ft 5¾ in (1.97 m); diameter 6.4 in (163 mm)
Guidance: semi-automatic radar homing (SARH)

A pair of AIM-4 Falcons nestle in the weapons bay of a Convair F-106, either side of the M61 Vulcan cannon pack fitted retrospectively to replace the nuclear-tipped Genie missile. These are the infra-red guided version, identified by the transparent nose cone.

Boeing/MARC F-99 Bomarc

History and notes

The F-99 designation was assigned in the late 1940s to the Bomarc surface-to-air missile (SAM) developed jointly by Boeing and the Michigan Aeronautical Research Center. The first example was test-launched on 1 September 1952 and, shortly thereafter, was redesignated IM-99A as an 'intercept missile'. Roughly contemporary with the US Army's Nike-Ajax and the Soviet Union's SA-2 'Guideline', the IM-99A was launched by a 23,000-lb (10432.8-kg) thrust, fuselage-mounted Aerojet General LR59-AG-13 liquid-fuel rocket motor. Second-stage power was provided by two 10,000-lb (4536-kg) thrust Marquardt RJ43-MA-3 ramjet engines. The Bomarc's warhead of about 1,000 lb (454 kg), which could be conventional or nuclear, was detonated by proximity fuse from the same ground-control centre which directed the Bomarc to its target.

The IM-99B designation was assigned in 1955 to what became the Super Bomarc SAM with first-stage power provided by a Thiokol solid-fuel rocket motor. On 18 September 1962, the IM-99A and IM-99B were redesignated CIM-10A and CIM-10B. In this instance, C for Coffin described the intercept missile's launch environment, i.e. horizontally stored in a protective enclosure and launched from the ground. Bomarc missiles served well into the 1960s with the USAF's Air Defense Command (ADC) and with Canadian forces.

Specification
F-99

Type: surface-to-air intercept missile
Powerplants: (first stage) one 23,000-lb (10432.8-kg) thrust Aerojet General LR59-AG-13 liquid-fuel rocket motor and (second stage) two 10,000-lb (4536-kg) thrust Marquardt RJ43-MA-3 athodyd ramjet engines
Performance: maximum speed attained during launch/intercept 2,275 mph (3661.2 km/h) or Mach 3.45 at 105,000 ft (32004 m)
Weights: launch 15,500 lb (7030.8 kg); at intercept about 8,500 lb (3855.6 kg)
Dimensions: span 18 ft 2 in (5.54 m); length excluding first-stage nozzle 47 ft 4 in (14.43 m); height 10 ft 3 in (3.12 m); wing area about 65 sq ft (6.04 m²)

Bomarc launches from Cape Canaveral during a test launch. Redesignated IM-99 shortly after its first launch, the Bomarc gave many years of NORAD service, based both in Canada and the United States. Nuclear warheads were an option for destruction of bomber formations.

North American F-100 Super Sabre

North American F-100D Super Sabre of the 20th Tactical Fighter Wing based in England during 1961. One other English base and two West German ones held F-100s at the time.

History and notes

When, at noon on 20 October 1953, the US Air Force released photos of the already-flown YF-100A (52-5754), it ushered in a new era and a 'century series' of level-flight supersonic fighters a generation more advanced than any then in service. North American Aviation, Inc., still led by J. H. 'Dutch' Kindelberger with a design team headed by Ray Rice, had produced a fighter which, if never to excel in air-to-air combat, earned the affection of countless airmen and chalked up more air hours in Vietnam than any other type.

Ordered by the USAF on 1 November 1951 in a contract calling for two service-test YF-100s and 110 production aircraft, the F-100 Super Sabre was conceived from lessons learned while Sabres and MiGs clashed in Korean skies. It was first flown on 24 April 1953 by George Welch and went supersonic on its first flight. The first production F-100A (52-5756) flew on 29 October 1953 again piloted by Welch and was soon delivered to the 479th Tactical Fighter Wing at George AFB, California.

At first, there seemed every possibility that this 10,000-lb (4536-kg) thrust Pratt & Whitney J57-powered supersonic day fighter might prove a failure. Stability problems were encountered in tests at Edwards AFB, California. Several aircraft were lost as a result of roll-coupling which turned a hard dive pullout into an uncontrolled swerve to the right. On 12 October 1954 a crash claimed the life of Welch, a 16-kill air ace and crack test pilot. Eventually, the roll/stability problem was solved with a raised vertical tail which became standard on the 'Hun', as the F-100 was now informally known. Development continued, and in October 1954 one F-100A (52-7659) was flying at Edwards with a typical payload of two 1,000-lb (454-kg) bombs, two 750-lb (340-kg) bombs and two 275-US gal (1041-litre) drop tanks. A total of 203 F-100As was delivered,

Seen on test from Edwards AFB, this is one of the first production machines (there were two prototypes but no pre-production aircraft). The first 70 of these F-100As were originally built with this short tail. The larger tail was retrofitted to most.

some later serving with Nationalist China or Taiwan, though the USAF service-life of this variant was brief. Under Project Slick Chick, six airframes were modified to RF-100A configuration with bulging camera bays to each side of the lower fuselage, some possibly flying with the Nationalist Chinese, and at least one was painted with the spurious serial 53-2600 (an F-89D Scorpion serial). The designation F-100B was initially applied to what was really a

The Thunderbirds Aerial Demonstration Squadron had a long and distinguished association with the F-100, flying the type for many years. Here the team perform an immaculate formation take-off at the start of their display. F-100Cs replaced Republic F-84s, and flew 641 displays between May 1956 and December 1963. Six displays were flown on the F-105 before the team switched back to the 'Hun', this time the F-100D. These flew a further 471 displays between May 1965 and November 1968.

This 120th Tactical Fighter Squadron, 35th TFW F-100C at its base at Phan Rang shows the sturdy and purposeful lines of the type. This was the first ground attack model of the F-100, the earlier F-100A being designed as a day fighter.

wholly new fighter, this being quickly redesignated YF-107A.

The production F-100C variant signalled the USAF's decision to employ the 'Hun' principally in the air-to-ground role. The first F-100C (53-1709) flown 9 September 1955 by George Hoskins, introduced a strengthened wing, with capability for up to six 750-lb (340-kg) bombs and an improved system for the ASM-N-7 Bullpup missile. The first machine was delivered by the manufacturer at Inglewood, California, and a second production source at Columbus, Ohio, added 25 F-100Cs to the 451 turned out in California. On 20 August 1955, Colonel Horace A. Hanes set a world absolute speed record of 822.09 mph (1323.03 km/h) in the first F-100C, an airframe which enjoyed an unusually long career and was still flying with NASA in 1975. One modified JF-100C (53-1715) was used for ordnance-separation tests at Holloman AFB, New Mexico. The F-100C eventually served the USAF in Europe and Asia and was exported to the Turkish air force. F-100Cs served with 14 USAF and 11 Air National Guard fighter wings, and at least one example (54-1951) performed the electronic countermeasures role with the 4758th Defense Systems Evaluation Squadron. Another (54-1966) was converted to the TF-100C two-seat trainer configuration and first flown 3 August 1956 by Robert White.

The definitive variant was the F-100D, intended for both the conventional and nuclear strike mission. The first F-100D (54-2121) was flown 24 January 1956 by Dan Darnell. Because of its pioneering role in the use of tactical nuclear and thermonuclear ordnance, the F-100D was equipped with the Skyspot radar system which allowed ground units to score hypothetical drops. Skyspot proved more effective for the pathfinder role, however, one of many missions the

F-100D would fly in conventional war. During the 1965-8 'Rolling Thunder' campaign against North Vietnam, F-105D Thunderchiefs and F-4C Phantoms were frequently guided to their targets by F-100Ds, which managed to fly their own strike missions unaided. Some 940 F-100Ds were manufactured at Inglewood and 334 in Columbus, including about 100 supplied new to France and Denmark.

The F-100E designation was assigned to an improved F-100D not built. The final new-built model was the two-seat F-100F, with a fuselage lengthened by 36 in (0.914 m) to house the second crew member. Following the sole two-seat TF-100C, the first production F-100F (56-3725) was flown 7 March 1957 by George Mace. A total of 339 F-100Fs was built in Inglewood, initially for conversion and proficiency training. Some were delivered to Denmark, France and Turkey. In Vietnam, the USAF machines became 'fast FAC' (forward air controller) craft, directing other fighter-bombers to their targets. The F-100F was used in the ECM or 'Wild Weasel' role employing special sensors to detect and analise enemy radio and radar emissions, including those from surface-to-air missile (SAM) sites.

'Huns' remained in Air National Guard (ANG) service until 1980 and with the air forces of Denmark and Turkey until 1982. Civil-registered F-100s are used in various flight test programmes today.

Fighter pilots and the F-100 were old friends by the time they went into combat together in Vietnam, 'Hun' drivers often having

Originally designed for the day fighter role, the 'Hun' found its niche as a fighter-bomber. Here an aircraft on test at Eglin AFB lets fly with a full salvo of 2.75-in rockets in a firepower demonstration.

F-100s flew more missions in South East Asia than P-51s did in World War II, notching up more than 300,000. This 35th TFW aircraft flew with the 352nd TFS, seen here dropping a napalm canister near Bien Hoa in South Vietnam.

Leading this pair is a two-seat F-100F, the 'SM' tailcode denoting the 308th TFS, 31st TFW flying from Tuy Hoa in South Vietnam. The accompanying F-100D is from the 352nd TFS, 31st TFW at Phan Rang. 'Huns' spent most of their war fighting over the South, where their vulnerability to MiGs and missiles was not such a liability.

hundreds of hours' more experience than pilots of other types. Colonel George (Bud) Day, who won the Medal of Honor for conduct as a prisoner of war after bailing out of an F-100D, arrived in theatre with more than 2,500 hours' flying time in the type. Like the men, the aircraft were tried and proven, early stability problems long ago resolved. Though it encountered some maintenance difficulties, the F-100 proved remarkably adaptable to rough-field operations in tropical heat and rain. For a time F-100s enjoyed the best maintenance record of any aircraft type in the combat zone.

F-100s were in South East Asia even before the beginning of the 1965 American build-up. In fact, the first recorded combat loss was an F-100D (56-3085) of the 428th Tactical Fighter Squadron, downed over Laos on 18 August 1964. On 1 April 1965, F-100s flew MiG combat air patrol (MiGCAP) for a strike force of F-105s attacking the Thanh Hoa Bridge in North Vietnam. No F-100 ever fought a MiG, however. It was quickly determined that the type was unsuited for operations over the North, having neither the range nor the survivability of the F-105. From mid-1965, F-100D fighter-bombers operated only in the south, although F-100F 'Wild Weasels' continued to range into the North.

The dangers inherent in the F-100F 'Wild Weasel' missions were illustrated on 20 December 1965 when Captain John Pitchford and Captain Robert Trier failed to return from a mission. Pitchford, at the controls of the ECM-equipped F-100F (58-1231) was guiding four F-105s on a strike against North Vietnamese targets. After detecting a 'Fan Song' SAM-associated radar near Haiphong, Pitchford was attacking the radar site when a 37-mm shell struck his craft. Pitchford pulled up and found that he had some control over the airplane. He fired his marker rockets into the SAM radar site, enabling the F-105s to hit it, and turned for the Gulf of Tonkin, but then his hydraulics went out. A full hydraulic failure meant total loss of control so, with the shoreline in sight, Pitchford and Trier ejected. Pitchford became a prisoner of war while Trier joined the missing.

On 11 August 1967, Lieutenant Colonel James E. McInerney Jr and Captain Fred Shannon in an F-100F led a mission that destroyed six SAM sites and damaged four, clearing the way for a strike on Hanoi's Paul Doumer Bridge. Eventually, the 'Wild Weasel' F-100F was replaced by the bigger, further-ranging F-105F, but only after providing yeoman service, just as did the fighter-bomber F-100D. So intense was the fighter-bomber's contribution that by 1969, the four tactical fighter wings in Vietnam (3rd, 31st, 35th and 37th) had exceeded the number of combat sorties flown by over 15,000 P-51 Mustangs in World War II! The F-100D was finally replaced in 1972 when its place was taken by the A-7, A-37, and F-4.

Specification
F-100D

Type: single-seat fighter-bomber
Powerplant: one 16,950-lb (7688.5-kg) afterburning thrust Pratt & Whitney J57-P-21A turbojet engine
Performance: maximum speed, clean 770 mph (1239.2 km/h) or Mach 1.013 at low altitude and 864 mph (1390.4 km/h) or Mach 1.3 at 40,000 ft (12192 m); initial climb rate, clean 16,550 ft (5044 m) per minute; service ceiling 46,000 ft (14021 m); range with two drop tanks 1,550 miles (2494 km)
Weights: empty 21,000 lb (9525.6 kg); maximum take-off 34,832 lb (15799.8 kg)
Dimensions: span 38 ft 9½ in (11.82 m); length excluding probe 47 ft 1¼ in (14.36 m); height 16 ft 2⅔ in (4.94 m); wing area 385 sq ft (35.77 m²)
Armament: four 20-mm M39E cannon, plus provision for up to 7,500 lb (3402 kg) of external ordnance

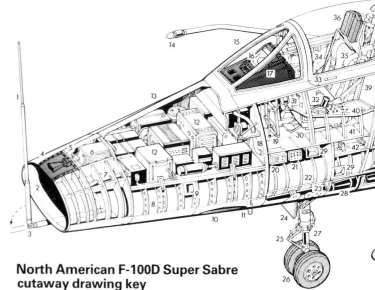

North American F-100D Super Sabre cutaway drawing key

1 Pitot tube, folded for ground handling
2 Engine air intake
3 Pitot tube hinge point
4 Radome
5 IFF aerial
6 AN/APR-25(v) gun tracking radar
7 Intake bleed air electronics cooling duct
8 Intake duct framing
9 Cooling air exhaust duct
10 Cannon muzzle port
11 UHF aerial
12 Nose avionics compartment
13 Hinged nose compartment access door
14 In-flight re-fuelling probe
15 Windscreen panels
16 A-4 radar gunsight
17 Instrument panel shroud
18 Cockpit front pressure bulkhead
19 Rudder pedals
20 Gunsight power supply
21 Armament relay panel
22 Intake ducting

North American F-100

The two-seat F-100F was primarily used for conversion training, but in Vietnam was used as a 'fast-mover' FAC and 'Wild Weasel' aircraft. This machine is configured for the latter role, with additional RWR aerials.

23 Cockpit canopy emergency operating controls
24 Nosewheel leg door
25 Torque scissors
26 Twin nosewheels
27 Nose undercarriage leg strut
28 Philco-Cord M-39 20-mm cannon (four)
29 Kick-in boarding steps
30 Ejection seat footrests
31 Instrument panel
32 Engine throttle
33 Canopy external handle
34 Starboard side console panel
35 Pilots ejection seat
36 Headrest
37 Cockpit canopy cover
38 Ejection seat guide rails
39 Cockpit rear pressure bulkhead
40 Port side console panel
41 Cockpit floor level
42 Control cable runs
43 Gun bay access panel
44 Ammunition feed chutes
45 Ammunition tanks, 200-rpg
46 Power supply amplifier
47 Rear electrical and electronics bay
48 Cockpit pressurization valve
49 Anti-collision light

50 Air conditioning plant
51 Radio compass aerial
52 Intake bleed air heat exchanger
53 Heat exchanger exhaust duct
54 Secondary air turbine
55 Air turbine exhaust duct (open)
56 Starboard wing integral fuel tank, capacity 174 Imp gal (791 litres)
57 Starboard automatic leading edge slat, open
58 Slat guide rails
59 Wing fence
60 Starboard navigation light
61 Wing tip fairing
62 Fixed portion of trailing edge
63 Starboard aileron
64 Aileron hydraulic jack
65 Starboard outer plain flap
66 Flap hydraulic jack
67 UHF aerial
68 Engine intake centre-body

69 Wing attachment fuselage main frames
70 Fuselage fuel tanks: total internal capacity 641 Imp gal (2915 litres)
71 Wing spar centre section carry through beams
72 Engine intake compressor face
73 Main engine mounting
74 Pratt & Whitney J57-P-21A afterburning turbojet engine
75 Dorsal spine fairing
76 Fuel vent pipe
77 Engine oil tank
78 Engine accessory gearbox
79 Compressor bleed air blow-off valve
80 Compressor bleed air blow-off valve
81 Fuselage break point
82 Rear fuselage attachment bolts (four)
83 Fin root filet
84 Engine turbine section
85 Engine rear mounting ring
86 Afterburner fuel spray manifold
87 Fin attachment sloping frame
88 Rudder hydraulic jack
89 Fin sub attachment joint
90 Tailfin construction
91 Fin leading edge
92 Fin tip aerial fairing
93 Upper UHF aerial
94 Fixed portion of trailing edge
95 AN/APR-26(v) radar warning antenna
96 Tail navigation light
97 Fuel jettison pipe

98 Rudder construction
99 Rudder trim control jack
100 Externally braced trailing edge section
101 Brake parachute cable fixing
102 Variable area afterburner, exhaust nozzle
103 Parachute cable 'pull-out' flaps
104 Afterburner nozzle control jacks
105 Brake parachute housing
106 Port all-moving tailplane
107 Tailplane spar box construction
108 Pivot fixing
109 Tailplane mounting fuselage double frames
110 Engine afterburner duct
111 Tailplane hydraulic jack
112 Fuselage lower longeron
113 Rear fuselage fuel tank
114 Port inner plain flap
115 Flap rib construction
116 Main undercarriage wheel bay
117 Undercarriage leg pivot fixing
118 Flap hydraulic jack
119 Flap interconnecting linkage
120 Port outer flap

121 Flap hydraulic jack
122 Aileron jack
123 Wing fence
124 Port aileron
125 Fixed portion of trailing edge
126 Wing tip fairing
127 Port navigation light
128 Compass master transmitter
129 750-lb (340-kg) HE bomb
130 SUU 7A CBU 19-round bomblet dispenser
131 Outboard wing pylon
132 Leading edge slat rib construction

133 Hinged leading edge attachment joint
134 Outboard pylon fixing
135 Wing rib construction
136 Rear spar
137 Port wing integral fuel tank, 174 Imp gal (791 litres)
138 Multi-spar inner wing panel construction
139 Centre pylon fixing
140 Multi-plate disc brake
141 Port mainwheel

142 Main undercarriage leg strut
143 Undercarriage mounting rib
144 Front spar
145 Wing/fuselage attachment skin joint
146 Aileron cable control run
147 Inboard pylon
148 Airbrake hydraulic jacks (two)
149 Retractable landing/taxiing lamps, port and starboard

150 Ventral airbrake
151 166.5 Imp gal (757 litres) drop tank or napalm container
152 AGM-12C Bullpup B tactical missile
153 Centre wing pylon
154 279 Imp gal (1268 litres) air refuellable supersonic fuel tank
155 Tank side bracing strut

AVIAGRAPHICA

© Pilot Press Limited

The Century Series

This 416th TFS, 37th TFW F-100D from Phu Cat is typical of the large numbers committed to the 'in-country' war against the Viet Cong in South Vietnam. Although the type had mixed with MiGs during the first few missions over the North, it spent the rest of its time carrying bombs, rockets and napalm into the jungle. 1968 was the busiest time for the aircraft, when regular Air Force units were reinforced by four Air National Guard squadrons. 'Hun' left South Vietnam in June 1971, having amassed over 360,000 combat sorties, and having lost 186 of its number to gunfire, 7 to airfield attacks and 45 to operational causes.

McDonnell F-101 Voodoo

History and notes

The McDonnell F-101 Voodoo was the inevitable follow-on to the company's XF-88 and was intended for the same purpose. Though the 1950 penetration fighter competition among XF-88, XF-90 and YF-93A resulted in no production contract, the Strategic Air Command still wanted an aircraft conceived from the outset as an escort fighter, its F-84F being seen as only an interim solution. McDonnell's design team under Herman Barkey responded with the heaviest single-seat fighter ever built. Powered by two 11,700-lb (5307.1-kg) Pratt & Whitney J57-P-13 turbojets, the F-101 would carry four 20-mm cannon plus three Hughes GAR-1D or GAR-2A Falcon missiles or 12 5-in (127-mm) high-velocity aircraft rockets (HVAR) mounted on rotary bomb doors. The first F-101A (53-2418) flew on 29 September 1954 at St Louis with Robert C. Little at the controls, and exceeded Mach 1 on its maiden flight. This was a production craft, there being no service-test machine. SAC dropped its requirement and the 77 F-101As built went to the Tactical Air Command. The first delivery was made 2 May 1957 to the 27th Tactical Fighter Wing. Seven of these airframes were later designated JF-101A while being used for temporary tests.

The first of two YRF-101A (54-149/150) service-test reconnaissance Voodoos flew on 10 May 1956, followed by 35 RF-101A airframes delivered to TAC's 363rd Tactical Reconnaissance Wing at

An F-101B demonstrates the launch of a Hughes AIM-4 Falcon missile. Note the lengthened jet pipes that distinguished this variant from the single-seaters. The 'B' also served the Canadian Armed Forces, backed up by twin-stick CF-101F trainers.

Shaw AFB, South Carolina. The reconnaissance Voodoo had a lengthened nose with space for downward or oblique cameras and other sensors. An RF-101A was shot down during the Cuban missile crisis of October 1962.

Above: The F-101A was a TAC-dedicated fighter version, able to carry internal stores in addition to unguided rockets and Falcon missiles. Visible in the nose are the ports for the 20-mm cannon also fitted. The similar F-101C was a more potent machine, optimised for nuclear strike.

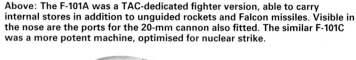

The F-101A and similar F-101C were used in Europe as fighter-bombers, equipped to carry nuclear weapons. This F-101A flew with the 81st TFW at the twin bases of Woodbridge and Bentwaters in England.

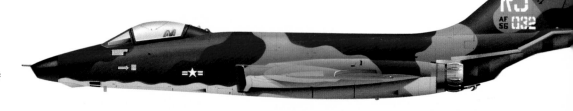

After their service with USAFE, surviving F-101As and Cs were converted into reconnaissance platforms as the RF-101G and H respectively. This is an RF-101H of the 192nd TRS, Missouri ANG.

Probably the most fearsome air-to-air weapon ever, the nuclear-tipped Douglas AIR-2A Genie missile equipped both F-101B and F-106A interceptors. The F-101B had a long career guarding North America, surviving into the 1980s with Air National Guard units such as Maine (illustrated).

The F-101B was the tandem two-seat all-weather interceptor version of the Voodoo for the Air Defense Command, powered by two 11,990-lb (5438.7-kg) thrust afterburning J57-P-55 turbojets. The first F-101B (56-232) flew on 27 March 1957 at St Louis. For long-range intercept, it could carry two Douglas MB-1 Genie nuclear un-guided rockets as well as three Falcons. Deliveries began on 18 March 1959 to the 60th Fighter Interceptor Squadron. Eventually, the F-101B equipped 16 ADC squadrons, guarding against the Soviet bomber threat to North America. The JF-101B designation was applied to two machines used for temporary tests. One NF-101B was structurally modified for development work. Very late in their careers, with reconnaissance Voodoos still needed long after the interceptor variant was retired, 22 of the two-seat airframes were converted to RF-101B. The TF-101B was a version of the interceptor with full dual controls.

The F-101C single-seat tactical fighter differed from the F-101A primarily in having the capability to carry a US tactical nuclear weapon, and 47 were delivered to TAC. The RF-101C, the first of which (56-40) was flown 12 July 1957, was an improved development of the RF-101A; 166 went to TAC squadrons. The USAF began operating the RF-101C in South East Asia in 1964 and suffered its first combat loss on 21 November 1964 when an RF-101C (56-320) of the 15th Tactical Reconnaissance Squadron was shot down over Laos. Though not as much publicised as other combat types, the RF-101C remained in combat until 1970. No fewer than 31 airframes were lost in battle, plus another six to operational causes. In the mid-1960s, a

few RF-101Cs served with the Nationalist Chinese air force, flying clandestine missions over the mainland.

Other Voodoo variants were the F-101F, the USAF designation for the CF-101F interceptor operated by Canadian forces; the RF-101G, a conversion of high-hour RF-101A airframes for reconnaissance duties with the Air National Guard; and the RF-101H, another reconnaissance conversion. One F-101B (58-234) appeared briefly on the US civil register, as N8234, used for thunderstorm research by Colorado State University. A few CF-101Fs remain in service with Canadian forces for electronic warfare operations. Total production was 807 Voodoos.

Specification

RF-101C

Type: single-seat tactical reconnaissance aircraft
Powerplant: two 14,880-lb (6749.6-kg) afterburning thrust Pratt & Whitney J57-P-13 turbojet engines
Performance: maximum speed 1,120 mph (1802.4 km/h) at 40,000 ft (12192 m); initial climb rate 10,000 ft (3048 m) per minute; service ceiling 52,000 ft (15850 m); range with drop tanks 2,400 miles (3862 km)
Weights: empty 25,610 lb (11616.7 kg); maximum take-off 48,270 lb (21895.3 kg)
Dimensions: span 39 ft 8 in (12.09 m); length 69 ft 3 in (21.11 m); height 18 ft 0 in (5.49 m); wing area 368 sq ft (34.19 m^2)
Armament: none

The dedicated tactical reconnaissance RF-101C was the only version of the Voodoo to see combat in South East Asia. This example served with the 45th TRS, 460th TRW at Tan Son Nhut.

ANG units operated the F-101B between 1970 and 1982. This Voodoo flew with the 179th Fighter Interceptor Squadron, Minnesota ANG in 1973.

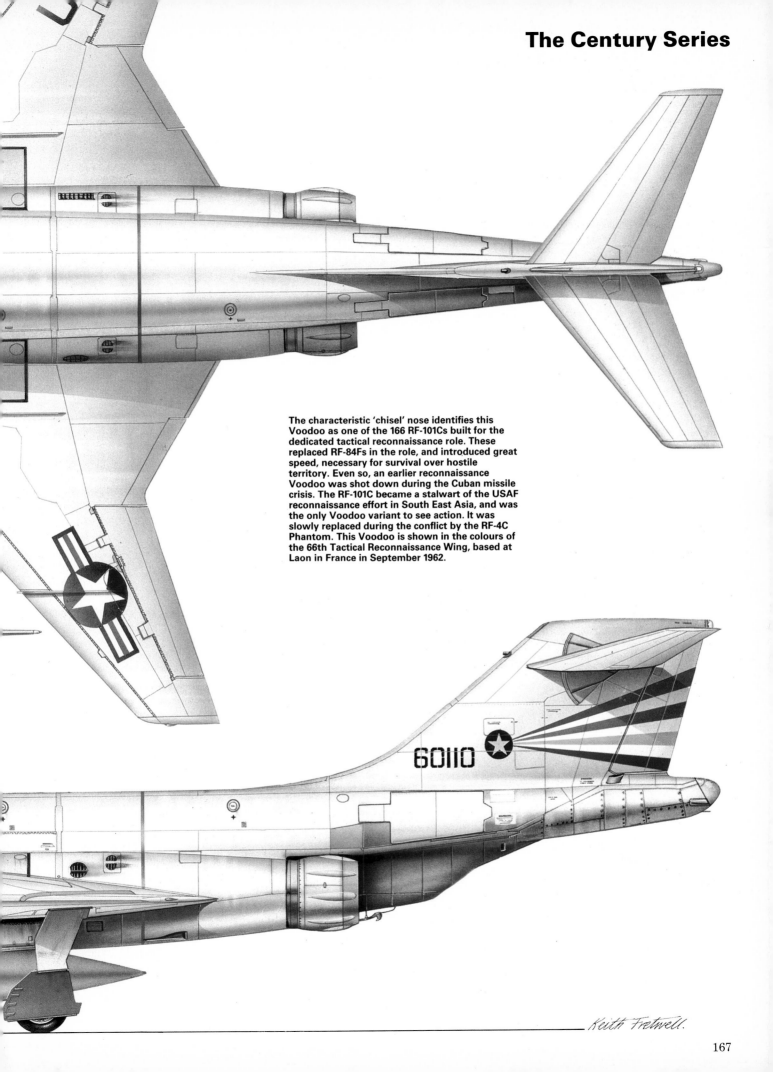

The characteristic 'chisel' nose identifies this Voodoo as one of the 166 RF-101Cs built for the dedicated tactical reconnaissance role. These replaced RF-84Fs in the role, and introduced great speed, necessary for survival over hostile territory. Even so, an earlier reconnaissance Voodoo was shot down during the Cuban missile crisis. The RF-101C became a stalwart of the USAF reconnaissance effort in South East Asia, and was the only Voodoo variant to see action. It was slowly replaced during the conflict by the RF-4C Phantom. This Voodoo is shown in the colours of the 66th Tactical Reconnaissance Wing, based at Laon in France in September 1962.

60110

Keith Fretwell.

Convair F-102 Delta Dagger

History and notes

The Convair F-102 Delta Dagger resulted from a 1950 USAF design competition for an integral all-weather interceptor weapon system. Combining the Hughes Falcon air-to-air missile, the delta wing platform first flown on the XF-92A, and the 10,900-lb (4944.2-kg) thrust Pratt & Whitney J57-P-11 turbojet, the first of 10 YF-102s (52-7994/7995 and 53-1779/1786) flew at Edwards AFB, California, on 24 October 1953. The prototype was lost in a mishap nine days later, but tests with other YF-102 airframes revealed a disappointing truth: the type was sorely underpowered and incapable of level supersonic flight. Rarely had the Air Force invested so much in a system which performed so poorly.

Convair designers went back to the drawing board and the indented fuselage or 'area rule' configuration developed by NACA's Richard Whitcomb was hastily introduced in the much-altered YF-102A, which was assembled in a scant 117 days. The first of four YF-102As (53-1787/1790) flew at Edwards AFB on 20 December 1954, not merely with 'area rule' but with cambered wing, new canopy (except on 53-1788) and 12,000-lb (5443.2-kg) thrust Pratt & Whitney J57-P-23. The new design was supersonic and met USAF expectations.

The production F-102A began to reach Air Defense Command squadrons in June 1955. The first two-seat TF-102A combat proficiency trainer (54-1351) flew at Edwards AFB 8 November 1955 and operated alongside F-102As in ADC service. Total Delta Dagger production was 873 airplanes.

The F-102B designation was briefly assigned to a new aircraft completed as the F-106. The little-known YF-102C (53-1806), a con-

One of the ten YF-102s in flight shows the small fin that characterised the early aircraft. Woefully inadequate in terms of performance, it took something of a miracle to design and construct the much better YF-102A in a short enough time to appease the Air Force.

verted F-102A model, tested change in the internal fire control system, but these were not adopted.

A rakish, well-liked and easily-handling aircraft, popular out of proportion to its importance, the F-102A eventually served with 27 ADC and 23 ANG squadrons. Air Defense Command machines went through several modernisation programmes before being relegated to the ANG, the internal provision for rockets being eventually omitted. A few F-102As went to Greece and Turkey. A few camouflaged F-102As were deployed to South East Asia in 1964-6, and to trouble-plagued Korea in 1968 but, while they flew a few missions over North Vietnam, they are not thought to have actually been in combat.

The PQM-102A is a Sperry-converted airframe under the Pave Deuce programme for use as a fully manoeuvrable manned or unmanned target drone. About 30 have been converted. Numerous F-102A airframes have been saved, the 199th Fighter Interceptor Squadron of the Hawaii Air National Guard having retained no fewer than four non-flyable F-102As for display purposes after transitioning to the F-4C Phantom.

Above: This anonymous F-102A displays the triangular fin and split tailcone airbrake that were major features of the type. The large fairings either side of the rear fuselage were purely aerodynamic in function, preserving the 'area rules' that gave the type its good performance. For obvious reasons they were known as 'Marilyns'.

Above and below left: This F-102A flew with the 317th Fighter Interceptor Squadron at Elmendorf AFB, Alaska in 1958. These northern units were key assets in the defence of the North American continent.

Right: Convair F-102A Delta Dagger of the 57th Fighter Interceptor Squadron, Keflavik, Iceland. This was the last operating unit of the 'Deuce'.

Convair F-102

One hundred and eleven TF-102As were built, these featuring side-by-side seating for two and full combat capability. In Vietnam a small number were used as high-speed FAC platforms and chase aircraft for B-52 raids.

Specification
F-102A

Type: single-seat all-weather interceptor
Powerplant: one 17,200-lb (7801.9-kg) afterburning thrust Pratt & Whitney J57-P-23 or -25 turbojet engine
Performance: maximum speed 825 mph (1327.7 km/h) or Mach 1.25 at 36,000 ft (10973 m); initial climb rate 13,000 ft (3962 m) per minute; service ceiling 51,000 ft (15545 m); range 1,350 miles (2173 km)
Weights: empty 20,160 lb (9144.6 kg); maximum take-off 31,276 lb (14186.8 kg)

Dimensions: span 38 ft 1½ in (11.62 m); length 68 ft 4½ in (20.84 m); height 21 ft 2½ in (6.46 m); wing area 661.5 sq ft (61.45 m²)
Armament: up to six AIM-4A/C/D Falcon semi-active radar-homing missiles or other missile combinations

Assigned to the 405th TFW, the 509th FIS was based at Clark AB, Philippines with F-102As. For air defence of South Vietnam the squadron sent detachments to Tan Son Nhut and Da Nang under the 'Water Glass' and 'Candy Machine' codenames. One was believed lost to a MiG-21 in action.

Republic F-103

History and notes

The Republic XF-103 of 1952 would have been a giant, hypersonic interceptor employing mixed turbojet and ramjet power to intercept Soviet bombers over the North Pole at 75,000 ft (22860 m) at Mach 2.2. Two prototypes were ordered and Republic completed a mock-up of the extraordinary delta-winged craft, built of titanium and stainless steel with a flush canopy and periscope for the pilot. In 1955, the periscope concept was tested on a specially-modified F-84G Thunderjet which was flown on a long cross-country hop with the pilot's vision blocked in front.

The XF-103 project was, simply, too ambitious. The 15,000-lb (6804-kg) thrust, Wright XJ67-W-3, licence-built version of the Bristol Olympus, to have comprised half of the turbo-ram power combination,

never materialised. Plans to substitute the Wright J65 were unrealistic. The XF-103 also had other design liabilities, including a low-slung, sugar-scoop engine intake which invited foreign object damage. The USAF determined that the programme was too costly and offered too little advantage over the Convair F-102 then under development. On 21 August 1957, the XF-103 project was terminated.

Specification
XF-103

Type: single-seat interceptor
Powerplant: (planned) one 15,000-lb (6804.0-kg) thrust, Wright XJ67-W-3 turbojet engine coupled with one 18,800-lb (8527.7-kg) thrust, Wright XJR55-W-1 ramjet

Performance: (estimated) maximum speed 2,400 mph (3862.3 km/h) or Mach 3.6 at 60,000 ft (18288 m); initial climb rate 19,000 ft (5791 m) per minute; service ceiling 75,000 ft (22860 m); range 810 miles (1303 km)
Weights: (estimated) empty about 25,000 lb (11340.0 kg); maximum take-off about 42,000 lb (19051.2 kg)
Dimensions: (planned) span 35 ft 10 in (10.92 m); length 81 ft 11 in

(24.97 m); height 18 ft 4 in (5.59 m); wing area 401 sq ft (37.25 m²)
Armament: (planned) six Hughes GAR-3 Falcon semi-active radar homing missiles and 36 2.75-in (69.86-mm) Mighty Mouse, folding-fin, aircraft rockets (FFAR)

This artist's impression shows the overall configuration of the F-103, with flush canopy and fuselage-side weapons bays for the Falcon and Genie missiles.

The Century Series

This F-102A served in West Germany with the 525th TFS, 36th TFW, at Bitburg, providing air defence for southern Germany (a task the squadron still performs with F-15C Eagles). The open weapon bay doors are noteworthy, revealing the four AIM-4 Falcon missiles that were the standard fit. One of the regular radar-guided weapons could be replaced by an AIM-29 Nuclear Falcon for anti-bomber sorties. The underwing fuel tanks were a standard 'Deuce' fit.

AIR FORCE FC-III

6IIII

Keith Fretwell.

The 'Century' Series Goes to War

With the 'Century' series of fighters established in service, the US Air Force believed itself to be the best-equipped air force in the world, and certainly in key areas it was. The North American F-100 was still a potent force in the day fighter/fighter-bomber role, the McDonnell F-101 was a good long-ranging interceptor while the elegant F-102 Delta Dagger and its F-106 Delta Dart successor were the last word in quick-reacting interceptors, able to defend the United States easily against any aggressor. In the tactical arena the Republic F-105 Thunderchief was a beast of an aircraft, with weapons to match. This only left the Lockheed F-104 Starfighter in the air superiority role, and this was too short-legged to be of any real use.

The parlous state of the true fighter in the US Air Force was cruelly exposed during the

The mighty AIR-2A Genie was the most fearsome air-to-air weapon ever available to USAF interceptors. Carried by the Convair F-106A (illustrated) and McDonnell F-101B, the Genie was unguided but had a nuclear warhead. It was designed to explode in the middle of incoming bomber formations.

mid-1960s when the service found itself back in Asia fighting MiGs again. This time the enemy was the Vietnam People's Air Force, and the foe MiG-17s, 19s and 21s. At once the vaunted 'Century' series fighters proved to be inferior to the simple MiGs in the oldest aerial battle of all: dogfighting, a discipline that had all but been ignored by military planners in the Pentagon.

'Century' series v MiGs

The Starfighter was supposed to have taken on the MiGs, but as one (F-100) pilot put it, they could only take about 'three giant steps outside the crew room door' before having to turn back for fuel. The MiGs simply stayed out of their way. F-100s got involved during 1965, and scored the first kills of the war (although not confirmed), but they too were not suited to life over North Vietnam. Similarly F-102s were out-and-out interceptors and although they provided air defence of South Vietnam, they only got into one scrape with the communists, and that resulted in a Dagger going down. Of the original 'Century' aircraft, it was the most unlikely that became a MiG-

killer – the nuclear bomber F-105. The pugnacious 'Thud' racked up an impressive victory list, but only at the expense of many losses.

What was needed was a dedicated air-to-air fighter, and that came in the shape of the McDonnell Phantom. Just as World War II made the P-51 a world-beater, and Korea the Sabre, so Vietnam turned the Phantom into an all-time classic. Despite its success, it had been developed as an attack aircraft, and the lack of gun armament in the early versions had proved embarrassing over North Vietnam, where the MiGs were getting in close with heavy-calibre cannon to make their kills. Of course the Phantom story had begun with the Navy back in the 1950s, but it could be regarded as a member of the 'Century' series as it had originally borne the F-110 designation.

The last member of the series showed all the high technology sophistication of the earlier aircraft. The North American F-107 was a very good fighter-bomber that was narrowly beaten by the F-105 in competition. The F-108 from the same company was an over-ambitious Mach 3 interceptor

F-105Ds from the 355th TFW, Takhli AB, Thailand, formate off the wing of a KC-135 after tanking during an April 1968 bombing mission. Both aircraft carry ECM pods on the outer wing pylons.

The F-4 Phantom rapidly became the most important tactical aircraft in South East Asia, performing not only the air-to-air mission but taking over many air-to-ground sorties from the F-105. These are 8th TFW F-4Ds, the nearest one carrying laser-guided bombs.

armed with nuclear-tipped missiles, while the F-110 (later F-4) introduced two-seats and all-missile armament to the air superiority fighter world. Finally there was the F-111.

Swing-wing problems

No aircraft can have had a more difficult passage into service than the radical swing-wing fighter-bomber, but such were its capabilities that when it eventually reached South-East Asia in full operation, it at once greatly enhanced the war-fighting ability of the US Air Force. Able to carry huge bomb-loads to distant targets, and deliver them with astonishing accuracy in the worst weather, the 'Aardvark' eventually proved right the protagonists who had fought for its existence for years. Consistent updates have kept it at the forefront of warplane technology, illustrated by the fact that it is, along with Tornado, NATO's prime strike platform in today's hostile combat environment.

With the F-111, the long series of US fighters came to an end, and in 1962 (long before the F-111 had flown), the Navy and Air Force got together and amalgamated their designation systems, choosing to start again at F-1 for fighters. Along the way the fighter had developed from the biplane Curtiss P-1 armed with light machine-guns to the variable-geometry nuclear bomber F-111. All that in just 38 years.

With the aerial conflict in South-East Asia ending a decade later in 1973, and with the often harsh lessons of that war fresh in the mind, the US Air Force prepared to embark on a new era, an era in which new words would be heard when discussing new fighters: agility, cost effectiveness, multi-role capability and combat persistence.

The General Dynamics F-111 introduced the swing-wing revolution, allowing the aircraft to take off with huge loads yet still fly supersonically at very low level. The long nose contained advanced attack radar, allied to a sophisticated weapon system.

Lockheed F-104 Starfighter

Lockheed F-104C Starfighter of the
435th Tactical Fighter Squadron,
Udorn, Thailand in 1966.

History and notes

The Lockheed F-104 Starfighter, the 'missile with a man in it', was conceived in 1952 by Clarence L. (Kelly) Johnson's design team for the noble purpose of outfighting anything the Soviets might throw into the Korean War. The intent was to produce a small, simple fighter with a high thrust-to-weight ratio and outstanding dogfight performance. Johnson designed a wide-chord short-span unswept wing with a maximum thickness of only 4 in (10.16 cm) and a leading edge so sharp that it needed protective felt-cap covering on the ground to prevent injury. Two XF-104 prototypes (53-7786/7787), each powered by a 7,800-lb (3538.1-kg) thrust Wright XJ65-W-6 Sapphire turbojet, began flight tests at Edwards AFB, California, on 28 February 1954 with Tony LeVier accomplishing the first flight. There followed 17 YF-104A airframes (55-2955/2971) which entered service-tests with the 14,800-lb (6713.3-kg) thrust afterburning General Electric YJ79-GE-3. Evaluation of the Starfighter proceeded, not without problems, and an F-104A crash claimed the life of Korean War ace Captain Iven C. Kincheloe. By 29 January 1958, the first of 153 F-104As was reaching the Air Defense Command's 83rd Fighter-Interceptor Wing at Hamilton AFB, California.

An RF-104A reconnaissance variant was ordered by the USAF, then cancelled. Three NF-104A aircraft were fitted with 6,000-lb (2721.6-kg) thrust Rocketdyne AR-2 booster motors in the tail for astronaut training and for a celebrated altitude attempt by Colonel Charles E. Yeager. A few aircraft became QF-104A target drones. The F-104B was a two-seat combat trainer for the USAF, a few of which were eventually transferred to Jordan and Taiwan. After the single-seat F-104A models were withdrawn from USAF and Air National Guard service, surplus aircraft were supplied to Taiwan (25), Jordan (36), Pakistan (12) and Canada (1).

The principal American Starfighter was the F-104C for the Tactical Air Command with 15,800-lb (7166.9-kg) afterburning thrust J79-GE-7 turbojet, and provision for Sidewinder missiles and con-

ventional or nuclear bombs or rockets; 77 F-104Cs were built. Though the Starfighter is not widely remembered for its relatively brief career in USAF colours, a squadron of the 8th Tactical Fighter Wing at Udorn, Thailand, operated F-104Cs in 1966-7; F-104Cs participated in Operation 'Bolo', the 2 January 1967 fighter sweeps over North Vietnam in which F-4C Phantoms shot down seven MiGs. Eight F-104Cs were lost in combat in South East Asia while six more were written off in operational incidents.

The F-104D was another two-seat combat trainer version, 20 of which were purchased for the USAF. It was known as the F-104DJ in Japan. All of the remaining Starfighters were for export, including the F-104F for West Germany; the F-104G manufactured in the USA, Canada and Europe for several NATO users; the RF-104G reconnaissance and TF-104G trainer variants for the Luftwaffe; the F-104H proposed export variant which was never built; the F-104J assembled principally by Mitsubishi for Japan; and the CF-104 and CF-104D for Canada. The ultimate machine in the series is Italy's Aeritalia-built F-104S developed in the late 1970s for the Italian and Turkish air forces and powered by 15,800-lb (7166.9-kg) afterburning thrust J79-GE-19.

Specification
F-104C

Type: single-seat tactical strike aircraft
Powerplant: one 15,800-lb (7166.9-kg) afterburning thrust General Electric J79-GE-7 turbojet engine
Performance: maximum speed, clean 1,150 mph (1850.7 km/h) or Mach 1.74 at 50,000 ft (15240 m); maximum climb rate 54,000 ft (16459 m) per minute; service ceiling, clean 58,000 ft (17678 m); range with drop tanks 1,500 miles (2414 km)
Weights: empty 12,760 lb (5787.9 kg); maximum take-off 27,853 lb (12634.1 kg)
Dimensions: span clean 21 ft 9 in (6.63 m); length 54 ft 8 in (16.66 m); height 13 ft 5 in (4.09 m); wing area 196.1 sq ft (18.22 m²)
Armament: one 20-mm M61A1 cannon, plus provision for two or four AIM-9 Sidewinder air-to-air missiles or up to 2,000 lb (907.2 kg) of ordnance

Intended as a fast-reacting interceptor, the F-104 had short range but blistering Mach 2 performance. The initial F-104A model had air-to-air capability only, armament consisting of two Sidewinder missiles on the wingtip rails and an internal 20-mm M61A1 cannon.

Republic F-105 Thunderchief

Republic F-105B Thunderchief of the 335th TFS, 4th TFW, the first operating unit. Note the small diameter nose cone.

History and notes

The Republic F-105 Thunderchief, or company model AP-63, was conceived in 1951 as a nuclear strike aircraft with an internal bomb bay, but won renown for hauling bombs externally in a conventional war. Alexander Kartveli's design team originally intended a straight fuselage for the craft but, after seeing NACA data assembled by Richard Whitcomb, was won over by the wasp-waist or 'area rule' configuration which enhanced transonic flight performance. At first intended for the Allison J71 engine and powered in prototype form by the Pratt & Whitney J57, the F-105 attained its successes with the 17,200-lb (7801.9-kg) thrust Pratt & Whitney J75-P-19W turbojet which provided 24,500-lb (11113.2-kg) thrust with afterburning. Its mid-mounted wing, swept 60 degrees, the F-105 stood high on its tricycle gear and was a big, brutish machine, yet it conveyed an image of sleekness and grace slicing through the air. Development of the aircraft was by no means without its difficulties, and things had only begun when two J57-powered YF-105As (54-98/99) commenced flying 22 October 1955, soon followed by 15 aircraft designated JF-105B and F-105B for test programmes.

Production F-105Bs, long delayed by development problems, began to roll from Republic's Farmingdale line during 1958 and the USAF accepted its first machine on 27 May 1958. The 335th Tactical Fighter Squadron, temporarily moved to Eglin AFB, Florida, began to work up in the new aircraft only to find that, given its complexity and production slippages, it would not become operational until 1960. Meanwhile, a two-seat strike variant, the F-105C, had reached the mock-up stage but was not built. Though technical problems persisted and critics were calling the 'Thud' a maintenance nightmare, Republic proceeded with the F-105D variant which afforded true, all-weather capability by introducing General Electric FC-5 fully integrated automatic flight fire-control system. The F-105D's fuselage was lengthened by 1 ft 3 in (0.381 m). Some 610 were manufactured, and first flight took place at Farmingdale 9 June 1959. The F-105D model soon equipped all three squadrons of the 4th Tactical Fighter Wing at Seymour Johnson AFB, North Carolina. United States Air Forces in Europe (USAFE) were the first overseas recipient of the F-105D, the 36th TFW at Bitburg AB, West Germany re-equipping from 12 May 1961 and the 49th TFW at Spangdahlem soon following. In the early 1960s, with a war growing in Asia,

The bulged dorsal spine of these F-105Ds denote them as 'T-Stick II' modifications, this programme adding all-weather bombing equipment. These aircraft served the 457th TFS/301st TFW, part of the Air Force Reserve flying from Carswell AFB, Texas.

F-105Ds joined the 18th TFW at Kadena AFB, Okinawa.

The F-105D was by now a proven ordnance-carrier. With multiple ejector racks (MER), it could carry an impressive load of external fuel, ECM gear, and eight 750-lb (340-kg) bombs on long-range missions. The F-105D could also operate with the Martin AGM-12 Bullpup air-to-surface missile, which was to prove remarkably ineffective against 'hard' targets in Vietnam and would be observed bouncing off the Thanh Hoa Bridge. In addition, the F-105D model could carry 2.75-in (69.85-mm) rocket pods, napalm canisters and the AIM-9 infra-red (IR) air-to-air missiles, while its integral M61A1 Gatling-type 20-mm cannon proved invaluable in the dual roles of air-to-air combat and air-to-ground strafing. A late-model variant of the F-105D was the F-105D T-Stick II fitted with additional avionics which bestowed all-weather bombing capability, housed in a prominent dorsal fairing extending along the spine of the fuselage to the tail.

Early F-105Ds sit in their original natural metal finish, complete with 'FH' buzz numbers. The D-model introduced a fully-automated fire control system, and was able to carry a large load of stores including nuclear weapons, the armament for which it was originally devised.

Republic F-105

Republic F-105D 'T-Stick II' of the
563rd TFS, 23rd TFW, McConnell
AFB, Kansas.

The F-105E was another two-seat variant that was not developed. A two-seat Thunderchief was inevitable, however, and in May 1962 Republic proceeded with the F-105F. This model, which made its first flight 11 June 1963, was some 2,000 lb (907.2 kg) heavier as well as slightly longer than earlier Thunderchiefs in order to accommodate the second crewman in tandem; 143 F-105Fs were delivered and 61 were later reconfigured for the electronic warfare or 'Wild Weasel' role in Vietnam, at first under their original designation and later as the F-105G.

The F-105D, F-105F and F-105G all fought in North Vietnamese skies, the F-104D model fighter-bomber so extensively that over half of the 610 built eventually fell to Hanoi's air defences. After withdrawal from South East Asia in 1969-70, the Thunderchief soldiered on in Reserve and Air National Guard units, eventually flying its final sortie in 1984. At one time no fewer than 14 USAF and 11 ANG squadrons operated the type, which was built to the extent of 833 examples. Perhaps because of its complexity, no F-105 was ever exported and it is exceedingly unlikely that any will ever be seen flying in civil registration.

Combat

At one point in 1965-8, it was calculated that an F-105 pilot stood only a 75 per cent chance of completing 100 missions over North Vietnam. From its first mission on 2 March 1965, when F-105s took part in a strike against the Xom Bong ammunition storage area near the 17th Parallel, F-105s were committed against some of the heaviest defences the world had seen. With its size and range, the F-105 could carry twice the bombload further and faster than the F-100, so the 355th and 388th Tactical Fighter Wings based in Thailand used the type to carry the brunt of the war to Hanoi.

Because of its immense size, the 'Thud' was also called 'Lead Sled', 'Ultra Hog', 'Iron Butterfly' and other names. Used with affection, these terms denoted a machine which, at first, sorely needed redundancy in its hydraulic system, frightened pilots with its long take-off run, and had wing-loading too high to manoeuvre effectively against MiGs. Once the hydraulic system was improved, the

A two-seat combat proficiency trainer was produced in the form of the F-105F, which was slightly longer to accommodate the tandem cockpits. These saw action in South East Asia, many being converted to 'Wild Weasel' configuration with extra antennae and Shrike-launch capability.

Few came tougher than the Thunderchief, although its flying qualities were often likened to a brick! Nevertheless it became the stalwart of the early air war against Vietnam. Shown here is an F-105G 'Wild Weasel' aircraft, identified by the fuselage-side ECM fairings.

F-105 could take severe battle damage and keep flying: on 28 June 1966 attacking a highway bridge in North Vietnam, Major William McClelland was hit by an 85-mm shell which exploded in his underwing pylon, continued laterally along and through the wing, and tore out everything for about 4 ft (1.22 m). Despite the great drag generated by this enormous hole and protruding wing sections, McClelland nursed his craft safely home.

The armed F-105F 'Wild Weasel', which fought North Vietnamese SAM sites, also produced two winners of the Medal of Honor, the only men to receive the award for actions while piloting fighter aircraft. On 10 March 1967, Captain Merlyn H. Dethlefsen in an F-105F (63-8354) pressed an attack on SAM sites while surrounded by anti-aircraft fire, missiles and MiGs. On 19 April 1967, Major Leo K. Thorsness's F-105F (63-8301) was at the limits of fuel and endurance when Thorsness covered a rescue operation and drove off a flight of MiG-17s, destroying one and damaging another. On these and other occasions, Thunderchief crews repeatedly submitted themselves to anti-aircraft, small-arms, SAM and MiG opposition, often all at the same time. Although the F-105 had never been conceived as a dogfighter, its pilots did shoot down 29 MiGs in Vietnam.

Republic F-105 Thunderchief cutaway drawing key

1 Pitot tube
2 Radome
3 Radar scanner dish
4 Radar mounting and tracking mechanism
5 Forward electronic countermeasures (ECM) antenna
6 Aft-facing strike camera
7 Radome hinge
8 ADF sense aerial
9 Fire control radar transmitter/receiver
10 Cannon muzzle
11 Instrument electronics
12 Inflight refuelling position light
13 Air refuelling receptacle
14 Cannon ammunition drum, 1,028 rounds
15 Liquid oxygen converter
16 Angle of attack transmitter
17 Cannon barrels
18 Nosewheel doors
19 M-61 20-mm six-barrel rotary cannon
20 Ammunition feed chute
21 Gun gas venting pipe
22 Air refuelling probe housing
23 Alternator and electrical bay
24 Air driven turbine
25 Air refuelling probe
26 Windshield rain dispersal duct
27 Bullet proof windscreen panels
28 Radar attack sight
29 Instrument panel shroud
30 Navigation radar display
31 Rudder pedals
32 Cockpit front pressure bulkhead
33 Cannon mounting
34 Nosewheel leg strut

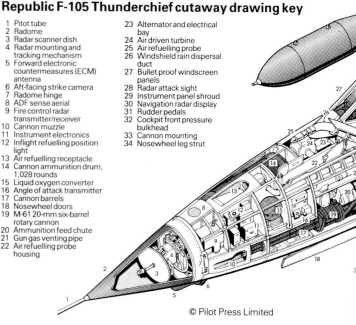

F-105G 'Wild Weasel' of the 561st TFS, 388th TFW, Korat, before the unit received its special 'WW' tailcode. The 'G' featured ECM fairings scabbed on to the fuselage sides, thus freeing wing pylons for extra missiles or fuel.

35 ILS system radar reflector
36 Taxiing lamps
37 Nosewheel
38 Torque scissor links
39 Hydraulic steering controls
40 Flight control system hydraulics bay
41 Electronics cooling air outlet
42 IFF aerial
43 UHF aerial
44 Underfloor radio and electronics bay
45 Cockpit pressure floor level
46 Pilot's side console panel
47 Engine throttle
48 Control column
49 Pilot's ejection seat
50 Seat back parachute pack
51 Headrest
52 Cockpit canopy cover
53 3,000-lb (1360-kg) HE bomb (inboard pylon)
54 Cockpit air intake
55 Cockpit canopy jack
56 Canopy hinge
57 Air conditioning pack
58 Cockpit rear pressure bulkhead
59 Secondary electronics bay
60 Air data computer
61 Port air intake
62 Bomb bay fuel tank, 390-US gal (1476 litres)
63 Boundary layer splitter plate
64 Intake duct variable area sliding ramp

65 Forward group of fuselage fuel tanks; total internal fuel capacity, 1,160 US gal (4391 litres)
66 Gyro compass platform
67 Bomb bay fuel tank fuel transfer lines
68 Fuselage/front spar main frame
69 Dorsal spine fairing
70 Starboard mainwheel, stowed position
71 450-US gal (1703-litre) external fuel tank
72 AIM-9 Sidewinder air-to-air missile
73 Missile launcher rail
74 Twin missile carrier (outboard pylon)
75 Starboard leading edge flap
76 Outboard pylon fixing/drop tank filler cap
77 Starboard navigation light
78 Static dischargers
79 Starboard aileron
80 Starboard Fowler flap
81 Trim tab, starboard only
82 Flap guide rails
83 Roll control spoilers
84 Anti-collision light
85 Air intake ducting
86 Ground running secondary air intake
87 Wing spar attachment joint
88 Fuselage/rear spar main frame

89 Engine compressor face
90 Forward engine mounting frame
91 Rear fuselage group of fuel tanks
92 Fuel pipe ducting
93 Drop tank tail fins
94 Afterburner duct cooling ram air intake
95 Starboard all-moving tailplane
96 Tailfin construction
97 Fin tip ECM aerials
98 Tail position light
99 Static discharger
100 Rudder mass balance
101 Rudder
102 Formation light
103 Water injection tank; 36 US gal (136 litre) capacity
104 Rudder power control unit
105 Brake parachute housing
106 Parachute door
107 Petal-type airbrakes, open position
108 Republic convergent/ divergent ram air ejector nozzle flaps
109 Airbrake/nozzle flap jacks
110 Internal variable area afterburner nozzle
111 Afterburner nozzle actuators
112 Afterburner ducting
113 Tailplane pivot fixing
114 Port all-moving tailplane construction
115 Tailplane titanium box spar
116 Leading edge nose ribs

122 Engine turbine section heat shroud
123 Engine bay venting ram air intake
124 Rear fuselage frame and stringer construction
125 Runway arrester hook
126 Ventral fin
127 Accessory cooling air duct
128 Cartridge starter
129 Fuselage top longeron
130 Engine driven accessory gearbox
131 Oil tank, 4.5-US gal (17-litre) capacity
132 Pratt & Whitney J75-P-19W afterburning turbojet engine
133 Port Fowler flap construction
134 Five section roll control spoilers
135 Flap screw jacks
136 Aileron mass balance
137 Port drop tank tail fins
138 Honeycomb aileron construction
139 Static dischargers
140 Wing tip fairing
141 Port navigation light
142 AGM-45 Shrike anti-radar missile
143 ECM pod

144 Outboard stores pylon
145 Pylon fixing/fuel filler cap
146 Aileron hinge control
147 Aileron/spoiler mixer linkage
148 Multi-spar wing construction
149 Aileron power control unit
150 Inboard pylon fixing
151 Inboard stores pylon
152 Mainwheel leg door
153 Port mainwheel
154 450-US gal (1703 litre) drop tank
155 Main undercarriage leg torque scissor links

156 Landing lamp
157 Port leading edge flap
158 Leading edge flap rotary actuators
159 Main undercarriage pivot mounting
160 Undercarriage side breaker strut
161 Hydraulic retraction jack
162 Diagonal wing spar

117 Ventral fuel vent
118 All-moving tailplane control jack
119 Rear fuselage break point
120 Engine firewall
121 Rear engine mounting

163 Mainwheel housing
164 Inner mainwheel door
165 Leading edge flap actuator
166 Leading edge flush aerial
167 650-US gal (2461-litre) centreline fuel tank
168 Fuel tank filler cap
169 Centreline stores pylon
170 Triple ejection rack
171 Six M117 750-lb (340-kg) HE bombs
172 Anti-personnel extended bomb fuse
173 AGM-78 Standard ARM anti-radar missile
174 AGM-12C Bullpup air-to-ground missile

Specification

F-105D

Type: single-seat fighter-bomber

Powerplant: one 24,500-lb (11113.2-kg) afterburning thrust Pratt & Whitney J75-P-19W turbojet engine

Performance: maximum speed 1,390 mph (2236.9 km/h) or Mach 2.1 at 36,000 ft (10973 m); initial climb rate, clean 34,400 ft (10485 m) per minute; service ceiling 45,000 ft (13716 m); range with maximum external fuel 2,390 miles (3846 km)

Weights: empty 27,500 lb (12474.0 kg); maximum take-off 52,838 lb (23967.3 kg)

Dimensions: span 34 ft 9 in (10.59 m); length 64 ft 4 in (19.61 m); height 19 ft 7 in (5.97 m); wing area 385 sq ft (35.77 m²)

Armament: one 20-mm M61A1 cannon, plus various combinations of up to 20,000 lb (9072 kg) of under-wing ordnance including typical load of eight 750-lb (340-kg) bombs

Bearing the fin-tip colours of the 4th Tactical Fighter Wing's 334th Tactical Fighter Squadron, this F-105D was one of the first camouflaged examples to see combat action, deploying to Da Nang in South Vietnam during 1965 prior to the organisation of permanently-based units at Takhli and Korat in Thailand. Surviving this tour of duty, this aircraft's luck eventually ran out on 31 March 1967 when it was brought down over North Vietnam while serving with the 388th TFW.

USAF
91745

Keith Fretwell.

Convair F-106 Delta Dart

History and notes

The Convair F-106 Delta Dart all-weather interceptor began its life as the F-102B but was essentially an entirely new aircraft design, having only a delta wing in common with its F-102 precursor. While development of the earlier fighter was delayed by various teething troubles in 1955-6, progress with the later machine became possible with the development of the Hughes MA-1 integrated fire-control system. In November 1955, the USAF placed an order for 17 F-102Bs and in December, a mock-up of the proposed cockpit with radically new equipment and pilot displays was completed. On 17 June 1956, the F-102B was redesignated F-106.

The USAF was tasking Convair to develop an interceptor which could intercept Soviet bombers in all weather at altitudes up to 70,000 ft (21336 m) and over a radius of 430 miles (692 km). Armed with guided missiles and/or unguided rockets with nuclear warheads, the F-106 was data-linked to the semi-automatic ground environment (SAGE) air-defence network and was expected to carry out intercepts at high altitude on the automatic mode.

The first of two YF-106A service-test aircraft (56-451/452) flew on 26 December 1956 at Edwards AFB, California. Like most new fighter types in the 'century series', the F-106 was initially a disappointment. Maximum speed, rate of climb and overall acceler-

Above: A two-seat F-106B heads this line-up of Delta Darts. The two-seater retained full combat capability, although none were among the aircraft retrofitted with a 20-mm cannon under Project 'Sixshooter'.

Below: For its principal interception role, the F-106 needed to react swiftly to incoming threats. With its J57 in full 'burner, the 'Six' could accelerate and climb rapidly, cutting interception times considerably.

In its heyday the F-106 equipped over half of Air Defense Command. This frontline aircraft served with the 87th Fighter Interceptor Squadron at K.I. Sawyer AFB, Michigan.

This F-106A served with the 101st FIS, 102nd FIW, Massachusetts Air National Guard. The squadron flew from Otis ANGB and was one of the last F-106 operators.

The 49th FIS at Griffiss AFB, New York, was the last F-106 front-line unit. When it retired the type it left only four ANG units which themselves retired the type in 1988.

Along with the New Jersey ANG, the Montana Guard were the last users of the F-106 in front-line service. The 186th FIS, 120th FIG flew from Great Falls International Airport, where it currently has F-16s.

ation were significantly below Air Defense Command expectations with the Pratt & Whitney J57-P-9 turbojet employed in the initial machines and the Wright J67, licence-built Olympus, being contemplated. When the latter powerplant failed to materialise, the USAF sharply reduced its requirement from 1,000 to 360 of the new interceptors. Coincidentally, performance was improved sharply with the installation of the 17,200-lb (7801.9-kg) thrust Pratt & Whitney J75-P-17 turbojet which could provide 24,500-lb (11113.2-kg) thrust with afterburning.

The F-106A attained its initial operating capability with the 498th Fighter-Interceptor Squadron at Geiger AFB, Washington, in October 1959 and subsequently served with 15 ADC and eight Air

Interceptors on guard: the Convair F-106 stood guard over America for nearly thirty years, aircraft standing on five-minute alert around the nation to ward off any potential threat. After its front-line days were over, the 'Six' served until 1988 on Air National Guard units, the last being New Jersey.

National Guard squadrons. Except for brief deployments to Europe and to Korea in 1968, the type served exclusively in North America. Totals of 277 F-106A single-seat interceptors served in company with 63 F-106B two-seat combat trainers, 340 machines actually being completed, and the types remained on active duty until 1982.

Specification

F-106A

Type: single-seat all-weather interceptor
Powerplant: one 24,500-lb (11113.2-kg) afterburning thrust Pratt & Whitney J75-P-17 turbojet engine
Performance: maximum speed, clean 1,487 mph (2393.0 km/h) or Mach 2.25 at 40,000 ft (12192 m); sustained ceiling 58,000 ft (17678 m); combat radius on internal fuel 575 miles (925 km); range with external tanks 1,950 miles (3138 km)
Weights: empty 23,814 lb (10802.0 kg); maximum take-off 38,250 lb (17350.2 kg)
Dimensions: span 38 ft 3½ in (11.67 m); length with probe 70 ft 8½ in (21.55 m); height 20 ft 3½ in (6.18 m); wing area 697.8 sq ft (64.83 m^2)
Armament: one 20-mm M61A1 cannon, four AIM-4E and/or AIM-4G Falcon air-to-air missiles, and two AIM-2B Genie nuclear-tipped air-to-air missiles

Convair F-106A Delta Dagger cutaway drawing key

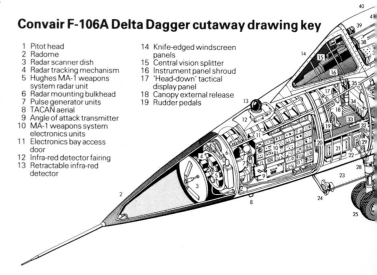

 1 Pitot head
 2 Radome
 3 Radar scanner dish
 4 Radar tracking mechanism
 5 Hughes MA-1 weapons system radar unit
 6 Radar mounting bulkhead
 7 Pulse generator units
 8 TACAN aerial
 9 Angle of attack transmitter
10 MA-1 weapons system electronics units
11 Electronics bay access door
12 Infra-red detector fairing
13 Retractable infra-red detector
14 Knife-edged windscreen panels
15 Central vision splitter
16 Instrument panel shroud
17 'Head-down' tactical display panel
18 Canopy external release
19 Rudder pedals

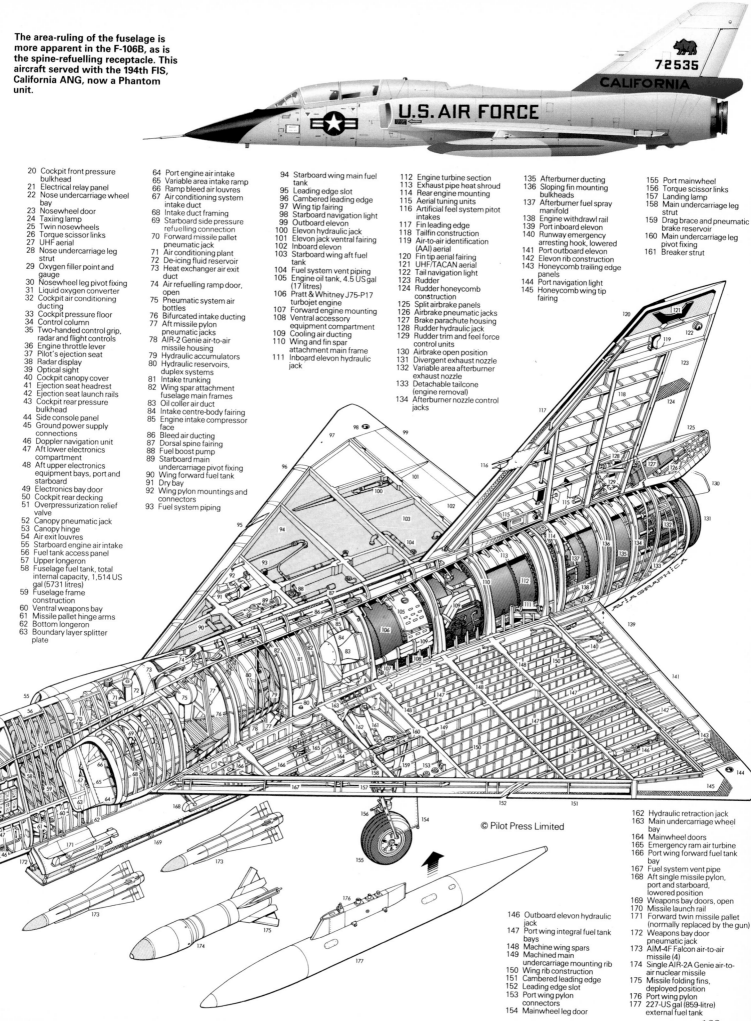

The area-ruling of the fuselage is more apparent in the F-106B, as is the spine-refuelling receptacle. This aircraft served with the 194th FIS, California ANG, now a Phantom unit.

72535
CALIFORNIA
U.S. AIR FORCE

20 Cockpit front pressure bulkhead
21 Electrical relay panel
22 Nose undercarriage wheel bay
23 Nosewheel door
24 Taxiing lamp
25 Twin nosewheels
26 Torque scissor links
27 UHF aerial
28 Nose undercarriage leg strut
29 Oxygen filler point and gauge
30 Nosewheel leg pivot fixing
31 Liquid oxygen converter
32 Cockpit air conditioning ducting
33 Cockpit pressure floor
34 Control column
35 Two-handed control grip, radar and flight controls
36 Engine throttle lever
37 Pilot's ejection seat
38 Radar display
39 Optical sight
40 Cockpit canopy cover
41 Ejection seat headrest
42 Ejection seat launch rails
43 Cockpit rear pressure bulkhead
44 Side console panel
45 Ground power supply connections
46 Doppler navigation unit
47 Aft lower electronics compartment
48 Aft upper electronics equipment bays, port and starboard
49 Electronics bay door
50 Cockpit rear decking
51 Overpressurization relief valve
52 Canopy pneumatic jack
53 Canopy hinge
54 Air exit louvres
55 Starboard engine air intake
56 Fuel tank access panel
57 Upper longeron
58 Fuselage fuel tank, total internal capacity, 1,514 US gal (5731 litres)
59 Fuselage frame construction
60 Ventral weapons bay
61 Missile pallet hinge arms
62 Bottom longeron
63 Boundary layer splitter plate

64 Port engine air intake
65 Variable area intake ramp
66 Ramp bleed air louvres
67 Air conditioning system intake duct
68 Intake duct framing
69 Starboard side pressure refuelling connection
70 Forward missile pallet pneumatic jack
71 Air conditioning plant
72 De-icing fluid reservoir
73 Heat exchanger air exit duct
74 Air refuelling ramp door, open
75 Pneumatic system air bottles
76 Bifurcated intake ducting
77 Aft missile pylon pneumatic jacks
78 AIR-2 Genie air-to-air missile housing
79 Hydraulic accumulators
80 Hydraulic reservoirs, duplex systems
81 Intake trunking
82 Wing spar attachment fuselage main frames
83 Oil coller air duct
84 Intake centre-body fairing
85 Engine intake compressor face
86 Bleed air ducting
87 Dorsal spine fairing
88 Fuel boost pump
89 Starboard main undercarriage pivot fixing
90 Wing forward fuel tank
91 Dry bay
92 Wing pylon mountings and connectors
93 Fuel system piping

94 Starboard wing main fuel tank
95 Leading edge slot
96 Cambered leading edge
97 Wing tip fairing
98 Starboard navigation light
99 Outboard elevon
100 Elevon hydraulic jack
101 Elevon jack ventral fairing
102 Inboard elevon
103 Starboard wing aft fuel tank
104 Fuel system vent piping
105 Engine oil tank, 4.5 US gal (17 litres)
106 Pratt & Whitney J75-P17 turbojet engine
107 Forward engine mounting
108 Ventral accessory equipment compartment
109 Cooling air ducting
110 Wing and fin spar attachment main frame
111 Inboard elevon hydraulic jack

112 Engine turbine section
113 Exhaust pipe heat shroud
114 Rear engine mounting
115 Aerial tuning units
116 Artificial feel system pitot intakes
117 Fin leading edge
118 Tailfin construction
119 Air-to-air identification (AAI) aerial
120 Fin tip aerial fairing
121 UHF/TACAN aerial
122 Tail navigation light
123 Rudder
124 Rudder honeycomb construction
125 Split airbrake panels
126 Airbrake pneumatic jacks
127 Brake parachute housing
128 Rudder hydraulic jack
129 Rudder trim and feel force control units
130 Airbrake open position
131 Divergent exhaust nozzle
132 Variable area afterburner exhaust nozzle
133 Detachable tailcone (engine removal)
134 Afterburner nozzle control jacks

135 Afterburner ducting
136 Sloping fin mounting bulkheads
137 Afterburner fuel spray manifold
138 Engine withdrawl rail
139 Port inboard elevon
140 Runway emergency arresting hook, lowered
141 Port outboard elevon
142 Elevon rib construction
143 Honeycomb trailing edge panels
144 Port navigation light
145 Honeycomb wing tip fairing

155 Port mainwheel
156 Torque scissor links
157 Landing lamp
158 Main undercarriage leg strut
159 Drag brace and pneumatic brake reservoir
160 Main undercarriage leg pivot fixing
161 Breaker strut

© Pilot Press Limited

146 Outboard elevon hydraulic jack
147 Port wing integral fuel tank bays
148 Machine wing spars
149 Machined main undercarriage mounting rib
150 Wing rib construction
151 Cambered leading edge
152 Leading edge slot
153 Port wing pylon connectors
154 Mainwheel leg door

162 Hydraulic retraction jack
163 Main undercarriage wheel bay
164 Mainwheel doors
165 Emergency ram air turbine
166 Port wing forward fuel tank bay
167 Fuel system vent pipe
168 Aft single missile pylon, port and starboard, lowered position
169 Weapons bay doors, open
170 Missile launch rail
171 Forward twin missile pallet (normally replaced by the gun)
172 Weapons bay door pneumatic jack
173 AIM-4F Falcon air-to-air missile (4)
174 Single AIR-2A Genie air-to-air nuclear missile
175 Missile folding fins, deployed position
176 Port wing pylon
177 227-US gal (859-litre) external fuel tank

183

The once great Air Defense
Command was slowly dismantled
during the 1970s and 1980s until
today, with only two remaining
front-line squadrons (and one is
based on Iceland). Even the great
command itself is now relegated to
the status of 1st Air Force of Tactical
Air Command. Increasingly the air
defence commitment passed to the
Air National Guard, which now flies
F-4s and F-16s on alert duty. Before
this the F-106 was the backbone of
the force, typified by this F-106A of
the 125th Fighter Interceptor
Squadron, Florida Air National
Guard, based at Jacksonville.

USAF

U.S. AIR FO

AIR FORCE

Florida

80786

14

AIR FORCE

14

Keith Fretwell 185

North American F-107

The second prototype of the North American YF-107 as seen at Air Force Plant 42, Palmdale, California during 1957 weapons tests (carrying nuclear 'shape').

History and notes

The North American F-107, or company NA-212, was the last USAF fighter to bear this famous manufacturer's name. Originally designated F-100B, it was an all-weather fighter-bomber version of the F-100 powered by a 23,500-lb (10659.6-kg) thrust Pratt & Whitney YJ75-P-9 turbojet fed via an air inlet above and behind the cockpit, so positioned to create space in the nose for radar.

Design work began in June 1953 and a year later the USAF ordered nine aircraft (55-5118/5126), although only three were actually completed. In 1955, the F-107 lost out to the Republic F-105 in a paper competition even though it had not yet flown and its competitor did not, then, have all-weather capability. Thus, the future of the F-107 was already clouded on 10 September

1956 when Robert Baker made the first flight at Edwards AFB, California, in the first of three servicetest YF-107As.

Considering the early difficulties encountered by other 'century series' fighters, the YF-107A was relatively troublefree and might well have played an important role in the Tactical Air Command. But despite good performance, the three YF-107As were soon relegated to permanent test status. Features of the aircraft warranting further evaluation included a flush centreline fuel tank mounted in the indented fuselage bottom, spoilers on the wing surface instead of ailerons, and a one-piece all-moving rudder, later adopted on the A-5 Vigilante attack bomber. The first YF-107A eventually found itself in a scrap

heap, the second is now on display at the Air Force Museum in Dayton, Ohio, and the third was lost in a crash landing while on loan to NACA.

Specification
YF-107A

Type: single-seat all-weather fighter-bomber
Powerplant: one 23,500-lb (10659.6-kg) thrust Pratt & Whitney YJ75-P-9 turbojet engine
Performance: maximum speed 1,300 mph (2092.1 km/h) or Mach 2.0 at 20,000 ft (6096 m); initial climb rate, clean 31,000 ft (9449 m) per minute; service ceiling 46,000 ft (14021 m); range 1,550 miles (2494 km)
Weights: empty about 28,000 lb

(12700.8 kg); maximum take-off about 40,000 lb (18144 kg)
Dimensions: span 36 ft 7 in (11.15 m); length excluding probe 60 ft 10 in (18.54 m); height 19 ft 6 in (5.94 m); wing area 376.02 sq ft (34.93 m²)
Armament: four 20-mm fixed forward-firing cannon (installed on second aircraft only), plus provision for 10,000 lb (4536 kg) of underwing ordnance

The first YF-107 flies in formation with the single TF-100C two-seater near Edwards AFB during the type's first flight on 10 September 1956. The similarities between the two are obvious, but the F-107 had all-weather avionics and a powerful J75 engine.

North American F-108 Rapier

History and notes

The North American F-108 Rapier was designed in 1957 as a modified-delta, twin-engined two-seat fighter larger by far than any previous fighter ever built. Its two crewmen were to wear pressure suits and ride inside individual ejection capsules. In 1959, two B-58 Hustler bombers were allocated to Hughes Aircraft for development of the AN/ASG-18 fire-control system for the nuclear-tipped GAR-9 (AIM-47A) air-to-air missile intended for the F-108. The

F-108 was apparently seen as both a long-range polar interceptor and an escort for the company's very similar and only slightly larger XB-70 Valkyrie bomber.

Development of the colossal F-108 proved too costly for its apparent benefits and the programme was terminated on 23 September 1959.

Specification
XF-108

Type: two-seat long-range fighter

Powerplant: (planned) two 30,000-lb (13608-kg) afterburning thrust General Electric YJ93-GE-3 turbojet engines
Performance: (estimated) maximum speed 2,000 mph (3218.6 km/h) or Mach 2.0 at 40,000 ft (12192 m); initial climb rate 18,000 ft (5486 m) per minute; service ceiling 60,000 ft (18288 m); range 1,150 miles (1850 km)
Weights: (estimated) empty 48,000 lb (21772.8 kg); maximum take-off 102,000 lb (46267.2 kg)

Dimensions: (planned) span 52 ft 10½ in (16.12 m); length 84 ft 10½ in (25.87 m); height 22 ft 1 in (6.73 m); wing area 1,400 sq ft (130.06 m²)
Armament: (planned) various missiles including Hughes GAR-9 nuclear-tipped semi-active radar homing missiles

History and notes

In 1955, the USAF rejected a proposal that the designation F-109 be assigned to a two-seat variant of the McDonnell F-101A Voodoo. The aircraft became the F-101B instead.

In February 1958, the USAF rejected a proposal that the Bell D-188A vertical take-off fighter project, completed in mock-up form only, be designated F-109. Although some published reports have quoted serial numbers, in fact the Bell design never received a USAF designation.

Throughout the 1950s, published reports associated the F-109 designation with vertical research by the Ryan Aeronautical Company which produced the X-13 aircraft. But the USAF never assigned the F-109 designation to Ryan.

The fact is, the designation was never assigned at all. Of 131 US fighter designations, 20 pertained to real aircraft which were planned but never built: P-11, P-14, P-18, P-19, P-27, P-28, P-32, P-33, P-34, P-44, P-48, P-52, P-53, P-57, P-65, P-68, P-69, P-71, F-103, F-108. Four designations simply were never assigned at all: P-73, P-74, F-109, F-13.

McDonnell F-110 Phantom II

History and notes

In 1961, the USAF ordered the US Navy's McDonnell F4H-1 Phantom II carrier-based interceptor with minor changes for the Tactical Air Command and gave it the designation F-110A. The USAF also ordered YRF-110A and RF-110A reconnaissance variants. While awaiting delivery, the USAF borrowed a number of US Navy Phantoms and one of these (149405) appeared at Edwards AFB, California, in 1962 with the F-110A appellation painted on its nose, though this was incorrect for this particular airframe. The actual F-110A never flew with that designation.

On 18 September 1962, the designation system for US aircraft was unified to bring the other military services in line with the method the USAF and its predecessor services had already been using. Under the new arrangement, the F-110 and 10 US Navy types were given new numbers to facilitate uniformity. The F for fighter series began again at F-1. The F-110A, YRF-110A and RF-110A thus became the F-4C, YRF-4C and RF-4C respectively.

Specification
F-110A
Type: two-seat fighter

Powerplant: two 17,700-lb (8028.7-kg) afterburning thrust General Electric J79-GE-15 turbojet engines
Performance: maximum speed, clean 1,432 mph (2304.5 km/h) or Mach 2.17 at 20,000 ft (6096 m); initial climb rate, clean 40,000 ft (12192 m) per minute; service ceiling 62,250 ft (18974 m); range 1,600 miles (2574 km)
Weights: empty 27,640 lb (12537.5 kg); maximum take-off 54,600 lb (24766.6 kg)
Dimensions: span 38 ft 5 in (11.71 m); length 58 ft 1 in (17.7 m); height 16 ft 3 in (4.95 m); wing area 530 sq ft (49.24 m²)

Armament: four AIM-7 Sparrow semi-active radar homing missiles and four AIM-9 Sidewinder infrared homing missiles, plus provision for up to 12,000 lb (5443.2 kg) of underwing ordnance

This aircraft was the first of 29 F-4B aircraft loaned to the USAF by the US Navy, pending delivery of their first true F-4Cs, hence the strange serial (in reality BuNo 149405). These aircraft were known as F-110A prior to the 1962 redesignation.

General Dynamics F-111

History and notes

The General Dynamics F-111 resulted from the Tactical Fighter Experimental (TFX) project of 1961, in which an attempt was made to create a swing-wing fighter for several roles for the US Navy and US Air Force. After edging out a Boeing design, General Dynamics teamed up with Grumman so that the latter firm, an experienced builder of carrier-based aircraft, could build the F-111 variant seen as early as 1961 as a replacement for the US Navy F-4 Phantom. The first USAF General Dynamics F-111A (63-9768) flew on 21 December 1964 and the first US Navy Grumman F-111B (BuNo 151970) went aloft on 18 May 1965. Although its variable-geometry configuration was the principal advancement found in the F-111, the swing-wing worked perfectly from the outset. But the F-111B proved too heavy and in other ways unsuited to carrier-deck operations and was cancelled in May 1968 after only nine airframes had been delivered.

In addition to 17 F-111As for development work, 141 went to Tactical Air Command, with first deliveries to the 474th Tactical Fighter Wing at Nellis AFB, Nevada beginning in 1968. These were powered by two 18,500-lb (8391.6-kg) afterburning thrust Pratt & Whitney TF30-P-3 turbofans. In March 1968, six F-111As of the wing's 428th Tactical Fighter Squadron under Colonel Ivan H. Dethman were rushed to Takhli, Thailand, to begin combat operations against North Vietnam. The first three aircraft launched on the first three missions vanished for ever, although the detachment later flew 55 missions successfully. The USAF discovered, as a prisoner of war from this deployment would later confirm, that a tailplane problem caused uncontrollable pitch-up and roll. This failure in the flying control system caused the aircraft to break up in flight without North Vietnamese assistance! A separate fatigue problem caused wing spar cracks and, in 1969, resulted in the loss of an F-111A when its wing was torn off. In 1969, the entire fleet of 300 aircraft was grounded while an exhaustive structural review programme remedied these problems.

Powerful FB-111A

The Strategic Air Command's FB-111A, operating with two wings, is a very long-range variant powered by two 20,350-lb (9230.8-kg) afterburning thrust Pratt & Whitney TF30-P-7 turbofans, with modified inlets, long-span wing, and provision for nuclear or thermonuclear weapons or up to 50 750-lb (340-kg) HE bombs; 76 FB-111As were built.

The third F-111 shows the then revolutionary swing-wing, here in the fully-forward position for low-speed flight. Although there were no official prototypes, the first 17 F-111As were retained for development work, the rest entering service in 1968.

The EF-111A, officially named Raven but called 'Electric Fox', is a Grumman conversion of the airframe, resulting in a dedicated tactical jamming system and electronic warfare aircraft. Painted off-white and distinguished by a large fincap radome housing receiver antennae, the EF-111A flew in production form on 28 June 1981 and entered service with a USAFE unit in England in 1984.

Twenty-four F-111C 'Aardvarks', the informal nickname for all fighter-bomber variants (67-125/148) were delivered to Australia in 1973 after lengthy delays. The F-111C differs from the F-111A model in having a longer-span wing and stronger landing gear. Four F-111Cs have been converted to the reconnaissance role and the remainder, like many USAF 'Aardvarks', are being equipped with Pave Tack pods for laser acquisition of ground targets.

The F-111D, F-111E and F-111F are variants of what has become a

The 'Combat Lancer' deployment saw F-111s rushed to Thailand to evaluate their performance in South East Asia, but this first deployment suffered heavy attrition. The 'Aardvarks' returned in 1972 with much better success, proving to be the only Air Force aircraft capable of making blind first-pass attacks with pinpoint accuracy in all weathers.

General Dynamics F-111F of the 493rd Tactical Fighter Squadron, 48th TFW, based at RAF Lakenheath in the 1980s. This Wing was responsible for the 1986 attack on Tripoli.

The hybrid designation FB-111A referred to the more strategic role of the two Wings delivered to SAC. With longer wings and uprated engines, these were optimised for long-range pinpoint nuclear attacks, with either free-fall weapons or SRAM missiles. These are being reworked as F-111Gs for tactical operations.

highly specialised long-range strike aircraft ideal as a counter to the Soviet Sukhoi Su-24 and as a means of hitting targets in eastern Europe from the British Isles. These variants are located respectively at Cannon AFB, New Mexico, RAF Upper Heyford and RAF Lakenheath, England. Production amounted to 96 F-111D (68-85/180), 94 F-111Es (67-115/124 and 68-1/84) and 106 F-111Fs.

The F-111H was a proposed strategic bomber once perceived as an ideal interim step for the 1980s when it appeared that the Rockwell B-1 had been cancelled. The F-111K was the intended version for the UK's Royal Air Force. Neither was built, and total production amounted to 562 airplanes.

The F-111 crew sits side-by-side, the pilot (aircraft commander) routinely referring to his weapons systems officer as a YOT ('you over there'). Both are enclosed in a capsule which separates from the aircraft in an emergency, a proven escape system which obviates the need for ejection seats. When F-111s returned to North Vietnam in 1972, this two-man, terrain-hugging attack system proved eminently successful, a success repeated during the 1986 raid on Tripoli by F-111Fs flying from RAF Lakenheath. F-111s will remain part of the NATO commitment for years to come, though some will be replaced around 1990 by the McDonnell Douglas F-15E Eagle.

Loaded with low-drag bombs, an F-111A from the 391st TFS, 366th TFW at Mountain Home, Idaho, practises low-level delivery over the Nellis ranges. Two wings fly the type in the United States, the other being the 27th TFW with F-111Ds at Cannon AFB, New Mexico.

Specification

F-111A

Type: two-seat tactical strike fighter

Powerplant: two 18,500-lb (8391.6-kg) afterburning thrust Pratt & Whitney TF30-P-3 turbofan engines

Performance: maximum speed 912 mph (1467.7 km/h) or Mach 1.2 at sea level; climb rate , clean 22,000 ft (6706 m) per minute; service ceiling 58,000 ft (17678 m); combat radius 1,190 miles (1915 km); ferry range about 4,190 miles (6743 km)

Weights: empty 44,948 lb (20388.4 kg); maximum take-off 98,850 lb (44838.4 kg)

Dimensions: span 63 ft 0 in (19.20 m); length 73 ft 6 in (22.40 m); height 17 ft 1 in (5.21 m); wing area 525 sq ft (48.77 m^2)

Armament: one M61A1 20-mm cannon, plus one or two bombs in internal weapons bay and up to 25,000 lb (11340 kg) of bombs on four external pylons

This F-111A bears the 'NA' tailcode of the 474th Tactical Fighter Wing, based at Nellis AFB, Nevada. The 474th TFW was the first USAF unit to receive the aircraft, with deliveries starting in 1968. It was from this unit that the 'Combat Lancer' detachment to Thailand was made.

Vietnam to Tomorrow

In the post-Vietnam period, budgetary constraints have bitten deep into the USAF's purse. At the same time, the Air Force has shifted the emphasis from anti-bomber operations to anti-fighter, resulting in far more agile fighters than those of the 1960s.

From the earliest days of the Vietnam air war, it was the F-4 Phantom that emerged as the USAF's number one fighter, yet it carried many penalties into battle, being large, relatively unmanoeuvrable, smoky and gun-less. Considering that the enemy was a nation that could only be classed as second-rate at best, the USAF found itself fighting some embarrassingly hard battles against simple aircraft flown by not very good pilots. Yet it was just this kind of war (Korea) that had shaped the fighters that were being used in Vietnam. What had gone wrong?

Korea had erroneously led fighter designers to believe that speed was all, and the advent of the missile had finally killed the use of the airborne gun. Despite the fact that over 800 MiG-15s had been shot down in Korea, a decade later it was not thought likely that fighters would ever fight fighters again. Of course Vietnam changed that, and

hastily-introduced rectifying measures carried the day for the Americans, these including the adoption of cannon and manoeuvring slats on the Phantoms and dedicated air combat training for their crews.

New aircraft needed

This was blatantly not enough for the future, and although the Phantom was to provide the backbone of the USAF's fighter squadrons for the remainder of the 1970s, new types were needed to meet the threats of new Soviet aircraft. The first answer was the McDonnell Douglas F-15 Eagle. At last here was an aircraft that was designed from the outset for fighting against fighters, although it was large enough and powerful enough to carry out the interceptor mission as well. But it was expensive, and whereas once upon a time money was little object to a

major new aircraft programme, the 1970s and beyond were not the period in which to embark on major re-equipment with sophisticated aircraft.

The USAF faced the reality that only a limited number of F-15s could be bought, and that a much cheaper fighter was needed to augment it with large numbers rather than sophistication. The Lightweight Fighter competition was born to provide such an aircraft, and involved the YF-16 and YF-17, both superb designs with excellent agility and visibility – the two traditional assets of fighting aircraft that had all but disappeared by the time of Vietnam. No

The McDonnell Douglas F-15 Eagle is the spearhead of the US fighter force today. As well as defending the United States, they are based in Europe and Japan to protect those areas. This trio is from the 33rd TFW at Eglin, seen on detachment to West Germany.

One of the lessons learned from Vietnam was that all USAF tactical pilots needed to be well-versed in the art of air-to-air combat. The Northrop F-5E was procured to simulate the MiG-21 in exercises, its pilots flying Soviet-style tactics.

Above: Representing the high-tech approach to fighters was the Lockheed YF-12A (background), although this was quickly relegated to test purposes with NASA. Here one flies in formation with NASA's single SR-71A, spuriously designated 'YF-12C' and bearing the equally fictitious serial '06937', previously worn by a CIA A-12.

Below: F-16s began to replace the F-4 Phantom as the standard tactical fighter of the USAF in 1979. Extremely agile and able to undertake air superiority and attack missions with equal ease, Fighting Falcons serve in large numbers at home and overseas. These are from the Nellis-based 474th TFW.

more would US fighters be outgunned in close combat by MiGs – the two LWF contenders could 'turn-and-burn' with anything and come out on top every time.

The YF-16 picked up the lucrative USAF contract, and later large export orders. The losing YF-17 had to be content with a major reworking as a naval fighter. By the time the F-16 reached service in 1979, it had changed considerably from its original concept. It had become much more sophisticated and therefore expensive, but it had picked up the ground attack mission, introducing real multi-role capability. It was superb at both its roles, and as such is now the USAF's principal tactical aircraft, having virtually ousted the Phantom from front-line service and semi-replaced it with reserve units. In 1989 the Eagle belatedly joined the multi-role ranks with the F-15E version, although only a small number will be procured.

'Stealth' warplanes introduced

On the dedicated attack front, the F-111 has remained the most potent tactical aircraft, a position it will keep for some time. Continual improvements have kept it at the forefront of its field. A more exciting attacker is the Lockheed F-117, the first of the 'stealth' warplanes. Its technology has been another by-product of the Vietnam war, spurred by the successes of communist SAMs during the latter part of the war (and in the 1973 Yom Kippur war). Dedicated to attack and reconnaissance, it is the first of many low-observable warplanes that will emerge from the United States.

What of the future? The US Air Force has recognised the fact that the F-15 is getting on in years now, and while the F-16 is new enough and has enough growth potential for service into the next century, the Eagle needs replacement soon. The Advanced Tactical Fighter will do just that, and it will bring together all the latest in warplane technology. It will be 'stealthy', employ new missiles and highly-capable radar, it will have thrust-vectoring for undreamt-of agility, and it will be able to operate away from fixed airfields. With all this capability it will naturally be expensive, but the key to any battle since the arrival of the warplane has been air superiority, and the winning ATF design will be procured to provide that.

North American F-1

On 18 September 1962, the Department of Defense introduced a new designation system common to all services. Consequently many Navy types then in service were allocated new designations in the F- range. The North American FJ Fury series was re-designated F-1.

McDonnell F-2

Although hardly any McDonnell F2H Banshee fighters remained in Navy or Marine use, these were allocated the F-2 designation in 1962.

McDonnell F-3

Another redesignation was the McDonnell F3H Demon carrier-borne missile-equipped fighter. Its service life ended shortly after receiving the F-3 designation.

McDonnell Douglas F-4 Phantom II

The elderly F-4Cs are all but out of service, the last survivors flying with ANG units. This colourful example served on air defence duties with the 171st FIS, 191st FIG, Michigan ANG, now an F-4D user.

History and notes

For a quarter-century, the McDonnell F-4 Phantom II has risen from land and sea to take command of the air, to carry out the strike mission, to fight MiGs, and to join the Thunderbolt, Mustang and Sabre among the immortals of American fighter aviation. Its bent wings, drooped tail and twin-engine configuration a trademark, the Phantom was the first aircraft which could detect, intercept and destroy any target within its radar range without assistance from surface-based radar. Built as an interceptor, it became a MiG killer, but it also excelled at ground attack, 'fast FAC', reconnaissance, and other duties.

The F-4A (US Navy F4H-1F) was a developmental variant, the first (BuNo. 142259) making its maiden flight at St Louis on 27 May 1958 with Robert C. Little at the controls. It was followed by the US Navy's operational F-4B (F4H-1), powered by two 17,000-lb (7711-kg) afterburning thrust General Electric J79-GE-8 engines. The F-4B model attained an altitude record of 98,556 ft (30040 m) on 6 December 1959, a speed record of 1,606.51 mph (2585.36 km/h) on 22 November 1961, and a low-altitude speed record of 902 mph (1452 km/h) on 20 August 1962, the last-named not being beaten for 16 years!

The EF-4B designation went to one airframe used for ECM training, and two modified, development airframes bore the NF-4B de-

signation. The QF-4B is a drone conversion. The RF-4B reconnaissance derivative served only with the US Marine Corps.

The F-4C (F-110A) was the US Air Force's first Phantom, the first example (62-12199) being flown on 27 May 1963. The F-4C became operational with the 12th and 15th Tactical Fighter Wings at MacDill AFB, Florida, in January 1964. Some 583 were built, 40 being transferred to Spain. The service-test YRF-4C (YRF-110A) led to the RF-4C (RF-110A), 499 of which were constructed for the photo-reconnaissance role. The F-4D Phantom fighter-bomber introduced a capability to deliver precision-guided munitions (PGM), or 'smart' bombs. Some 825 were built, including 32 delivered new to Iran and 36 transferred to South Korea.

Once in action in Vietnam in 1965, the Phantom seemed to need a gun to augment its missile armament in close-quarter battles with MiGs. The SUU-16/A 20-mm external gun pod was an interim measure. The F-4E, first flown on 7 August 1965, introduced more powerful J79-GE-17 engines but its principal change was the in-

The USAF's first Phantoms were F-4Bs loaned from the Navy. Deliveries of the definitive Air Force F-4C began in 1964. Early F-4s still retained the AIM-4 Falcon missiles, although these gave way to Sidewinders early in the fighter's career.

McDonnell Douglas F-4

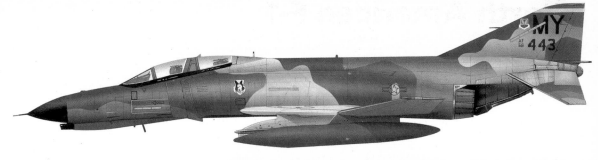

The 347th TFW at Moody AFB, Georgia, was one of the last active-duty F-4E units, but has now transitioned to the F-16.

ternally-mounted M61A1 20-mm cannon. Although superior pilot training would later prove more important than the cannon in establishing a 2.5-to-1 kill advantage over North Vietnamese MiG-17, MiG-19 and MiG-21 fighters, the F-4E became the definitive Phantom, and 1,397 rolled off the line. Examples were supplied to Australia (on loan), Greece, Iran, Israel, Turkey, South Korea and West Germany; and 140 F-4EJs were licence-built by Mitsubishi in Japan. The RF-4E was an export reconnaissance derivative, supplied to Greece, Iran, Israel, Japan and West Germany.

By the mid-1960s, the Phantom was just about the best-known fighter in the world. On 2 January 1967 in Operation 'Bolo', F-4Cs of the 8th TFW under Colonel Robin Olds shot down seven North Vietnamese MiGs. Increasingly, F-4Ds took over from the Republic F-105 the job of bringing ordnance to bear on Vietnamese ground targets. Visitors to St Louis, where McDonnell took over Douglas in 1967, wanted not merely to see the heavy, complex fighter put together by Herman Barkey's design team, but to buy it.

The F-4F was a specialised air superiority version for the West German Luftwaffe, and 175 were delivered. The F-4G designation had been used initially for 12 aircraft taken from the US Navy F-4B production line. They had the two-way ASW-21 data-link system for automated carrier landings, and all later reverted to F-4B standard. In the 1970s, the F-4G appellation was used again for the US Air Force's 'Advanced Wild Weasel' electronic warfare aircraft, 116 of which were converted from F-4E standard. Originally seen as a counter to enemy SAM missile sites and associated radars, the F-4G now carries out a wide portfolio of electronic missions. Aircraft are stationed as far afield as the 3rd TFW Clark Field, Philippines, and 52nd TFW, Spangdahlem AB, West Germany.

The F-4J was an improved production fighter for the US Navy with 17,900-lb (8119-kg) afterburning thrust J79-GE-10 engines, enlarged wing and improved avionics. The F-4K was developed for the UK's Royal Navy and the F-4M for the Royal Air Force, though both

Following the F-4C, the F-4D was externally similar but featured upgraded avionics, including a new radar in an enlarged radome. Cannon pods were often carried on the centreline to redress the lack of guns. This example is seen during service with the 52nd TFW at Spangdahlem.

are now operated by the latter service which, with expanded commitments following the 1982 Falklands war, has also inherited 15 ex-US Navy F-4Js. The F-4N is an upgraded 'rebuild' of the F-4B, and has in turn been converted to the QF-4N drone. The F-4S is an upgraded F-4J with wing manoeuvre slats and was the final Phantom variant to serve aboard an aircraft carrier, with VF-151 and -161 aboard the USS Midway.

Phantoms serve widely with the Reserve and Air National Guard and are likely to remain in front-line service with some air forces into the 21st century.

During the latter part of the South East Asia war, the F-4 Phantom was the principal tactical aircraft in the theatre. Here F-4Ds of the 13th Tactical Fighter Squadron formate with F-4Es of the 58th TFS, both squadrons flying as part of the 432nd TFW at Udorn in Thailand.

McDonnell Douglas F-4

McDonnell Douglas F-4E Phantom II cutaway drawing key

1. Starboard tailplane
2. Static discharger
3. Honeycomb trailing edge panels
4. Tailplane mass balance weight
5. Tailplane spar construction
6. Drag chute housing
7. Tailcone/drag chute hinged door
8. Fuselage fuel tanks vent pipe
9. Honeycomb rudder construction
10. Rudder balance
11. Tail warning radar fairing
12. Tail navigation light
13. Fin tip antenna fairing
14. Communications antenna
15. Fin rear spar
16. Variable intensity formation lighting strip
17. Rudder control jack
18. Tailplane pivot mounting
19. Tailplane pivot seal
20. Fixed leading edge slat
21. Tailplane hydraulic jack
22. Fin front spar
23. Stabilator feel system pressure probe
24. Anti-collision light
25. Stabilator feel system balance mechanism
26. Tailcone cooling air duct
27. Heat resistant tailcone skinning
28. Arresting hook housing
29. Arresting hook, lowered
30. Starboard fully variable exhaust nozzle
31. Rudder artificial feel system bellows
32. Fin leading edge
33. Ram air intake

34. Fuselage No 7 fuel cell, capacity 84 US gal (318 l)
35. Engine bay cooling air outlet louvres
36. Arresting hook actuator and damper
37. Fuel vent piping
38. Fuselage No 6 fuel cell, capacity 213 US gal (806 l)
39. Jet pipe shroud construction
40. Engine bay hinged access doors
41. Rear AIM-7E-2 Sparrow air-to-air missile
42. Semi-recessed missile housing
43. Jet pipe nozzle actuators
44. Afterburner jet pipe

45. Fuselage No 5 fuel cell, capacity 180 US gal (681 l)
46. Fuel tank access panels
47. Fuel system piping
48. Tailplane control cable duct
49. Fuselage No 4 fuel cell, capacity 201 US gal (761 l)
50. Starboard engine bay construction
51. TACAN aerial
52. Fuselage No 3 fuel cell, capacity 147 US gal (556 l)
53. Engine oil tank
54. General Electric J79-GE-17A turbojet engine
55. Engine accessories
56. Wing rear spar attachment
57. Mainwheel door
58. Main undercarriage wheel well
59. Lateral control servo actuator
60. Hydraulic accumulator
61. Lower surface airbrake jack
62. Flap hydraulic jack
63. Starboard flap
64. Honeycomb control surface construction
65. Starboard aileron
66. Aileron power control unit
67. Flutter damper

68. Spoiler housing
69. Wing tank fuel vent
70. Dihedral outer wing panel
71. Rear identification light
72. Wing tip formation lighting
73. Starboard navigation light
74. Radar warning antenna
75. Outer wing panel construction
76. Outboard leading edge slat
77. Slat control linkage
78. Slat hydraulic jack
79. Outer wing panel attachment
80. Starboard wing fence
81. Fuel vent system shut-off valves
82. Top of main undercarriage leg

83. Outboard pylon attachment housing
84. Inboard slat hydraulic jack
85. Starboard outer pylon
86. Mainwheel leg door
87. Mainwheel brake discs
88. Starboard mainwheel
89. Starboard external fuel tank capacity 370 US gal (1400 l)
90. Inboard leading edge slat, open

91. Slat hinge linkages
92. Main undercarriage retraction jack
93. Undercarriage uplock
94. Starboard wing fuel tank, capacity 315 US gal (1192 l)
95. Integral fuel tank construction
96. Inboard pylon fixing
97. Leading edge ranging antenna
98. Inboard pylon fixing
99. Twin missile launcher
100. AIM-9 Sidewinder
101. Hinged leading edge access panel
102. Wing front spar
103. Hydraulic reservoir
104. Centre fuselage formation lighting
105. Fuselage main frame
106. Engine intake compressor face
107. Intake duct construction
108. Fuselage No 2 fuel cell, capacity 185 US gal (700 l)
109. Air-to-air refuelling receptacle, open

110. Port main undercarriage leg
111. Aileron power control unit
112. Port aileron
113. Aileron flutter damper
114. Port spoiler
115. Spoiler hydraulic jack
116. Wing fuel tank vent pipe
117. Port outer wing panel
118. Rearward identification light
119. Wing tip formation lighting
120. Port navigation light
121. Radar warning antenna
122. Port outboard leading edge slat
123. Slat hydraulic jack
124. Wing fence
125. Leading edge dog tooth
126. Inboard leading edge slat, open
127. Port external fuel tank capacity 370 US gal (1400 l)
128. Inboard slat hydraulic jack
129. Port wing fuel tank, capacity 315 US gal (1192 l)
130. Upper fuselage light
131. IFF antenna

132. Avionics equipment bay
133. Gyro stabiliser platform
134. Fuselage No 1 fuel cell, capacity 215 US gal (814 l)
135. Intake duct
136. Hydraulic connections
137. Starter cartridge container
138. Pneumatic system air bottle
139. Engine bleed air supply pipe
140. Forward AIM-7 missile housing
141. Ventral fuel tank, capacity 600 US gal (2271 l)
142. Bleed air louvre assembly, lower
143. Avionics equipment bay
144. Variable intake ramp jack
145. Bleed air louvre assembly, upper
146. Radar operator's Martin-Baker ejection seat
147. Safety harness

148. Face blind seat firing handle
149. Rear cockpit canopy cover
150. Front canopy hinges
151. Inter-canopy bridge section glazing
152. Radar operator's instrument console
153. Canopy jack
154. Port intake
155. Pilot's Martin-Baker ejection seat

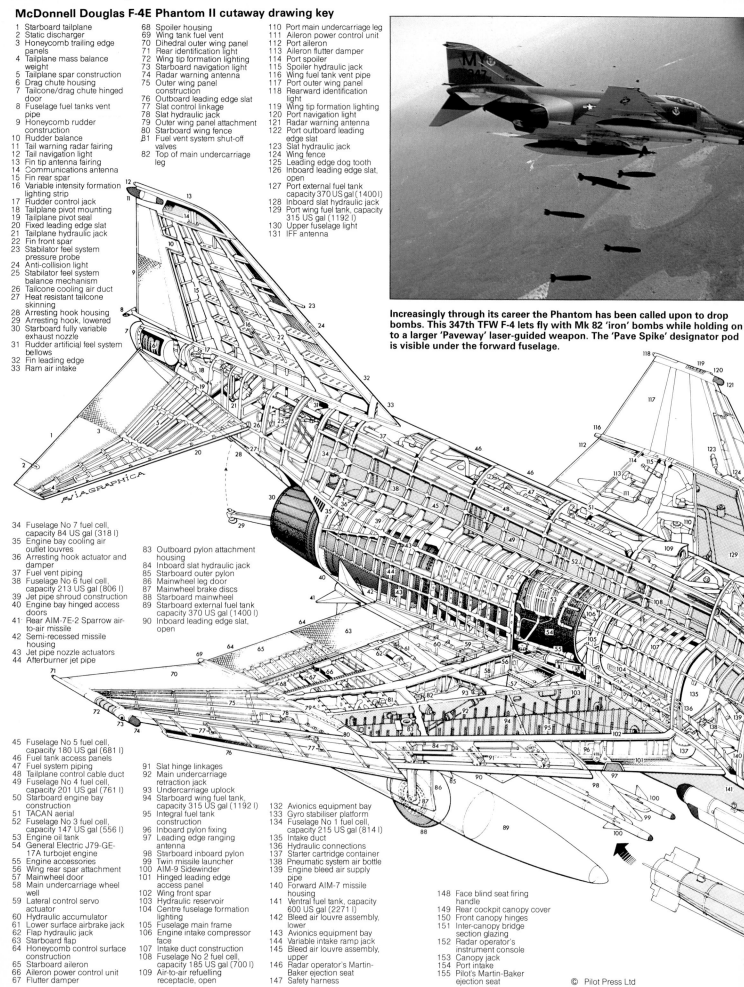

Increasingly through its career the Phantom has been called upon to drop bombs. This 347th TFW F-4 lets fly with Mk 82 'iron' bombs while holding on to a larger 'Paveway' laser-guided weapon. The 'Pave Spike' designator pod is visible under the forward fuselage.

© Pilot Press Ltd

McDonnell Douglas F-4

This F-4E of the 51st Tactical Fighter Wing is resplendent in the latest 'Egyptian One' camouflage scheme. The wing operated Phantoms and A-10s from Suwon, Taegu (illustrated) and Osan in Korea. It has now settled at Osan with the F-16.

Combat

The first action for the F-4 Phantom came just after the Cuban missile crisis of October 1962, when US Marine squadron VMFA-531 was rushed to NAS Key West, Florida, for 'hot pad alert'. Colonel Robert Foxworth recalls: "We came within a half-mile of a formation of Castro's MiG-17s and spent 20 minutes clawing for position but neither of us quite got a shot at the other." In August 1964, F-4Bs were catapulted from the USS *Constellation* in the Gulf of Tonkin air strikes. On 17 June 1965, the first air-to-air victory was achieved when Commander Louis Page and Lieutenant John C. Smith Jr of VF-21 from USS *Midway* flying an F-4B (BuNo. 151488), callsign SUNDOWN 101, used an AIM-7 Sparrow missile to shoot down a MiG-17 near Hanoi. On 10 July 1965, two MiG-17s fell to US Air Force F-4Cs of the 45th Tactical Fighter Squadron operating from Ubon, Thailand.

Not everything about the Phantom was perfect. Early F-4Cs sprang wing tank leaks that required resealing after each flight. Eighty-five of them developed cracked ribs on outer wing panels. The F-4C and RF-4C were at times grounded due to dripping potting compound. Teething problems with missile armament continued well past the first decade of the Phantom's service life. Captain

The RF-4C is a dedicated tactical reconnaissance version, carrying a fan of cameras in the nose. Further reconnaissance capability comes from a small side-looking airborne radar and infra-red linescan equipment.

Richard S. (Steve) Ritchie, first US Air Force ace and one of but five men to attain ace status in Vietnam, railed furiously about poor location of the Phantom's only radio, beneath the pilot's ejection seat. Ritchie also reported to General William W. Momyer, commander of the 7th Air Force, that the Phantom could be effective only if its two men operated as a 'hard' crew, staying together for a full combat tour and complementing each other's strengths and weaknesses.

Phantoms fought over North Vietnam in the 1965-8 'Rolling Thunder' campaign and again in the 1972 'Linebacker' campaign. On 10 May 1972, Lieutenant Randall Cunningham and Lieutenant (j.g.) William P. Driscoll, flying an F-4J (155800), callsign SHOWTIME 100, shot down three MiGs to become the first aces of the war. The last MiG kill of the war came on 12 January 1973 when Lieutenant Victor T. Kovaleski and Lieutenant (j.g.) James A. Wise, flying from the *Midway* in an F-4B (153045), callsign ROCK RIVER 102, used a Sidewinder to shoot down a MiG-17. Thus, the F-4B model and the *Midway* scored the first and last kills of the war, eight years apart.

Combat success of the F-4 Phantom with foreign air arms is outside the scope of this work, but it must be said that in the 1973 Yom Kippur conflict Israel lost not a single Phantom in air-to-air combat.

As a 'mud mover', in the fighter-bomber role where it replaced the F-105 in South East Asia, the Phantom performed well but had its

Intake front ramp
Starboard intake
Blee air holes
Boundary layer splitter plate
ALQ-72 electronic countermeasures pod (replaces forward Sparrow missile)
HOBOS 2000-lb (907-kg) guided bomb
Nosewheel door
AIM-7E-2 Sparrow missile semi-recessed housing
Forward formation lighting
Air conditioning plant
Pilot's starboard side console

168 Ejection seat safety harness
169 Engine throttles
170 Port intake front ramp
171 Forward cockpit canopy cover
172 Port inboard wing pylon
173 Pylon attachments
174 Triple ejector release unit
175 Mk 84 low profile 500-lb (227-kg) bombs
176 Extended bomb fuses
177 Windscreen panels
178 Pilot's lead computing sight
179 Instrument panel shroud
180 Control column
181 Rudder pedals
182 Cockpit front pressure bulkhead

183 Refrigeration plant
184 Communications antenna
185 Nosewheel jack
186 Nose undercarriage leg strut
187 Twin nosewheels
188 Nosewheel torque links
189 Landing and taxiying lamps
190 Air conditioning ram air intake
191 Angle of attack probe
192 Ammunition drum 639 rounds
193 Rain dispersal duct nozzle
194 ADF antenna
195 Gun bay frame construction
196 M61A-1 20-mm rotary barrel cannon
197 Cannon fairing
198 AN/APQ-120 fire control radar
199 Radar antenna mounting
200 Gun muzzle fairing
201 Radar scanner
202 Radome
203 Pitot tube

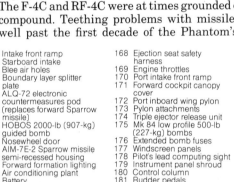

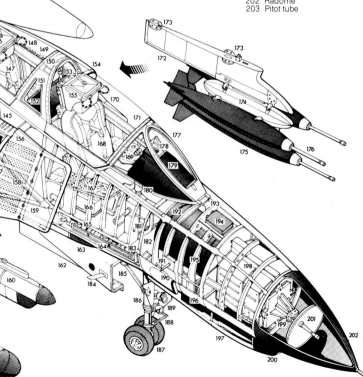

Major refits applied to the F-4E included manoeuvring slats and the TISEO optical acquisition equipment, visible on this 52nd TFW aircraft pointing forward of the port wing leading edge.

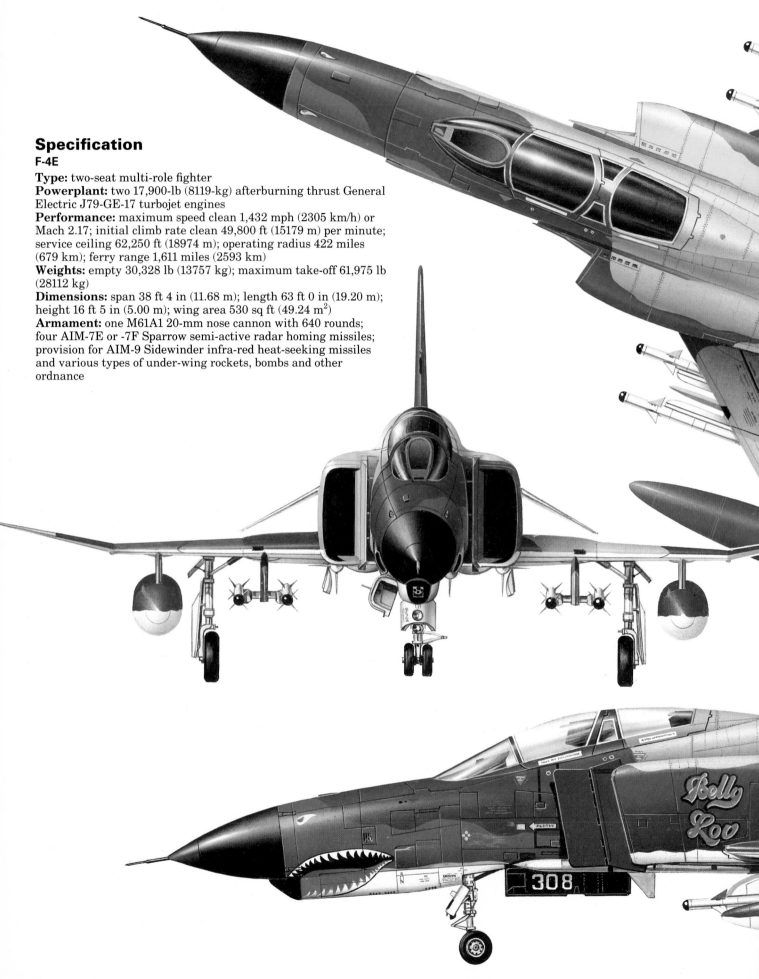

Specification

F-4E

Type: two-seat multi-role fighter

Powerplant: two 17,900-lb (8119-kg) afterburning thrust General Electric J79-GE-17 turbojet engines

Performance: maximum speed clean 1,432 mph (2305 km/h) or Mach 2.17; initial climb rate clean 49,800 ft (15179 m) per minute; service ceiling 62,250 ft (18974 m); operating radius 422 miles (679 km); ferry range 1,611 miles (2593 km)

Weights: empty 30,328 lb (13757 kg); maximum take-off 61,975 lb (28112 kg)

Dimensions: span 38 ft 4 in (11.68 m); length 63 ft 0 in (19.20 m); height 16 ft 5 in (5.00 m); wing area 530 sq ft (49.24 m^2)

Armament: one M61A1 20-mm nose cannon with 640 rounds; four AIM-7E or -7F Sparrow semi-active radar homing missiles; provision for AIM-9 Sidewinder infra-red heat-seeking missiles and various types of under-wing rockets, bombs and other ordnance

Despite its age, the Phantom is still a viable force in the modern air battle, although newer and more capable types are replacing it rapidly in USAF units. Its heyday was in the South East Asia war, particularly in the later stages when it accounted for a large proportion of US tactical airpower. This is a typical example: an F-4E serving with the 469th Tactical Fighter Squadron, 388th Tactical Fighter Wing at Korat in Thailand.

The F-4E was in many ways the definitive Phantom, equipped with a new slimmer radar and most importantly an internal cannon. Large numbers still serve, although they are rapidly passing to the National Guard. The 86th TFW at Ramstein shown here is now an F-16 operator.

detractors. The fighter-bomber mission exposes plane and crew to intense defences, and throughout much of its career the F-4 produced telltale smoke exhaust which told the enemy when it was coming. Some fliers felt that the F-4 lacked the capacity to absorb punishment found in other aircraft types and was especially vulnerable in the 'belly' while pulling away from target. Early F-4Cs ran into difficulty with crew ejection because departure of the back-seater generated a vacuum which held the front-seat pilot's canopy fast. In recent years, revision of internal systems has tended to 'clutter' the once-roomy cockpit, making the two-man crew less comfortable and more isolated from each other. The criticisms were often uttered along with praise. None detracts from the simple truth that the F-4 Phantom was, and is, among the finest fighters of its era.

Below: Most Phantoms now wear the grey 'Egyptian One' camouflage. The F-4G 'Wild Weasel V' is an important variant, equipped for locating and tracking SAM radars. With the 52nd TFW at Spangdahlem, it forms the 'clever' part of the F-4G/F-16C hunter-killer anti-radar team.

Above: The 'bullet' fairing on the fin-top and extended undernose fairing identify this aircraft as an F-4G 'Wild Weasel', seen in company with an F-4E. Both aircraft carry Shrike anti-radiation missiles, while the 'G' has a Standard ARM as well.

Northrop F-5

Vietnam to Tomorrow

History and notes

The highly successful Northrop F-5 is largely the result of private initiative. In 1955, Northrop undertook development of its N-156F fighter for the export market. The purpose was to achieve a simple, inexpensive, easily-maintained multi-role fighter for sale to less-developed countries, but the project also led to the T-38 Talon trainer. With Lew Nelson as pilot, the US-financed N-156F flew on 30 July 1959 and the type later became known as the F-5A Freedom Fighter. The F-5B two-seat combat trainer actually became operational first, joining the 4441st Combat Crew Training Squadron at Williams AFB, Arizona, on 30 April 1964. By late 1964, both were being evaluated by the USAF, primarily to determine suitability for export to South Vietnam. The ultimate such test was Operation 'Skoshi Tiger', an extended deployment of USAF F-5As to South Vietnam over 1965-7. American pilots found the F-5A well-suited for the ground-attack mission and were bitter that, after these machines were turned over to the South Vietnamese in 1967, their own air force had none.

The F-5A and F-5B were exported to a dozen countries and were manufactured in Canada (CF-5A and CF-5D), the Netherlands (NF-5A and NF-5B) and Spain (SF-5A, SRF-5A and SF-5B). The RF-5A reconnaissance variant with four nose cameras was also widely used abroad, and the improved F-5C went to Vietnam during the empty years of the late 1960s when the US Air Force operated no aircraft of the type.

For a 1970 USAF-sponsored international fighter (IFX) competition, Northrop designed an improved version powered by two 5,000-lb (2268-kg) thrust General Electric J85-GE-21 turbojets pro-viding 23 per cent more power than the engines of the F-5A. Chosen over Lockheed, McDonnell and Vought submissions, this was initially called the F-5A-21 but became the F-5E Tiger II. The F-5E had increased fuel capacity and an integrated fire-control system (though without radar) but it retained the simplicity and ease of operation which made it a prime candidate for third-world countries. The first production F-5E was flown on 11 August 1972 with Hank Chouteau at the controls and was soon followed by the F-5F two-seat combat trainer with lengthened fuselage, which retained the fire-control system and combat capability. F-5Es were assembled under licence in Taiwan. Only long after foreign countries had purchased them did the USAF and US Navy acquire the F-5E and F-5F for 'Aggressor' squadrons to simulate MiG threat aircraft in dissimilar air combat training (DACT).

The F-5G designation was assigned to a single-engine variant originally intended for Taiwan although sales to that customer became impossible after the US normalised relations with China in December 1978. The F-5G first flew at Edwards AFB on 30 August 1982 piloted by Russ Scott. By November, this variant had been renamed the F-20A Tigershark.

Some 818 F-5As (including the almost identical F-5C) and 290 F-5Bs were built. The F-5E and F-5F second-generation machines are likely to remain in service for some time. The F-20A represents a third generation of an aircraft already used by Brazil, Canada, Chile, Egypt, Ethiopia, Greece, Iran, Jordan, Kenya, Libya, Malaysia, Morocco, the Netherlands, Norway, the Philippines, Republic of China (Taiwan), Republic of Korea, Saudi Arabia, Singapore, Sudan, Switzerland, Spain, Thailand, Turkey and Vietnam.

Below: The Northrop F-5's combat career in USAF colours was brief, amounting to an evaluation deployment to South East Asia during 1965-67 under the programme name 'Skoshi Tiger'. Although the type could not carry a vast load, it was fast and very agile, making it ideal for dodging Viet Cong guns during attack runs. Following the successful evaluation, the F-5As and two-seat F-5Bs were all handed over to the South Vietnamese, who made full use of them until the end of the conflict.

Representing Soviet fighters during dissimilar air combat exercises, the Northrop F-5E became well-known on 'Aggressor' duties. This gaudy example served the 527th Aggressor Squadron at RAF Alconbury, until the unit moved to Bentwaters and picked up the F-16C as its sole equipment.

Specification

F-5E

Type: single-seat fighter

Powerplant: two 5,000-lb (2268-kg) afterburning thrust General Electric J85-GE-21 turbojet engines

Performance: maximum speed 1,082 mph (1741 km/h) or Mach 1.64 at 40,000 ft (12192 m); initial climb rate 34,300 ft (10455 m) per minute; service ceiling 52,500 ft (16002 m); ferry range 1,880 miles (3025 km)

Weights: empty 9,683 lb (4392 kg); take-off, clean 15,450 lb (7008 kg); maximum take-off 24,680 lb (11195 kg)

Dimensions: span 26 ft 8 in (8.13 m); length 48 ft 2 in (14.68 m); height 13 ft 4 in (4.06 m); wing area 186.2 sq ft (17.30 m²)

Armament: two 20-mm cannon, plus up to 7,000 lb (3175 kg) of disposable ordnance on seven stations

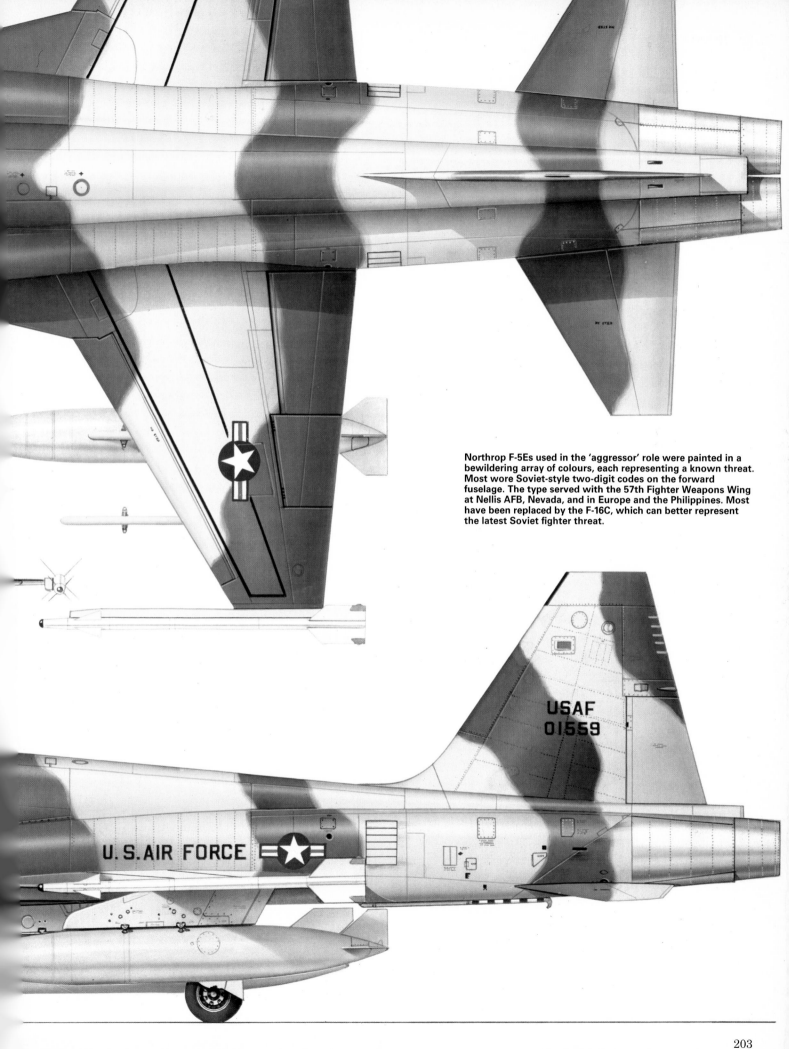

Northrop F-5Es used in the 'aggressor' role were painted in a bewildering array of colours, each representing a known threat. Most wore Soviet-style two-digit codes on the forward fuselage. The type served with the 57th Fighter Weapons Wing at Nellis AFB, Nevada, and in Europe and the Philippines. Most have been replaced by the F-16C, which can better represent the latest Soviet fighter threat.

Douglas F-6

Serving under this designation for only a short while was the Douglas F4D Skyray, in use with both the Navy and Marine Corps.

Convair F-7

For some inexplicable reason, the experimental Convair F2Y Sea Dart jet-powered seaplane fighter was allocated the F-7 designation in 1962, six years after the project had been abandoned.

Vought F-8

The excellent F8U became the F-8 in 1962, and served virtually throughout the war in South East Asia with the Navy and Marine Corps, downing several MiGs with the former. The RF-8 reconnaissance version eventually retired from the US Navy Reserve in 1987.

Grumman F-9

The Grumman F9F Panther/Cougar naval fighter series received the designation F-9 in 1962. TF-9J Panther aircraft served in the forward air control role in Vietnam.

Douglas F-10

The elderly Douglas F3D naval all-weather fighter was allocated the F-10 designation. During its later years, it was best remembered for its use with the Marine Corps as an ECM platform (EF-10B) during the war in Vietnam.

Grumman F-11

Serving only with the Navy, the F11F Tiger was redesignated F-11 in 1962. These aircraft equipped the 'Blue Angels' display team during the mid-1960s.

Lockheed F-12

History and notes
During the late 1950s, Lockheed's Advanced Development Projects office ('Skunk Works') at Burbank, California, was involved in the design and construction of a Mach 3+ high-altitude strategic reconnaissance platform to replace the U-2 then in service with the CIA and US Air Force. With expert direction from Clarence L. 'Kelly' Johnson, the resultant A-12 was fabricated largely of titanium alloy to maintain the structural integrity of the airframe when subjected to kinetic heating. At the design speed in excess of Mach 3, some components could reach 300°C. Because aerodynamic drag increases exponentially with speed, the slimmest possible fuselage and thinnest delta wing went into the design, together with integral lifting chines along the forward fuselage to prevent pitch-down at increasing speed.

Power was to come from two giant turbo-ramjet engines, the 14742 kg thrust Pratt & Whitney J58-P-1. A complex mechanical sensing system provided air data information to allow the complicated series of bleed/inlet doors to be opened or closed correctly for optimum airflow, as well as the optimum position for the huge centrebody inlet spike. A high flashpoint fuel, JP-7, was especially developed for high-altitude flight.

The first A-12 flew in great secrecy with Lou Schalk at the controls from Lockheed's test plant at Groom Dry Lake, Nevada, on 26 April 1962 and despite several problems during the flight test phase, aircraft were soon flying clandestine missions for the CIA. Included in the initial A-12 batch were three aircraft configured as interceptors as a spin-off of the main reconnaissance programme.

These YF-12As differed considerably from the A-12. Firstly they had two cockpits, the second containing a Weapon Systems Officer (this work incidentally being of great value to the upcoming two-seat SR-71 derivative of the A-12). Secondly the YF-12A had its chines cut back to allow the carriage of a Hughes ASG-18 radar, which was later augmented by two infra-red sensors. Weaponry was carried in bays in the chine area, these being four Hughes XAIM-47 air-to-air missiles. Ventral fins were fitted to offset the loss of directional stability caused by the nose radome.

If the aircraft had been developed further as an interceptor, it would have done exactly what the MiG-25 and SA-2 missile did to the American B-70 bomber, namely neutralise the threat of high-altitude strategic bombing forever. It is widely believed that the YF-12As were used to test systems for the cancelled North American XF-108 Rapier interceptor.

Three YF-12As were built (60-6934, 6935, 6936), and the first public viewing came on 30 September 1964, its debut marked by the heat from its engines setting off a sprinkler system and drenching onlookers! The A-12 aircraft had been made public in February (President Johnson erroneously calling it the A-11), and when the YF-12A appeared these were widely assumed to be the same aircraft.

To further publicise the aircraft, a series of 12 world records was established by 60-6936 on 1 May 1965, including the absolute speed mark of 3331.35 km/h and sustained altitude record of 24462.59 m, since only beaten by its offspring, the SR-71A. All three YF-12As quickly passed to NASA Dryden at Edwards AFB, California, where they undertook high altitude, high speed trials in a programme that lasted until 1979. 60-6934 was badly damaged in an accident at Edwards, and its rear half was used (together with an engineering mock-up) to create 64-17981, the SR-71C two-seat trainer. 60-6936 crashed at Edwards in 1971, but 60-6935 continued until the completion of its trials in 1979. It flew to a well-earned rest in the US Air Force Museum.

The F-12B designation was not accounted for, but the YF-12C (60-6937) was a test aircraft for NASA. In fact it was the second SR-71A (64-17951) assigned a spurious serial (60-6937) had already been applied to a CIA A-12). Stripped of military equipment, the YF-12C was better-performing than the standard SR-71As, and it too had a long and fruitful career on trials with NASA Dryden. Its last disposition was in store with some A-12s at Lockheed's Palmdale plant.

Specification
YF-12A

Type: single-seat research aircraft
Powerplant: two 32,500-lb

With a powerful radar in the nose and infra-red sensors in the front of the fuselage chines, the YF-12A would have had considerable long-range detection capabilities. Weapons were housed internally. All three aircraft ended their days with NASA on high-speed research work.

Lockheed F-12

The first Lockheed 7F-12A seen as it appeared during early flight testing from the Groom Dry Lake facility in the Nevada desert. Note the additional ventral fins and the pod-mounted test camera.

(14742-kg) thrust Pratt & Whitney J58-P-1 continuous-bleed turbojets
Performance: maximum speed 2,189 mph (3523 km/h) at 70,000 ft (21336 m); initial climb rate 39,600 ft (12070 m) per minute; service ceiling 105,000 ft (32004 m); range 3,300 miles (5311 km)
Weights: empty about 60,000 lb (27216 kg); maximum take-off about 145,000 lb (65772 kg)
Dimensions: span 55 ft 7 in (16.94 m); length 107 ft 5 in (32.74 m); height 18 ft 6 in (5.64 m); wing area 1,800 sq ft (167.22 m^2)
Armament: four Hughes AIM-47 air-to-air missiles

F-13

The F-13 designation was not assigned by the US Department of Defense. In the pursuit/fighter series, unassigned designations were P-73, P-74, XF-109 and F-13.

Grumman F-14

The mighty Grumman F-14 Tomcat forms almost the bulk of the fighter fleet of the US Navy, being deployed on all but two carriers. As such it will remain in service for many years.

McDonnell Douglas F-15 Eagle

1st Air Force (ex-Air Defense Command) assets now include only three Fighter Interceptor Squadrons with the F-15 Eagle. The 5th FIS operated this F-15A from Minot AFB, North Dakota, but is now disbanded.

History and notes

The first McDonnell Douglas F-15 Eagle made its maiden flight on 27 July 1972, giving the US Air Force by far its most potent fighter aircraft, albeit one of its most complex and expensive. The Eagle was developed to rival the MiG-25. Powered by two 23,930-lb (10855-kg) thrust Pratt & Whitney F100-PW-100 afterburning turbofans, the Eagle, unlike its Soviet counterpart, is not a stand-off interceptor but a close-combat dogfighter with AIM-7 Sparrow air-to-air missiles along the bottom of its large inlet ducts and 20-mm cannon mounted in the right inboard wing. The two-seat F-15B combat trainer which first flew on 7 July 1973 is about 800 lb (363 kg) heavier than the F-15A fighter, but retains most of its combat capability.

The Eagle is equipped with Hughes APG-63 pulse-Doppler radar with computerised data-processing to leave nothing on the pilot's head-up or head-down displays except items of genuine interest. All-round visibility is superb and the F-15 pioneered the HOTAS (hands on throttle and stick) concept to ease the pilot's task in combat. The single-seat F-15C has now replaced its predecessors on the McDon-

Making the F-15 Eagle such a formidable fighter is its high surplus power, excellent manoeuvrability and all-round firepower. The standard load is illustrated here, comprising four AIM-7 Sparrow missiles under the engine nacelles, four AIM-9 Sidewinders on the wing rails and the internal 20-mm M61A1 Vulcan cannon in the starboard wing root.

The air defence of the 4th ATAF region (southern Germany) is entrusted to the 36th Tactical Fighter Wing at Bitburg, which has three squadrons of F-15C/Ds. These maintain a 24-hour ground alert, with four aircraft at five-minute readiness.

Operating as part of 2nd ATAF, a single squadron (32nd TFS) is based at Soesterberg in Holland with F-15Cs.

McDonnell Douglas F-15C Eagle cutaway drawing key

1 Tailplane honeycomb construction
2 Boron fibre skin panel
3 Tailplane spars
4 All-moving tailplane pivot fixing
5 Leading edge dog-tooth
6 Low-voltage formation lighting strip
7 Fin root attachment frames
8 Rudder hydraulic rotary actuator
9 Rudder honeycomb construction
10 Fin spar construction
11 Boron fibre skin panel
12 Anti-collision light
13 Electronic countermeasures aerials (ECM)
14 Variable area afterburner exhaust nozzles
15 Nozzle sealing flaps
16 Fueldraulic nozzle actuators
17 Afterburner duct
18 Engine bay titanium ring frames
19 Rear engine mounting frame
20 Engine bay titanium frame and stringer construction
21 Titanium skin panelling
22 Port tailplane hydraulic actuator
23 Tailplane hinge arm
24 Port rudder
25 Tailboom fairing
26 ECM aerial
27 Port tailplane
28 Tail navigation light
29 ECM aerial
30 Radar warning aerials
31 Boron fibre skin panelling
32 Fin leading edge
33 Port air system equipment bay
34 Forward engine mounting
35 Engine mounting frame
36 Bleed air system ducting
37 Engine support link
38 Engine bay fireproof bulkhead
39 Pratt & Whitney F100-PW-100 afterburning turbofan engine
40 Starboard air system equipment bay
41 Engine bleed air primary heat exchanger
42 Heat exchanger ventral exhaust duct
43 Retractable runway arrester hook
44 Wing trailing edge fuel tank
45 Flap hydraulic jack
46 Starboard plain flap
47 Flap and aileron honeycomb panel construction
48 Starboard aileron
49 Aileron hydraulic actuator
50 Fuel jettison pipe
51 Aluminium honeycomb wing tip fairing
52 Low-voltage formation lighting
53 Starboard navigation light
54 ECM aerial
55 Westinghouse ECM equipment pod
56 Outboard wing stores pylon
57 Pylon attachment spigot
58 Cambered leading edge ribs
59 Front spar
60 Machined wing skin/stringer panels
61 Outboard pylon fixing
62 HF flush aerial
63 Leading edge fuel tank
64 Inboard pylon fixing
65 Wing rib construction
66 Starboard wing integral fuel tank, total internal fuel load, 13,455-lb (6103-kg)
67 Wing root rib support struts
68 Titanium wing spars
69 Wing spar/fuselage attachment pin joints
70 Machined fuselage main bulkheads
71 Wing/fuselage fuel tank interconnections
72 Airframe mounted engine accessory gearbox
73 Standby hydraulic generator
74 Jet fuel starter (JFS)/auxiliary power unit (APU)
75 Engine intake compressor face
76 Cooling system intake bleed air spill duct
77 Port wing trailing edge fuel tank
78 Port plain flap
79 Flap hydraulic jack
80 Aileron control rod
81 Aileron hydraulic actuator
82 Port aileron
83 Fuel jettison pipe
84 Wing tip fairing
85 Low-voltage formation lighting
86 Port navigation light
87 ECM aerial
88 Cambered leading edge
89 Outboard pylon fixing
90 Port wing internal fuel tank
91 Fuel system piping
92 Inboard pylon fixing
93 Leading edge fuel tank
94 Anti-collision light
95 Boom-type air refuelling receptacle
96 Bleed air duct to air conditioning plant
97 Control rod runs
98 Dorsal airbrake, open
99 Airbrake glass-fibre honeycomb construction
100 Airbrake hydraulic jack
101 Centre fuselage fuel tanks
102 Intake ducting
103 Ammunition feed chute
104 M61A1 Vulcan 20-mm cannon
105 Hydraulic rotary cannon drive unit
106 Starboard anti-collision light
107 Ventral main undercarriage wheel bay
108 Main undercarriage leg strut
109 Starboard mainwheel
110 Inboard stores pylon
111 Air-to-air missile adaptor
112 Bomb rack
113 Mk 82 low drag 500-lb (227-kg) HE bombs
114 Bomb triple ejector rack
115 Missile launcher rail
116 AIM-9L Sidewinder air-to-air missile
117 AIM-7F Sparrow air-to-air missile
118 Sparrow missile launcher unit
119 Cannon muzzle aperture
120 Cannon barrels
121 Central ammunition drum, 940-rounds
122 Airbrake hinges
123 Forward fuselage fuel tanks
124 UHF aerial
125 Intake duct bleed air louvres
126 Intake by-pass air spill duct
127 Variable area intake ramp hydraulic actuator
128 Air conditioning system cooling air exhaust duct
129 Canopy hinge point
130 Air conditioning plant
131 Intake incidence control jack
132 Intake duct variable area ramp doors
133 Intake pivot fixing
134 Starboard engine air intake
135 Nosewheel leg door
136 Nose undercarriage leg strut
137 Nosewheel
138 Landing/taxiing lamps
139 Nosewheel retraction strut
140 Rear underfloor equipment bay
141 Tactical electronic warfare system (TEWS) racks
142 Cockpit coaming
143 Rear pressure bulkhead
144 Canopy jack
145 Cockpit pressurization valves
146 Structural space provision for second crew member (F-15D)
147 Cockpit aft decking
148 Canopy arch
149 Port intake external compression lip
150 Fuel and sensor tactical (FAST) pack, conformal fuel pallet, capacity 5,000-lb (2268-kg)
151 600-US gal (2271-litre) external fuel tank
152 Cockpit canopy cover
153 Ejection seat headrest
154 Seat safety handle/arming lever
155 Canopy emergency jettison linkage
156 Ejection seat launch rails
157 Safety harness
158 McDonnell-Douglas ACES II 'zero-zero' ejection seat
159 Cockpit sloping bulkhead
160 Pilot's side console panel
161 Air conditioning duct
162 Forward underfloor equipment bay, built-in test equipment (BITE) and liquid oxygen converter
163 Low-voltage formation lighting strip
164 Port side retractable boarding ladder
165 TACAN aerial
166 Angle of attack probe
167 Rudder pedals
168 Control column
169 Pilot's head-up display (HUD)
170 Instrument panel shroud

Vietnam to Tomorrow

After being developed by the manufacturer and tested on a converted airframe (71-291), the concept of using the F-15 as a long-range, all-weather interdiction aircraft was accepted by the USAF and the F-15E Enhanced Eagle was ordered in 1984, almost certainly as replacement for the General Dynamics F-111. McDonnell has moved in two directions to develop the F-15E's capability, concentrating on avionics and ordnance-carrying potential. The rear cockpit of the prototype has been fitted with four multi-purpose cathode ray terminals (CRT) for information display to the systems operator, and three more CRTs are to be installed for the pilot in production versions. Beneath the nose cone, high-resolution radar provides long-range ground-mapping of remarkable clarity while forward-looking infra-red (FLIR) gives close-range images of the best quality. In combination, these systems allow rapid target indentification and all-weather weapons delivery. Production F-15E aircraft have about 25 per cent greater load-carrying ability and range than the current fighter variants.

Versions of the F-15 have been exported to Israel, Japan and Saudi Arabia. The Israeli Defence Force/Air Force aircraft have been involved in several dogfights with Syrian MiG-21s and MiG-23s and are officially confirmed as having shot down at least one MiG-25. On 7 June 1981, Israeli F-15s escorted F-16s making the strike against Iraq's Osirak nuclear powerplant, covering a radius of 600 miles (966 km).

The 1st Tactical Fighter Wing at Langley AFB, Virginia, was the first USAF recipient of the F-15A, while the first operational aircraft in Europe were assigned to the 36th TFW at Bitburg AB, West Germany. USAF F-15s also operate in the Netherlands, Okinawa, and Alaska as well as the continental USA. Some have also reached Air National Guard units.

Specification

F-15C

Type: single-seat fighter
Powerplant: two 23,930-lb (10855-kg) thrust Pratt & Whitney F100-PW-100 augmented turbofans
Performance: maximum speed, clean except AAMs, 1,650 mph (2655 km/h) at 40,000 ft (12192 m); initial climb rate 44,000 ft (13411 m) per minute; service ceiling 85,000 ft (25908 m); range

Full combat capability is retained by the F-15B/D two-seat conversion trainer, which, apart from the second seat and enlarged canopy, differs little from the single-seat aircraft. Although large numbers are concentrated in the training units, they are issued to each operational unit.

nell production line in St Louis, along with the two-seat F-15D. In both, internal fuel is increased, FAST (fuel and sensor, tactical) pallets fitting against the sides of the fuselage giving 9,750 lb (4423 kg) of extra fuel.

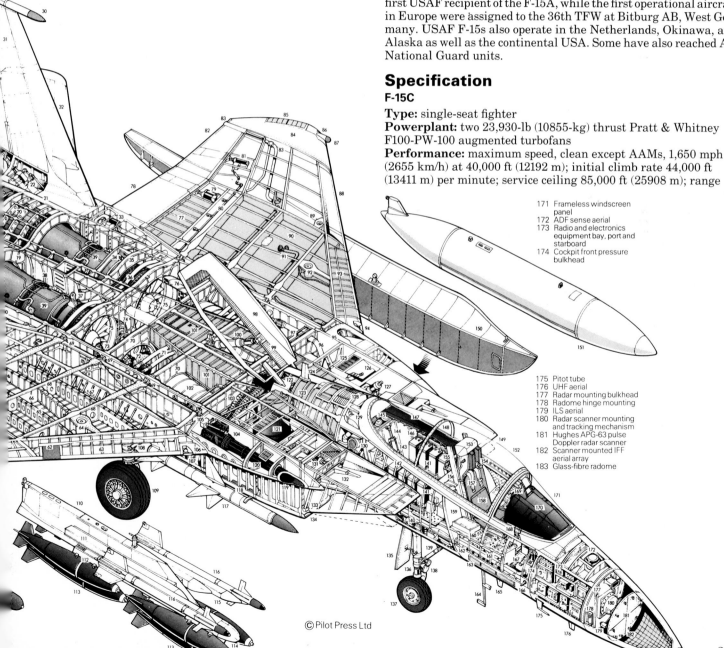

171 Frameless windscreen panel
172 ADF sense aerial
173 Radio and electronics equipment bay, port and starboard
174 Cockpit front pressure bulkhead

175 Pitot tube
176 UHF aerial
177 Radar mounting bulkhead
178 Radome hinge mounting
179 ILS aerial
180 Radar scanner mounting and tracking mechanism
181 Hughes APG-63 pulse Doppler radar scanner
182 Scanner mounted IFF aerial array
183 Glass-fibre radome

© Pilot Press Ltd

207

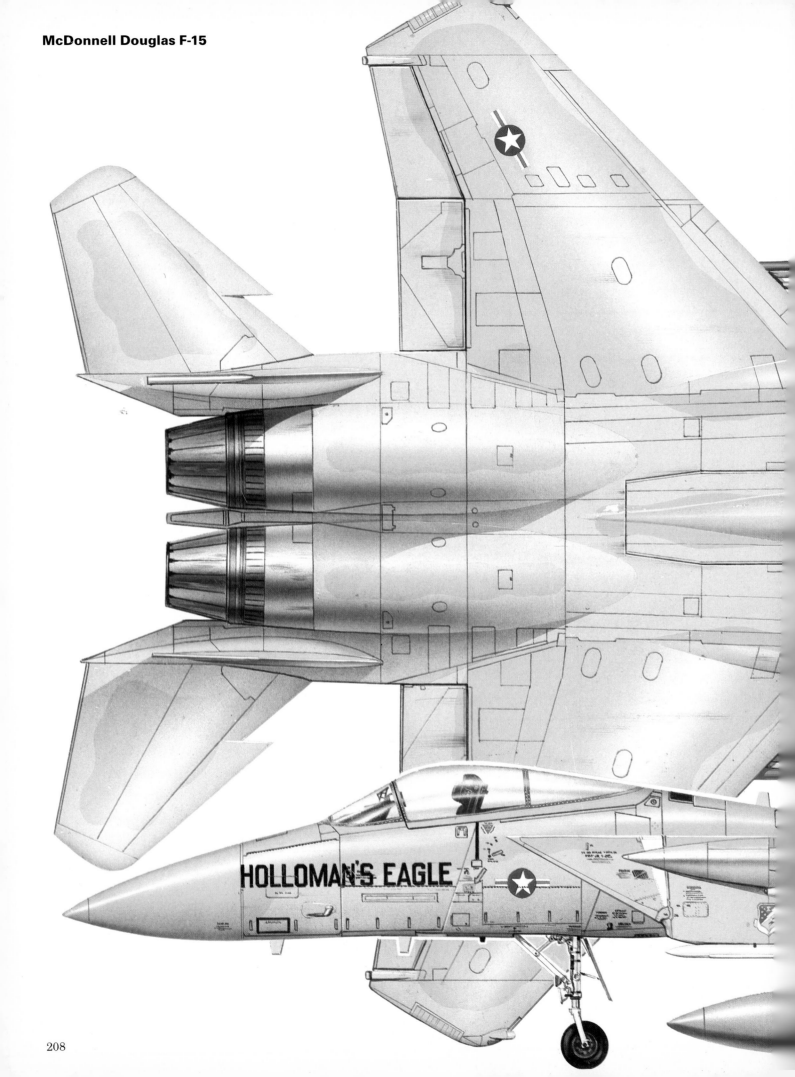

HOLLOMAN'S EAGLE

Still the West's most potent fighter, the McDonnell Douglas F-15 Eagle has power and manoeuvrability in abundance, although its large size makes it more visible in combat than its pilots would prefer. This is an early F-15A, as flown by the commander of the 49th TFW from Holloman AFB, New Mexico. This unit, like other front-line wings, now flies the improved F-15C model, the older aircraft passing slowly to the reserve forces.

Piercing the Alaskan sky, a 21st TFW F-15A demonstrates the standard air-to-air missile load of the type. Carried conformally along the engine ducts are four AIM-7 Sparrows, radar-guided for medium-range engagements. On the wing pylons are four AIM-9 Sidewinders with heat-seeking heads for short-range attacks, while for close work the Eagle has an internal 20-mm M61A1 six-barrel rotary cannon.

McDonnell Douglas F-15

3,460 miles (5568 km)
Weights: empty 31,600 lb (14334 kg); maximum take-off 68,000 lb (30845 kg)
Dimensions: span 42 ft 9¾ in (13.05m); length 63 ft 9 in (19.43 m); height 18 ft 5½ in (5.63 m); wing area 608 sq ft (56.48 m²)
Armament: one M61A1 20-mm cannon; four AIM-7 Sparrow or AMRAAM semi-active radar homing missiles plus four AIM-9 Sidewinder or ASRAAM air-to-air missiles; up to 16,000 lb (7258 kg) of ordnance

The latest version of the Eagle is the F-15E, now operational with the 4th TFW at Seymour-Johnson AFB, North Carolina. It has upgraded avionics (including radar) to perform a dual-role mission, carrying large loads of external stores on fuselage sides and wing pylons.

General Dynamics F-16 Fighting Falcon

History and notes

The General Dynamics F-16 Fighting Falcon seems likely to be the most important fighter in the West for the remainder of the century. Yet it took to the air for the first time by accident. On 20 January 1974, pilot Phil Oestricher was having difficulty in taxi trials of the first YF-16 (72-1567) at Edwards AFB and, rather than make an abrupt and risky halt, took off and flew the aircraft for six minutes.

Designed in 1971 for the USAF's lightweight fighter competition (LWF), the two YF-16 prototypes won out over the Northrop YF-17 in a fly-off contest. If not as lightweight as once envisaged, grossing the scales at 35,400 lb (16057 kg), the F-16A production fighter and its two-seat F-16B derivative clearly had great stretching potential for future development. On 7 June 1975, in what was called the 'deal of the century', it was announced that the F-16 had been chosen by Belgium, Denmark, the Netherlands and Norway to re-equip their air forces. Though these NATO air arms were always seen as the prime customers for the type, subsequent foreign purchasers have included Egypt, Greece, Indonesia, Israel, South Korea, Pakistan, Thailand, Turkey and Venezuela.

First deliveries to the USAF reached the 388th Tactical Fighter Wing at Hill AFB, Utah, on 6 January 1979 and its first overseas unit, the 8th TFW at Kunsan AB, South Korea, on 1 November 1980. The first USAF unit in Europe to re-equip with Fighting Falcons was the 50th TFW at Hahn AB, West Germany on 1 December 1981.

As part of a major policy decision to upgrade the equipment operated by second-line units, the F-16 has already reached the South Carolina Air National Guard, deliveries beginning in mid-1983, followed by other ANG units, as the aircraft were replaced in USAFE by later models.

Characterised by a pointed nose and low-slung inlet for its 23,840-lb (10814-kg) afterburning thrust Pratt & Whitney F100-PW-200 turbofan, the F-16 has swept wings which are blended into the fuselage, saving weight, increasing lift at high angles of attack and reducing drag in the transonic speed range. Moveable leading- and trailing-edge flaps, controlled automatically by the aircraft's speed and attitude, enable the wing to assume an optimum configuration for lift under all conditions of flight. All flying controls are operated by a 'fly-by-wire' electronic system.

Variants of the Fighting Falcon include the F-16/79, a company-financed F-16 powered by a lower-cost 18,000-lb (8165-kg) thrust General Electric J79-GE-119 afterburning turbojet engine. First flown 29 October 1980 and extant in F-16/79A (single-seat) and F-16/79B (two-seat) versions, the craft is intended as a reduced-cost ex-

The 388th TFW at Hill AFB, Utah, was the first recipient of the F-16A in January 1979. This base also lays claim to being the home of the F-16 as the Ogden Air Logistics Center which handles F-16 depot-level maintenance is also based here.

Like the F-15, the two-seat F-16B/D suffers little from the addition of an extra seat. This aircraft belongs to the 6512th Test Squadron of the Air Force Flight Test Center at Edwards AFB, seen during trial firings of the AGM-45 Shrike anti-radiation missile.

The F-16s assigned to USAFE units are dual-role, with ground attack duties being as important as air-to-air fighting. These F-16As from the 50th TFW at Hahn carry rocket pods and ALQ-131 ECM protection. Today the wing flies F-16Cs.

Two examples of the F-16 were fitted with a double delta wing under the F-16XL/F-16E project, a company-funded programme to enhance the performance and load-carrying ability of the type. These were beaten to a USAF dual-role requirement by the F-15E Strike Eagle.

port machine. The F-16/101 was a similarly re-engined example powered by a 28,000-lb (12701-kg) thrust General Electric F101 turbojet of the same type as that which powers the Rockwell B-1 bomber. This machine first flew 19 December 1980 and its evaluation has now been concluded.

The F-16XL is a company-funded development with a new highly-swept 'cranked-arrow' wing with an area more than 120 per cent greater than standard, and a lengthened fuselage to increase internal fuel capacity by 82 per cent. This doubles the capacity for underwing ordnance. The prototype F-16XL was flown on 3 July 1980. The F-16E is a proposed production variant.

The F-16C (single-seat) and F-16D (two-seat) are improved versions of the F-16A and F-16B and have replaced them on General Dynamics' Fort Worth production line by early 1985. The F-16R is a reconnaissance version with an underfuselage pod, and the F-16N is an 'Aggressor' version for the US Navy.

Above: With refuelling, three ferry tanks and a baggage pod, the F-16 is ready to deploy swiftly to any part of the world. This is a 474th TFW F-16B.

Below: The best-known F-16s are the aircraft equipping the USAF Aerial Demonstration Squadron, better known as the 'Thunderbirds'.

F-16 cutaway drawing key

1 Pitot tube
2 Radome
3 Planar radar scanner
4 Scanner drive motors
5 ADF antenna
6 Front electronics equipment bay
7 Westinghouse radar electronics
8 Forward radar warning antenna
9 Cockpit front bulkhead
10 Instrument panel shroud
11 Missile control electronics
12 Fuselage forebody strake fairing
13 Marconi-Elliot head-up display.
14 Side stick controller (fly-by-wire control system)
15 Cockpit floor
16 Frameless bubble canopy
17 Canopy fairing
18 Ejection seat (30° tilt-back)
19 pilot's safety harness
20 Throttle
21 Side control panel
22 Cockpit frame construction
23 Ejection seat headrest
24 Cockpit canopy seat
25 Canopy hinge
26 Rear avionics bay (growth area)
27 Cockpit rear bulkhead
28 Boundary-layer splitter-plate
29 Fixed-geometry air intake
30 Antenna
31 Air retracting nosewheel
32 Shock absorber scissor link
33 Retraction strut
34 Nosewheel door
35 Intake trunking
36 Cooling louvres
37 Gun gas suppression nozzle
38 Air conditioning system pipes
39 Forward fuselage fuel tanks
40 Canopy aft glazing
41 Drop tank, capacity 370 US gal (1400 litres)
42 Forebody blended wing root
43 TACAN aerial
44 Fuel tank access panel
45 Cannon barrels
46 Forebody frame construction
47 M61 rotary cannon
48 Ammunition feed and link return chutes
49 Ammunition drum (500×20-mm rounds)
50 Ammunition drum flexible drive shaft
51 Hydraulic gun drive motor
52 Leading edge control shaft
53 Hydraulic service bay
54 Hydraulic reservoir

57 No. 2 hydraulic system reservoir
58 Leading edge control shaft
59 Inboard pylon
60 Wing centre pylon
61 Mk 82 500-lb (227-kg) bombs
62 Outboard wing pylon
63 Missile launcher shoe
64 AIM-9 Sidewinder missile
65 Starboard navigation light
66 Aluminium honeycomb leading edge construction
67 Static dischargers
68 Fixed trailing edge section
69 Multi-spar wing construction
70 Integral wing fuel tank
71 Starboard flaperon
72 Fuel system piping
73 Access panels
74 Centre fuel tank panels
75 Centre fuselage fuel tank
76 Intake duct
77 Wing mounting bulkheads
78 Flight refuelling receptacle
79 Pratt & Whitney F100-PW-100(3) turbofan
80 Engine gearbox, airframe mounted
81 Gearbox drive shaft
82 Ground pressure refuelling receptacle
83 Flaperon servo-actuator
84 Rear fuselage frame construction
85 Integral fuel tank
86 Front engine mounting
87 Antenna
88 Fin root fairing
89 Flight control system hydraulic accumulators
90 Anti-corrosion light power supply
91 Starboard tailplane
92 Graphite-epoxy fin skins
93 Fin construction
94 Aluminium honeycomb leading edge construction
95 Steel leading edge strip
96 Antenna
97 Anti-collision light
98 Tail radar warning antenna

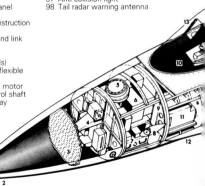

99 Aluminium honeycomb rudder construction
100 Rudder servo-actuator
101 Radar warnings power supply
102 Tail navigation light
103 Fully variable exhaust nozzle
104 Split trailing edge airbrakes (upper and lower surfaces)

55 Leading edge manoeuvre flap drive motor
56 Antenna

So far, the F-16 has been taken into combat by Israel, which used the type on 7 June 1981 to strike Iraq's Osirak nuclear powerplant and has subsequently employed Fighting Falcons in combat in Lebanon. Pakistan has shot down Communist aircraft along the Afghan border using its F-16s. Though a decade has passed since its inception, the F-16 is believed by pilots to be the most advanced fighter operational in the world today.

While most ANG and Reserve units receive F-16A/Bs passed on from front-line units, the 944th Tactical Fighter Group (302nd TFS) has received new-build F-16C/Ds. The unit is based at Luke AFB, amid the magnificent scenery of Arizona, where low-level training fills the major proportion of its time. Currently two AFRes units have F-16s, the other being the 466th TFS at Hill AFB, Utah, with F-16As.

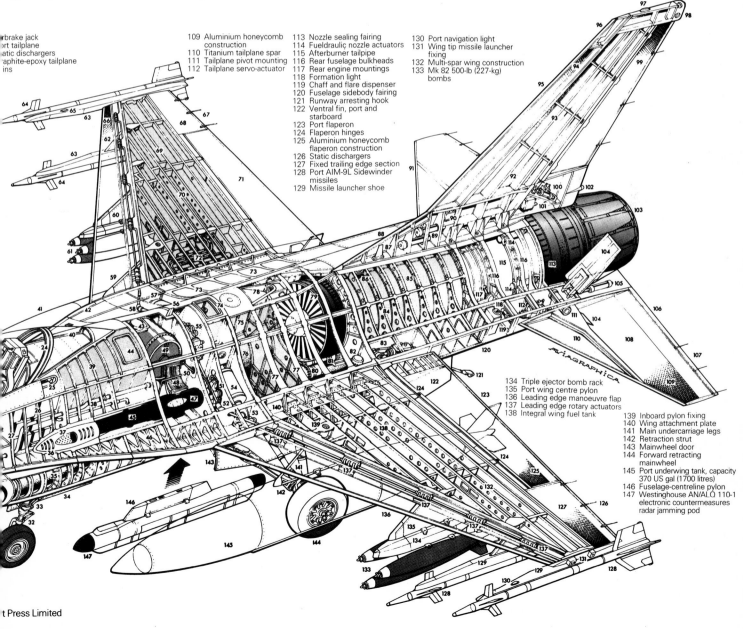

rbrake jack
rt tailplane
tic dischargers
aphite-epoxy tailplane
ins

109 Aluminium honeycomb construction
110 Titanium tailplane spar
111 Tailplane pivot mounting
112 Tailplane servo-actuator
113 Nozzle sealing fairing
114 Fueldrauliç nozzle actuators
115 Afterburner tailpipe
116 Rear fuselage bulkheads
117 Rear engine mountings
118 Formation light
119 Chaff and flare dispenser
120 Fuselage sidebody fairing
121 Runway arresting hook
122 Ventral fin, port and starboard
123 Port flaperon
124 Flaperon hinges
125 Aluminium honeycomb flaperon construction
126 Static dischargers
127 Fixed trailing edge section
128 Port AIM-9L Sidewinder missiles
129 Missile launcher shoe
130 Port navigation light
131 Wing tip missile launcher fixing
132 Multi-spar wing construction
133 Mk 82 500-lb (227-kg) bombs

134 Triple ejector bomb rack
135 Port wing centre pylon
136 Leading edge manoeuvre flap
137 Leading edge rotary actuators
138 Integral wing fuel tank
139 Inboard pylon fixing
140 Wing attachment plate
141 Main undercarriage legs
142 Retraction strut
143 Mainwheel door
144 Forward retracting mainwheel
145 Port underwing tank, capacity 370 US gal (1700 litres)
146 Fuselage-centreline pylon
147 Westinghouse AN/ALQ 110-1 electronic countermeasures radar jamming pod

t Press Limited

213

As the 'bread-and-butter' aircraft of today's US Air Force, the F-16 is widely deployed overseas in both Europe and the Far East. The 50th TFW at Hahn AB, West Germany, was the first to get the aircraft in Europe, followed by the 52nd TFW at Spangdahlem, the 86th TFW at Ramstein and the 401st TFW at Torrejon in Spain. Most of these aircraft have a multi-role mission, ranging from close air support to battlefield air superiority. Those of the 52nd TFW fulfil a specialist defence suppression role in concert with F-4Gs. Depicted is an F-16A, since replaced by F-16Cs.

HR
AF
81 731

Keith Fretwell.

Large numbers of F-16s are based with Stateside units (such as the 31st TFW at Homestead AFB, Florida), ready to deploy swiftly around the world in the event of conflict. Obviously Europe is seen as the main area of operation, and US-based aircraft regularly deploy to the theatre to train in the conditions found there.

388th TFW F-16s cruise over the pyramids during a 'Bright Star' exercise. These take place in Egypt to test US Central Command's ability to rapidly deploy large numbers of forces to the Middle East. Several air force units are assigned to these deployments.

F-16As assigned to the Air National Guard are taking an increasingly important share of the air defence of the United States. Stationed strategically around the nation's borders, they stand alert to ward off potential attackers. This F-16 from New Jersey is shown in company with the aircraft it replaced, the Convair F-106.

Specification

F-16A

Type: single-seat fighter

Powerplant: one 23,840-lb (10814-kg) augmented thrust Pratt & Whitney F100-PW-200 turbofan engines

Performance: maximum speed 1,320 mph (2142 km/h) or Mach 2.0 at 40,000 ft (12192 m); initial climb rate 44,000 ft (13411 m) per minute; service ceiling 59,000 ft (17983 m); range 1,350 miles (2173 km)

Weights: empty 15,586 lb (7070 kg); maximum take-off 35,400 lb (16057 kg)

Dimensions: span 31 ft 0 in (9.45 m); length 49 ft 6 in (15.09 m); height 16 ft 8½ in (5.09 m); wing area 300 sq ft (27.87 m²)

Armament: one General Electric M61A1 20-mm cannon; provision for an air-to-air missile at each wingtip; provision for a maximum external weapons load of 20,450 lb (9276 kg)

Northrop F-17

History and notes

The Northrop F-17 was developed for the USAF's 1972 lightweight fighter competition (LWF) from the company's P-530 Cobra design, which had been intended principally for export. Two YF-17A prototypes (72-1569/1570) were built, the first making its maiden flight on 9 August 1974. A trim and attractive machine characterised by outward-canted twin vertical-tail surfaces and wing leading-edge root extensions blended into the forward wing, the YF-17A was powered by two 15,000-lb (6804-kg) thrust General Electric YJ101 continuous-bleed turbojets.

Although the YF-17A lost out in a fly-off competition with the General Dynamics F-16, the US Navy continued to be interested in the aircraft and evaluated it at NAS Patuxent River, Maryland. Based upon an agreement with Northrop and McDonnell Douglas, the basic design with very few changes re-emerged as the F/A-18A Hornet strike fighter. When evolution went full-circle, however, and Northrop attempted to sell an F-18L land-

The Northrop YF-17 was the unsuccessful candidate for the USAF's Lightweight Fighter competition. It was reworked as the navalised F-18 Hornet, emerging as less manoeuvrable but more capable than the F-16 it had originally competed against.

based variant, there were no purchasers. The two YF-17As are no longer flying.

Specification

YF-17A

Type: single-seat fighter

Powerplant: two 15,000-lb (6804-kg) thrust General Electric YJ101 continuous-bleed turbojets

Performance: maximum speed 1,390 mph (2237 km/h) or Mach 2.13 at 44,000 ft (13411 m); initial climb rate 44,900 ft (13686 m) per minute; service ceiling 55,000 ft (16764 m); range 980 miles (1577 km)

Weights: empty about 15,000 lb (6804 kg); maximum take-off 21,000 lb (9526 kg)

Dimensions: span 35 ft 0 in

(10.67 m); length 55 ft 6 in (16.92 m); height 14 ft 6 in (4.42 m); wing area 350 sq ft (32.52 m²)

Armament: one 20-mm M61A1 cannon; provision for an air-to-air missile at each wingtip; provision for a maximum external weapons' load of 20,450 lb (9276 kg)

F-112 to F-116

The announcement by the USAF in November 1988 that the Lockheed 'Stealth' fighter is designated F-117A raised much speculation about the designation system used by the Department of Defense. The 'F-19' number had long been attributed by the popular press to the aircraft, but with the revelation (expected by most well-informed observers) that it was F-117, it left them wondering what the 'F-19' actually is. The most likely explanation is that it was never assigned

and was a deliberate 'red herring' to further shield the F-117 programme. However, chronologically the F-117 does fit into the 'F-19' time-frame, and may have once carried the designation.

However, the choice of F-117 refers to a continuation of the 'Century' series which had been stopped at F-111 in 1962. What, then, were the F-112 to F-116? Once again this may be US Air Force disinformation, but a possible (and attractive!) explanation has been put forward. Operat-

ing within the vast Nellis ranges, and most probably sharing the Tonopah Test Range facility with the F-117s is the USAF's MiG Squadron. Acquired from several sources, the US Air Force operates a variety of MiG and Sukhoi types (MiG-17, MiG-19, MiG-21, MiG-23 and Su-7/20) for evaluation and dissimilar combat. In order to ease security problems surrounding flight plans and radio traffic, the aircraft may have been assigned the F-112 to F-116 designations. These aircraft

have been known to exist for some time, so the use of F-117 for the Lockheed aircraft would further hide the highly-secret 'Stealth', particularly as it flies in the same vicinity as the Soviet types.

McDonnell Douglas F-18

Now serving in large numbers with the Marine Corps and Navy, the F-18 Hornet is a most useful multi-role fighter. Navy aircraft are deploying aboard carriers, replacing F-4 Phantoms and A-7 Corsairs.

Lockheed F-117

History and notes

Low observable technology, or 'stealth', has been under study at least since the end of World War II, but it was not until the 1960s that computing capacity became available to design truly stealthy aircraft. Naturally Lockheed's Advanced Development Projects department ('Skunk Works') was in the forefront of these developments. Spurred on by the lethal effect of Egyptian SAMs on Israeli warplanes during the 1973 Yom Kippur war, Lockheed began construction of a proof-of-concept aircraft in the mid-1970s, flying this XST aircraft from Groom Lake, Nevada, in 1977.

The following year Lockheed was authorised to begin development of a full-scale fighter based on XST technology (codenamed 'Senior Trend'), and in June 1981 the first such aircraft flew, again from Groom Lake. The 'stealth fighter' exhibited the concept of faceting, whereby the surface is made up of many small flat surfaces to split up the incoming radar beams into many small lobes. The split intake was complicated,

shielding the compressor blades of the engines from radar. The General Electric F404 engines were non-afterburning, exhausting through a diffused section to limit infra-red signature to a minimum. Other detection areas such as engine smoke and noise were also reduced significantly.

In October 1983 the fighter became operational, flying from Tonopah Test Range airfield in the northwest corner of the vast Nellis ranges. The operating unit was the 4450th Tactical Group, officially based at Nellis AFB and flying the Vought A-7D Corsair ('LV' tailcode). In fact these Corsairs were used for daylight training, the A-7's low thrust/weight ratio, modest manoeuvrability and non-afterburning performance closely resembling that of the new aircraft.

Meanwhile the world's press was working itself into a frenzy over the new aircraft, assigning it the designation 'F-19' and bestowing upon it the most amazing shapes imaginable in a host of artists' impressions. Throughout, the US Air Force refused to admit its existence – who can forget the stony face of General Lawrence Skantze, then chief of Aeronautical Systems Division, repeating over and over "There is no such aircraft as the F-19". Of course, technically he was right, for after ten years of flight trials and five years of service, the Pentagon finally revealed the aircraft as the F-117A in November 1988.

By this time some aviation journalists were quoting this designation, and the facts concerning the aircraft matched some of the more educated rumours. 59 aircraft were ordered (believed to be reduced from 100) of which 52 had been delivered by 1988. Little more information has been released, and although the USAF can now use the F-117s in less secure areas, it still remains a highly-classified programme.

Operations of the F-117 are aimed at pinpoint attacks against high-value targets. Accordingly the crew members are drawn from experienced F-111 or 'Wild Weasel' pilots. Reports suggest that the F-117 was considered for strikes against Libya, and it has certainly operated from bases in the United Kingdom. With removable wings, it is easily transportable in the hold of a C-5 Galaxy. Until the relaxation of security, all operations were made at night.

Specification (speculative)
F-117

Type: single-seat reconnaissance/strike fighter
Powerplant: two 12,566-lb (5700-kg) thrust non-afterburning General Electric F404 turbofan engines
Performance: maximum speed Mach 0.95; range more than 1,864 miles (3000 km)
Weight: maximum take-off 44,092 lb (20000 kg)
Dimensions: wing span 45 ft (13.7 m); length 30 ft (9.1 m)
Armament: up to 4,000 lb (1815 kg) of bombs or air-to-ground missiles carried in two internal bays

This photograph of the Lockheed F-117A does not give too much away concerning the details of the type. Precision attack and reconnaissance are its main roles, its low performance and modest agility not equipping it for air-to-air fighting.

Northrop F-20 Tigershark

History and notes

The Northrop F-20 Tigershark is a third-generation, single-engine development in the company's F-5 series and was, in fact, still designated F-5G when the first example (82-0062) flew at Edwards AFB on 30 August 1982 piloted by Russ Scott. The new designation was assigned a few weeks later, emphasising the Tigershark's differences from its forebears, includ-

ing its single 17,000-lb (7711-kg) afterburning thrust General Electric F404-GE-100 turbofan engine. Originally intended for sale to Taiwan, the F-20 became in the mid-1980s a symbol of Northrop's enterprise. It was also a

The F-20 prototypes were originally known as the F-5G, but the new designation was applied to reinforce the considerable redesign of the fighter.

credit to the Northrop design team headed by Lee Begin.

To retain the excellent high-AOA (angle of attack) handling of earlier F-5 models, Northrop decided to adhere to the same underfuselage shape, building shelves on each side of the more slender rear fuselage. At the same time it was found that a flattened 'shark nose' improved handling, so this was introduced. Other changes in the F-20A included a two-shock inlet ramp to ensure efficient operation at Mach 2.0, the insertion of a 5-in (12.7-cm) structural plug to accommodate the larger engine, an enlarged canopy (improved still further on the second airframe) and a modernised cockpit. Equipment options included the General Electric G-200 radar, and AIM-7 Sparrow or AMRAAM missiles.

The F-20A had been shown to enthusiastic crowds at the Paris Air Show (1983) and at Farnborough (1984), and Northrop had invested more than $800 million into the aeroplane and into an ambitious programme to demonstrate it to potential customers. Once regarded as a possible new 'Aggressor' aircraft for the US Navy, the F-20A was not entered in the competition because Northrop needed a significantly larger order to commence production.

Three F-20A Tigersharks were completed, before the programme was officially shelved, two crashing during aerobatic sequences. Despite aggressive selling and an excellent product, Northrop could not break the grip on the world and home markets held by the F-16.

Specification
F-20A

Type: single-seat fighter
Powerplant: one 17,000-lb (7711-kg) afterburning thrust

turbofan engine
Performance: maximum speed 1,400 mph (2253 km/h) or Mach 2.1 at 40,000 ft (12192 m); initial climb rate 50,000 ft (15240 m) per minute; service ceiling 60,000 ft (18288 m); range 1,700 miles (2736 km)
Weights: empty about 9,600 lb (4355 kg); maximum take-off about 27,100 lb (12293 kg)
Dimensions: span 26 ft 8 in (8.13 m); length 46 ft 6 in (14.17 m); height 13 ft 10 in (4.22 m); wing area 180 sq ft (16.72 m²)

A company prototype Tigershark looses off with a Sidewinder. In all trials the F-20 proved to be a superb fighter, in most respects superior to the F-16. However, without a USAF contract, the aircraft had little hope of getting export orders, a problem compounded by two crashes (pilot error in both cases).

Armament: two 20-mm cannon; provision for AIM-7 Sparrow or AMRAAM air-to-air missiles; provision for up to 20,000 lb (9072 kg) of external ordnance

---

IAI F-21

The F-21 designation covers IAI Kfirs leased from the manufacturer to the Marine Corps and Navy. They are employed on dissimilar air combat duties.

Lockheed F-22

History and notes

The US Air Force's next generation Advanced Tactical Fighter (ATF) will be chosen from between the YF-22A, being developed by a three-company team headed by Lockheed, and the YF-23A being built by Northrop. These competitors for the USAF fighter of the 1990s are being developed in unusual secrecy, making use of "Stealth" and other advanced technologies, and relatively little information has been disclosed.

The October 1986 contract for $691 million charged Lockheed with developing an ATF with high manoeuvrability, advanced low-observable technologies and the ability to cruise at supersonic speeds for sustained periods. The company asserts that the YF-22A will "fly sortie after sortie with minimum ground time for rearming, refuelling and maintenance."

Lockheed will develop and construct all forward-fuselage structures and components, including crew station. General Dynamics will develop and construct mid-fuselage structures, tail assembly, nose and main landing gears, and electrical, hydraulic, fuel and flight control

systems. Boeing is to provide radar and the infra-red search and track system (IRST) and to test these systems aboard a company-owned 757 transport. Numerous other manufacturers have lesser roles, such as General Electric which is to provide multifunctional cockpit displays.

Apart from a decision on crew size (the YF-22A will be a single-seater), almost no details of the fighter's configuration have been revealed. It is understood that both ATF candidates are to be powered by wholly new engines chosen from between Pratt & Whitney and General Electric designs. First flight date for both aircraft is set for October 1990. It is unlikely that many details will be revealed even by then.

The specification which follows is notional, intended to typify the kind of aircraft being built.

Specification (speculative)
F-22

Type: single-seat fighter
Powerplant: one or two 30,000-lb (13695-kg) thrust each Advanced Technology Engines (ATE) to be chosen from designs by General

Electric and Pratt & Whitney
Performance: maximum speed Mach 2.5 or 1,903 mph (3045 km/h) or higher at altitude; cruising speed Mach 1.1 or 835 mph (1336 km/h) or higher at sea level; initial climb rate 50,000 ft (15240 m) per minute; service ceiling 60,000 ft (18288 m) or higher; range 1,350 miles (2175 km)
Weights: empty 19,975 lb (9061 kg); maximum take-off 36,047 lb (16351 kg)
Dimensions: span 56 ft 10 in

(17.32 m); length 67 ft 7 in (20.6 m); height 15 ft 9 in (4.8 m); wing area 610 sq ft (56.67 m²)
Armament: guns and missiles to be developed

Lockheed's impression of its YF-22 fighter shows the 'stealth' features and manoeuvring nozzles that will characterise the type. Designed to replace the F-15, the winner of the F-22/F-23 fly-off can expect orders for up to 750 units for service from the mid-1990s onwards.

Northrop F-23

History and notes

The Northrop candidate for the US Air Force's Advanced Tactical Fighter, the YF-23A, is being developed under conditions of, if anything, even greater secrecy than the Lockheed candidate. The aircraft will be 'revolutionary, not evolutionary' according to Northrop's Tom McNiff who hastily adds that he

won't have much else to say about it. The Northrop YF-23A will make the same use of 'Stealth' and other advanced technologies and will be especially intended for high manoeuvrability, this having been proven to be more important in a fighter than is high speed.

Almost no other details of the

YF-23A are available. The notional details on the YF-22A can be considered to be equally illustrative of the YF-23A. Like its Lockheed competitor, one prototype of the YF-23 will fly with Pratt & Whitney YF119 engines and one with General Electric YF120s.

INDEX

Note: Page numbers printed in **bold** refer to an illustration

221